Two Strategies for Europe

Two Strategies for Europe

De Gaulle, the United States,
and the Atlantic Alliance

Frédéric Bozo

Translated by
Susan Emanuel

ROWMAN & LITTLEFIELD PUBLISHERS, INC.
Lanham • Boulder • New York • Oxford

ROWMAN & LITTLEFIELD PUBLISHERS, INC.

Published in the United States of America
by Rowman & Littlefield Publishers, Inc.
4720 Boston Way, Lanham, Maryland 20706
http://www.rowmanlittlefield.com

12 Hid's Copse Road
Cumnor Hill, Oxford OX2 9JJ, England

This work was published with the assistance of the Ministère Français Chargé de la Culture–Centre National du Livre.

British Cataloguing in Publication Information Available

Library of Congress Cataloging-in-Publication Data

Bozo, Frédéric.
   [Deux stratégies pour l'Europe. English]
   Two strategies for Europe : De Gaulle, the United States, and the Atlantic Alliance / Frédéric Bozo ; translated by Susan Emanuel.
    p. cm.
   Includes bibliographical references and index.
   ISBN 0-8476-9530-1 (alk. paper)—ISBN 0-8476-9531-X (pbk. : alk. paper)
   1. North Atlantic Treaty Organization. 2. France—Politics and government—1958—
3. Gaulle, Charles de, 1890–1970. 4. France—Foreign relations—1958–1969 5.
France—Foreign relations—United States. 6. United States—Foreign relations—
France. I. Title.
UA646.5.F7 B6913 2000
355'.031091821—dc21   00-040301

Printed in the United States of America

♾™ The paper used in this publication meets the minimum requirements of American National Standard for Information Sciences—Permanence of Paper for Printed Library Materials, ANSI/NISO Z.39.48-1992.

Contents

Contents

Acknowledgments

As is the case with all scholarly work, this book has its own history. I recall it here as a means of acknowledging the support from individuals and institutions without which its writing would have been impossible. The book's first draft was completed in 1992 at the University of Paris X-Nanterre; I want to thank my colleague and friend Pierre Melandri for his support, advice, and encouragement during this formative period. Throughout those years, my research gained enormously from the financial support and the intellectual impulse of the Groupe d'étude français de l'armement nucléaire (GREFHAN). I want to express my appreciation to Maurice Vaïsse, to whom this book owes a great deal, and to honor the memory of Jean-Baptiste Duroselle. Because GREFHAN was the French branch of the international Nuclear History Program (NHP), I also want to thank the promoters of the NHP, in particular John L. Gaddis, Catherine Kelleher, Wolfgang Krieger, Ernest May, Uwe Nerlich, and Robert O'Neill. The French Institute for International Relations (IFRI), where I have conducted most of my research over these years, proved to be an incomparable asset both in terms of logistics and intellectual work, and I am grateful to Thierry de Montbrial for his support. I also thank the Fondation Charles de Gaulle, in particular Chantal Morelle, for making the publication of the French version possible. Last but not least, I want to express my gratitude and affection to Stanley Hoffmann, to whom I owe so much in so many regards, starting with two of his favorite themes: de Gaulle and French-American relations.

Not much of course would have been possible without access to appropriate sources. In the United States, I want to thank the librarians and staff of the John F. Kennedy Library in Boston and of the Lyndon B. Johnson Library in Austin, where I was fortunate enough to do research respectively in 1988 and 1990. In France, my appreciation goes to archivists and senior staff in the Archives Diplomatiques in the Ministry of Foreign Affairs, in particular Monique Constant and Pierre Fournié, for allowing me to consult theretofore inaccessible archival material from 1990 to 1992 and again from 1993 to 1995 as I worked to complete the French version of the book. I also thank those in charge of the Bibliothèque de Documentation Internationale Contemporaine (BDIC) in Nanterre, the Fondation Nationale des Sciences Politiques in Paris, and the Benjamin Franklin Center in the U.S. Embassy in Paris. Finally, I am grateful to all the former officials involved in the momentous events of that period who kindly agreed to be interviewed and serve as witnesses, thus providing a much-needed complement to archival and other sources.

Although it would be impossible to name all those who have contributed, one way or another, to this book, I am sure that those not personally mentioned here, whether friends, colleagues, or both, will recognize themselves in my gratitude.

For the help on the English version of this book, one last word of sincere appreciation is in order to those who have made it possible: Stanley Hoffmann again for his advice; Susan McEachern, executive editor, and Dawn Stoltzfus at Rowman & Littlefield; Susan Emanuel, the translator; Steven Long, the copy editor; as well as the institutions that have helped with the funding, including the NATO Office of Information and Press and the French Ministry of Culture.

Finally, a word of caution is in order: This is the translation of a book published in French in 1996. It includes a substantive new concluding chapter, but I have not tried to incorporate some of the material that has been made available or published since the publication of the original volume. This does not in my view affect the findings of this book in any substantial way, whether of fact or interpretation. However, when useful, I have acknowledged new evidence and/or recent scholarly work by referring to it in endnotes or in the bibliography.

Introduction

"France proposes to regain full sovereignty over its territory, currently undermined by the permanent presence of allied military units and their routine use of its airspace, to cease its participation in 'integrated' commands, and no longer to put its forces at NATO's disposal."

Thus on March 7, 1966, General Charles de Gaulle announced to U.S. president Lyndon B. Johnson that his country had decided to withdraw from the joint military arm of the Atlantic Alliance while remaining a full member of the latter. One year later, more than twenty thousand American soldiers stationed in France, along with their logistical support, equipment, and command apparatus, had left French national territory and the principal interallied staffs, starting with Supreme Headquarters of Allied Powers in Europe (SHAPE), had moved to Belgium or the Netherlands. Finally, the headquarters of the Alliance itself, the seat of the Atlantic Council and the civilian structure of NATO, left Paris for the Brussels suburbs. Starting in the summer of 1966, French forces in Germany were no longer assigned under the supreme allied commander Europe (SACEUR), nor was the French air force deployed in the Federal Republic of Germany.

It was a turning point. France had for a while been subject to American dictates; it now put an end to a foreign presence that was generally unwelcome and disengaged from an Atlantic integration structure that it felt was prejudicial to its freedom of international maneuver. This was the apogee of the policy of independence pursued by de Gaulle since his return to power in 1958, a policy that was increasingly perceived across the Atlantic as being directed against the United States, where the 1966 decision seemed an affront. It appeared to question not just U.S. leadership in Europe but the whole strategy of containment at a time when the military escalation in Vietnam threatened former certainties about U.S. power. Although it already had experienced serious crises, the Atlantic Alliance itself was now enduring one of the most uncertain

periods in its history. Indeed, military integration, implemented at the start of
the 1950s and now denounced by de Gaulle, symbolized the permanence of
U.S. engagement in Europe and the solidity of common defense under the
Atlantic Pact.

Since 1966, the relationship between France and the Alliance has fueled many
debates and much commentary. It has given rise to cut-and-dried, even carica-
tured, interpretations. In France, de Gaulle's decision rapidly became the founding myth of restored national independence; in the United States, the General's
Atlantic policy was interpreted as essentially anti-American. Finally, in Alliance
circles, the 1966 rupture certainly consecrated "Gaullism" as a kind of major
heresy within the Atlanticist religion.

The reason is that the political stakes—differing according to viewpoints—
have profoundly influenced interpretations of the event. From the 1960s
through the 1980s, the nature of transatlantic relations remained essentially
unchanged and continued to affect interpretations of this period, whether in
France, the United States, or the rest of the Alliance. Moreover, the character
of the relevant issues, which, if not always classified, then at least politically
sensitive, aggravated the classic problem for scholars, limited to secondhand
sources and prevented for years from examining the archives. This problem
was accentuated, and not only in the French case, by a characteristic gap
between "declaratory" policy and "operational" policy, that is, between discourse and reality.

Yet the end of the Cold War has largely removed these obstacles. Because the
very logic of transatlantic misunderstandings and Franco–U.S. disagreements,
along with the system of power blocs, has been called into question, we are now
finally allowed a more judicious reading of events. The lowering of the stakes
permits a more liberal policy of access to firsthand sources and thus the ability to
draw on more balanced and more complete documentation. Meanwhile, the declaratory and operational dimensions are at last reunited in the strategies of actors
on the transatlantic playing field.

Accordingly, the goal of this book is to offer a reinterpretation of transatlantic and especially Franco–U.S. relations throughout the decisive 1958 to
1969 period. Moving beyond the schematic interpretations that have hereto-
fore prevailed on both sides, it appears that de Gaulle's policy largely sur-
passed the narrow nationalist objectives that have long been attributed to it. As
for the United States, faced with what might be called the Gaullist grand design, while maintaining at first only a reactive attitude, it gradually learned
how to take the measure of this challenge. While still seeking to keep French
policy from affecting the rest of the Alliance, it eventually adopted a more dynamic and constructive approach. New light can thus be shed on the transatlantic relations that took shape in this period; indeed, the Alliance, for a time
shaken by the French offensive, was, as a result, forced to adapt and emerged
in some ways strengthened.

THE POLITICS OF GRANDEUR OR A GRAND DESIGN?

Power, independence, and grandeur are to be found, of course, at the heart of de Gaulle's Atlantic policy. The September 1958 memorandum on the Alliance, addressed to Dwight D. Eisenhower and Harold Macmillan, marked the country's return to institutional stability, to general financial equilibrium, and to international influence. The end of the Algerian War four years later, by ridding the country of its colonial burden, put the finishing touches to a phase in which the General sought to redefine French power. It also inaugurated a new era of assertive French diplomacy, bolstered by France's emerging nuclear capability. Later, the culminating phase of Gaullist contestation over the Atlantic system in 1965–1967 coincided with an apogee of French power, unprecedented economic expansion, political stability confirmed by the reelection of de Gaulle, and operational nuclear capacity. This was the foundation on which was built a policy of contesting the role of the dollar, of denouncing blocs, and of withdrawing from integration within NATO. And after the crisis of May 1968, when this foundation splintered along social, economic, and political fault lines, de Gaulle's Atlantic policy softened somewhat—though less in principle than in practice.

This was because independence was the immutable bedrock of Gaullist policy within the Alliance. First, military independence. After his return to power, de Gaulle decided to disengage France from the machinery of Atlantic integration which, in combination with a foreign military presence whose grave dangers he had witnessed during the Middle East crisis during the summer of 1958, appeared to him wholly incompatible with national sovereignty. Second, strategic independence. In his view, nuclear weapons, guarantor of the very existence of the nation, could not be shared, and this merely reinforced the logic of secession from NATO integration. Finally and above all, political independence. In contrast to his predecessors, de Gaulle's objective was not to place France on a par with Great Britain as second fiddle to the United States, but actually to make its allies recognize its status as a world power—a goal he judged incompatible with integration within NATO.

Yet Gaullist policy, in its operational mode, paradoxically revealed the General's profound awareness of the inequality of power that separated France from the United States. Hence the necessity, in order to hold its rank, of a politics of grandeur, composed of both strategic intransigence and tactical flexibility. Hence, too, a style characterized by strong language, a certain taste for the surprise effect, and impatience with regard to negotiation, a style particularly pronounced in Franco-American relations and in policy regarding the Alliance.

If this is indeed a politics of grandeur, it is above all a grand design. As Stanley Hoffmann[1] has expressed better than anyone, power, independence, and grandeur were for de Gaulle inseparable from the much wider objective of transforming the international system. The "possession goals" were for him inseparable from the "milieu goals." Atlantic policy indeed belonged to a project extending beyond the simple quest for rank, as much in its West-West as in its East-West dimension.

With respect to the West-West dimension, it is now established that (contrary to accepted wisdom) de Gaulle's objective was not so much to weaken NATO as to transform the Western group of nations, if not somehow to reinforce transatlantic ties. The General throughout this period never seriously questioned the Atlantic Alliance (even at the height of his grand design in 1965–1967), nor did he contest the need for U.S. involvement on the Old Continent (even as NATO forces quit French national territory). However, he considered that the alliance between the United States and Europe, which remained indispensable as long as a Soviet threat persisted, would not remain viable unless it adapted to the profound changes that had occurred in the international context since its creation in 1949–1950. The unchanging maintenance of NATO in its Cold War configuration, that is, as a military organization tightly integrated under U.S. command, could only, according to him, uphold the illusion of security because it no longer corresponded to the new politico-strategic realities, most important the nuclear factor. The balance of terror, heralded in 1957 with the launching of *Sputnik*, overturned the initial calculation of Western strategists who had believed they could base European security on the sole guarantee of the United States. Now, faced with the prospect of Soviet intercontinental nuclear capacity, U.S. involvement could no longer be considered unconditional, which was confirmed in de Gaulle's eyes by the concept of *flexible response*. Hence the necessity of a European strategic organization that would rely heavily on French nuclear power and would guarantee an ensured and permanent transatlantic tie.

The goal of Western European autonomy constituted an essential constant in the General's policy. Implicit in his 1958 memorandum (Europe would have been represented by France in the "tri-directorate" proposed to the "Anglo-Saxons"), this objective became the veritable driving force of his policy after 1960. With the Fouchet Plan, he was calling for a Western Europe that was united and autonomous and that would transform the Atlantic Alliance. And if the Western European dimension of Gaullist policy faded after the failure of the plan in 1962 and the relative failure of the Elysée Treaty in 1963, it remained present in the background as a long-term objective, even after the crisis of the "empty chair" in 1965–1966. It was confirmed by the Soames affair in 1969, the final but abortive Gaullist attempt to lay the foundation of a political and strategic Europe. In short, the politico-strategic construction of Europe and the rebalancing of the Atlantic Alliance were, in the General's policy, two sides of the same coin.

The gradual retreat from military integration (which in 1966 merely reached its logical conclusion), far from signaling a desire to break with France's allies, constituted for de Gaulle the *sine qua non* condition for the buildup of France's military and strategic power in relation to the Alliance. The image maintained since (both by Gaullist tradition and by Atlanticist common wisdom) of a position near to armed neutrality within the Alliance, was in fact very far from de Gaulle's conception. For him, the defense of France, faced with a Soviet threat "two stages of the *Tour de France* away," was inseparable from defense of the other allies, starting with Germany. This position was confirmed to a large extent (in spite of a declaratory policy that chose to dramatize the rupture between France and NATO in order to maximize political and diplomatic advantages) by the Ailleret-Lemnitzer agreements in 1967. These discreetly but surely laid the foundation for a new military cooperation between France and NATO.

The Atlantic policy of de Gaulle also had an East-West or pan-European dimension. At its height, in the mid-1960s, it even held out the genuine prospect of transforming the international system beyond its old Cold War logic. To be sure, the first years, marked by the Berlin and Cuba crises, demonstrate a de Gaulle particularly firm when faced with Soviet threats and concerned for Western cohesion (although already sketching a new approach to East-West relations and to the German question). Yet, after 1964 his Atlantic policy was more and more clearly governed by the triad "détente, entente and cooperation." The refusal of integration, the search for autonomy from the United States, and the rejection of the strategic logic of flexible response were all tied to the idea of overcoming blocs, the veritable spearhead of French security policy in the years 1964–1968. Until the crushing of the Prague spring, which dealt a serious blow to de Gaulle's vision of one Europe from the Atlantic to the Urals, his policy with respect to NATO, beyond the goal of national independence, aimed to lay the foundation for what the General foresaw as a durable pan-European settlement. And if after 1968 this objective became unrealistic in the short or medium term, it remained, despite the Czechoslovak "*incident de parcours*" (hitch), at the heart of French national security policy.

Hence, whether in their national, West-West, or East-West dimensions, the permanence of the goals of Gaullist policy prevailed over changes of circumstance. And if the 1966 decision could appear to consecrate a narrow national interest, in reality it belonged to an ambitious international perspective. Liberated from the constraints of integration, France offered itself, alone, as the champion of European autonomy and the overcoming of blocs.

THE UNITED STATES AND THE GAULLIST CHALLENGE

Gaullist policy from its inception represented a challenge for the United States, a challenge that went to the very heart of U.S. conceptions of its own power, of its Atlantic leadership, and, at the end of the day, of the world order. Americans thus would be constantly tempted to reduce the General's policy to its narrow nationalist expression and to ignore its ambitions to transform the international system. They conveniently assimilated de Gaulle's diplomatic conceptions as a sort of archaic survival of the European balance of power, as opposed to the postnational approach to relations among states that they advocated and for which the "Atlantic community" might serve as paradigm. In the same way, especially after de Gaulle's double "No"—to the Nassau Accords and to the entry of Great Britain into the Common Market in 1963—the United States would systematically interpret French policy as an expression of anti-Americanism, as a wish to exclude the United States from Europe in order to better assert an exclusive French hegemony. In fact, faced with the General's policy, the United States had a tendency to confuse form and substance—which incidentally contributed to some extent to his own goals, especially *rang* (status).

Yet, while contesting the international dimension of Gaullist policy, the United States long seemed devoid of a truly constructive vision to pit against de Gaulle's grand design. If Eisenhower did answer the September 1958 memorandum (contrary to what some people in France let on), he in fact opposed it with what amounted to a flat refusal, sticking to a narrow defense of the Atlantic status quo. Similarly, when John F. Kennedy in 1962–1963 offered his own "grand design" of "Atlantic partnership" against de Gaulle's grand ambition for a "European Europe," the Americans had trouble hiding (behind the rhetoric of "interdependence") their concern to maintain indefinitely, within the framework of an Atlantic Alliance of which they could remain the uncontested leaders, their hold over emerging European unity. Finally, when the General developed his trilogy of "détente, entente and cooperation," and announced his ambition to move beyond blocs to put an end to the division of Europe, the Americans countered with the necessity of conserving a tightly integrated Alliance, which they considered had allowed the stabilization of the Cold War in Europe and the establishment of détente between East and West. Until 1965 at least, U.S. policy thus remained "wait and see"; faced with a Gaullist challenge whose implications they minimized, it essentially consisted of reasserting the leadership of the United States in an Atlantic Alliance consolidated around its own Cold War model.

French withdrawal from the integrated organization confirmed the failure of this dilatory strategy and placed the Americans in a dilemma, one which was first felt in the early months of 1965 when it became clear that de Gaulle was indeed intending to follow the logic of "dis-integration" from NATO to its conclusion. The leaders of the Johnson administration were convinced that the United States should and could prepare for a French withdrawal (in fact de Gaulle's decision in the spring of 1966 caused no surprise in Washington); the withdrawal, they reckoned, would have surmountable military consequences for the Alliance only if the United States managed to avoid the French example spreading like wildfire to the rest of the Alliance. Yet there remained a major question: Was it necessary to demonstrate firmness toward de Gaulle and make him pay dearly for his decision in order to prevent a possible propagation of his ideas among the other allies, even if at the risk of radicalizing the General's policy, which might then lead to a more serious break within the Alliance? Or on the contrary, was it necessary to demonstrate flexibility and so manage a quiet French withdrawal in order to maintain the possibility of a calm cooperation between France and its allies, even at the risk of fostering the General's objectives? This alternative was hotly debated between the State Department, which maintained a position of intransigent Atlanticism and wanted to give de Gaulle a hard time, and the Pentagon, which favored a much more pragmatic attitude. In these conditions, it was President Johnson himself who had to choose. Reckoning that the United States would place itself in a humiliating position with respect to an ungrateful ally if it had to contest de Gaulle's decision, he imposed on his administration a position closer to the Pentagon's, thus avoiding a confrontation with de Gaulle.

It was this choice, undoubtedly more personal and intuitive than truly strategic, that allowed the United States to "rebound" from the French withdrawal and to take the Atlantic Alliance in hand, eventually elaborating a constructive policy in the face of the challenge presented by de Gaulle. In fact, the pragmatic management of the French withdrawal by the Americans rested on a wager: By solving the "de Gaulle problem," they would solve the Alliance problem as a whole; this wager proved to be won, once France chose to put itself on the margins of NATO. The French retreat from integrated working bodies allowed the United States to reassert its leadership within the Alliance and to surmount the vetoes previously provoked by Paris. In parallel, U.S. diplomacy expertly exploited the now open dissidence of France within the Alliance in order to rebuild, starting in 1966–1967, a political and strategic consensus that was to a large extent defined by opposition to French conceptions, which were now isolated from other Europeans. This consensus was notably confirmed through the 1967 adoption of the Harmel report on the future tasks of the Alliance and by the strategy of flexible response, previously blocked by Paris. To this was added reinforcement of NATO's military cohesion, which the Americans obtained on the heels of the French withdrawal by exploiting (aided by the Mansfield Amendment) the risk of the integrated military structure falling apart.

TWO STRATEGIES FOR EUROPE AND FOR THE ALLIANCE

The 1966 decision was thus paradoxically an opportunity for the United States to reassert its managerial role in an Alliance whose leadership it retained, while recognizing at last the necessary character of its adaptation to new realities. This takeover of the Atlantic Alliance put a provisional end to transatlantic misunderstandings. However, if these misunderstandings had become confused during the 1960s with Franco–U.S. disagreements, the Atlantic crisis that culminated in 1966 cannot be reduced, without minimizing its bearing, to a quarrel between de Gaulle and the United States.

The Gaullist policy was indeed as much a revealer of the Atlantic crisis as its catalyst. When the General returned to power, this crisis was already latent and his actions in the years that followed served less to provoke it than to precipitate it. Thus, the deeper origins of this crisis are to be found in the ongoing transformations of the power relations that underpinned the international system: transformations that were strategic (the probable loss of U.S. nuclear supremacy after *Sputnik*), economic (the end of the cycle of reconstructing and setting Western Europe on its feet), and even political (France's return to stability and the international reestablishment of Germany). These were the structural developments that led the Alliance at the end of the 1950s and beginning of the 1960s to enter a phase of questioning fundamentals, in which Gaullist France played an active, but by no means exclusive role by questioning the strategic equation of extended deterrence (whose credibility was being undermined by the balance of power) and by questioning U.S. supremacy in the conduct of the Alliance.

In the middle of the 1960s, the structural crisis of NATO was transformed into an existential crisis. The growing military implication of the United States in Vietnam brutally posed (as the Suez crisis had once) the question of the Alliance's limits: How far should Atlantic solidarity extend? Should it cover U.S. policy in Southeast Asia, a policy whose rationale the allies were contesting? Above all, the gradual establishment of détente between the superpowers, then in Europe itself, posed the question of the *raison d'être* of a NATO whose creation had been shaped under the massive and imminent threat of the USSR.

Gaullist policy, even if it clearly diagnosed this situation, was not itself at the origin of a crisis that was both structural and existential. On the contrary, until 1963 at least (when the French gave up proposing reform of the Atlantic Alliance), it was a matter of de Gaulle trying to find a solution by seeking to win over his partners to his views. It is in this sense that opposition between France and the United States was paradigmatic of transatlantic misunderstandings as a whole: Two strategies for Europe and for the Alliance confronted each other against the backdrop of profound transformations in the international environment. The two strategies relied on the same objective realization about the evolution of the context from the early days of the Alliance, but they arrived at opposite solutions: de Gaulle's was revisionist, and America's one was attached to the status quo. (This is particularly clear with respect to nuclear problems, where the French and Americans agreed on diagnosing the lost credibility of massive retaliation after *Sputnik*, but proposed to remedy this in radically opposed manners, the former by European nuclear autonomy, and the latter by flexible response.)

Does this mean that French withdrawal (which sanctioned de Gaulle for his failure to rally his partners to his vision of the Alliance, but did not signify the abandonment of this vision) marked a victory for Atlantic immobility? No, because the Alliance was in a way revitalized by the Gaullist episode, to the extent (as has been said) to which the French withdrawal allowed the United States to finally reestablish its Atlantic leadership and thus to strengthen the cohesion of NATO. As Americans foresaw, the simple fact that the Alliance had resisted the shock of 1966 would powerfully contribute to consolidate it once this shock was absorbed.

Moreover, the Atlantic Alliance was in many ways different in 1967 from what it had been in 1958 or even in 1962, because the political and strategic consensus that the Americans managed to reconstitute in the wake of the French secession paradoxically integrated the Gaullist vision within it, at least to some extent. In the political domain, the new legitimacy of the Alliance, which the Harmel report found to be compatible with détente, owed much to de Gaulle's policy on Eastern Europe, even if the NATO conception of détente was different from the General's, since it postulated the maintenance of blocs. In the strategic domain, the adoption of flexible response was basically possible only because the Americans had agreed after 1965 to temper initially maximalist conceptions by revising their calculations of the nuclear threshold, and to some extent integrate the European strategic conceptions of which France had made itself the spokesman. Finally, in the military domain, the acceptance by the United States and its integrated allies, even if against their will, of a new form of military cooperation at the heart of the Alliance (as defined by the Ailleret-Lemnitzer agreements) carried within itself an incipient questioning of the dogma of integration that, even if it remained limited to the French case, already prefigured (we will return to this in our conclusion) what an Atlantic Alliance might be if liberated from the logic of power blocs.

In short, if French dissidence within an Alliance now of "14 + 1" marked the failure of a veritable renewal of the Atlantic Alliance, and even if the Alliance continued after the Gaullist episode to function in a crisis mode, de Gaulle's politics had by and large contributed to strengthen it. This is not the smallest paradox of what was truly a grand design, which at the end of this book we will review and then evaluate the legacy.

NOTE

1. See Stanley Hoffmann, *Decline or Renewal? France Since the 1930s*, New York, Viking, 1974.

Acronyms and Abbreviations

ABM	Antiballistic missile
ACCHAN	Allied Command Channel
ACLANT	Allied Command Atlantic
ACE	Allied Command Europe
AEC	Atomic Energy Commission (U.S.)
AFCENT	Allied Forces Central Europe
AFMED	Allied Forces Mediterranean
BAOR	British Army of the Rhine
CAP	Common Agricultural Policy
CATAC	Commandement aérien tactique
CDU	Christian Democratic Union (FRG)
CFSP	Common Foreign and Security Policy
CEA	Commissariat à l'énergie atomique
CEMA	Chef d'état-major des Armées
CENTAG	Central Army Group
CHEM	Centre des hautes études militaires
CIA	Central Intelligence Agency
CINCENT	Commander in Chief, Central Europe
CINCHAN	Commander in Chief, Channel
CINCMED	Commander in Chief, Mediterranean
COMCENTAG	Commander, Central Army Group
DDEL	Dwight D. Eisenhower Library
DOT	Défense opérationnelle du territoire
DPC	Defense Planning Committee
DPWG	Defense Planning Working Group
EDC	European Defense Community
EEC	European Economic Community
ESDP	European Security and Defense Policy
EU	European Union

FAS	Forces aériennes stratégiques
FATAC	Force aérienne tactique
FFA	Forces françaises en Allemagne
FRG	Federal Republic of Germany
GATT	General Agreement on Tariffs and Trade
GDR	German Democratic Republic
GREFHAN	Groupe d'étude français sur l'histoire de l'armement nucléaire
ICBM	Intercontinental Ballistic Missile
IFRI	Institut français des relations internationales
IHEDN	Institut des hautes études de défense nationale
IRBM	Intermediate Range Ballistic Missile
JCAE	Joint Committee on Atomic Energy (U.S.)
JFKL	John F. Kennedy Library
LBJL	Lyndon B. Johnson Library
MBFR	Mutual and Balanced Forces Reductions
MC	Military Committee
MLF	Multilateral Force
MRP	Mouvement Républicain Populaire
NADGE	NATO Air Defense Ground Environment
NATINAD	NATO Integrated Air Defense
NATO	North Atlantic Treaty Organization
NHP	Nuclear History Program
NPG	Nuclear Planning Group
NPT	Nonproliferation Treaty
NSAM	National Security Action Memorandum
NSC	National Security Council
NSF	National Security File
NTB	Nuclear Test Ban
OPCOM	Operational Command
OPCON	Operational Control
OSCE	Organization for Security and Cooperation in Europe
SAC	Strategic Air Command (U.S.)
SACEUR	Supreme Allied Commander Europe
SACLANT	Supreme Allied Commander Atlantic
SALT	Strategic Arms Limitation Talks
SFIO	Section française de l'internationale ouvrière (Socialist Party)
SGDN	Secrétariat général de la défense nationale
SHAPE	Supreme Headquarters Allied Powers Europe
SPD	Social Democratic Party (FRG)
TNWs	Tactical Nuclear Weapons
UNR	Union pour la République nouvelle (Gaullist Party)
USAREUR	U.S. Army Europe
USCINCEUR	U.S. Commander in Chief Europe
USIA	U.S. Information Agency

Chapter One

1958: De Gaulle Hoists His Colors

In 1948–1949, when the establishment of blocs appeared irreversible, France had played a decisive role in the creation of the Alliance. Even though this Atlantic choice was not made without certain questions or afterthoughts, it seemed that only an engagement in force by the United States in the defense of Western Europe could ensure the security of the Old Continent faced with the gravity of the Soviet danger. Then, in the face of rising perils, the French had been anxious to give weight to the U.S. guarantee to Europe and had favorably welcomed the setting up of a military organization that would concretize the Atlantic Pact in the wake of the Korean War. But very soon, numerous international crises (wars in Indochina and Algeria, the European Defense Community (EDC) affair, the Suez crisis, the launch of *Sputnik*) were going to make membership in NATO problematic for a France undermined by internal instability and by colonial decomposition. Against the background of an almost permanent Franco-American crisis, French participation in the Alliance—a reflection of all the national and international dilemmas that the Fourth Republic had to face—constantly gave rise to more frustrations and dissatisfactions. In this sense, the General's return to power in June 1958 would consecrate a profound evolution in France's Atlantic policy, which, at least since the last years of the Fourth Republic, was marked by a veritable loss of faith in NATO. In taking on this heavy heritage, de Gaulle was going to use an approach that seemed to have some continuity with that of his predecessors, but his return to public affairs also marked a break in France's relations with the Atlantic Alliance. This was illustrated by the memorandum addressed in September 1958 to the American president and the British prime minister, which aimed not only to state the new orientations of the Atlantic policy, but also to clearly mark France's comeback as a major Western power.

A LOSS OF FAITH

In 1958, after a decade of Western alliance, French experience of NATO participation was already long. It had been significantly marked from the start by certain reservations, which the evolution of the political and strategic context had
gradually transformed into many frustrations.

Reservations and Frustrations

Since the Alliance's formation, France's Atlantic policy had been colored by worries, if not second thoughts. The Washington Treaty signed on April 4, 1949,
brought a properly existential guarantee—that of the United States—against a Soviet threat that was at that time muted and latent, but that the Korean War would
soon render massive and imminent. But the Atlantic Pact also bore certain risks
in the medium or long term that were already well identified by the French and
that future events would confirm. In the first place, wasn't the rearmament of
Germany contained within the Alliance like "the germ in the egg," in Hubert
Beuve-Méry's famous phrase?[1] While a Germany divided and under surveillance
no longer represented a direct military danger to France as the main continental
power (with the exception of the USSR), the possible remilitarization of the Federal Republic of Germany (FRG) remained, four years after the war's end, more
or less unacceptable to the French. Next, what would happen to French interests
overseas? Of course Paris had obtained the inclusion of Algerian territory (then
constituted as French *départements*) within the zone covered by Article 6 of the
treaty, but such was not the case with colonial possessions properly speaking. In
a general context of decolonization, could France, in the midst of the war in Indochina, obtain its Atlantic allies' recognition of the rationale of its overseas policy? And inversely, would Atlantic integration not constrain its margin of maneuver and its military autonomy outside Europe? Finally, in an Atlantic Alliance
in which the influence of *les Anglo-Saxons* could only predominate, wouldn't
France find itself marginalized, if not contested, as a world power? This explains
the desire of French decision makers at the time the treaty was negotiated to establish a sort of directorate composed of the United States, Great Britain, and
France, a body that would guarantee the latter parity status with its major allies—
a wish that was not satisfied, however, despite the establishment of a tripartite
"Standing Group" that in practice was given limited power and a wish that de
Gaulle was to some extent going to take over.

The evolution of the Alliance in the 1950s would justify the initial fears of the
French negotiators. After the vicissitudes of the EDC, whose failure in 1954 culminated in the first major Franco-American and Atlantic crisis, France found itself constrained by the Paris Agreements to accept the entry into NATO (and
hence the rearmament) of Germany. In parallel, the war in Algeria, and the recently ended one in Indochina, distracted it more and more from the European

theater. The dual consequence was that a rise in German power threatened France's status as the foremost continental member of NATO at a time when its contribution to the defense of Europe happened to be weakening and when the allies, starting with the United States, were proving less and less disposed to recognize that—as French diplomats tried to demonstrate—France's actions in Algeria were part of the West's grand combat against international subversion.

By the mid-1950s, the French, as a result, were already appearing to allied eyes as the "bad pupils" in the Atlantic class. The allies proved all the more critical of the weakening of the French contribution to Western defense because it resulted from a colonial policy that they were less and less prone to endorse. The French, aware of the extent of the gap between their means and their ambitions, and presented with a difficult choice between their European and their overseas commitments, increasingly resented NATO as a constraining burden upon their interests, status, and international margin of maneuver. The Suez crisis in October 1956 would act both to reveal and catalyze these frustrations. From Paris's viewpoint, it demonstrated that Western solidarity went in only one direction, since the United States had not hesitated to abandon its European allies, France and Great Britain, in the name of its own interests, especially those in the Arab world. Worse, Washington had enjoined Paris and London to put an end to an operation aimed at both defending their positions in the Middle East and reasserting their status as world powers. Hence the affair culminated in a new and very serious Franco-American and Atlantic crisis.

After the crisis, France's frustration with the United States naturally carried over principally onto NATO, the expression *par excellence* of a U.S. guardianship that was accepted with increasing difficulty. More specifically, France started to question that which appeared largely responsible for the weakening and obliteration of its power: NATO integration. The inverse reaction took place on the British side, with London trying after Suez to reinforce its "special relationship" with Washington—which in repercussion would only aggravate French frustration by feeding its obsessive fear of an Anglo-Saxon directorate at the core of the Alliance. At the end of 1956, only 10 percent of the French, according to a survey, considered that the United States treated their country on an equal basis (this figure would be only 4 percent at the end of 1957) and 39 percent judged American influence on French policy to be excessive.[2] As for the politicians, most of them, like Minister of Foreign Affairs Christian Pineau, thought that "the principal victim" of the Suez Affair was in fact the Atlantic Alliance.[3]

Two years before the General's return, Suez had significantly modified France's relationship with the rest of the Alliance. The crisis and its consequences, against the background of the aggravation and internationalization of the Algerian conflict, already marked a clear turning point. French diplomacy had focused since the end of the war on maintaining France alongside Britain and the United States as the third "Great" Western power. But even if it had somehow managed to do so up to Suez, after the crisis it had become very difficult for those in charge of this diplomacy to maintain this pretence. "Within the Three, France possesses the least strong voice and sometimes risks isolation," the French representative to the Atlantic Council modestly recognized in the spring of 1958, when de Gaulle returned to public affairs.[4] This was an understatement: In reality, the Suez crisis had opened a decisive phase in the relations between France and NATO, a phase in which the disadvantages of the latter now appeared greater than its advantages. In short, the initial questioning had given way to frustrations, and these now threatened to turn French participation in the Alliance into a loss of faith, if not dispute.

Strategic Uncertainties

The Suez crisis marked not only a political turning point in the relations between France and the Alliance, it also inaugurated a period of strategic uncertainties that were all the more pressing in that they concerned the country's vital interests. Seen from Paris, the Soviet ultimatum issued in the midst of the Suez crisis by Nikolay Bulganin to France and Great Britain, backed up by atomic threat, far from being stymied by the American nuclear guarantee, had neutralized it. To the French at least, this demonstrated that the United States, faced with the risk of an atomic confrontation with the USSR, privileged de-escalation—be it at the expense of their allies' own interests. In short, American extended deterrence, from the start the cornerstone of the Atlantic Alliance, was no longer entirely unconditional. In these circumstances, the launch of *Sputnik* that in autumn 1957 seemed to announce a Soviet strategic breakthrough, would again sharpen French disquiet about the reliability of the U.S. nuclear guarantee, since the credibility of "massive retaliation" could only diminish as the United States became itself vulnerable. John Foster Dulles himself recognized, in private, that the buildup of the Soviet nuclear arsenal, of which *Sputnik* was the symbol, diminished the plausibility of a massive American response in case of an attack against Western Europe—hence the necessity for the United States to adopt a military posture that did not necessarily imply escalation to nuclear extremes in responding to limited aggression.

All this just confirmed the advent of a situation of mutual deterrence that the strategist Albert Wohlstetter would theorize some months later in a landmark article.[5] Nevertheless, U.S. nuclear strategy remained unchanged in principle after *Sputnik*. Despite pressure from the military, notably General Maxwell Taylor, the U.S. Army chief of staff, Eisenhower was opposed to abandoning massive retaliation. The president in effect did not believe in the possibility of waging "limited" wars: any confrontation, even local, with the USSR, especially in Europe, could only lead to a total nuclear confrontation, for which the United States ought to remain prepared. Moreover, he was hostile to an increase in military expenditure that would unfailingly result if the role of conventional arms were increased, and he judged as politically dangerous any measure that in the eyes of the European allies called into question the absolute character of the American nuclear guarantee. In fact, the directive NSC 5810, adopted in April 1958, re-affirmed "that nuclear weapons will be used, as necessary, to defend Free World interests."[6]

These U.S. reassurances were insufficient to appease French strategic preoccupations, already sensitive in the mid-1950s and reanimated by the *Sputnik* launch—all the more so because France was largely kept in ignorance of nuclear affairs by the United States. When in 1953 the Americans introduced atomic weapons into the U.S. Army arsenal in Europe, the French were hardly involved in the process—unlike the British, who were involved to a limited extent. The strategic influence of France within NATO found itself even more narrowly limited, if not marginalized, thus leading to a gradual—but from 1954 to 1958 more and more clear—choice for a national nuclear option by the Fourth Republic. This choice was even more unavoidable because it clearly appeared that the United States was by no means disposed to aid France in acquiring atomic weapons. Tied by the McMahon Act of 1946 that in principle (even after the 1954 amendment) forbade any assistance in this matter to foreign countries, the Americans remained fundamentally hostile to France's more or less declared nuclear ambitions. This did not prevent them, however, in the post-Suez context, from ultimately consenting to inflect this legislation to the benefit of the British, who, reputed to have achieved "substantial progress" in the mastery of the atomic bomb, could then, under the terms of a new amendment passed in 1958, profit from U.S. atomic assistance. With this unequal treatment, and confronted with the difficulty of realizing and especially financing a national atomic weapon, the last governments of the Fourth Republic had tried to give their atomic policy a European dimension, reckoning that if it was up to France to correct the nuclear imbalance favorable to *les Anglo-Saxons* in the Alliance, it could not do so "entirely alone" and that it had at the very least a "need for the understanding and support of its European partners."[7] In the greatest secrecy, negotiations between France, Germany, and Italy had even been held in 1957–1958 with a view to tripartite cooperation in the military nuclear area. This project, named "FIG" (France-Italy-Germany) by some insiders, gave rise in February 1958 to agreements between Franz-Josef Strauss, Jacques Chaban-Delmas, and Paolo Emilio Taviani, respectively the West German, French, and Italian defense ministers.[8] If the concrete significance of these accords remained unclear, things nonetheless went sufficiently far (at least until de Gaulle's return put an end to the affair in June 1958[9]) to disturb the Americans.

Due to the still-distant character of a real French nuclear capability, it was especially within NATO, in other words by trying to affect the strategic choices of the United States, that France in these years tried to gain some influence over the Alliance's nuclear affairs. In the spring of 1957, Paris had suggested through Christian Pineau that the United States commit itself to put nuclear weapons at the eventual disposal of the Europeans.[10] Accordingly, Washington made formal

proposals at the Alliance summit in December 1957 to respond to European and
especially French strategic anxieties: the installation in Europe of intermediate
range ballistic missiles (IRBMs) to be put into operation by Europeans, and the
creation of a NATO nuclear stockpile in Europe to be used by allied national
armies—the warheads in both cases under U.S. control in peacetime, in accordance with the McMahon provisos. In short, for the Americans it was a matter of
introducing into the NATO framework both tactical and theater atomic weapons
placed under "double key," in order to satisfy European demands for nuclear
sharing, but without abandoning ultimate control. Moreover, Washington proposed cooperating with "interested" allies concerning the technology of nuclear
submarine propulsion, which lay outside the McMahon Act—an offer that particularly interested Paris. Thus, without questioning the fundamental choice of
nuclear nondissemination partially inflected to benefit the British alone, this set
of measures aimed to reassure Europeans about the efficacy of the American um-
brella in the context of new strategic equilibria. Nevertheless, these measures did
not manage to convince the French of the futility of their own nuclear effort.

Integration in Question

Questions about France's place in NATO also—after 1956 at least—carried
over onto more specific military issues, in other words, onto the question of integration. Here again, the Suez crisis had served to expose latent problems. The
Franco-British intervention had resulted in an integration of forces under
British command, and consequently the failure of the operation was widely ascribed, on the French side, to the situation of dependence in which the French
forces found themselves. The very notion of military integration, though at the
basis of the organization of Atlantic defense since the early 1950s, was now
openly criticized. It was more and more felt as a constraint upon the French military, all the more so because operations in North Africa, taking over from the
war in Indochina, had necessitated withdrawing forces normally assigned to
NATO in Central Europe, which aroused acerbic criticism from the allies, who
were concerned, as we have seen, not to drain the Alliance's line of defense. As
a result, even if in the last analysis France kept full sovereignty over its own
forces, the mechanics of Atlantic integration were going to nourish the sentiment of an amputated military autonomy, hence of a limited sovereignty.[11] This
sentiment was aggravated by the intensive allied use of national airspace and
territory (the NATO Secretariat, SHAPE, AFCENT, lines of communication,
pipelines, supply depots, and air and naval bases). This use was all the more
visible and politically sensitive because with a foreign military presence of
about fifty thousand men (mostly Americans) in peacetime, this logistical
contribution to NATO was by definition passive, and so it was resented as
something required if not imposed, and overshadowing an active operational
contribution that by then was very reduced.

This negative perception of integration was accentuated by the fact that the military responsibilities held by France within NATO seemed marginal. With the important exception, it must be admitted, of Allied Command Europe's (ACE) main subordinate command, the Central Europe command (AFCENT, established at Fontainebleau), France did not hold any major command. Of the thirteen principal NATO commands, only AFCENT belonged to it, as opposed to seven to the United States and five to Great Britain.[12] So certain French demands recurred, which the Fifth Republic would take over, concerning a larger share of military responsibility within NATO, notably in the Mediterranean. Moreover, starting in 1955–1956 when the operations in Algeria substantially lowered the level of French military contribution to the defense of the central front, the FRG set up a Bundeswehr destined in a few years to become the principal conventional army of NATO on the Old Continent, thus threatening French primacy. Paradoxically, it was therefore at the very moment when they could least legitimately claim greater responsibility, due to the weakness of military means placed at NATO's disposal, that the French, who were kept out of nuclear affairs, began to feel a real frustration about their weak influence within the integrated military structure.

Finally, this was compounded by an older dissatisfaction. When NATO was being set up in the early 1950s, Paris had hoped that the integrated commands would be placed under the politico-military responsibility of the higher organizational bodies, specifically the Atlantic Council, the supreme body in the Alliance, and the Military Committee. In Paris's view, a subsidiary of the latter, of which it was the executive, called the Standing Group, based in Washington and composed exclusively of French, British, and American officers, should have been confided a major role in the direction of NATO. But in 1958, the inverse situation prevailed in actuality.[13] The integrated staffs, and SHAPE for a start, where the Americans inevitably predominated, held the real military and strategic influence. The Military Committee and the Standing Group, and in the last analysis, the Council, were *de facto* short-circuited by the integrated commands, which actually were U.S. commands. All this aggravated French disillusionment with Atlantic integration still more. In fact, though originally ardently desired by the French to give weight to the American guarantee, this integrated organization was — already at the end of the 1950s — being strongly contested by them.

De Gaulle and NATO before 1958

From 1949 to 1958, de Gaulle's ideas about the Alliance had changed considerably. The General had generally approved the concluding of the Atlantic Pact, reckoning that only the United States was in a position to defend a Western Europe faced with the Soviet threat. Yet, he had then announced certain reservations that would recur again, in their overall orientations, in his policy toward the Alliance after 1958, notably deploring that the Washington Treaty carried no guarantee of automatic assistance in its Article 5, unlike the Brussels Treaty of 1948.

Moreover, he was already disturbed that the zone covered by the Washington Treaty, limited to the North Atlantic, was too narrow with respect to the more global realities of the Soviet threat. He feared, in short, that France would find itself, from a political and strategic viewpoint, marginalized within the Atlantic ensemble.

The General's attitude with respect to the Alliance would quickly be transformed into a critique with no concessions, particularly after the1954 EDC crisis. His criticism was fed simultaneously by the objective deterioration of the French position within the Alliance and by the discrediting of the rulers of the Fourth Republic, now being castigated by de Gaulle for their "Atlantic docility."[14] Not only was the Alliance becoming, he thought, a shackle on France's international action, particularly overseas, but it also no longer entirely ensured its security. By 1955, the General thought the value of NATO to be at best relative, considering that for France what really mattered was the nuclear power that it ought to give itself, as well as its bilateral relations with the United States and Great Britain. Two years later, he wondered if France should remain within NATO, concluding: "I would not want to withdraw myself from NATO. I would like NATO to be seriously modified." But in February 1958, at the time of the Sakhiet affair (which culminated in the last Franco-American crisis under the Fourth Republic and demonstrated France's disastrous situation on the international scene), he broke step. "If I governed France, I would quit NATO. NATO is against our independence and our interest," he confided. Undoubtedly he was already distinguishing, as he would constantly after 1958, between the Alliance properly speaking, that is, adherence to the Washington Treaty, which was not in question, and what he called NATO, that is to say, the integrated military organization, which he clearly called into question. But it still remained true, as the American journalist Cyrus L. Sulzberger (who met him regularly) noted, that "the nearer his comeback approached, the more dismal his view of NATO became."[15]

By the mid-1950s, de Gaulle had grasped the long-term implications of the modification of the U.S.–Soviet nuclear balance. When in the spring of 1956 Colonel Pierre Gallois, then assigned to SHAPE and associated with the elaboration of allied strategy, had briefed de Gaulle on the subject at the Hotel La Pérouse, he had not failed to draw his attention to the foreseen consequences of future Soviet capabilities on the credibility of massive retaliation.[16] And the *Sputnik* launch told de Gaulle that, given the new vulnerability of U.S. territory, "the United States would not fight for us."[17] By 1958, then, the General had already made the strategic diagnosis on which he would later base his critique of extended deterrence and by which he would justify French nuclear choices: that of the inevitable erosion of the U.S. guarantee in Europe.

However, the focal point of de Gaulle's criticism of the Atlantic organization, at the time of his return to public affairs, was the military question. The fact of integration properly speaking, that is to say, the permanent assignment of French forces to NATO commands—hence, in the final analysis, to the United States—

just as much as the presence of foreign forces on national territory, were both in contradiction with the idea he had of the international role and status of France. His hostility to integration was long-standing. He had already had experience of it during World War II, notably during the winter operations of 1944–1945, during which he opposed Eisenhower over the defense of Strasbourg. He came out of it convinced that the principle of a single allied command in wartime was only worthwhile to the extent that the missions of national forces assigned to the coalition were compatible with the specific interests of the country in question. In 1951, while Allied Command Europe was being set up under the initiative of Eisenhower, then the supreme allied commander, de Gaulle, while recognizing that only the United States was in a position to defend Europe, was on guard against the dangers of Atlantic integration: "If American support must aid Europeans, it is not done to absolve them of their responsibilities, let alone to encroach upon their independence."[18] From that time on, he supported a system of combined staffs entrusted with preparing and executing strategic plans, but placed under the direct control of governments. He made the same warning in 1954 at the time of the EDC affair, the plan for which envisaged an even tighter integration than that foreseen within NATO: "How can our policy have vigor and impact when our defense is systematically placed in total dependence on others?"[19] Finally, in 1956, de Gaulle more than anyone else drew from the Suez affair the conclusion that integration was harmful, as he would later say to Guy Mollet.[20] It was really military organization that during the last years of the Fourth Republic crystallized the essence of his criticism of the Atlantic Alliance and of French policy: "I refuse to admit," he told his son-in-law, "that France's defense depends on a foreign general who himself depends totally on the President of the United States."[21]

THE MEMORANDUM

If there was one orientation clearly announced upon his return, it was the necessary French disengagement from military constraints that he had long considered to be unacceptable: "to disengage France, not from the Atlantic Alliance, which I intended to maintain by way of ultimate precaution, but from the integration realized by NATO under American command."[22] These ideas were known to key allies, which explains the lukewarm reaction to his return to power. While it was thought that France would return to stability and once again become a reliable ally, the probable counterpart was equally pressed: As a more solid member of the Atlantic Alliance, France would also be a more demanding partner, and the frustrations it felt since Suez would no doubt result in an active rethinking of the Atlantic status quo. But de Gaulle's return was in fact welcomed, notably in Washington, where, according to French ambassador Hervé Alphand, many Americans had the impression of finally rediscovering "the half-erased image of the France they loved and admired."[23]

De Gaulle's prime preoccupation at the start of June 1958 was the Algerian question, which was directly responsible for his return (and which would actually condition Franco-American relations to an increasing extent). When the General met with Maurice Couve de Murville to whom he had just entrusted the Ministry of Foreign Affairs, the international overview he went on to present was essentially devoted to the Algerian problem that had the country "by the throat," and only a few words were said on Atlantic and European matters.[24] That did not prevent them from being at the forefront of the General's mind when he publicly judged "our international position disparaged even within our alliances," [25] and he gave France the goal, once Algeria was pacified and the links with the French Union were redefined, of "taking the place that is ours, undertaking actions that are our own actions" in the Western world, to which "we belong without having to confine ourselves to it." [26]

The June 17 Meeting

De Gaulle made his views on the question of NATO known very quickly. On June 17, he called an important meeting at the Hotel Matignon on defense questions, to which came Minister of Foreign Affairs Couve de Murville, Minister of Armed Forces Pierre Guillaumat, and General Paul Ély, chief of staff of the army. Reviewing the principal dossiers concerned with national defense and the Atlantic Alliance, the new president of the Council abandoned the reserve he had publicly maintained until then. The statement was very clear:

> Our place in the NATO organization must be reconsidered. The Americans have at their disposal commands of an overwhelming preponderance. We are the object of discrimination that is not acceptable. By leaning on the McMahon Act, they keep us out of an essential area of common defense. This law is an American affair; it's up to them to modify it. . . . Essential conceptions of common defense lie outside our reach. We are completely in the dark about the plans developed by SAC and the British Bomber Command. [SACEUR] possesses means whose use is completely outside our decision-making power. We cannot accept this exclusion of which we are the object in matters of atomic war, all the less so in that our territory might eventually be used. . . . Without us, NATO would not exist. This is a situation from which we ought to draw consequences.[27]

Above all else, it was the nuclear topic that was on the meeting's agenda (it was at this meeting that the General put an end to the project of atomic cooperation with Germany).[28] It was a matter of deciding on the response to give to Eisenhower's proposals to the Atlantic summit in December 1957 concerning the creation of a nuclear stockpile and the installation of IRBMs within the NATO framework in Europe. While French national territory had been exempt up until then, as General Ély confirmed, acceptance of these proposals by France would lead for the first time to the introduction into France of American nuclear weapons. This evidently posed a question of principle, de Gaulle thought, inseparable from the general context of the Alliance that he had just evoked. While he did not reject it *a priori*, the presence of U.S. nuclear weapons in France should be subject to a triple condition: first, these weapons—whose simple presence on the ground "questions our national existence"—should in peacetime be placed under French control, if necessary with U.S. participation, and should not be used without the French government "giving its consent"; second, France ought to participate actively in the elaboration of the strategy under which these weapons would be activated as a last resort, in other words, be implicated in the "conception and planning of an atomic war"; and finally, France had to be able to have access to atomic secrets by being associated "with the development of military atomic research by the United States," from which France must be in a position to receive "assistance" in this domain.[29]

These demands were essentially in line with those of the Gaillard government, but they marked a hardening that disturbed the Ministry of Foreign Affairs, which thought the General's position "maximalist," especially concerning the control of IRBM warheads. The Americans, tied by the McMahon Act, would not be able to accept sharing such control, they thought at the Quai d'Orsay.[30] But de Gaulle had firmly decided to place the nuclear question at the center of his first talks with top NATO officials and *les Anglo-Saxons*, starting with the Americans.[31] And he undertook these conversations with a key idea: "France is already virtually an atomic power."[32] For him two implications followed: first, the United States, France, and Great Britain should set up a tripartite body charged with strategic coordination among the nuclear powers of the Alliance; second, France should be able to count on help to allow it to attain effective nuclear capability more rapidly. Depending on the response to these demands, France would study the question of nuclear stocks and IRBMs.

The new president of the Council received in turn the secretary general of the Alliance, the Belgian Paul-Henri Spaak; the supreme allied commander, American general Lauris Norstad; British prime minister, Harold Macmillan; and finally American secretary of state, John Foster Dulles. In these first exchanges; de Gaulle proved circumspect. While confiding his sentiments about the insufficiently recognized role of France, he stressed his overall reflections on the Alliance. While he clearly expressed the view—which could not surprise them—that France "does not approve of NATO,"[33] and that he attached a great importance to a "reorganization" of the Atlantic Alliance,[34] he was hardly precise about the forms it might take. Less than a month after his return to public affairs, he intended more to sound out the allies, but not without indicating that he would soon be making his own proposals.[35] Spaak, the first senior Atlantic figure to meet the new head of government, came out of the meeting rather reassured. The General, he recalled, was not hostile to NATO, even though he judged there was insufficient French influence in it.[36]

"France Is There"

The principal conversation during the start of the summer of 1958 took place on July 5 during Dulles's visit to Paris. The secretary of state, conscious of the importance of this first contact with de Gaulle, wanted to show that he recognized the historic and political impact of the General's return. France, he said, "has in the course of recent years not enjoyed the consideration that is due it in American opinion, but we hope that under your direction it will recover its position" as "the most loved country of all our allies." Yes, replied de Gaulle, Americans had been "disappointed by French flagging." But today, "France is there. It reassumes its means. It is a considerable element in the world and the proof is that you and I are both here." But the country must have the certainty of exercising world responsibilities, without which it will lose interest in the defense of the free world. He added that these world responsibilities were above all atomic.[37]

This was the core of a meeting clearly dominated by the nuclear issue. Dulles, who had prepared for his visit, tried to forestall the observations he was expecting from de Gaulle. At first, the secretary of state broached the question of the U.S. nuclear guarantee, which he ensured him remained effective, as much at the strategic level (where the United States would keep superiority over the USSR for a few more years) as at the European level (where U.S. IRBMs, soon to be deployed, would allow equilibrium to be maintained). Thus, the United States remained resolute on using atomic weapons to defend Europe. As for the deployment of theater nuclear weapons, it ought to prove to the allies that their security did not depend exclusively on strategic weapons stationed in the United States. From this arose the second point, concerning atomic responsibility. Dulles reminded him—reiterating in passing the American proposal to help France regarding nuclear submarine propulsion—that the United States had decided, within the limits of the MacMahon law (meaning while keeping full control in peacetime), to eventually put nuclear weapons at the disposal of the NATO allies. But while recognizing France's right to become a complete nuclear power ("it is up to you to decide"), the secretary of state did not disguise his prejudice against possible nuclear efforts independent of the United States. These would be, he stressed, a fruitless waste: only the United States was in a position to develop an effective nuclear force. It would be better for the allies, starting with France, to have the certainty that American nuclear weapons, when the time came, would be effectively available for the defense of Europe within the NATO framework.

Dulles scarcely concealed his hostility to the French nuclear effort as de Gaulle conceived it, that is, as resolutely autonomous. The calculation was clear: The United States hoped that as France became aware of the difficulties and costs of autonomous deterrence, it would be persuaded, prompted by well-designed American aid, to place its nuclear effort back within the NATO framework—in other words, under U.S. control.[38] Such would be, with variations, American policy regarding the *force de frappe* (strike force) in years to come.

On the first point Dulles raised, de Gaulle did not contradict him; faced with the Soviet menace, the American arsenal remained the best rampart. He proved rather serene about the validity of the American nuclear guarantee. Consciously or not, it was instead Dulles who entertained doubts in evoking the new atomic equilibria and their consequences for Western strategy, because by advancing the necessity of no longer making extended deterrence rest solely on weapons based in the United States, he implicitly expressed an uncertainty about the strategy of massive retaliation. With such a strategy being seriously criticized in the United States itself, Dulles's remarks could only encourage de Gaulle to question, deep down inside, the permanence of U.S. strategic nuclear engagement in Europe. This doubt was further fed by a meeting he had had a few days previously with General Norstad, during which the supreme allied commander had not given him a satisfactory response to the question of plans for employing nuclear weapons.[39]

However, de Gaulle was more on the offensive on the question of sharing atomic responsibilities and secrets. France, he told Dulles, intended to become an atomic power in its own right ("it is now a matter of months"), even if its arsenal would be on a wholly different scale from that of the United States. France would willingly accept, he argued, receiving or making nuclear weapons with the help of the United States, which would save money, but always on condition that it had the effective responsibility for and control over those weapons—it being understood that they were to be used under a NATO plan on which France had agreed. But if it was a matter of subordinating their use to a decision by the U.S. president or by SACEUR (which amounted to the same thing), then Dulles's proposal had no interest, since the disadvantages of deployment on French territory had no compensation in an increased role for France within the Western bloc. This in turn raised the issue of the sharing of responsibilities within the Alliance, with which de Gaulle was not satisfied. NATO, he explained, only covered a limited zone, that of Europe and the North Atlantic, whereas for France security mattered also in North Africa and the Middle East, among other places. In short, NATO as a regional alliance did not reflect the new strategic realities, nuclear or not. For a country like France these realities were worldwide. This was why, de Gaulle concluded, "one must establish a system" that lets France participate "in the planning of world security and strategic atomic armament." And that, he observed, "would necessarily involve a reorganization of the command structure."

The Crises of Summer 1958

After the July 5 meeting, the nuclear question remained a priority in Franco-American relations. The ball was in the French court: Should it respond formally to the American proposals by laying out the conditions for their acceptance? Paris seemed to hesitate over such an approach.[40] Over the summer, draft memoranda on the subject were prepared at the Quai d'Orsay. It would be a matter of responding to Dulles's proposals and restating the French position on the deployment on French territory of U.S. atomic weapons—that is, joint control of weapons to be used according to plans agreed in advance.[41] But the Quai was anxious to avoid offending the susceptibilities of the other allies by demanding for atomic affairs an overly visible tripartite consultation.[42] This was why in the end no move was undertaken for the time being.

The crises of July and August 1958 would get things going again. In fact they were the prelude to the initiative that de Gaulle, convinced now of the need to act, would take at the end of the summer. In fact, the Middle East crisis of July 1958 constituted the first large-scale illustration of France's mediocre influence on its U.S. and British allies and, more seriously, of the limited character of its strategic autonomy.

In the first months of the year, events in the Middle East were marked by Egypt's Gamal Abdel Nasser's activism and by increasing Soviet influence, in Syria especially. The proclamation in February of the United Arab Republic (UAR), a fusion of Syria and Egypt, seemed to undermine Western interests. Wouldn't countries favorable to the West, like Iraq, Lebanon, and Jordan, find themselves caught in a pincer? As summer approached, there was acute agitation in Lebanon. UAR partisans threatened the country's political equilibrium. France had particular responsibilities in the region, established by a long, historic tradition and reaffirmed in 1950 in a French, British, and American tripartite declaration. During his visit at the end of June, Macmillan agreed with de Gaulle on the necessity of Western nations acting in common.[43] Several days later, Dulles came to agree with the General's opinion that Western military intervention would be harmful and that it ought to be avoided, if possible (as he thought it was). The secretary did not hide his belief that France, on account of its Algerian situation, should keep out of the Middle East scene. De Gaulle added, though, that if there had to be U.S. and British intervention, then France, which had many interests in the Levant, "would be in any case present, whether the intervention was joint or whether it was between you and the English."[44]

Events rushed on: A coup d'état against the pro-Western monarchy in Iraq on July 14 precipitated Anglo-American intervention. The British sent three thousand parachutists into Jordan, and the Americans sent ten thousand marines to Lebanon. Paris was not informed in advance, but at most "simultaneously advised" of the operation by the British.[45] De Gaulle took very badly what he considered a serious injury to Western solidarity in a region where France had historic responsibilities. The Quai d'Orsay, in an unusually frosty note to Washington and London, pointed out "the extremely regrettable and worrying impression it had of the conditions in which the decisions had been taken by the two allies," decisions that "were not the subject of the least consultation with the French government," whereas France "is one of the three Western powers principally involved in the Middle East."[46] De Gaulle, who saw a bad precedent in this, decided to send the Mediterranean Fleet to cruise off the Lebanese coast and ordered the limitation to a minimum of contact between French and Anglo-Saxon warships; the cruiser *Colbert*, especially, was sent "to mark our presence separately." [47]

From a political standpoint, this crisis revealed Anglo-American attitudes toward France. It was all the more gravely resented by de Gaulle due to one of its military aspects: The Americans had had recourse, without informing Paris, to the Evreux base to set up an aerial bridge to Beirut.[48] He judged this an unacceptable affront to French sovereignty, since, as the Quai d'Orsay noted, "the utilization of French territorial bases or communications or airspace by the forces of the United States or Great Britain might have the effect of engaging France in certain implications that might not have been preceded by any consultation with France." [49] The affair clearly demonstrated what the General felt increasingly throughout the 1950s: Atlantic integration and the foreign military presence hobbled national independence.

The crisis of Quemoy and Matsu at the end of August was equally rich in lessons. It was potentially more serious, because it could appear linked to nuclear risk. Maurice Couve de Murville thought that events might degenerate, if not "lead to a war between China and the United States," and that in such a situation, "Taiwan would profit from the occasion to drag the United States into the reconquest of the continent." [50] On the night of August 22, Communist China resumed bombardment of the two small islands in the Formosa Straits occupied by the Nationalists. The United States quickly sent numerous naval and marine forces to Taiwan's aid. An escalation was feared—even though de Gaulle was not convinced in his heart of the grave risk of nuclear war.[51] Whatever the case, for the General, the United States had once again managed a very serious crisis with significant military means and without the least cooperation.[52] The affair confirmed the view that in the era of missiles, the zone covered by the Western alliance was too narrow, since the United States was inclined under Dulles's influence to "systematic interventionism" and could lead the world to the edge of a nuclear crisis without consulting its closest allies.[53]

The Memorandum

The crisis in the straits of Formosa, after the one in the Middle East, is at the direct origin of the initiative of September 1958. The idea of a memorandum on tripartite relations had been there, as we have seen, since the start of the summer, and atomic and strategic problems were at the heart of it. But the September initiative was taken personally by de Gaulle and it was more encompassing than the nuclear issue. The memorandum was incontestably "his affair." [54] He wrote a rather dry note himself on September 9, and then asked his diplomatic advisor, Jean-Marc Bœgner, and Maurice Couve de Murville to put it into proper form.[55]

Between Matignon and the Quai d'Orsay there were, if not fundamental differences of opinion on such an initiative, then at least differences over its nuances. Couve de Murville originally was hardly favorable to sending the document at all and saw it as "a fantasy that would be short-lived."[56] The Quai d'Orsay especially thought it was blowing in the wind to the extent that the memorandum had scarcely any chance of being accepted by *les Anglo-Saxons*. In a general manner, officials at the Ministry of Foreign Affairs remained marked by the policies of the Fourth Republic. They were desirous to avoid affronting the susceptibilities of the other allies. They wanted to carry on with tripartite demands and the Atlantic policy, with the latter leading France not to "disdain NATO" but rather to develop its presence and actions within it.[57] Couve de Murville himself was by nature prudent and he hesitated over the General's audacious initiatives, which he sought to temper. Perhaps more fundamentally, he did not have the same confidence as the other in the capacity of France to actually influence *les Anglo-Saxons* and feared that overly constraining tripartite mechanisms might oblige it to fall into alignment even more.[58]

The French initiative was confidential. It was addressed exclusively to the two English-speaking allies: De Gaulle made no mention of it to Konrad Adenauer whom he met two days before in Colombey and with whom he had decisive talks on Franco-German relations, in the course of which Atlantic problems were mentioned.[59] This denotes less a double game with regard to Germany than an important political reality, at least as de Gaulle perceived it: France was a world power, and the memorandum concerned the organization of Western security at a planetary level. The FRG was thus not concerned.

Dated September 17, 1958,[60] the memorandum was transmitted the following week to its recipients. It was July 25 when Hervé Alphand gave it to Dulles with a covering letter from the General to Eisenhower. The secretary of state did not conceal his skepticism: This document, he told him, raised considerable problems and would require careful consideration in both the State and Defense departments. This reaction did not surprise Alphand who, even before delivering the memorandum, had little hope that the United States would accept the French proposal and thought the approach futile, if not counterproductive.[61] This was also the opinion of Paul-Henri Spaak, whom de Gaulle received on September 24 and to whom he communicated the memorandum "as strictly personal, asking him not to mention it under any circumstances."[62]

What, then, was the tenor of this note, which this same Spaak estimated as "of exceptional importance"?[63] It was a short document that can be summarized as follows.[64] First came the motivations: The "recent events in the Middle East and in the Formosa Straits" have only confirmed the inadequacy of the "Western alliance" to the new international situation. While there was in effect a sharing of "risks incurred," there was no sharing of "decisions" or of "responsibilities." The threat was no longer limited to the North Atlantic zone (that defined in Article 6 of the Washington Treaty) and the security of Europe depended on "what happens" in Africa and in the Middle East; the "indivisible responsibilities" of France (i.e., the French Union) extended to Africa, the Indian Ocean, and the Pacific, "in the same way as those of Great Britain and the United States." Moreover, "the sphere of action of ships and planes and the range of missiles" capable of carrying nuclear weapons rendered the NATO system too "narrow." The result was that while it was justified in the beginning to delegate "in practice" decisions concerning defense "on a world scale" to the United States, it was otherwise today.

Hence the French proposal. Since "NATO in its current form" no longer satisfied the conditions of security, it was a matter of establishing a tripartite organization (United States, France, and Great Britain) on a "political and world strategic level" that would take political decisions "touching world security" and would prepare and if need be implement "plans for strategic action, notably regarding the use of nuclear weapons." Theaters of operation (Africa as well as the Atlantic, Pacific, and Indian oceans) were to be "organized and subordinated to the general organization" accordingly. And inasmuch as France saw such an evolution of the Western alliance as indispensable, it made it a condition of "any development in its current participation in NATO" and reserved an appeal, if necessary, to Article 12 of the Washington Treaty (which stipulates that "after the Treaty has been in force for ten years or at any time thereafter, the Parties shall, if any of them so requests, consult together for the purpose of reviewing the Treaty"). For the moment, the memorandum asked Great Britain and the United States to engage "as soon as possible" in consultations bearing on these propositions at the ambassadorial level in Washington and within the Standing Group of NATO, also located in Washington.

Problems of Interpretation

Although written in a clear style, the content of the memorandum of September 17, 1958, raised problems of interpretation from the start. Mentioning in turn the "Atlantic Alliance," the "Western alliance," and "NATO," de Gaulle proposed instituting within them a tripartite "organization." This gave rise to an ambiguity: The memorandum seemed to suggest simultaneously a reform of NATO (which in de Gaulle's words meant the integrated organization), a modification of the treaty properly speaking, and the creation of a new organization with a worldwide political and strategic mission. In reality, there was a hierarchy among these elements, though only implicitly so in the document, it is true. Because although NATO had to be reformed, this is not what was principally at stake in the memorandum, which did not detail the content of a possible reform of the integrated military organization.[65] In fact, de Gaulle thought the latter was a "secondary" question, because it covered only the North Atlantic zone. The real problem "lay on top." [66] And this problem was precisely that of relations among the three great Western nations. France did not intend to propose a reform of NATO proper as long as an agreement was not achieved over tripartite relations. One had "to begin with a general accord on world, political and strategic problems, and move down from there to precise questions," confirmed Couve de Murville.[67] For de Gaulle,

this could be summarized as follows: The aim was to reach a tripartite organization of Western security and to reorganize NATO accordingly, but if an agreement
were not possible on a tripartite organization, then France reserved the right to
modify unilaterally its position within NATO.[68] This way of seeing things, tending to organize problems and to subordinate the military to the political, would
remain at the core of French policy in the years to come.

But should this tripartite organization be formal or informal, *de jure* or *de
facto*? The memorandum might appear to suggest a formalization of tripartism,
since it proposed modifying the Washington Treaty. At the start, it was in this way
that the principal interested parties perceived it—or pretended to perceive it. But
de Gaulle had no preconceived ideas about the institutional form his initiative
ought to take. This was confirmed by Hervé Alphand to his American contacts: It
was not a matter of "creating a directorate of three" but of "establishing organized consultations aiming at all the problems of world security, with a concern for
finding a solution and a common plan of action." [69] In short, the approach was
pragmatic, and for the General the essential thing was to know if it were "possible or not to establish a common program of action by the West regarding problems posed in the world," with the institutional question coming afterward. It was
a matter of avoiding facing the USSR "in dispersed order," [70] for example, in the
Third World and more generally anywhere not pertaining strictly to NATO. On
these affairs, consultations with a view to elaborating a common position ought
to take account of realities and to adopt the line of whichever power was the most
implicated in any issue or any zone. In Morocco or Tunisia, for example, such a
common position "ought to be France's position." [71]

Yet it was the nuclear issue that really lay at the core of the tripartite approach.
In this respect *les Anglo-Saxons* at first interpreted the memorandum as a formal
requirement of a right of veto over U.S. nuclear forces on the world scale. This
was an interpretation the French tried immediately to dissipate: It was clear, the
Quai d'Orsay stressed, "that nobody could oppose a decision taken by a government on a problem that for it corresponds to an essential national interest," [72] as
was the case with nuclear issues. If de Gaulle offered as a condition for the stationing of American nuclear weapons in France the obtaining by Paris of a right
of veto over their use, it was in no way the same for the rest of the U.S. arsenal
in Europe and *a fortiori* in the world. Such a demand would be in contradiction
not only with the strictly national conception the General had of atomic weapons,
but also with his concern to avoid any U.S. *droit de regard* (right to examine) over
the future French nuclear force.[73] In fact, what the memorandum asked for was
that "the three Western powers act strategically in common, in conformity with
prepared plans," and do so first of all "about the decision to use atomic
weapons." [74] It would be a matter of "a sort of permanent and organized concerted
effort," [75] allowing the three powers to agree on a common strategy by defining
in peacetime the modes of possible recourse to nuclear arms. What de Gaulle
sought above all was to create the conditions for a fundamental agreement on the

role of nuclear arms within the Alliance and, more particularly, between a France that would soon be a nuclear power and its Anglo-Saxon partners, at a time when he feared that new strategic realities, because of the balance of terror, would make such an agreement difficult in the future. In sum, for the General it was a matter of trying to avoid a strategic divorce between Europe and America that he strongly feared, without yet believing it inevitable.

A decisive question remained, however: What were de Gaulle's intentions in writing this document? For some, it was a pretext: His goal was to broadcast France's new ambitions, but he did not really aim at the objectives being advanced, which were evidently unacceptable to his partners; the memorandum might even aim at provoking a negative reaction on their part so as to justify a policy of withdrawal from Atlantic integration. For others, on the contrary, the memorandum was by no means a feint: It simply corresponded with the idea de Gaulle had of the new strategic context and of the role of France in that context, and he drew the consequences they spelled for the Western alliance. The second interpretation is doubtless closer to reality, even if de Gaulle had scarcely any illusions about the possibility of his propositions being retained as they were.[76] To be sure, it cannot be ruled out that he may have desired, if not to justify his policy of calling military integration into question, then at least to make an announcement, to "hoist his colors," [77] in his own expression, before putting into effect a gradual withdrawal from NATO. But sending the memorandum cannot be reduced to tactical gesture or pretence. While remaining aware that tripartite proposals could not be accepted as such by his partners, de Gaulle did not necessarily exclude their coming about someday: he would continue to advance them for months, even years. And for the time being, he thought that "logically, everything runs toward an agreement." [78]

THE REACTIONS

So the memorandum had to be taken literally. This was France's policy, and these were its proposals; if they were rejected, this policy would be pursued unilaterally and French participation in NATO would be reduced. The first reactions to the sending of the memorandum would quickly push de Gaulle toward the latter course, even if the General would not try to accelerate things.

A Polite but Blunt Refusal

On July 5, Dulles had responded in anticipation of the memorandum. Alerted to de Gaulle's ideas on the Atlantic Alliance, he foresaw that the latter would formulate tripartite proposals. Indeed, from the start, while admitting the necessity of a greater solidarity and closer political consultation among the Western nations, Dulles had presented NATO as the natural framework for this cooperation and stressed that important progress had been made in this direction. And while recognizing that the great powers had "special" political and strategic responsibilities, he had immediately specified that these responsibilities "should be exercised with wisdom to avoid giving the impression that the major countries were acting out of pure nationalism and to take account of the principle of the sovereign equality of all nations." Finally, without ruling out better cooperation in practice among the three, he had warned de Gaulle against "any formal association designed to direct the free world." [79] NATO, and only NATO, was the proper venue for political and strategic cooperation among Western nations, and any measure making officially evident the managing role of some countries in the Western ensemble should be avoided. After the memorandum was sent, it was this line of argument that would be used to reply to de Gaulle.

The document immediately unleashed manifest disquiet among the Americans and top NATO officials on grounds of procedure. Both wanted to avoid at all costs letting other Alliance members feel that Washington was ready to give satisfaction to de Gaulle by lowering them to the role of second-rate powers. This concern applied as a priority to the two great European countries that could not pretend to the status of world powers, the FRG and Italy. U.S. diplomacy was especially anxious to preserve a feeling of equality among the allies, maybe factitious, but favorable to its own leadership. When Dulles proposed to Eisenhower, three weeks after the memorandum was sent, organizing (as the General suggested) a first series of tripartite discussions on his proposals, the president, in mid-October, gave a green light to such discussions on condition that the meetings take place at a level below that of secretary of state,[80] and he recommended that Dulles explain fully to the Italians and Germans that it was only a matter of discussing the proposals formulated by the French. This did not prevent Paris from congratulating itself that the Americans accepted the upcoming opening of tripartite conversations.[81] As for Macmillan, he let it be known to de Gaulle at the end of October, through his ambassador in Paris, that Great Britain, while disapproving of the orientation of the memorandum, was disposed to engage in tripartite discussions, even if London considered that it was not possible for the Big Three to speak of NATO, that is, without the other allies.[82]

Eisenhower's prudence was motivated by the fact that Adenauer had already reacted negatively to the affair, which he got wind of through Macmillan,[83] and which he broached directly with de Gaulle, to whom he complained bitterly about not having had communication about the memorandum when the General had spoken to him "in very general terms" about the NATO question at Colombey.[84] The Italians, for their part, protested vigorously in advance to the Americans and objected to the French on grounds of "method." [85] As for Spaak, who had discussed the memorandum with Dulles shortly beforehand, he thought the procedure proposed by de Gaulle "detestable": Though he had nothing against conversations at the ambassadorial level in Washington, he thought it dangerous to undertake them behind the backs of other members of the Alliance, since "in-

evitable indiscretions" could only "exacerbate feelings and increase distrust."
Above all, he considered that the proposal in the memorandum to make use of the
Standing Group, "a body which was subordinate to NATO and on which all the
fifteen member countries were represented" but on which sat only the three powers concerned, was a perversion of procedure. For him, too, it was a matter of
avoiding an ostensible treatment of "small countries" as inferior.[86] Thus, from the
standpoint of the immediate impact of the document issued by de Gaulle, allied
reactions were characterized by a very clear distrust of the French initiative, even
if those parties principally involved, the Americans and British, did not refuse
discussions, on condition that they take place in the least visible manner.

Reactions of substance confirmed this. The reply Eisenhower gave in due form
was dated October 20; this correspondence would become the subject of a
Franco-American polemic some years later, with Washington complaining that
Paris let it be known that the memorandum had languished without a response.[87]
Nevertheless, although it indeed exists, Eisenhower's response is practically a polite but blunt refusal. While recognizing that the memorandum raised "serious
questions" that merited attentive examination—the problem of defending the free
world was, he ensured, at the core of his own preoccupations—the president in
fact praised the status quo. The globalism of the communist threat, its multiform
and not strictly military character, were already taken into account by American
policy, and was even its principal postulate. As for the Atlantic Alliance, it had
adapted itself in the past two years to the new conditions of security, and consultations within NATO had long outstripped the framework of the European zone
in order to cover the Middle and Far East. In short, Eisenhower concluded,
though the Western alliance "must constantly evolve and find means to make itself more useful in the face of changing conditions," there was no question for
Washington of envisaging modifying the Washington Treaty.[88]

As de Gaulle would write, it was really an evasive response that eluded the nuclear question that was at the heart of the memorandum.[89] Eisenhower's response
was very close to the position of high NATO officials, led by Spaak, who wrote
a memorandum on the subject on October 15. The secretary general of NATO felt
that one had to acknowledge the experience of political consultation among allies, which in fact already had bearing on extra-European questions. These issues,
moreover, interested countries other than the Big Three—for example, Portugal,
the Netherlands, and Belgium. As for the idea of a tripartite organization, it would
not be tolerated by countries like Italy or Germany, not to mention the "small"
states of the Alliance. A directorate of three, he insisted, would be injurious to Alliance cohesion.[90] The same note was sounded in Bonn, where Adenauer thought
that a directorate of three would risk weakening NATO, and that it would be
preferable to seek to "strengthen the position of continental Europe" within the
Alliance,[91] and also in Rome, where President of the Council Amintore Fanfani
let it be known loudly and long that Italy could not accept a role as executor of
decisions taken by "three figureheads." [92]

Rupture or Continuity?

The memorandum, whose content was very quickly leaked and by the same token altered, inspired reticence among its recipients and irritation among other Alliance countries. Washington and London did not forbear entertaining this irritation, while pretending to dissipate it by better informing allies,[93] but de Gaulle — who had certainly anticipated it — declared himself "indifferent" to this irritation.[94] It was in this context that two tripartite meetings took place in Washington that brought together, on December 4 and 10, the ambassadors of France and Great Britain and Undersecretary of State Robert Murphy, during which Alphand clarified the memorandum. These discussions remained introductory; what was at issue was the method of following up on the French initiative. But if the conversations did not lead anywhere, they already dramatized what would quickly become a dialogue of the deaf: to the concern for pragmatism strongly pressed by Paris (there was no question of a "directorate"), London and Washington opposed a petition of principle (do nothing that could hurt the current functioning of NATO).[95]

Faced with evidence of the differences that separated him from his allies, de Gaulle in the fall of 1958 was manifestly tempted to hurry things along. "There was nothing to prevent us from taking action," [96] he would write in his *Memoirs*. On October 13, moreover, during a meeting on National Defense — even before receiving Eisenhower's reply — he had solemnly reaffirmed the double principle of his policy: defense of France must be "national," its "organization" must be "worldwide." [97] Did this mean that (anticipating the probable refusal by his allies) he counted immediately on putting into operation the policy announced on September 17, 1958, by responding with unilateral measures to what he perceived as a blunt refusal? The answer is no, for at least three reasons. First, even if the previous reactions of his partners confirmed his impression that they were not ready to accept his proposals, he could not draw at this initial stage any definitive conclusions because the position of *les Anglo-Saxons* was still far from being clear on certain problems such as the nuclear issue, the most determining of all. Then, the Americans and British consented to undertake discussions on these points, and it was only on the basis of the experience of these conversations that their positions would appear more clearly. Second, a rupture was not on the agenda of de Gaulle's Western policy, whose objective was, on the contrary, to work toward the reinforcement of the Alliance while promoting French interests. In the course of the summer of 1958, the General had certainly issued a number of firm options, starting with a necessary distancing from military integration; but although he had a strategic vision of the evolution of the Alliance, de Gaulle was also concerned with tactics, and these obliged him to proceed pragmatically — due to the evolution in the positions of other actors and by dint of circumstances. Finally, France did not yet have the means to adopt a unilateral policy, and international circumstances did not lend themselves to one; and while de Gaulle thought that

France should assert its own orientations, he thought "circumstances decreed that we should act with circumspection. We did not yet possess any bombs. Algeria still held our Army, our Air Force and our Navy in its grip. We did not know what direction the Kremlin would eventually take in its relations with the West." [98] As long as French power was burdened with the Algerian conflict, as long as its atomic capability remained virtual, and as long as Soviet ambitions remained aggressive, then France's margin of maneuver within the Alliance would remain narrow. To the extent that these three variables would evolve favorably, so would de Gaulle's Western policy be affirmed in practice, in accordance with the direction outlined in the memorandum.

A last question remains: To what extent did de Gaulle's initiative mark a change of policy from that of Fourth Republic governments? In a strategic context that in 1958 remained that of post-Suez and post-*Sputnik*, numerous elements of continuity stick out: a growing frustration about the integrated military organization; an increasing dissatisfaction in the nuclear domain; the long-standing demand to formalize tripartism; and a renewed demand for enlarging the zone covered by NATO toward the Mediterranean and the Middle East.[99] Nevertheless, the memorandum above all marked a rupture with the past. For the governments of the Fourth Republic, it had fundamentally been a matter of making NATO change in a direction favorable to French interests and ideas, but for them NATO would remain the irreplaceable framework of France's defense and security policies, whether at the European or world level. But it was totally otherwise for de Gaulle, whose proposals of September 1958 outstripped the NATO framework as strategically too narrow, and whose principal characteristic, military integration, he rejected. In fact, the memorandum proposed less to make NATO worldwide than to step outside its overly restrained and confining frame. This is precisely what made his orientation inadmissible from the British and American standpoint. This is why de Gaulle had already resolved "to take appropriate steps in the direction of Atlantic disengagement," while maintaining "direct cooperation with the United States and Britain." [100] Such were no doubt his leanings when, in the last weeks of 1958, one of the most serious trials in the East-West confrontation burst forth: the second Berlin crisis.

NOTES

1. *Le Monde*, 6 April 1949.

2. IFOP Surveys, cited in Jean Charlot, *Les Français et de Gaulle*, Paris, Plon, 1971, p. 262.

3. Quoted in Maurice Vaïsse, "Aux origines du mémorandum de septembre 1958," *Relations Internationales,* no. 58, Summer 1989, pp. 253–68.

4. Note de M. de Crouy-Chanel, "Position française à l'OTAN," 17 June 1958, Ministry of Foreign Affairs (MAE), Diplomatic Archives, Pactes 1948–1960, box 31.

5. Albert Wohlstetter, "The Delicate Balance of Terror," *Foreign Affairs*, vol. 37, January 1959, pp. 211–34.

6. NSC 5810, Basic National Security Policy, 15 April 1958, quoted by Jane E. Stromseth, *The Origins of Flexible Response: NATO's Debate over Strategy in the 1960s*, London, Macmillan, 1988, p. 22.

7. Note de M. de Crouy-Chanel, "Position française à l'OTAN," 17 June 1958.

8. See Georges-Henri Soutou, "Les Accords de 1957 et 1958: vers une communauté stratégique et nucléaire entre la France, l'Allemagne et l'Italie?" *Matériaux*, no. 31, April–June 1993, pp. 1–12.

9. See note 28.

10. See Vaïsse, "Aux origines du mémorandum de septembre 1958."

11. On the concrete significance of integration, see Frédéric Bozo, *La France et l'OTAN. De la guerre froide au nouvel ordre européen*, Paris, Masson, "Travaux & Recherches de l'IFRI" series, 1991, pp. 34 ff.

12. See André Beaufre, *L'OTAN et l'Europe*, Paris, Calmann-Lévy, 1966, p. 58.

13. Beaufre, *L'OTAN*, pp. 63 ff.

14. Charles de Gaulle, *Memoirs of Hope (MH)*, trans. Terence Kilmartin, London, Weidenfeld & Nicolson, 1971, p. 201.

15. Cyrus L. Sulzberger, *The Last of the Giants*, New York, Macmillan, 1970, p. 61.

16. Testimony of General Pierre Gallois in the roundtable proceedings of GREFHAN of 8 November 1988.

17. Sulzberger, *Last of the Giants*, p. 61.

18. Speech at Nîmes, 7 January 1951, in Charles de Gaulle, *Discours et Messages (DM)*, vol. 2, "Dans l'attente (février 1946–avril 1958)," Paris, Plon, 1970, p. 404.

19. Press conference at Hotel Continental, 7 April 1954, in de Gaulle, *DM*, vol. 2, p. 601.

20. See Vaïsse, "Aux origines de mémorandum de septembre 1958."

21. General Alain de Boissieu, *Pour servir le Général*, Paris, Plon, 1982, p. 238.

22. De Gaulle, *MH*, p. 202; personal interviews.

23. Telegram from Washington, 12 June 1958, Alphand to Couve de Murville, MAE, Amérique 1952–1963.

24. Testimony of Couve de Murville in *Espoir* no. 26, March 1979, pp. 38–49.

25. Declaration to the National Assembly, 1 June 1958, *Major Addresses, Statements and Press Conferences of General Charles de Gaulle (MA)*, New York, French Embassy, n.d., p. 7.

26. Radio broadcast speech from the Hotel Matignon, 13 June 1958, in de Gaulle, *DM*, vol. 3, "Avec le renouveau" (mai 1958–juillet 1962), pp. 17–19.

27. "Réunion du 17 juin 1958 à 15h. chez le Général sur des questions d'armements," MAE, Pactes 1948–1960, box 35.

28. "Réunion du 17 juin . . ." This programme, declared the General, "should be set aside for the moment."

29. " Réunion du 17 juin . . ."

30. Note pour le ministre, "Ogives des IRBM," 30 June 1958, MAE, Pactes 1948–1960, box 247.

31. Note, "Préparation des conversations avec les États-Unis sur les questions militaires," 26 June 1958, MAE, Pactes 1948–1960, box 247.

32. Note de J. de Beaumarchais et J-M Bœgner, "Problèmes stratégiques et armes nucléaires," 1 July 1958, reviewed and corrected by General de Gaulle, MAE, Pactes 1948–1960, box 34.

33. De Gaulle, *MH*, p. 209.

34. Meeting between de Gaulle and Macmillan, 30 June 1958, *Documents diplomatiques français (DDF) 1958*, vol. 1, Paris, Imprimerie Nationale, 1992–1993, p. 873.

35. Meeting between de Gaulle and Macmillan.

36. Paul-Henri Spaak, *The Continuing Battle: Memoirs of a European 1936–1966,* trans. Henry Fox, London, Weidenfeld & Nicolson, 1971, p. 313.

37. Meeting between de Gaulle and Dulles, 5 July 1958, *DDF*, *1958,* vol. 2, pp. 22 ff.

38. Meeting between de Gaulle and Dulles, p. 24. See also Christian Herter, interim Secretary of State, to John McCone, Chairman, AEC, 18 September 1958, Dwight D. Eisenhower Library (DDEL), Dulles and Herter papers, Chronological Correspondence Series, box 5.

39. De Boissieu, *Pour servir le Général*, p. 238.

40. Note manuscrite consécutive à une réunion chez le général de Gaulle le 12 juillet 1958, no date, MAE, Pactes 1948–1960, box 34.

41. Draft memoranda, 12 July 1958 and 17 July 1958, MAE, Pactes 1948–1960, boxes 34 and 35.

42. Projet de mémorandum communiqué par les Affaires étrangères, 5 August 1958, sent to de Gaulle by M. Couve de Murville, MAE, Pactes 1948–1960, box 34.

43. Meeting between de Gaulle and Macmillan, 30 June 1958, *DDF*, *1958*, vol. 1, pp. 867–68.

44. Meeting between de Gaulle and Macmillan, 5 July 1958, *DDF*, *1958*, vol. 2, p. 28.

45. Maurice Couve de Murville, *Une Politique étrangère, 1958–1969*, Paris, Plon, 1971, 33; personal interviews; telegram from London to Paris, 18 July 1958, #2434–41, MAE, Amérique 1952–1963, États-Unis 9.5.5.

46. Telegram from Paris to London and Washington, 18 July 1958, #7492–7500 and 8011-19, *DDF*, *1958*, vol. 2, p. 90.

47. "Directive pour le général d'Armée, CEMGA," 15 July 1958, Charles de Gaulle, *Lettres, notes et carnets (LNC) (juin 1958–décembre 1960)*, Paris, Plon, 1985, pp. 46–47; de Gaulle, *MH*, p. 204.

48. Maurice Ferro, *De Gaulle et l'Amérique, une amitié tumultueuse,* Paris, Plon, 1973, p. 169; personal interview.

49. *DDF*, *1958*, vol. 2, p. 91.

50. Interview of 18 June 1976, in *Espoir,* no. 26, March 1979, pp. 38–49.

51. Telegram from Washington to Paris, #5061–64, 29 August 1958, *DDF*, *1958*, vol. 2, p. 302; personal interview.

52. Couve de Murville, *Une Politique étrangère, 1958–1969*, p. 33.

53. Maurice Couve de Murville, interview of 18 June 1976, *Espoir,* no. 26, March 1979, pp. 38–49.

54. Personal interview.

55. Handwritten note by Jean-Marc Bœgner to Maurice Couve de Murville, 9 September 1958, MAE, Pactes 1948–1960, box 34.

56. Jean Chauvel, *Commentaire*, vol. 3, "De Berne à Paris (1952–1962)," Paris, Fayard, 1973, p. 265.

57. Note de M. de Crouy-Chanel, "Position française à l'OTAN," 17 June 1958.

58. Interview with Maurice Couve de Murville in *Espoir*.

59. Pierre Maillard, *De Gaulle et l'Allemagne. Le rêve inachevé*, Paris, Plon 1990, p. 164; de Gaulle, *MH*, p. 194.

60. And not September 14 as de Gaulle would write, see de Gaulle, *MH*, p. 204.

61. Letter from Dulles to Eisenhower, 25 September 1958, DDEL, Dulles and Herter Papers 1953–1961, WHCM, box 6; Hervé Alphand, *L'Étonnement d'être. Journal (1939–1973)*, Paris, Fayard, 1977, p. 292.

62. Note pour le ministre des Affaires étrangères, 25 September 1958, Jean-Marc Bœgner, Ministry of Foreign Affairs, Pactes 1948–1960, box 35.

63. Spaak, *The Continuing Battle*, p. 312.

64. Document published for the first time in Jean-Raymond Tournoux, *Jamais dit*, Paris, Plon, 1971, pp. 191–92; see also *Espoir*, no. 15, June 1976.

65. Personal interview.

66. Sulzberger, *Last of the Giants*, p. 21.

67. Sulzberger, *Last of the Giants*, p. 562.

68. Sulzberger, *Last of the Giants*, p. 62.

69. Telegram #6980–7007, 4 December 1958, Washington to Paris, MAE, Pactes 1961–1970, box 35.

70. "Note manuscrite pour Hervé Alphand," 10 December 1958.

71. Entretien entre le général de Gaulle et M. Foster Dulles, December 15, at Hôtel Matignon, 15 December 1958, MAE, Pactes 1948–1960, box 35.

72. Note d'audience avec Sir Gladwyn Jebb, 27 October 1958, MAE, Pactes 1948–1960, box 35.

73. Personal interviews.

74. "Note manuscrite pour Hervé Alphand," 10 December 1958.

75. Telegram #12499–12504, Paris to Washington, 10 December 1958, MAE, Pactes 1948–1960, box 35.

76. Couve de Murville, *Une Politique étrangère, 1958–1969*, pp. 33, 55; Maillard, *De Gaulle et l'Allemagne*, pp. 164 ff.; personal interviews.

77. De Gaulle, *MH*, p. 202.

78. Sulzberger, *Last of the Giants*, p. 21; personal interview.

79. Meeting between de Gaulle and Dulles, 5 July 1958, *DDF, 1958*, vol. 2, p. 25.

80. "Memorandum of conversation with the President," 13 October 1958, DDEL, Dulles and Herter Papers, White House Correspondence and Memoranda Series, WHCM, box 7.

81. Telegram, Paris to Washington, #11795–11800, 3 November 1958, MAE, Pactes 1948–1960, box 35.

82. Note d'audience avec l'ambassadeur de Grande Bretagne (unsigned), 23 October 1958, MAE, Pactes 1948–1960, box 35.

83. "Memorandum of conversation with the President," 13 October 1958.

84. Letter from Adenauer to de Gaulle, 11 October 1958, French version, MAE, Pactes 1948–1960, box 35.

85. Telegrams, Washington to Paris, #5941–45, 8 October 1958, and Rome to Paris, #995–999, 15 October 1958, MAE, Pactes 1948–1960, box 35.

86. Spaak, *The Continuing Battle*, pp. 316–18.

87. Eisenhower to de Gaulle, 20 October 1958, Lyndon B. Johnson Library (LBJL), National Security File, France, box 172; see also EMBTEL, Paris, 6 March 1963, and DEPTEL, Paris, no. 4265, 9 March 1963, John F. Kennedy Library (JFKL), National Security File, France, box 72.

88. Eisenhower to de Gaulle, 20 October 1958.

89. De Gaulle, *MH*, p. 203.

90. Memorandum sent by Spaak on 15 October, 1958, *DDF, 1958*, vol. 2, pp. 523 ff.

91. Telegram, Bonn to Paris, #2536–54, 31 October 1958, MAE, Pactes 1948–1960, box 35.

92. Telegram, Rome to Paris, #995–99, 15 October 1958.

93. Telegram, Washington to Paris, #6820-23, 26 November 1958, MAE, Pactes 1948–1960, box 35.

94. Note de Jean-Marc Bœgner pour le ministre des Affaires étrangères, 22 October 1958, proceedings of a meeting with the British ambassador at Matignon on 21 October, 1958, MAE, Pactes 1948–1960, box 35.

95. Telegrams, Washington to Paris, #6980–83 and #7105–20, 10 December 1958, MAE, Pactes 1948–1960, box 35.

96. De Gaulle, *MH*, p. 203.

97. Note d'information, "Conclusions de la réunion de Défense nationale du 13 octobre 1958," MAE, Pactes 1948–1960, box 140.

98. De Gaulle, *MH*, p. 203.

99. See Vaïsse, "Aux origines du mémorandum de septembre 1958."

100. De Gaulle, *MH*, p. 203.

Chapter Two

The Time of Crises (1959–1960)

For the two years following the sending of the memorandum, French policy followed in the direction set by the September 1958 initiative. De Gaulle maintained the perspective he had announced to his allies, first and foremost the search for an entente among the three great Western nations. Indeed the Berlin crisis that erupted at the end of November and henceforth constituted the backdrop to French policy confirmed his ideas by dramatizing what was at stake in Western solidarity. Yet this serious upsurge in East-West tension would also paradoxically limit French margin of maneuver. The country remained otherwise burdened by the pursuit of the Algerian conflict, which continued to mobilize its military and weighed on France's diplomatic initiatives, while the nuclear effort had not yet produced operational results. In that period, the relations between de Gaulle, Eisenhower, and Macmillan were good, but Paris's principal allies were scarcely inclined to give him satisfaction. Eisenhower's administration, not disposed to any substantial change, at the close of his second term entered into a phase of more or less passive management of Atlantic affairs. Meanwhile, de Gaulle gradually sensed the limits of his tripartite approach, though he did not renounce it or push it toward the breaking point. While announcing his ambition for a more autonomous defense, he started to inflect his approach to the Western alliance and to sketch an alternative to an Atlantic policy oriented toward *les Anglo-Saxons,* a continental alternative built on a Europe in which France and Germany would constitute the axis.

THE BERLIN CRISIS AS BACKDROP AND PROP

During this period, the Berlin affair was the backdrop to international relations. Just as with the first one ten years earlier, the second Berlin crisis concentrated all aspects and all stakes of the Cold War. France's attitude during this affair, as it turned out, was clearly much firmer than that of its allies, and de Gaulle's perception of the tenets and upshots of the crisis represent a determining aspect of his Western policy.

Yet, the relations between this policy and its Berlin background are complex. On the one hand, the crisis appeared to validate the tripartite orientation of the memorandum, but on the other hand, it slowed down its concrete application. The Berlin affair was the backdrop to relations among Western nations, and de Gaulle did not hesitate to use it to promote his own ideas. In sum, the Berlin crisis was during this period both the backdrop and the prop of the General's Western policy.

A Certain Idea of the Crisis

On November 27, 1958, Nikita Sergeyevich Khrushchev addressed to the three Western powers that along with the USSR were the guarantors of the status of Berlin (France, the United States, and Great Britain) as well as to the West German government, a note proposing making West Berlin a free and demilitarized city under international supervision. If this procedure was less bellicose than during the 1948 blockade, the objectives were not fundamentally different. Moscow proposed nothing less than the abandonment by the three powers of their prerogatives over the former capital of the Reich. Once the quadripartite status inherited from the war was abolished, the city would be *de facto* dependent on the German Democratic Republic (GDR), in particular regarding access by Westerners, and would be fated in time to probable incorporation into the Communist bloc. The Soviet proposal would result in a political and strategic retreat for the West and the probable loss of their liberty for West Berliners; meanwhile, it implied recognition of the legitimacy of the GDR and of the division of Germany, that is to say, of the *fait accompli* of the Soviet occupation. This is obviously not what the Federal Republic or its Western allies wanted at any price; since 1955 Bonn had stuck to the "Hallstein Doctrine" (threatening to break off diplomatic relations with states that recognized the GDR) and demanded reunification by means of free elections.

Yet the Berlin crisis revealed at least as much about West-West rapport as about East-West relations, and on the evidence Khrushchev's ultimatum aimed first and foremost to put Western solidarity on trial. In the autumn of 1958, the Soviets were indeed worried about the cohesion proclaimed by the Alliance, especially since the Atlantic summit of December 1957. For Moscow, the installation of IRBMs in Europe would annul the strategic advantage garnered by the *Sputnik* success. Thus, if the November 27 note aimed to obtain the consecration of the division of Germany, it also tried more immediately to drive a wedge into the Alliance.

From the first day of the crisis, de Gaulle set the tone: The French position would be absolutely firm. This intransigence can be explained by a series of factors: the very personality of the General who was by nature little given to compromise; his refusal of a bargaining process that might signal abandonment; his certainty that Khrushchev would not go all the way for Berlin, and especially not risk war; his concern to carefully treat the newfound trust and friendship of Adenauer (whom he had again met at Bad-Kreuznach on the very eve of the ultimatum), and more generally, to maintain Western cohesion; and finally, his conviction that the Western position was just as a matter of principle and that the allies should remain united while faced with Soviet threats.[1] John Foster Dulles took the measure of the General's determination at their second meeting on December 15, 1958. The day before, on the margins of the ministerial session of the Atlantic Council, the ministers of foreign affairs of France, the United States, and Great Britain had published a communiqué rejecting the Soviet ultimatum. The two men agreed on what was essential: The West could by no means cede before the threat; if the East Germans took control of access to Berlin with Soviet backing, the Western nations must accept a show of force, which would allow them to see what the communist reaction would be. "If Khrushchev says 'this is war,' we must say the same thing as he does. It's the best way to prevent war," de Gaulle declared; we will not get to that point, Dulles countered, because the Soviets have measured the allies' military might and will not take this risk.[2]

At this stage, there were no disagreements over the Berlin affair. It is true that the conversation remained very general and that concrete options had scarcely been broached. However, in the first months of 1959, while the crisis intensified, what made the French attitude different appeared more distinctly. De Gaulle, who wanted to demonstrate his solidarity with German positions, did not seek to lower the tension at any price, while Macmillan went to Moscow at the end of February to explore avenues of compromise. The Americans, for their part, tried to make their allies accept a middle position. This was Dulles's goal in February 1959, on what would be his last tour of Europe. Arriving in Paris on February 6, he was welcomed at Orly International Airport by Maurice Couve de Murville, who did not conceal his disquiet. The situation reminded him of 1936 and the inability of democracies to react to the remilitarization of the Rhineland. The minister insisted that one had to be ready for recourse to military force in case of a Soviet or East German attempt to hinder access to Berlin.[3]

In fact, the rising tension led the three Western powers that were militarily present in Berlin to agree on measures to take if this situation came about. So Dulles and Couve de Murville discussed contingency plans to be put into effect in case access to the city was closed. A Franco-Anglo-American general staff (baptized "Live Oak") would be established for this purpose at the headquarters of the U.S. commander in chief in Europe (the other hat of SACEUR), at the Camp des Loges near Paris.[4] De Gaulle, who received Dulles, fully approved of a plan aiming to coordinate, among the Western Three, possible military operations around the Reich's former capital. He thought that one must "respond with force to any attempt at interference in our communications with Berlin."[5]

France's participation in the Live Oak activities, during the whole crisis and beyond, would be wholehearted. For de Gaulle, this tripartite general staff was justified by the Berlin situation and was in no way to be confused with integration within the NATO framework.[6]

Dulles, weakened by the illness that would soon kill him, was once more struck by the General's determination and by the apparent commonality of French and U.S. views. But convergence was not perfect: Dulles wished to bend French intransigence somewhat, whereas de Gaulle feared a certain lack of resolution behind the firmness of the secretary of state's proposals, despite the elaboration of common emergency plans. Yet several weeks later, Christian Herter, who had just succeeded Dulles as secretary of state, would underscore that firmness by declaring that atomic weapons could be employed to defend access to the city.[7] In any case, the military dimension of the Berlin crisis was primary, especially because it was a nuclear crisis, potentially at least.

The French difference in the crisis was also political in nature. In his press conference on March 25, 1959, de Gaulle outlined the terms of what might become a long-term settlement of the German question: recognition of the Oder-Neisse Line and the full and entire renunciation of nuclear weapons; and practical and progressive establishment of relations between the two Germanys (but the General forbore suggesting diplomatic recognition of the GDR, which was unacceptable to Bonn). In doing this, while continuing to advance intransigence in the short term, he demarcated himself from the others in two ways. On the one hand, he implicitly broke with a Western and West German doctrine he considered untenable since it postulated "that the reunification of Germany was immediately necessary,"[8] which was unrealistic. On the other hand, and as a corollary, he recognized to a certain extent Soviet security interests with regard to the German question. This mixture of intransigence in the short term and openness in the long term would trigger, in the final phase of the crisis in 1961, a sharp confrontation between France and the United States, and it prefigured the policy of détente that de Gaulle would actively apply starting in 1964.

The spring of 1959 marked a calm in the Berlin crisis. In May a four-power conference opened in Geneva. De Gaulle had accepted its being held: As long as no one "cedes to any formal demand" and the Western "right of access" is respected, "we should not refuse a discussion," he wrote to Eisenhower, provided that the conference not take place at a summit but at the level of foreign affairs ministers. In passing, he deplored the fact that once again the French, British, and Americans were "rather badly out of agreement on this affair"[9]—a way of reminding Eisenhower of his proposals back in September 1958.

Western Solidarity on Trial

The conference would end in August with no concrete result. At the beginning of September 1959, Eisenhower met de Gaulle on a state visit in France and discussed the crisis. The two men were still in agreement to have a dialogue with the Soviets concerning Berlin on condition that the rights and responsibilities of the Western nations were not questioned, and they refused holding a summit they judged inopportune at this stage.[10] But this commonality of views had cracked by the autumn. Discussions between Eisenhower and Khrushchev at Camp David resulted in the American president to back down as he accepted the principle of a quadripartite summit in 1960, among other things, which contradicted the assurances he had given to de Gaulle shortly before. The latter did not conceal from Eisenhower that he deplored "the spirit of Camp David" that had run with public opinion; while wishing for détente, he said he "had many reservations about what could be obtained in a conference at the summit" in the present circumstances. At the least, he expected preparation by the Western side to be as rigorous as possible.[11] More than ever, the General was posing as champion of Western cohesion and as enemy of compromise with the East.

This cohesion would be tested again in December 1959 during meetings in Paris and Rambouillet among the Big Three, joined by Adenauer. Discussions that in principle should have arrived at a common Western position with a view to the summit, instead confirmed de Gaulle's fears. Macmillan, but also Eisenhower, were hostages to a public opinion that had been "aroused and shown itself keenly interested" and they leaned toward compromise. While saying they were prepared to take concrete measures to ensure communication with Berlin, the General discovered that they "were extremely reluctant to define them" and that, "if it came to that point they would be even less willing to put them into effect." De Gaulle had the feeling that *les Anglo-Saxons* might be tempted to make concessions in order to avoid the worst.[12] Along with Adenauer, he tried to get a message of firmness approved by Eisenhower and Macmillan. In the absence of Western support in the ongoing confrontation, he predicted, the FRG could "defect"—in other words be tempted to trade its neutrality for its reunification.

Despite these admonitions, the General could only deplore the absence of coordination among the Western nations in the preparation for the summit foreseen in Paris for the spring of 1960, whose approach was punctuated by important diplomatic events, namely Khrushchev's visit to France (March 23–31) and de Gaulle's to Britain and the United States (April 5–8 and 22–29, respectively). In this context, the General tried above all to play an equal game with the United Kingdom and the United States by acceding, symbolically for the moment, to the nuclear club: On February 13, 1960, the first French atomic explosion took place at Reggane in the Sahara. De Gaulle wanted in effect "to make 'his' bomb burst" before these important meetings.[13]

The Paris summit arranged for May 16, 1960, would give rise to a crisis within the crisis. De Gaulle, convinced that Khrushchev was above all trying to make pressure mount, did not expect anything much.[14] In fact, the U2 affair— a U.S. spy plane flying over USSR territory was brought down by a Soviet fighter plane—aborted the meeting of the four, which was adjourned even before any substantive discussion. Whatever the share of U.S. responsibility in this failure, the General was concerned to proclaim perfect Western solidarity and so chose to stand with Eisenhower. As host of the summit and convinced that the Soviet cries of rage were a bluff, he persuaded his allies not to concede to Khrushchev's injunctions, while Macmillan was guilty in his eyes of "whimpering Munichism."[15] De Gaulle's attitude of solidarity "warmed the heart" of the U.S. president, who was very sensitive to the wholehearted support lent by the French president.[16] After the failure of the summit, de Gaulle, faithful to a line of conduct that seemed to him validated by events, drew lessons from the crisis. In the future, he announced in a televised broadcast, peace must be made; but for now, the French must more than ever maintain and strengthen the Western alliance, especially among the Big Three; France should "have her own role in it, and her own personality." He confided to his son: "We have to exist by ourselves. In particular, an effective nuclear force is necessary for us."[17]

These were de Gaulle's perceptions on the Berlin crisis during the summer of 1960 when tension gave way to a period of respite lasting several months. He saw, as much in the adventurism of the Soviet Union as in the behavior of the Western nations—badly coordinated, weak, even defeatist—not just confirmation of the rationale of the concept of the Alliance he had formulated in 1958, but also of the effort France was making to build up its *force de frappe*.

TRIPARTITE PROPOSALS: CAUTION

The link between the Berlin crisis and the tripartite proposals is complex. While the Berlin contest was the only actual instance—and not very conclusive—of systematic cooperation among the Big Three, de Gaulle thought that the two matters were very distinct. Cooperation over Berlin flowed from the rights and responsibilities of the three great Western powers over the former Reich capital and more generally, over Germany, whereas the memorandum's proposals grew out of a wish to establish cooperation on a world scale. This distinction, basically rather theoretical, did not prevent frequent shifts from one matter to another. Yet despite the incitement to three-way political and strategic coordination represented by the Berlin crisis, the years 1959 and 1960 would not bring real progress in this area. The General's initial skepticism—he had realized from the start that his tripartite proposals ran up against allied caution—would be born out.

Extra-European Crises

The extra-European crises that studded these two years, particularly on the African continent where France thought it had its closest interests, were far from giving rise to an effective cooperation among Western nations. They actually threw into relief, as with Berlin, their divergences—very clearly so between

French and Americans, despite the excellence of the rapport between de Gaulle and Eisenhower. For de Gaulle, these crises exposed the limits of the solidarity that he might expect on the part of *les Anglo-Saxons* on a global level and more particularly in North Africa, which remained his principal preoccupation.

This appeared very clearly during the second meeting between de Gaulle and Dulles on December 15, 1958, against the Berlin backdrop, a meeting whose ambiance was much less good than the first five months earlier. The General, discontented with the U.S. attitude to the Algerian affair, gave the secretary of state a tepid welcome. Despite the relative goodwill of the Eisenhower administration, the Algerian conflict was increasingly poisoning Franco–U.S. relations since Suez and particularly since the last months of the Fourth Republic; it weighed down France's Atlantic policy and continued to tarnish relations between Paris and Washington—even though de Gaulle had been putting into effect in Algeria a policy more in line with American views. At the end of October he had indeed offered "a peace of the braves" and announced the very ambitious Constantine plan. This was a policy, he explained to Dulles, that aimed to push Algeria "in the direction of liberty" so as not to "let it slide" toward communism. He complained that France encountered among its allies only "reservations, to say the least," notably within the United Nations, where the United States did not support France when faced with the activism of Third World states.[18] While France carried out an action in North Africa he thought favorable to the West, and while he was affirming his solidarity in the current European crisis, de Gaulle thus deplored the absence of political solidarity from the United States, which, he believed, was trying above all to manage its interests in the Arab world.

The U.S. attitude appeared all the more unacceptable to de Gaulle because French policy was gradually orienting itself toward Algerian self-determination. Some weeks after the General's announcement in September 1959 of the referendum on self-determination that marked a decisive shift in the Algerian conflict, the United States once more abstained in the General Assembly from voting on an Afro-Asian resolution, which was rejected by only one majority vote. French diplomacy, in the voice of Couve de Murville, could only note again its disappointment.[19] De Gaulle spoke up, as well: to Eisenhower, who mentioned the incident while in Paris in December 1959, he coldly replied, "I regret that."[20] But at bottom, the General took this new let-down badly, and against the background of disagreements over Berlin, he saw it as confirmation of his doubts about U.S. solidarity.

After 1960, the Algerian affair, while the process leading to independence was put in place, did not weigh so heavily on Franco–U.S. relations.[21] But two other extra-European events in this period contributed to sustain the General's doubt with regard to Western solidarity. This time it concerned black Africa, which Dulles had himself suggested, at the end of 1958, serve as a testing ground for the tripartite cooperation proposed by de Gaulle. The first event was in Guinea, which was the only African territory in the French Union to reject the project for a commonwealth in 1958 and had *ipso facto* acceded to independence. De Gaulle subsequently decided to break off with Sekou Touré, who presented an obstacle to his project for a Franco-African community "of great importance for the West," and he reproached the Americans for not opposing the accession of Guinea to international recognition or its entry into the United Nations.[22] Once again, the United States, he believed, did not know how to reconcile Western solidarity with its own influence in the Third World. As to the second event, it concerned the Congo, which would be the subject of serious litigation with Kennedy, and about which de Gaulle put Eisenhower in the summer of 1960 on his guard against the risk that the West was managing the postindependence crisis there "in chaotic manner."

In the summer of 1960, the General's balance sheet of two years of management, or rather nonmanagement of crises by the Western nations was particularly negative, if not bitter. "In the events unfolding from one end of the world to the other," he wrote in total frankness to the American president, "my country notes every time that those whom it holds as allies behave as if they were not."[23]

Tripartite Discussions: Stalemate

Indeed the three Western nations had perspectives on world affairs that were often divergent, if not irreconcilable. In these circumstances it was not surprising that the matter of tripartite political and strategic planning, called for by de Gaulle in the September 1958 memorandum, made scarcely any progress during these two years. After the meeting with Dulles on December 15, 1958, we can see a distancing between French and U.S. positions on the tripartite question. On this subject, too, the General proved less cordial than in July; as for Dulles, he had left Washington rather exasperated with de Gaulle, whom he started to find "troublesome in his desire to be in on" everything that was happening throughout the world.[24] In more diplomatic language, the secretary of state repeated to his host that there was no question of accepting an "organic structure" for tripartite cooperation, even if the Big Three could do "much more" to "practice a common policy," on condition that this be on a "discreet basis." French and Americans nevertheless agreed to relaunch tripartite discussions in Washington (at this stage they had not moved beyond simple contact).[25] De Gaulle, at any rate, attached more importance to "the reality of things rather than their form," as Couve de Murville reminded Dulles, who said he was ready for tripartite discussions on subjects of common interest, such as the Far East, the Middle East, and Africa.[26] At the start of January 1959, the secretary of state confirmed to Hervé Alphand that he would wish to place the Far East at the head of the subjects to be tackled by the three. Thus a first meeting was planned on this theme for February 6 in Washington—with Paris's agreement.[27]

Far from renouncing his tripartite ideas, de Gaulle at the beginning of 1959 reasserted their necessity, notably during a Defense Committee meeting on January

31: France, he insisted, must continue the effort undertaken with the memorandum.[28] But this first phase of background consultations devoted, at the start of February, to Far East problems, got lukewarm appreciation by the French side, especially at the Elysée (the Quai d'Orsay, for its part, noted U.S. "goodwill"). On the one hand, *les Anglo-Saxons* accepted the principle of tripartite meetings, while since Suez Dulles had refused any formal Franco-Anglo-American discussion; but on the other, the practical outcome of these discussions appeared very limited. On the political level, they resulted in "neither precise conclusions nor common positions," Paris thought; and on the strategic level, the results were "insignificant." The General's entourage nevertheless judged that the experiment should be pursued, since the "bad will" of *les Anglo-Saxons* was not at this stage, "clearly demonstrated." De Gaulle was thus ready to make a "new attempt."[29]

In April, then, a new series of tripartite consultations took place in Washington, this time on Africa. For Paris, they brought nothing more than the preceding discussion and did not get beyond the stage of exchanging rather general information. At the start of May, the Elysée judged that things had clearly reached an impasse and that discussions "about some region of the world or other" would remain futile as long as the Americans would not broach the heart of the problem, meaning strategic coordination.[30] It was now patently clear that disagreements over form were actually basic disagreements. For de Gaulle, it was a question of establishing procedures for consultations that were not necessarily very institutionalized, but at least effective, and from which might emerge common positions to which each party would stick. On the contrary, Washington preferred to avoid anything that might resemble a three-party directorate that might undermine the cohesion of the Alliance as a whole, since the latter ought to remain the principal forum for Western cooperation. Things could hardly go any farther, and the systematic political consultations demanded by de Gaulle would not move beyond the informal and exploratory stage of the Washington discussions that were eventually suspended in the spring of 1959. The idea of reestablishing these consultations, in one form or another, would be the subject of agitation from time to time between 1959 and 1963, but without ever leading to a formal process for permanent cooperation.

Nuclear Responsibilities

Still more than tripartite political cooperation, it was the nuclear question, as the memorandum implied, that was at the center of General de Gaulle's policy regarding *les Anglo-Saxons* during these two years. The issue was over sharing strategic responsibilities on the one hand and atomic cooperation on the other. But in both these domains, his initial doubts about the possibility of an agreement with the Americans was soon confirmed—hence a less accommodating attitude on his part, which eventually would be translated into a definitive refusal of any U.S. nuclear presence in France.

The problem of strategic nuclear responsibilities was a determining one. The Berlin crisis, which could have led to an open conflict, posed very concretely the question of allied strategy. France could not accept, as de Gaulle told Dulles, atomic war "being unleashed or not unleashed" without her interests being taken into consideration. Hence the necessity of a preexisting strategic agreement among the three powers.[31] This was really the priority: "to determine the conditions for use of atomic weapons," that is, as the General clarified to the Defense Committee in early 1959, to agree on the timing, placing, and modes of recourse to nuclear weapons.[32]

Despite French insistence on broaching this question within the framework of the discussion begun in Washington at the end of 1958, the Americans shied away from this, which strongly contributed, as we have seen, to the failure of the whole round of discussions; Dulles refused to touch questions of atomic strategy, especially at the operational level. For the Americans, there was no question of a tripartite discussion of nuclear plans. But why should the Big Three continue to discuss problems in Africa, a zone of French influence, officials asked in Paris in the spring of 1959, when the United States refused to mention the issue of nuclear consultation?[33] In fact, the interruption in May of tripartite discussions in Washington pushed back *sine die* any examination of the French demand, especially since at the same time de Gaulle would make known his refusal of any American nuclear presence in France—as we shall see.

In the summer of 1959, nuclear consultation was thus at an impasse—at least at the diplomatic level. De Gaulle decided to reopen the issue at the summit during Eisenhower's visit to France in September, but without much illusion about his chances of succeeding. To his renewed formal demand for strategic cooperation in due course, Eisenhower limited his reply to the statement that "the United States would never launch a nuclear war without consultation," except in case of a totally unforeseen attack. He proposed to the General the creation of means of communication in case of emergency, analogous to those existing with Great Britain, which remained well short of the request. And Eisenhower objected once more to any institutionalization of tripartism.[34]

Discussion on sharing nuclear responsibilities among Western countries was not closed, but de Gaulle was more and more convinced that only an autonomous French nuclear capability would enable satisfaction to be obtained. The day after Eisenhower's visit, while French diplomacy was more than ever prone to describe the atmosphere of Franco-American relations as "extremely cordial,"[35] the question of nuclear strategy and responsibilities was beginning to seriously cloud these relations.

In the autumn of 1959, de Gaulle made a supplementary step in his challenge to the Alliance's nuclear status quo. He was now publicly pointing to the risk posed by the challenge to the strategic link between Europe and America that he had foreseen at least since *Sputnik*, and that appeared to him confirmed in the context of the Berlin crisis. Could one not in fact fear a nuclear war limited to Europe in which the two superpowers would spare each other as a result of the balance of terror? Inversely, was there not a risk of the United States dissociating itself from the nuclear defense of Europe when the time came?[36] This time, de Gaulle had hit a sensitive point. Eisenhower wrote to him indignantly about statements that he saw as casting doubt on the nuclear guarantee of the United States and constituting a gesture of defiance to the Americans.[37]

It was the beginning of a long misunderstanding between France and the United States, and at the same time the start of a strategic break within the Alliance that would be confirmed throughout the 1960s. But for the moment, de Gaulle wished to preserve Western solidarity and avoid a rupture. He took the greatest care to explain his position. On the one hand, he insisted in response to Eisenhower that he was not throwing into doubt *hic et nunc* the reality of U.S. involvement in the defense of Europe; he recognized that U.S. strategy remained unchanged, that it was still founded on the principle of massive retaliation, thanks notably to the personal determination of the American president. On the other hand, as someone supremely responsible for his country's security, how could he not wonder about the future? And how could he be assured of the fact that "the strategy adopted by you at this time in case of world conflict involving tight solidarity between the United States and Western Europe would remain forever without change?"[38] This was a prescient question since, with Kennedy, the United States would in fact proceed to the change of strategy that de Gaulle had publicly feared back in the autumn of 1959; yet at this stage, he undoubtedly thought it still possible to avoid strategic "decoupling" between Europe and America by means of the close nuclear consultation that he was precisely trying to establish among the French, Americans, and British.

"Atomic Secrets"

Parallel to nuclear consultation, the question of sharing "atomic secrets" was beginning to matter more and more in de Gaulle's Western policy after 1958. That question would crystallize the strategic differences between France and *les Anglo-Saxons*, at least until 1962.

We have seen that the question of atomic cooperation had been mentioned during de Gaulle's first contact with the Americans in the summer of 1958.[39] From that moment, a duality appeared. On one side, the United States, not enthusiastic about the prospect of a separate French nuclear power, was scarcely disposed to facilitate one, even if Eisenhower was not irreducibly hostile to it. American policy consisted in fact of trying to insert the French effort into a framework they controlled, preferably NATO. On the other side, the General would not refuse American assistance if it allowed France to save time and money and would put it on an equal footing with Great Britain (which since 1958 had benefited from nuclear cooperation with the United States after a modification of the McMahon

Act), but on condition *sine qua non* that such assistance did not involve a con-comitant strategic dependence on Washington.

When de Gaulle returned to power, the possibility of finding common ground between these two positions was not totally excluded but it would become grad-ually so in the coming months. The General was skeptical from the start about such an arrangement, since he thought that Congress would not authorize it.[40] On principle, then, he would not mention the subject himself to his U.S. contacts. De-spite the more optimistic attitude of Hervé Alphand and the relevant people at the Quai d'Orsay, who did not exclude the possibility of an agreement whose terms would be acceptable, and despite the more enterprising approach of Michel Debré, who did not hesitate placing France in a position of demander, de Gaulle's view—that significant American assistance to the French nuclear effort was impossible—grew stronger throughout 1959.[41]

The spring of 1959 brought the first confirmation of this, with a sharp check suffered by negotiations that had begun in September 1958 after the de Gaulle–Dulles meeting of July 5. These negotiations bore on U.S. help for the construction of a nuclear submarine engine (or even its simple handover) and the delivery of the necessary nuclear fuel. But the agreement signed on May 7, 1959, by Alphand and Herter turned out to be limited to the second part. The submarine engine promised by Dulles fell by the wayside. Moreover, the United States had delivered only a third of the specified quantity of enriched uranium.[42] The result was well below French aspirations, but both parties were to blame. The reluc-tance of the Americans, who since August 1958 used pretexts to slow things down over alleged "security" problems at the Commissariat à l'Energie Atomique (CEA; where, as Washington had not forgotten, there was formerly a very marked communist presence), was compounded in early March by the negative effect of the withdrawal of the French fleet from NATO commands in the Mediterranean.[43]

Whether or not this last decision (to which we will return) was just a pretext to justify Washington's very restrictive attitude, as was thought in Paris, the affair confirmed the General's impression that the United States was ill disposed to co-operation with France in this domain. He regretted this, but stood his ground. He also reminded Hervé Alphand that France was not asking for American "atomic secrets," even if it would not turn down help that would have allowed time and money to be saved,[44] and he made the same speech to Eisenhower during their meeting in early September 1959. If he was indignant that the Americans found it dangerous for France to know "what a thousand Soviet corporals already know," he quickly added, true to his line of conduct, that "I am not a demander." And as if to make himself better understood, he revealed to the American presi-dent that the first French nuclear explosion would take place in February 1960. From then on, the meeting made no progress on this issue, as Eisenhower was content to restate the offer formulated by Dulles to provide France with nuclear weapons that would remain under double key, an offer that de Gaulle considered without any interest since the ultimate decision would remain a U.S. one.[45] So by the end of 1959, even though contact was not interrupted, especially at the level of the CEA and the U.S. Atomic Energy Commission (AEC), French and American atomic cooperation was stalemated. Restricted to the limited supply of enriched uranium by the United States, it contributed only very marginally to France's nuclear effort,[46] whose success essentially depended on itself alone.

The progress achieved at home further reduced the practical interest of eventual American assistance, without making it more plausible. The explosion on February 13, 1960, that made France an effective nuclear power—while not yet an operational one—did not fundamentally change the givens of the problem, even if Eisenhower, referring to the *force de frappe*, had declared shortly beforehand that the United States should not refuse to its allies what their potential enemy already possessed.[47] Despite the success in Reggane, Alphand in the first months of 1960 no longer believed, as he had the preceding year, in the possibility of an agreement on military atomic cooperation with the United States. However much Eisenhower said he was not hostile to it, the resistance of the bureaucracies at the State Department and to a lesser extent at the Pentagon, and especially within Congress (the all-powerful Joint Committee on Atomic Energy), was simply too strong. It would be very difficult for the president, particularly in an election year, to obtain an adaptation of the McMahon Act. Moreover, the ambassador observed, this would not necessarily be to France's advantage, judging from the experience of the British, who complained of the constraints imposed on them by the Americans in exchange for their cooperation. Therefore, it was useless, said Alphand, to "force open doors that were solidly bolted," even though contact might be maintained with a view to cooperation in the long-term, when the Americans understand the necessity for it.[48]

On the eve of de Gaulle's visit to the United States in April 1960, Eisenhower thus had nothing to offer him in this domain. As for the General, he would not ask for anything, even if some people tried to refloat the idea of Franco-American nuclear cooperation, like Minister of Armed Forces Pierre Guillaumat, who thought "this door should not be closed," and like François de Rose, head of the Pacts directorate at the Quai d'Orsay, who was very keen despite the negative opinion of Alphand and Couve de Murville, and who deplored the fact that the question was not really debated within the government.[49] After June 1960, the question of nuclear cooperation was frozen by Eisenhower himself, now a lame duck president. Although the issue would be reopened under Kennedy in 1961 and 1962, it would be under even less favorable conditions, especially for personality reasons. Above all, it was now too late, since the French bomb, a political reality since February 1960, would gradually become a military reality.

At the end of 1960, de Gaulle seems to have reached a definitive opinion on the issue: "As for obtaining anything in the nuclear or missile area, I no longer believe in it. If I were in their place, I would do the same." There was no question of begging for U.S. aid, since "you must not ask for what you cannot get." From his viewpoint, even the British experience was negative, since London had paid dearly for nuclear cooperation with Washington. The English, he thought, had become the "satellites" of the United States, "stuffed with nuclear weapons which they don't control."[50] This remark clearly suggests what the General's attitude would be at the time of the Nassau Accords two years later.

Nuclear Stockpiles

One thing is certain: From now on, the nuclear question, and more particularly, the issue of atomic cooperation "was at the heart of relations" between France and the United States.[51] It is in the light of this nuclear misunderstanding that we must interpret de Gaulle's attitude to the possibility of a U.S. nuclear presence in France. In the spring of 1959, the General held to the position adopted since his return to power that there was no question of accepting the presence of U.S. nuclear warheads in France, unless "the disposal of atomic weapons stored *in* France belonged *to* France within the framework of a commonly agreed plan for their use."[52] This was a double condition that the Americans were manifestly still not disposed to grant, since, as we have seen, the principle of nuclear consultation appeared as seriously compromised as the hypothesis of Franco-American atomic cooperation, and already so in the spring of 1959. At the start of May, Eisenhower and Herter began to fear a negative decision on the General's part. In fact, de Gaulle confirmed to Eisenhower on May 25, 1959, that there was no question of storing U.S. nuclear missiles in France, although the subject was not formally closed.[53]

In reality, the issue was already understood. The French decision led Norstad, on instructions from Washington, to plan the transfer of two hundred U.S. Air Force F-100 bombers with nuclear capacity.[54] Deployed at the French bases of Toul, Étain, and Chaumont, these planes were intended to launch nuclear projectiles, and this move, completed only at the end of 1959, marked the first retreat of allied forces from French territory. It had but small operational consequences, however: The redeployment of F-100s to Great Britain and Germany indeed allowed them to maintain their missions "in the same conditions of effectiveness," as the highest allied military authorities stated.[55] The problem was really political. For the Americans, the French decision undermined Western solidarity: "Norstad will be obliged to move the planes; this will become known and it will be bad for the Alliance," warned Herter.[56] For the French, it was a matter of emphasizing that one "could not dissociate the question of storing atomic weapons in France from the problem of the world organization of security."[57] By postponing indefinitely the deployment of American nuclear weapons in France, de Gaulle was reminding people not only of the necessity of sharing control over atomic weapons that would be based on French territory, but also and especially of his wish for a strategic agreement in due course among the French, Americans, and British on the conditions for using them. This was a demand that the Berlin crisis threw into high relief, since as de Gaulle let it be known, the U.S. nuclear presence in France might pose a considerable risk, although it represented only a marginal military advantage.

The line announced in May–June 1959 fits in perfectly with the overall logic of de Gaulle's policy: the search for new, close, and substantial strategic cooperation with his partners through dialogue—and if necessary through unilateral decisions. In the course of 1959, the General was more and more persuaded that the latter were indispensable in moving toward his goal, and that he would obtain nothing decisive as long as France did not have the clout of a really operational nuclear capability. In the meanwhile, to refuse the presence of American nuclear weapons, in the context of East-West tensions, gave France an increased margin of maneuver.[58]

The problem was very different with regard to French forces in Germany. Like those of other allied countries, they were to receive under the December 1957 initiative the capability of executing nuclear strikes with weapons that the United States would, as the case may be, put at their emergency disposal within the NATO framework. This time, for Paris it was an "essentially technical" question:[59] France's interest, in the absence of a national capability, was eventually to have at its disposal, on German territory, tactical American nuclear warheads. Washington officially proposed this to Paris in the summer of 1959, and so in September 1960, after rather long negotiations (the subject was sensitive, after all), an agreement was signed between France and the United States.[60] The French Forces in Germany (FFA) were equipped with "Honest John" tactical missiles and the First Tactical Air Command (CATAC), partially deployed in West Germany, received Nike antiair missiles. Both kinds of nuclear devices were to remain under U.S. control until an eventual decision to use them; as to the question of nuclear free-fall bombs destined for the first CATAC planes, it would not be settled until 1963, for technical reasons. But the truth is that France did not refuse to participate in the nuclearization of Western defense under American control—as long as this did not threaten either its security or its sovereignty.

INTEGRATION: THE FIRST DECISIONS

Since essentially no visible progress occurred in tripartite relations, it was now, as de Gaulle had announced, on the terrain of France's participation in the integrated military organization properly speaking that the issue of relations between France and the Alliance was played out. As we have seen, the General had well-defined views on the subject: During a Defense Committee meeting in early 1959, he had stated once again that France could not "accept the integration of its forces, nor an organization of the Allied command, that would curtail its freedom of action"—which "did not exclude, of course, cooperation with our allies."[61] In the spring of 1959, France was going to begin a process, still measured and selective, of disengagement from Atlantic integration, and at the same time start to sketch what in the future might become a national defense organization that was freed of the latter's constraints. This double movement, announced in the memorandum, took place step by step. The pursuit of the Algerian conflict, even though a notable improvement occurred on the ground as a result of the Challe Plan, prevented any haste. Moreover, East-West tension prevented any weakening of the existing military links between France and its allies, all the more so since in this context de Gaulle wanted to proclaim strong solidarity with them.

The Mediterranean Fleet

De Gaulle, in line with Fourth Republic policies, nevertheless tried immediately to modify one particular situation, that of the Mediterranean Fleet, over which he thought in January 1959 the country should reassume "full disposition."[62] On March 6, 1959, the French representative on the Atlantic Council informed the allies of the decision taken by his government to keep under NATO command in time of war certain ships previously liable in case of conflict to come under the integrated naval command in Malta. This measure concerned about a third of French tonnage in the Mediterranean, with the rest of the fleet already under strictly national command.[63]

The announcement was related to NATO's naval situation in the Mediterranean. Since the beginning of the Alliance, the Mediterranean command (AFMED) belonged to a British admiral, headquartered in Malta, to whom were assigned, with the exception of the Sixth American Fleet, the other allied national fleets in the Mediterranean, including the French squadron. Six subordinate sectors belonged to AFMED, of which only one (the western Mediterranean command, which covered only a limited zone) belonged to a French admiral. This division of roles had never been well liked in Paris, but the frustration was all the more acute at the end of the 1950s because—thanks to the very large reduction in the British naval presence in the Mediterranean—the French fleet was now the largest after the Sixth Fleet. Its possible submission to a British admiral in wartime became unacceptable, all the more so because the navy was the principal logistical weapon in Algerian operations. For the French, the Mediterranean squadron belonged much more to a Euro-African axis, which naturally constituted a national strategic priority, than to an East-West axis. It was precisely because of this that de Gaulle thought the NATO framework too narrow and ill-suited to French interests, especially since the allies (starting with the Americans over Algeria) did not hesitate to take positions unfavorable to France and to its "vital interests" in this zone.[64]

The withdrawal of the Mediterranean Fleet was thus primarily a "warning shot" designed to stress French discontent with the lack of Anglo–U.S. solidarity and the absence of a satisfactory reply to the memorandum, and to prove that in these circumstances France intended to engage, alone if necessary, in the direction of transforming NATO—which meant both less integration and more cooperation.[65] The political significance of the French decision did not escape the Americans: The State Department was worried about the "psychological and political consequences, rather than the military ones" of what it considered a *fait accompli*, and Eisenhower wrote to de Gaulle to ask him to reverse his decision.[66]

The political dimension of the move was even clearer because its operational implications were limited. The ships concerned were only "earmarked," meaning that the prerogatives of the commander in chief, Mediterranean (CINCMED) were almost nonexistent in peacetime, and their transfer to effective command in wartime was by no means automatic. So in practice the decision changed nothing, especially since de Gaulle was proposing to discuss a formula for naval cooperation between France and NATO in the Mediterranean, one designed to replace the integrated situation that he was terminating.[67] The conclusion of such a formal agreement between France and NATO would not occur for several years (except on the holding of common naval exercises), but a first experiment of military cooperation between France and NATO was *de facto* put in place. It satisfied the U.S. Navy, for whom the March 1959 decision had practically no consequences whatsoever.[68]

"The Defense of France Must Be in French Hands"

Yet the withdrawal of the French Mediterranean Fleet marked the start of a unilateral redefinition of France–NATO relations in the area of military integration, which the General now publicly criticized during his press conference on March 25, 1959, and, more solemnly, in his important speech at the École Militaire on November 3: "The defense of France must be in French hands. This is a principle that has not always been current in recent years, as I know. It is indispensable it become so again. If a country like France is obliged to make war, it must be its own war; its effort must be its own effort. Otherwise our country would be in contradiction with everything it has always stood for, with its role, with its self-esteem, with its soul." He added that the "system" of integration "had had its day": if it had been justified in the beginning faced with "an imminent and unlimited threat" and when France still had not recovered its "national personality," it was today unacceptable. It followed that command must be national and could not be "inserted into a hierarchy that was not ours." This did not prevent, he insisted, a search for formulas of cooperation with the allies, since "it goes without saying that our defense, the activation of our means, the conception of the conduct of war, must for us be combined with that of other countries. Our strategy should be combined with the strategy of others. On the battlefield, it is infinitely probable that we will find ourselves side by side with allies. But each must play its own part!"[69]

Starting in 1959, these principles began to govern French defense policy at the national level. Although the Algerian conflict still prevented an overhaul of the military, the foundations were laid. The promulgation of the January 7,

1959, "*ordonnance*" on the general organization of defense gave the government the necessary legal tool for this reform, while the program-law on defense
for the period 1960–1965 was being worked out.[70] In addition, these principles
had the support of the French people. To be sure, the program-law did not pass
without difficulty in Parliament, where the government confronted several censure motions. But public opinion was behind France's nuclear effort: 65 percent
were pleased with the Reggane explosion—echoing de Gaulle's "hurrah for
France!"—and a majority of the French people were in favor of developing the
atomic bomb even further. France had confidence in itself again, and de
Gaulle's policy toward NATO led to the apparently paradoxical result of also
restoring French confidence in the Atlantic Alliance (28 percent were confident
about its organization of European defense in 1960, as opposed to 13 percent
two years earlier)—no doubt because they thought their country was more respected within it.[71]

Air Defense

The year 1960 marked a new phase in the redefinition of the French position toward NATO integration, this time in the air force domain. For several years,
SACEUR had been demanding an increased integration of the aerial defense systems of NATO countries in Europe so as to be able more effectively to face the
growing threat of Soviet aviation and especially its missiles. In December 1957,
the Atlantic Council had endorsed this request, and in April 1958, the Military
Committee had put forth a "concept of integrated aerial defense" (MC54/1) calling for a heightened integration of systems of alert, detection, and also aerial
interception. However, in early 1959, this program, called NATINAD (NATO
Integrated Air Defense), was judged "unacceptable" by the French side, in the
absence of progress on the discussion of the September memorandum. On this
matter as on others, the allies henceforth had to reckon with de Gaulle. Throughout 1959 discussions broke down over the French refusal. Paris was opposed to
any delegation to integrated commands of the authority to open fire without
ruling out "effective coordination between [national] systems of detection and
control of aerial defenses." The affair continued to plague relations between
France and the United States in the first months of 1960, especially during
de Gaulle's visit to the United States in April, during which Eisenhower wanted
to avoid touching on this delicate subject with him.[72]

It was only at the end of September 1960 that a compromise could be finally
refined, which took into account French anxiety about heightened integration
while permitting the indispensable operational effectiveness of NATO's aerial
defense. It called for an integration of the French means of alert and detection
according to the same schema as for the allies, as well as for the integration of air
defense forces properly speaking (planes and missiles) stationed in Germany and
in the northeast sector of France. On the other hand—and here lies the limit

imposed by Paris—this measure did not concern firing, which only a national authority could order. Moreover, the air defense forces stationed in the rest of France were not concerned and remained under solely national command. It was in line with this arrangement that de Gaulle then accepted French participation in the NADGE (NATO Air Defense Ground Environment) program, by limiting it to the transmission of data via the Drachenbronn Center in the Vosges and by excluding firing orders.[73]

The compromise of September 1960 thus allowed France to keep mastery of most of its military airspace and, at least for air defense forces stationed on national territory, to avoid the subordination of French forces to foreign command in peacetime, which integration within NATINAD would have implied. Above all, by excluding firing orders from the measures for partial integration of its air defense forces based in eastern France and in Germany, de Gaulle managed to avoid France being, in case of a Soviet attack, almost automatically implicated in a European conflict. From the operational viewpoint, this setup was less satisfying for NATO than a pure and simple integration of French forces would have been. De Gaulle was conscious of this, but while seeking the maximum cooperation between France and NATO, he chose, conforming to his overall policy, to privilege the political aspect rather than the military.[74]

"EUROPE D'OCCIDENT"

Since September 1958, in the name of a necessary strengthening of the Western alliance, de Gaulle had unflinchingly—but with scarcely any results—advanced tripartite political and strategic cooperation. While registering his partners' attitudes, which he thought dilatory, he gradually undertook what he had announced in the memorandum, that is, France's disengagement from integrated military structures. While recovering his country's margin of maneuver, he thus tried to underline to the British and Americans the importance that France attached to an overall reform of the Western alliance. But the second half of 1960 would mark a shift. While continuing to stress the memorandum's principles, de Gaulle would in effect take a European turn and lay the foundations of a Western policy that was more continental, and of which the Franco-German axis would be the backbone.

Tripartism Relaunched

In the spring and summer of 1960, de Gaulle tried once more to relaunch his tripartite project. Already in February he had confided to Cyrus L. Sulzberger that he hoped to do so during his visit to the United States in April. No doubt he counted on his good relationship with Eisenhower to advance things. His American trip was a veritable personal triumph for de Gaulle, an "extraordinary success," cabled Alphand, and marked the apex of the friendship between the two men. Amid the crises of the 1950s and the challenges of the 1960s, it also marked a high point in Franco-American relations, which despite accumulating differences were enjoying an unusual serenity. Ratings for France and de Gaulle in the United States were at their highest.[75]

For all that, the U.S. tour would not result in any substantial progress on the principal tripartite issues. But afterwards, de Gaulle remained convinced of the urgency of strengthening and reforming the Western alliance. The U2 crisis the following month confirmed his views on the need for tripartite cooperation. After the aborted summit, he confided to Eisenhower that he envisaged making new proposals to his partners, especially about adopting the principle of a semi-annual tripartite summit meeting.[76] During July, de Gaulle wrote to the U.S. president to recommend once again firmness over Berlin and to suggest a meeting with Macmillan to examine tripartite cooperation and Alliance reform. Without rejecting the proposal, Eisenhower asked de Gaulle for details about his conception of changes for NATO. On August 9, de Gaulle sent him and Macmillan a note on the possible reorganization of the Alliance. He felt more than ever how much relations among Western nations depended on the personal relationships among the three heads of state. He was particularly anxious, he told Macmillan, to make use of the last months of Eisenhower's presidency, since he feared that his successor would have very different views on the defense of Europe. This was why he hoped for a meeting of the Big Three in September.[77]

This summit would not take place. De Gaulle's proposals convinced neither Washington nor London of any urgency. The General was right: The U.S. president was at the end of his mandate and, as later confirmed with regard to the nuclear issue, he no longer had the will or the margin of maneuver necessary to change the course of events. Things remained as they were; even though, with Kennedy, other attempts at the tripartite project took place, the summer of 1960 marked the high point of the approach inaugurated two years earlier.

Summer 1960: First European Steps

In the summer of 1960, a shift took place, from a kind of diplomacy flowing from the 1958 memorandum to a policy that would privilege, for three years at least, relations with European partners, the Germans foremost. De Gaulle took the initiative on this policy "as soon as it became clear that France was going to get out of the Algerian drama."[78] This new phase of French diplomacy thus marked the first stage in France's return to power and influence.

On May 31, 1960, the French president, absorbing the lessons of the U2 crisis and the four-power summit fiasco, had insisted not only on the necessity of strengthening the Western alliance, faced with the persistent Soviet threat, but also on "building Western Europe into a political, economic, cultural and human grouping, organized for action, progress and defense." Building this "Europe d'Occident" was henceforth, he said, "the indispensable condition of the equilibrium of the world."[79] This theme was then taken up during the press conference of September 5, 1960, during which de Gaulle insisted on the fact that European ambitions must also be deployed in the military domain and take their place in the organization of defense.[80] He explained that it was a matter of making the Western alliance develop so as to take account of both the necessity of closer cooperation among the Big Three, which he continued formally to advocate, and the necessity for a properly European political and military grouping that should gradually be established. At the end of 1960, the slide from the first to the second objective was clearly perceptible within Gaullist priorities. It was a matter, no more nor less, of making the European ensemble "the greatest political, economic, military and cultural power that has ever existed" and of helping "this assembled Europe and its daughter, America, to reorganize their alliance in order better to defend the free world and to act together in all parts of the earth."[81]

This European inflection was far from being just rhetorical. At Rambouillet on July 29 and 30, de Gaulle and Adenauer laid out a European project that would now be at the core of his policy.[82] De Gaulle thought that Europe had to "become a real entity playing its own part in world affairs" and that to this end "it should organize by itself and for itself in the realms of politics, economics, culture and in defense." France's ambition was to transform the "*acquis communautaire*," for the moment essentially economic, into a real political—and in due course, military—project. The European Six should be able to contribute to the equilibrium of the whole, and France and the FRG in this respect had particular responsibilities; this was why, he stressed to Adenauer, Franco-German cooperation constituted a goal "of the first order" from the perspective of constructing an independent Europe.[83]

But which Europe? De Gaulle recognized that it "could currently consist only of an organized cooperation among States." He therefore envisaged the creation of new intergovernmental bodies, namely mixed commissions composed of national bureaucrats from each of the six countries, to be competent in four respective domains: foreign policy, economic and financial affairs, education and culture, and lastly defense. For de Gaulle, it was a matter of fashioning a Europe of States, and not a supranational Europe. If there must be supranational bodies, they should be "reformed, subordinated to governments and employed in the normal and technical tasks of advice."[84] The supranational system established by the treaties of Rome and for coal and steel should be confined to its proper domain and be subjected to new political arrangements: "One does not superimpose but rather creates anew, and one remodels what exists by a retroactive application of the intergovernmental principle."

This distinctive conception of the organization of Europe should not surprise us. While since the war the political unification of Western Europe had been for de Gaulle a historic necessity, unless it was to remain only a "chimera," it should take account of "realities,"[85] meaning the nation-states. Moreover, he slipped in,

Great Britain, which one day might take part in this construct, would only do so if it remained intergovernmental.[86] Adenauer's reactions were favorable. Even if, as a Rhineland Catholic, he was attached to a supranational concept (as a founding father, he had himself contributed to inspiring the European Community project), the chancellor at Rambouillet appeared to accept de Gaulle's overall approach—or at least he put up with it.[87] Maybe he thought that over the years de Gaulle would prove less hostile to the federal conception, maybe he also thought that a Germany whose own unity was suspended had nothing to lose from an approach to European unification that, by respecting nation-states, would eventually give German reunification a better chance. Whatever the case, Adenauer could not help but be sensitive to the place, significantly higher than at the Colombey meeting, that de Gaulle was now offering Germany in this gestational Europe.

Europe and NATO

At Rambouillet the question also arose of the defense of Europe and of its organization within the Atlantic framework. For de Gaulle, NATO reform and the political and strategic construction of Western Europe were in effect two sides of the same coin. In this domain, his ideas were further apart from those of Chancellor Adenauer, which he did not try to conceal. Adopting his conception of Europe, de Gaulle told him, "would put an end to American 'integration,' " which he judged contrary to the existence of a Europe "having its own international viewpoint, personality and responsibility." It was particularly difficult, he said, for France and Germany, "which assume great responsibilities and have great capabilities, to admit that it is not up to them to defend themselves."[88]

Adenauer could not have been totally surprised by these statements. He knew de Gaulle's views on NATO and on integration, views they had tackled together since the summer of 1958. What was new to him was that the General thought that the political unification of Europe should—not only for France but also for its partners, including the FRG—lead not to the end of the Alliance but to forms of military cooperation among the major nation-states (United States, France, Germany, Great Britain, and maybe Italy), forms that would substitute for NATO. De Gaulle, in addition, foresaw a certain geographic and strategic division of roles (Germany in the forefront on the east, Great Britain oriented to the north and charged with protecting maritime routes, France toward the Mediterranean and Africa and occupying a second-line position in continental Europe, and the United States with a global support role) and, in this ensemble, he envisaged particularly close Franco-German military cooperation. In this respect, he pronounced himself favorable to a growth in the FRG's military power and deplored the guardianship of NATO chiefs over it, and he even went so far, regarding nuclear weapons, as to hint to Adenauer that "one day it should be foreseen that Germany will possess them."[89]

These suggestions reveal de Gaulle's long-term vision, no doubt not unclouded by second thoughts, notably over atomic weapons. Yet Adenauer, for his part, could not support them. He could accept de Gaulle's wish to disengage France from Atlantic integration. Announced at Colombey, this determination was simply confirmed at Rambouillet. And he did not object when the General announced to him what would become a major principle of French defense policy: occupying a second-echelon, reserve position at the rear of NATO lines in Germany. Receiving the assurance that France, even in such a reserve position, would stand alongside Germany, Adenauer did not see in this principle a sign of French disengagement from the defense of Germany. The two countries, he concluded from de Gaulle's statements, would remain inextricably linked in the defense of the same ground in a single battle.[90]

Adenauer, while showing himself understanding about French policy toward NATO, could nevertheless not envisage his country adopting the same principles. He certainly had "boundless" confidence[91] in de Gaulle, strengthened by his firmness in the Berlin affair and his *sang-froid* during the U2 affair. He also shared his worry about the duration of the U.S. engagement in the defense of Europe, particularly due to the new strategic balances. But he drew different conclusions: For him, this engagement should be strengthened, especially through the integrated military structure of NATO that remained both the condition and the best guarantee of this engagement. And from the political point of view, the NATO framework could not be questioned by Adenauer's Germany, since it was within this framework that the FRG had from the start conceived and effected its return to international sovereignty and responsibility. The Atlantic primacy of Bonn's security policy was not negotiable in 1960 and if, overall, the chancellor could understand de Gaulle's position on NATO, he could not accept its transposition to the rest of the Alliance, least of all his own country.[92] For a long time this would remain the principal limit to de Gaulle's European and Franco-German projects.

The Franco-German Misunderstanding

During the Rambouillet meeting, this limit may not have been quite apparent to de Gaulle, thus leading at the end of the summer of 1960 to a certain misunderstanding between himself and Adenauer over the questions of defense and of NATO. If that meeting had not showed "a clear opposition"[93] between the two conceptions, it foreshadowed all the ambiguity in Franco-German relations in the realm of security in years to come. For the chancellor, the Alliance had to adapt to new geostrategic conditions, while conserving its essential structures that made possible the maintenance of American engagement in Europe; whereas for de Gaulle, the Atlantic Alliance had to be preserved, but the integrated system under American leadership had to be ended, while the strategic dimension of the Europe of Six had to be organized.

After the summit, this misunderstanding was soon made manifest when de Gaulle tried "to strike while the iron [was] hot." After the Rambouillet meeting, he asked his foreign minister to put into effect a Franco-German commission to work along the lines of the European perspective opened up by the two statesmen, including on defense questions.[94] This idea made progress and resulted at the start of 1961 in establishment of the Fouchet Commission in which the Six were represented. But things went less well on the Atlantic score. De Gaulle hoped that the Franco-German commission would study the reform of the Alliance, of which he thought he had persuaded Adenauer, and he intended to start by convening a "very restricted" defense committee to "quite fix" France's position on the matter.[95] But this was to no avail; at the end of September, de Gaulle had the clear feeling the Germans were backpedaling on Atlantic affairs. He even confided to Debré that he regretted having gone so far with Adenauer: "I thought him more truly European than he is in reality. So, without going back on what we said, let's pretend for now that the problem is not acute."[96]

After the Franco-German and European breakthrough at Rambouillet, the autumn of 1960 marked a veritable crisis in relations between Paris and Bonn on security matters. Important bilateral military agreements were signed at the end of October that for the first time granted to Germany logistical facilities on French territory. But in the background, Adenauer put on the brakes. On August 15, he had written to de Gaulle to tell him that the reform of the Alliance could not be examined before the arrival of Eisenhower's successor. It was indeed the question of NATO that would be at the core of difficult discussions he had with Debré and Couve de Murville during their visit to Bonn on October 7.[97]

Adenauer explained himself the day after this visit, in a long letter to de Gaulle. Germany, he wrote, could not accept a reform of NATO that would dissolve integration in peacetime and would transform the Alliance into a "coalition of national defense systems." Reform was necessary, but the aggravation in the international situation required NATO's strengthening at the moment. If the Europe of Six envisaged setting up their own military organization, "this would lead to duplication and to major dissension with our NATO partners and would inevitably be interpreted by the United States as our desire to act in total independence in Western Europe, even to renounce their cooperation." Hence the absolute need to avoid anything that might be perceived by the Americans as a European propensity to envisage their eventual withdrawal, except at the risk of encouraging their tendency toward disengagement. A defense of Europe without the United States, he insisted, was impossible. Hence the indispensable nature of integration and the necessity that "all the principal partners in the Alliance maintain along the first line of defense, the length of the iron curtain, sufficiently strong units."[98]

The message was clear. The French policy of questioning Atlantic integration was not acceptable to Germany, and the maintenance of France in the first line of defense of Germany was eminently desirable. Two months after the harmony of Rambouillet, de Gaulle and Adenauer appeared to be opposed over essentials, while speaking from the same standpoint about the uncertain future of the American presence in Europe. For the former, a strong Western alliance would be preserved by means of the political and strategic emergence of the Europe of Six, which would eventually compensate for the inevitable American disengagement. For the latter, on the contrary, NATO's existing structures must be strengthened, that is, maintaining Atlantic integration so as to forestall the American tendency to retreat, instead of encouraging it by measures that would make it seem that such a tendency could be compensated for by greater European autonomy.

The chancellor's switch may be explained in part by domestic pressures similar to those after Colombey, but also by the context within the Alliance, since in the autumn of 1960 the Americans unveiled their project for a multilateral nuclear force that would occupy center stage in the Atlantic strategic debate for several years to come.[99] The idea of a NATO atomic force, whose operation—though for the time being under American control—would involve the allies, even the nonnuclear ones starting with Germany—was seductive to Adenauer. The chancellor judged it propitious for German security interests, which he had always envisaged as having an Atlantic priority, as he confided to high NATO officials, including Norstad; for Adenauer, a nuclear force owned, serviced, and controlled in common within a NATO framework appeared as the best response to the strategic challenges faced by Europe and America. The multilateral force (soon identified by the acronym MLF), officially presented by Herter to the Atlantic Council on December 16, 1960, thus incited Bonn at the end of the year to make a clear pro-Atlantic switch that could only be made at the expense of Gaullist projects.[100]

De Gaulle came to terms with this volte-face. The situation was basically frozen in the autumn of 1960 by the impending U.S. presidential election. He could merely acknowledge the failure of his double initiative of that summer, toward the Americans and British on one hand, and the Germans and Europeans on the other. But 1960 also marked a first shift in his Western policy. While he still held to the tripartite orientation outlined in 1958, with John F. Kennedy's election in November, it is clear he had a keen awareness of the limits of this approach after two years' experience. Since sending the memorandum, he could measure the conservatism of his partners and their reluctance to envisage a fundamental reform of the Western alliance in the direction he proposed and beyond that, to recognize the new reality, in his view, of French power and influence. Moreover, as the Berlin crisis demonstrated, he was correct in his conviction that a growing danger existed of strategic decoupling between Europe and America, particularly from the nuclear standpoint.

De Gaulle had not, however, abandoned any hope of influencing the evolution of the Western bloc. His goal from the strategic standpoint remained still to work for the maintenance of Alliance cohesion and particularly for an understanding between France and its Anglo-American partners. Undoubtedly, he based this on the perceptible rise in his country's influence, now on its way to becoming a nuclear power and to freeing itself shortly of the burden of the Algerian War. At the same time, he thought that a new direction should be explored: a continental agreement built around the Franco-German axis and destined to give birth to a strong West European entity whose emergence would profoundly modify the givens of West-West—and maybe East-West—relations.

NOTES

1. Cyril Buffet, "La politique nucléaire de la France et la seconde crise de Berlin (1958–1962)," *Relations Internationales*, no. 59, Autumn 1989, pp. 347–58.

2. Meeting between General de Gaulle and J. Foster Dulles, 15 December 1958, at Hôtel Matignon, Archives diplomatiques, MAE, Pactes 1948–1960, box 35.

3. Memorandum of Conversation with Couve de Murville, 7 February 1959, Orly, DDEL, Papers of John Foster Dulles and Christian Herter, Chronological Correspondence Series (CCS), box 17.

4. Meeting between M. Couve de Murville and J. Foster Dulles, Friday 6 February 1959, MAE, Pactes 1948–1960, box 248; see also Gregory W. Pedlow, "Multinational Contingency Planning During the Second Berlin Crisis: The Live Oak Organization 1959–1963," paper for the NHP conference, Ebenhausen, June 1991.

5. Telegram SECTO #17, 6 February 1959, 1/2, quoted in Bernard Ledwidge, *De Gaulle et les Américains. Conversations avec Dulles, Eisenhower, Kennedy et Rusk,* Paris, Flammarion, 1984.

6. Comments by General Valentin and Henri Froment-Meurice at the GREFHAN roundtable, 31 May 1991. See also Henri Paris, "Berlin, symbole et enjeu stratégique," *Défense Nationale,* November 1987, pp. 33–46. (The Live Oak staff would remain operational until German reunificaiton in 1990.)

7. Cf. Ledwidge, *De Gaulle et les Américains*, pp. 71–73.

8. Letter to Khrushchev, 10 September 1959, in Charles de Gaulle, *Lettres, notes et carnets (LNC) (juin 1958–décembre 1960),* Paris, Plon, 1985, pp. 255–56.

9. Letter to Eisenhower, 11 March 1959, in de Gaulle, *LNC (1958–1960),* pp. 204–6.

10. Conversation between de Gaulle and Eisenhower, 2 September 1959, Paris, in Ledwidge, *De Gaulle et les Américains*, pp. 81 ff.

11. Letters to Eisenhower, 20 October and 26 October 1959, in de Gaulle, *LNC (1958–1960),* pp. 270–72, 275–77.

12. Charles de Gaulle, *Memoirs of Hope (MH)*, trans. Terence Kilmartin, London, Weidenfield & Nicolson, 1971, pp. 222–23.

13. Hervé Alphand, *L'Étonnement d'être. Journal (1939–1973)*, Paris, Fayard, 1977, p. 316; see also, Instruction manuscrite pour le général Lavaud, 4 February 1959, in de Gaulle, *LNC (1958–1960),* p. 326.

14. Cyrus L. Sulzberger, *The Last of the Giants*, New York, Macmillan, 1970, p. 668.

15. Quoted by Buffet, "La politique nucléaire . . ."

16. Memorandum of Conversation, 16 May 1960, DDEL, President Dwight D. Eisenhower's Office Files, part 2, International Series, box 39.

17. Radio and television broadcast speech given at the Elysée Palace, 31 May 1960, in *Major Addresses, Statements and Press Conferences of General Charles de Gaulle (MA)*,

New York, French Embassy, n.d., pp. 275–78; letter to Philippe de Gaulle, 18 May 1960, in de Gaulle, *LNC (1958–1960),* pp. 358–59.

18. Dulles–de Gaulle Meeting, 15 December 1958.

19. Meeting between Couve de Murville and Herter on 14 December 1959, MAE, Pactes 1948–1960, box 248.

20. Quoted by Pierre Melandri, "La France et le 'jeu double' des États-Unis," in Jean-Pierre Rioux, ed., *La Guerre d'Algérie et les Français,* Paris, Fayard, 1990.

21. See Melandri, "La France et le 'jeu double' des États-Unis." However, one must mention several incidents between 1960 and 1963 during which officials in France might have believed in the involvement of certain American services in activities considered subversive of the French military in Algeria and of the OAS. See Sulzberger, *Last of the Giants,* p. 893. There was the same scenario after the April 1961 putsch in Algiers. See EMBTEL, Paris 4580, 23 April 1961, JFKL, NSF, France, box 73. Nothing indicates that these elements, unconfirmed as they are, played an important role.

22. Dulles–de Gaulle Meeting, 15 December 1958.

23. Letter to Eisenhower, 9 August 1960, in de Gaulle, *LNC (1958–1960),* pp. 388–90.

24. Memorandum of conversation with the President, 12 December 1958, DDEL, Papers of John Foster Dulles and Christian Herter, WHCMS, box 7.

25. See chapter 1, p. 22.

26. Dulles–de Gaulle Meeting, 15 December 1958; Dulles–Couve de Murville Meeting, 17 December 1958, MAE, Pactes 1948–1960, box 35.

27. Telegram, Washington to Paris, 7 January 1959, #106–114; note from Couve de Murville to the embassy in Washington (n.d.); telegram from Washington to Paris, 3 February 1959, #633–42, MAE, Pactes 1948–1960, box 35.

28. Premier Ministre, Comité de Défense, Secrétariat, "Extrait de décisions du comité de défense (réunion du 31 janvier 1959)," 6 February 1959, MAE, Pactes 1948–1960, box 35.

29. Direction générale des Affaires politiques, note pour le ministre, 11 February 1959, Note with handwritten comments by Jean-Marc Boegner on the first phase of tripartite consultations, 9 February 1959, MAE, Pactes 1948–1960, box 35.

30. Note pour le Général, Jean-Marc Boegner, 4 May 1959; note du Service des Pactes, 14 August 1959, MAE, Pactes 1948–1960, box 35.

31. Dulles–de Gaulle Meeting, 15 December 1958.

32. "Extrait de décisions du comité de défense (réunion du 31 janvier 1959)."

33. Couve de Murville to Washington (n.d.), MAE, Pactes 1948–1960, box 35; "Note pour le Général," Jean-Marc Boegner, 4 May 1959.

34. Alphand, *L'Étonnement d'être,* p. 310; conversation between de Gaulle and Eisenhower, 2 September 1959.

35. Outgoing telegram, Circular #102, 7 September 1959, Lucet to Alphand, MAE, Amérique 1952–1960, EU 9.4.1., France–U.S. relations, box 1958–1960.

36. Press conference held at the Elysée, 10 November 1959, in *MA,* pp. 61 ff.; Vernon A. Walters, *Silent Missions,* Garden City, NY, Doubleday, 1978, p. 297.

37. DEPTEL, Paris #2080, 17 November 1959, DDEL, President's Office Files, Part 2, International Series, box 12.

38. Letter to Eisenhower, 24 November 1959, in de Gaulle, *LNC (1958–1960),* pp. 283–84. See also the recollection of Walters, *Silent Missions,* and de Gaulle's memoir, *MH,* pp. 213–15.

39. See chapter 1, pp. 12–13.

40. Sulzberger, *Last of the Giants*, p. 23.

41. Alphand, *L'Étonnement d'être*, p. 295; "Note en vue des conversations entre le président de la République et le président des États-Unis," 19 August 1959; and "Entretiens franco-américains à l'hôtel Matignon le vendredi 1 er mai de 15h30 à 16h30," MAE, Pactes 1948–1960, box 248.

42. Note, "Négociations franco-américaines pour les applications militaires de l'énergie atomique," 27 November 1959, MAE, Pactes 1948–1960, box 254; "Review of Negotiation History of Mutual Defense Agreement with France of 1959," LBJL, National Security File, Committee File, Committee on Nuclear Proliferation, box 5 (n.d.); Maurice Couve de Murville, *Une politique étrangère 1958–1969,* Paris, Plon, 1971, p. 62; see also the testimony of Bertrand Goldschmidt at the GREFHAN roundtable, 31 May 1991.

43. Memorandum for the President, "Your Meeting with French Foreign Minister Couve de Murville," Christian Herter, 21 August 1958, DDEL, President's Office Files, International Series, box 11; "Review of Negotiation History of Mutual Defense Agreement . . ."; and telegram from Washington to Paris #1353–63, 21 March 1959, MAE, Pactes 1948–1960, box 35; see also the testimony of Goldschmidt.

44. Letter to Eisenhower, 25 May 1959, in de Gaulle, *LNC (1958–1960)*, pp. 225–28; Alphand, *L'Étonnement d'être*, pp. 304, 311.

45. Walters, *Silent Missions*, p. 490; Ledwidge, *De Gaulle et les Américains*, p. 289.

46. "Négociations franco-américaines . . ."

47. McGeorge Bundy, *Danger and Survival: Choices about the Bomb in the First Fifty Years*, New York, Vintage, 1988, p. 483.

48. Note for Couve de Murville, "Coopération franco-américaine dans le domaine de la production des armes nucléaires," Hervé Alphand, 3 March 1960, MAE, Pactes 1948–1960, box 254.

49. Memorandum for the President, Christian D. Herter, "Visit of French President Charles de Gaulle," 19 April 1960, DDEL, Presidential Office Files, Part 2, International Series, box 12; note by Pierre Gauillaumat, "Politique nucléaire de la France," 8 March 1960; and de Rose to Alphand, 16 February 1960, MAE, Pactes 1948–1960, box 254.

50. Alphand, *L'Étonnement d'être*, p. 343.

51. De Rose to Alphand, 16 February 1960.

52. Note du général de Gaulle, 29 April 1959, MAE, Pactes 1948–1960, box 35.

53. Memorandum of Conversation with the President, 2 May 1959, DDEL, Papers of John Foster Dulles and Christian Herter, Herter Chronological Correspondence Series, box 7; and de Gaulle to Eisenhower. 6 October 1959, in de Gaulle, *LNC (1958–1960),* pp. 225–28, 262–64.

54. Telegrams, REPAN #50043 and 50044, 22 & 26 May, 1959, MAE, Pactes 1948–1960, box 96.

55. "Transfert hors de France des escadrons de chasseurs-bombardiers de l'OTAN," EMGDN, 3 July 1959; "Redéploiement des escadrons américains en Europe," Délégation française au Groupe permanent, 20 August 1959, MAE, Pactes 1948–1960, box 96.

56. "Entretiens franco-américains à l'hôtel Matignon le vendredi 1 er mai de 15h30 à 16h30," MAE, Pactes 1948–1960, box 248.

57. Telegram REPAN, 11 June 1959, MAE, Pactes 1948–1960, box 96.

58. See de Gaulle to Eisenhower, 6 October 1959; personal interview.

59. Letter from Michel Debré to Maurice Couve de Murville, 4 November 1960, MAE, Pactes 1948–1960, box 140.

60. Memorandum for the President, "Offer of Nuclear Capable Weapons to France," 1 July 1959, DDEL, Office Files, Part 2, International Series, box 11; "Texte de l'accord entre le gouvernement de la République Française et le gouvernement des États-Unis d'Amérique relatif aux stocks OTAN en Allemagne d'armes atomiques prévues pour le soutien des forces françaises affectées a l'OTAN et destinées à être utilisées par celles-ci," 6 September 1960, MAE, Pactes 1948–1960, box 140.

61. Extrait de décisions du comité de défense (réunion du 31 janvier 1959).

62. Présidence du Conseil, réunion de Défense nationale no. 0097, 7 January 1959, MAE, Pactes 1948–1960, box 83.

63. Telegram Paris REPAN #50063, 6 March 1959, MAE, Pactes 1948–1960, box 35; *Revue de Défense Nationale*, May 1959, pp. 920, 930; and *Le Monde*, 28 February 1959.

64. Couve de Murville to Washington (n.d., early 1959), MAE, Pactes 1948–1960, box 35; réunion de Défense nationale, 7 January 1959; *Le Monde*, 28 February 1959.

65. Michel Debré, *Mémoires*, vol. 3, "Gouverner 1958–1962," Paris, Albin Michel, 1988, p. 406; press conference of 25 March 1959, in Charles de Gaulle, *Discours et Messages (DM)*, vol. 3, "Avec le renouveau" (mai 1958–juillet 1962), p. 93.

66. Christian Herter, Memorandum for the President, "Status of French Mediterranean Fleet," 4 March 1959, DDEL, Papers of John Foster Dulles and Christian Herter, Herter Chronological Correspondence Series, box 7; DEPTEL, Paris #3470, 19 March 1959, DDEL, Eisenhower Office Files, Part 2, International Series, box 12.

67. Fiche, "Situation des forces navales françaises réservées pour affectation en Méditerranée," EMDN, 26 February 1959, MAE, Pactes 1948–1960, box 35; telegram #50003, 6 March 1959.

68. EMBTEL, Paris, #808, 20 August 1963, JFKL, NSF, France, box 72A.

69. Speech given at the École Militaire on 3 November 1959, in de Gaulle, *DM*, vol. 3, pp. 125–29.

70. Debré, *Mémoires*, p. 370; Pierre Messmer, *Après tant de batailles. Mémoires*, Paris, Albin Michel, 1992, p. 305.

71. Polls by IFOP, February 1960 and 23–31 May 1960, cited in Jean Charlot, *Les Français et de Gaulle*, Paris, Plon, 1971, p. 272.

72. Note, "Intégration aérienne européenne," (n.d., end of 1959), MAE, Pactes 1948–1960, box 248; memorandum for the President, "Visit of French President Charles de Gaulle," 19 April 1960.

73. *Revue de défense nationale*, April 1960 and November 1960, p. 1882; *L'Information*, 29 September 1960; *Le Monde*, 21 April 1960; personal interview.

74. *Le Monde*, 11 October 1960; *L'Information*, 29 September 1960; *The Times*, 29 September 1960; personal interview.

75. Sulzberger, *Last of the Giants*, p. 661; telegram Washington #2340–45, 3 May 1960, Alphand to Couve de Murville, MAE, Amérique 1952–1963, États-Unis 9.4.1.; personal interview.

76. Memorandum of Conversation, de Gaulle–Eisenhower, 18 May 1960, DDEL, President's Office Files, Part 2, International Series, box 39; Alphand, *L'Étonnement d'être*, p. 332.

77. Ledwidge, *De Gaulle et les Américains*, p. 291; letter to Macmillan, 9 August 1960.

78. Charles de Gaulle, *Mémoires d'espoir*, "Le Renouveau" (1958–1962), Paris, Plon, 1970, p. 210. See Alain Peyrefitte, *C'était de Gaulle*, vol. 1, "La France redevient la France," Paris, de Fallois/Fayard, 1994, pp. 61–62.

79. Radio and television broadcast, 31 May 1960, in *MA*, p. 78.

80. Press Conference, 5 September 1960, in *MA*, pp. 92–93.

81. Radio and television broadcast, 31 December 1960, in *MA*, p. 109.

82. Pierre Maillard, *De Gaulle et l'Allemagne. Le rêve inachevé*, Paris, Plon, 1990, p. 187.

83. Note au sujet de l'organisation de l'Europe, Rambouillet, 30 July 1960, in de Gaulle, *LNC (1958–1960)*, pp. 382–83; see also Maillard, *De Gaulle et l'Allemagne*, p. 189.

84. Note au sujet de l'organisation de l'Europe, Rambouillet; see also Maillard, *De Gaulle et l'Allemagne*, p. 189.

85. Press Conference of 5 September 1960, in *MA*, pp. 92–93.

86. Quoted by Maillard, *De Gaulle et l'Allemagne*, p. 189.

87. Maillard, *De Gaulle et l'Allemagne*, p. 193; Jean Lacouture, *De Gaulle*, vol. 3, "Le Souverain," Paris, Le Seuil, 1986, p. 335.

88. Maillard, *De Gaulle et l'Allemagne*, p. 191; note au sujet de l'organisation de l'Europe, Rambouillet, 30 July 1960.

89. Maillard, *De Gaulle et l'Allemagne*, p. 191.

90. Maillard, *De Gaulle et l'Allemagne*; personal interview.

91. Couve de Murville, *Une politique étrangère*, p. 245.

92. Maillard, *De Gaulle et l'Allemagne*, p. 194.

93. Maillard, *De Gaulle et l'Allemagne*.

94. Letter to Couve de Murville, 1 August 1960, in de Gaulle, *LNC (1958–1960)*, pp. 383–84.

95. Letter to Couve de Murville, 1 August 1960, in de Gaulle, *LNC (1958–1960)*, pp. 383–84.

96. Directive pour M. Debré, 30 September 1960, in de Gaulle, *LNC (1958–1960)*, pp. 398–99.

97. See Georges-Henri Soutou, "Les problèmes de sécurité dans les rapports franco-allemands de 1956 à 1963"; Couve de Murville, *Une politique étrangère*, pp. 246–47; and *Revue de Défense Nationale*, December 1960.

98. Letter from Adenauer to de Gaulle, 8 October 1960, MAE, Pactes 1948–1960, box 34.

99. Colette Barbier, "La force multilatérale," *Relations Internationales*, no. 69, Spring 1992, pp. 3–18.

100. Note pour le Ministre, "Force de frappe OTAN," Pierre de Leusse, 26 October 1960; REPAN telegram #618, 5 December 1960, MAE, Pactes 1948–1960, box 34.

Chapter Three

From Berlin to Cuba (1961–1962)

The years 1961 and 1962 were decisive for relations between France and the Alliance. The arrival of John F. Kennedy in the White House in January 1961 inaugurated a new American policy toward NATO. More dynamic, but also more directorial, this policy tended to reaffirm U.S. leadership in the Alliance and to bend it in a direction that would rapidly be revealed as opposite to de Gaulle's conceptions. Against the backdrop of the Berlin and Cuban crises, this tendency would become accentuated and would lead de Gaulle to demarcate himself more and more from U.S. policy—especially since the reestablishment of France's international status, with the end of the Algerian conflict and the pursuit of nuclear effort, would considerably increase his maneuverability.

The substantial differences between France and the United States that appeared in 1961 and 1962 and led to a serious degradation in relations between Paris and Washington went beyond simple conflict of interests. In a period of crises decisive for the evolution of the Cold War, they increasingly exposed more clearly two antinomic conceptions of power and international order. Kennedy's United States of America, animated by an internationalism both idealistic and hegemonic, was ready to "bear all burdens," to meet all challenges. De Gaulle's France, by contrast, on its way to shedding once and for all its colonial burden, was redefining its place in the world at the cost of a largely national effort. France, observed Stanley Hoffmann correctly, "repatriated" its power objectives.[1] De Gaulle tried with its resources, that of a medium power, to give it a role on a par with its grandeur, that of a world power. In short, the United States had a "grand design" on the one hand and France had a "grand ambition" on the other[2]—hence competition and soon a total clash between two rival visions of the Alliance and of Europe.

KENNEDY AND THE ALLIANCE: ACTIVISM OR *DIRIGI$\mathbb{C}$? 'E*?

In the first months of the new administration, the shift in U.S. policy made itself felt. The young Kennedy team arrived full of strategic certainties. As a senator, then as Democratic Party candidate in the presidential election, Kennedy had severely criticized the conservatism of his predecessor and had recommended a defense policy better adapted to the new context. Arriving in the White House, he intended therefore to put into practice a dynamic policy toward the Alliance and to reaffirm U.S. leadership of NATO. Most of the men who would assist in this task had already had, at the time of the "creation" of the Atlantic system, often direct experience of these affairs. This was the case with Dean Rusk, former assistant secretary of state in the Truman administration and now secretary of state; with George Ball, a friend of Jean Monnet and now assistant secretary of state, who was particularly influential in European affairs; as well as with Paul Nitze, the author in 1950 of the NSC 68 document that had marked the militarization of the containment doctrine, now assistant secretary of defense for international security affairs. Others such as McGeorge Bundy, who left Harvard University to take the decisive post of presidential advisor on national security, and Robert McNamara, the president of Ford Motor Company who became secretary of defense, were chosen less for their political experience than for their intellectual abilities. All of them, with variations in sensibility or approach, shared Kennedy's vision of an Alliance that would allow the West, with the United States at its head, to "win" the Cold War.[3]

A New Approach to the Alliance

The new U.S. approach to the Atlantic Alliance was defined in the spring of 1961 in a report Kennedy commissioned from the former secretary of state, Dean Acheson. The choice of the latter spoke for itself. Acheson had played a major role in U.S. policy toward Europe in the Truman era. If he had not taken a determining part in negotiating the Washington Treaty (he was not in government in 1948), it is he who had concluded it as secretary of state after January 1949 and who had secured ratification of the Atlantic Pact by the Senate. Acheson, one of the principal American protagonists of the initial "transatlantic bargaining," was in 1961 associated with the idea of a strong, indeed of a hegemonic Atlanticism, and without holding an official post in the Kennedy or Johnson administration would play a starring role in American policy toward the Alliance and toward Europe. The Acheson report, submitted in March 1961 to President Kennedy, who officially approved it on April 21, was not lacking in ambition: it aimed at integrating the political, military, and economic dimensions of transatlantic relations into a strategic vision of their development. The goal of this new policy was to strengthen U.S. leadership while renewing active management of the Alliance in a context of profound international mutations.[4]

In the political domain, the report unsurprisingly insisted that Western cohesion was imperative. Previously overlooked by Washington, systematic consultation should take place between the allies, Acheson suggested; while giving them the feeling that their views were taken into account, this would by the same token make the managing role of the United States more acceptable. In the eyes of the new administration, NATO should be more than ever the principal forum in which U.S. leadership was exercised. Beyond the current NATO situation, Washington in fact assumed a wider and more long-term goal: to arouse, organize, and become the head of a veritable "Atlantic community" that would link America to an "integrated" Europe—meaning free from national ambitions deemed to be archaic. This is why the Acheson report, strongly influenced by Europeanists like George Ball, insisted on the need for a "coherent" approach to Western European unification. This approach would in particular integrate what was becoming under Kennedy (who had vigorously criticized Eisenhower on this point) a prime concern for the United States: the need to preserve the country's economic and financial equilibrium. While America was seeing its balance of payments and economic competitiveness deteriorate under the weight of foreign engagements, Europe, it was argued, should avoid aggravating that situation by becoming, through a restrictive or even protectionist trade policy, a disloyal rival. This concern to link the economic and the military would become more predominant in the years to come in U.S. policy toward Europe and the Alliance.

It was above all in the military domain that the report announced a decisive—and predictable—change in policy. NATO, Acheson thought, had until now privileged the worst of strategic hypotheses (a massive nuclear attack by the USSR) and not the most probable (limited aggression, for example, in Berlin). Therefore, he advocated, like General Norstad who spoke out on this issue in November 1960, possessing conventional forces sufficiently powerful, in case of aggression, to be able to mark a "pause" before nuclear escalation. To avoid an "all or nothing" situation for the United States, the "threshold at which nuclear weapons are introduced," explained Acheson, "should be a high one"[5]—which moreover should occur through the strengthening by the Europeans of their potential for conventional defense, so as to ensure a better sharing of the burden of Western defense, of which the Americans already carried too heavy a share. In addition, one must avoid the overlapping of NATO's atomic weapons in Europe with those deployed in the United States, on which essential deterrence should rely and, accordingly, strengthen the centralization of the command and control of nuclear forces. Hence a categorical imperative for Washington: to abstain from lending assistance to the development of national nuclear forces.

But, paradoxically, while characterizing the reinforcement of conventional defense as a "top priority" and while pleading for better centralization of the Alliance's nuclear deterrence, the Acheson report proposed to strengthen European confidence (shaken since *Sputnik*) that a Soviet attack in Europe would indeed unleash U.S. strategic nuclear reprisals. The Europeans' fear that this might not be the case was unfounded, declared Acheson, for it postulated "the irrationality" of Soviet leaders; the allies should be persuaded "that nuclear weapons will be used effectively in their defense against a nuclear attack or against a non-nuclear attack which NATO non-nuclear forces cannot contain."[6] But how could one raise the nuclear threshold and at the same time reassure the allies about U.S. determination to defend Europe by all means necessary, even nuclear? The Acheson report left this difficulty alone; it would remain at the heart of the debate over "flexible response" that opened in the first months of the new administration.

Whether in the political, economic, or strategic dimension, there existed in this new approach to the Alliance a fundamental contradiction that would remain at the center of transatlantic misunderstandings in the coming years. Although Kennedy was favorable, as the Acheson report suggested, to the emergence of an Atlantic "community," which he insisted ought to be a community of "equals," he was determined above all to affirm the leading role of the United States within it.[7] This contradiction would soon materialize, in 1962, in the two decisive domains for transatlantic relations: the nuclear and European issues.

A New Approach to France

Meanwhile, the new approach to the Alliance developed by Acheson in the spring of 1961 already appeared distant from de Gaulle's ideas. The new administration from the start saw in the latter's policy one of the principal challenges that the United States had to face in transatlantic relations. In the wake of the Acheson report, the Kennedy team also tried to develop a "new approach" to France, the goal being to incite the French to work once again for the "common cause," meaning NATO. The planners thought Washington should "seek to go to the heart of de Gaulle's anxieties" but without necessarily remedying things by the methods he advanced, starting with the tripartism he had been proposing since 1958, the formalization of which might sap the Alliance's cohesion.[8] It was the same for France's nuclear demands, with the new administration proving even more hostile than the preceding one to the French atomic effort. Haunted by the prospect of multiplying the number of nuclear powers, it tried to forestall the risks of proliferation. These risks were considered particularly serious with respect to Germany, which was judged susceptible of being tempted in time to acquire a national nuclear capability—especially if Great Britain and France persisted in their own efforts, which would only sharpen Bonn's frustrations or even make it itch to go that way itself. Any U.S. help with French nuclear or missile efforts should therefore be avoided, so as to remove the peril of a "German missile and/or nuclear program" that the State Department feared above all else. Jean Monnet, akin to the Europeanists in the administration like Ball who were concerned to treat Germany on a par with the other allies, was in full agreement with them on that.[9]

Accordingly, the Kennedy team postulated that by suppressing the privileged status of Great Britain and inciting London to reduce its national nuclear effort and assign its arsenal to NATO, Washington would obtain a more cooperative attitude on de Gaulle's part, since what he wanted above all, the State Department thought, was to reduce the difference in treatment that existed between the two countries. In the longer term, meaning after de Gaulle's eventual departure, the United States could even manage to "discourage the French" from pursuing their nuclear effort.[10] Meanwhile, the goal was to respond to the French wish to be associated with the elaboration and application of strategy, by guaranteeing the Europeans "effective participation" in the "control" of American nuclear forces assigned to NATO and in the elaboration of "guidelines" for the use of these weapons. As for U.S. nuclear forces not assigned to NATO, the United States could "consider the long term possibility of some Allied influence" over them — and then contrive to never reach that point. In return for these "concessions," the United States could ask France to contribute actively to the rise in conventional power that Washington called for from its allies, and to assign its future nuclear forces to NATO.[11]

This "new" approach to France (which owed much to a misunderstanding of de Gaulle's goals, reduced to a demand for parity treatment with Great Britain) in fact merely corresponded to the general line of Eisenhower's policy. But it did so in a more dynamic and more systematic manner, and would therefore exacerbate its intrinsic contradictions. On the one hand, the Kennedy team tried taking on board all the Alliance's problems by giving durable responses to the Europeans' questions and de Gaulle's interpellations. More out of realism than gladly, the new administration admitted that it had to satisfy (within limits) the latter's desire for "grandeur" in order to preserve NATO cohesion.[12] But on the other hand, it was convinced that this cohesion would result from the reaffirmation of U.S. leadership. In short, while appearing sensitive to French arguments, the administration planned to strengthen U.S. hegemony within the Alliance. The effects of this contradiction, which interested parties could not indefinitely overlook, would soon be felt.

"Tell Me What That Young Man Is Like"

At the start of 1961, de Gaulle was not ill disposed to the new administration. His views were certainly unchanged: an Atlantic Alliance remained indispensable, even if its organization needed overhauling; tripartite cooperation, systematic and effective, remained eminently desirable; finally, the development of a French nuclear force was more than ever essential. But the General, remembering the blunt refusal of the preceding administration, did not expect with Kennedy to proceed to a fully fledged relaunch of the memorandum's ideas, "frozen" since the fruitless attempt of summer 1960.[13] While he did not exclude the possibility that the new U.S. president had ideas closer to his own than his predecessor, he was in a waiting position. "Tell me what that young man is like," he asked Jacques Chaban-Delmas, whom he sent as scout to Washington in early March.[14] Received at the

White House, the president of the National Assembly would "test" de Gaulle's ideas on Kennedy. The latter's election represented a unique opportunity, Chaban told him, to effect certain fundamental changes in the Alliance, notably in the direction of tripartite coordination. If Kennedy acceded to these views, "existing difficulties would be surmounted." He insisted that de Gaulle was not hostile to any form of this consultation, provided that it was efficient and occurred at the highest level (which Alphand had already explained to Rusk several times since the arrival of the new administration).[15] To which Kennedy responded politely that he was open to de Gaulle's proposals, which he awaited with interest.[16]

In the immediate future, it was quite the reverse that occurred: At the end of April, Acheson, dispatched by Kennedy, came to present to de Gaulle an outline of the new U.S. approach to the Alliance. This conversation already heralded future developments: The former secretary of state came more to inform the French head of state than to consult him, even if he affirmed that Kennedy awaited the result of this conversation before approving his report. De Gaulle's reaction to Acheson's presentation appeared lukewarm; he was skeptical about the political part of the new approach, and the idea advanced by Acheson in his report of extending consultation within NATO to all geographic zones seemed to him impractical. As a military organization, NATO was not adapted to this type of consultation, as the Congo affair demonstrated.[17] As for the strategic part, de Gaulle did not reject the central goal, at least not in front of Kennedy's emissary: to raise the nuclear threshold so as to escape all-or-nothing, through strengthening the conventional potential of NATO. And it was with apparent satisfaction, thought Acheson when he was reminded of European fears in this regard, that de Gaulle received the assurance that no nuclear weapon would be withdrawn from Europe and that Washington would use them if necessary in case of attack, nuclear or conventional, against the USSR.[18]

Yet, despite the polite interest he showed during the discussion, de Gaulle was in no way convinced by Dean Acheson's explanations. From this hour-long conversation with the former secretary of state, what he in fact retained was that the Kennedy administration intended to take a path that was decidedly not the one he recommended. The very next day, during a press conference, he hinted that the new American approach did not, in his opinion, resolve the Alliance's nuclear problem.[19] And in the following weeks, he let it be known to anyone who would listen that he no longer believed in the U.S. strategic guarantee, which justified France in pursuing its own nuclear effort to protect Western Europe from Soviet blackmail. This is what he confided in May to Paul-Henri Spaak, now Belgium's foreign affairs minister.[20]

As Kennedy's arrival in Paris at the end of May approached, French decision makers, like de Gaulle, already appeared generally skeptical of the Atlantic ideas of the new administration, as much from a political as from a strategic standpoint. The first contacts at the diplomatic level had promised "a sincere desire to ameliorate consultation," it was thought at the Quai d'Orsay, but they had also re-

vealed traditional U.S. disquiet about any institutionalization of this cooperation.[21] Alphand could thus observe that the three foreign ministers had consulted
with each other three times on the margin of international meetings, but that U.S.
diplomacy wished that "these exchanges do not take on a statutory character."[22]
As for the evolution of the Alliance's defense toward greater suppleness on the
ground, especially by means of an increase in conventional forces, the French
strategists were not opposed to it as such, but they feared "equivocation" in proposals that might well be interpreted as "translating a desire for U.S. disengagement."[23] This was the reserved position that French representatives to NATO
announced when in May 1961 the Atlantic Council began to discuss, at the request of the Americans, the Alliance's strategic concept that Washington, in line
with the Acheson report, wished to see change in the direction of the "pause" and
"limited war"—in other words, the flexible response.[24]

The Kennedy–De Gaulle Meeting

It was clear in this situation that strategic questions would be at the center of conversations between de Gaulle and Kennedy. En route to Vienna where he would
meet Khrushchev, the American president stopped in Paris from May 29 to June
2. When he left Washington, Kennedy appeared divided, even "ambivalent,"
about what was meant to be at the core of these strategic conversations, that is,
the nuclear issue and particularly atomic cooperation.[25] While wishing to keep to
the restrictive recommendation in the Acheson report, Kennedy, anxious to reconcile with de Gaulle, manifestly did not want to arrive in Paris empty-handed.
Perhaps, he was influenced by the advice of those like Spaak who were recom-
mending a supple approach to the issue, considering that all hope was not lost of
placing the French nuclear effort within the "NATO framework,"[26] on condition
that de Gaulle be given a "concrete" token of goodwill; or like General James
Gavin, his new ambassador to Paris, who made himself in the first months the
advocate of the French nuclear effort in Washington and declared himself favorable, like Spaak, to U.S. assistance in the ballistic sphere, not covered by the
McMahon Act.[27] This attitude aroused a certain interest on the French side.
Shortly before the two heads of state met, Hervé Alphand, in the presence of
François de Rose, hinted to Paul Nitze, "more personally than officially," that allowing for certain concessions, France might envisage inserting its future nuclear
capability into the NATO framework.[28]

En route to Paris, President Kennedy examined the different options regarding
atomic cooperation with France, options running from delivering a nuclear reac-
tor for submarines, mentioned back in 1958 and then shelved, to helping in the
domain of inertial guidance systems for ballistic missiles.[29] Nevertheless, if a
"good third" of the de Gaulle–Kennedy meetings concerned nuclear questions,
the issue of atomic cooperation properly speaking seems scarcely to have been
touched.[30] At most, Kennedy stressed a proposal announced several days before

in Ottawa to the Canadian Parliament (partially taking up a plan by the preceding administration) of placing five nuclear submarines of the Polaris type under SACEUR orders to strengthen deterrence in Europe and to constitute in time a nuclear multilateral force (MLF), controlled jointly by the allies. To which de Gaulle replied that he had no objection, but that this "partial solution" did not resolve NATO's nuclear problem since the use of the weapons in question "would continue to depend as in the past on solely American decisions."[31] Things went farther on the issue of nuclear consultation, but with scarcely more concrete results. To de Gaulle, who explained to him that he no longer believed in either the value of Atlantic military integration nor the American nuclear guarantee — both being in his opinion undermined by the "end of the American atomic monopoly and the establishment of a balance with the Russians" and by "the re-establishment of Western Europe, which justified its real participation in defense"[32] — Kennedy stressed (without convincing him) that a massive conventional attack by the USSR would undoubtedly unleash a U.S. nuclear response. He added he was ready to extend to France the agreement between Eisenhower and Macmillan whereby Washington "would take every possible step" to consult Great Britain over an eventual recourse to nuclear weapons "in the event of increased tension or of threat of war."[33]

Regional issues did not bring the two men any closer together. On Southeast Asia, and particularly Laos, two rationales confronted each other: Kennedy's, faithful to the domino theory that postulated that only military force would stop the spread of communism in the region, and de Gaulle's, for whom any military solution would only turn against the West and who encouraged Kennedy to play a political card, that of Souvanna Phouma and the neutrality of Laos.[34] Discussion was also lively about problems in Africa, especially the Congo. De Gaulle reminded Kennedy of his original hostility to the UN military role in this affair, which he thought counterproductive, and his often-unexpressed preference for concerted action by the three Western powers.[35] Even if the atmosphere was cordial, if not confident, the meetings revealed the range and width of disagreements that continued to exist between the two countries and that, especially over strategic issues, were liable to become aggravated. When Kennedy, taking up the General's ideas, mentioned as if remembering to do so at the end of discussions, the setting up of a mechanism for tripartite consultations, de Gaulle, even if he did not reject the idea that "senior figures designated specifically for this task" meet "regularly to examine on a world scale problems posed to the three countries,"[36] could only be skeptical about a proposal that had scarcely any more chance of succeeding than the previous times.

Kennedy's visit appeared at the time as a success, especially for public opinion and the press. It is true that the president's youth and presence and his wife's charm made a contrast with the preceding administration, which nowhere since his inauguration made as much of an impact as during his stay in Paris, where de Gaulle and the French gave the presidential couple a magnificent welcome. For his part, Kennedy wanted to show that he came to see de Gaulle as a young head of state desirous to profit from the experience and judgment of a man who had already entered into history (the American president had just suffered a severe setback with the Bay of Pigs, whereas de Gaulle was stronger after the aborted putsch in Algiers a month earlier). The press vied with itself to stress the mutual confidence the two men of state bore each other, even though they were so different and separated by a generation.

Very soon, the limits of this personal equation appeared. Kennedy said he was ready to follow up on his overtures about tripartite cooperation but, as always, U.S. diplomats wanted to avoid drawing the attention of the other allies and so finally issued watered-down proposals.[37] De Gaulle observed that "as one would expect," Washington really wished to maintain the current situation, that is, routine consultation between the secretary of state and the French and British ambassadors in Washington.[38] French diplomats did not see in the U.S. proposals, just a few months after the arrival of the new administration, anything more than a continuation of "previous bad habits." None of this, noted Couve de Murville, permitted really preparing decisions springing from a common policy.[39] And de Gaulle, more skeptical than ever, concluded that "the American attitude would change only when we have atomic bombs."[40] At the end of June, when Kennedy wrote to de Gaulle to formally confirm that "in case of a situation implying heightened tension or a danger of war, the United States has the intention of consulting with France," de Gaulle welcomed it coldly, content to "take note" of it in a rather dry acknowledgment.[41]

By all accounts, de Gaulle was not satisfied with these assurances, already formulated by Eisenhower two years earlier, which from his viewpoint had only limited weight. He was not wrong, however. The Americans themselves thought they were scarcely bound by their engagement to consult with the British (and now equally with the French) in the event of nuclear danger. For Washington, this engagement did not go beyond the declaration of intent.[42] Later events, particularly around Berlin and Cuba, would demonstrate this. It would take only a few months for it to be proved to de Gaulle that Kennedy, even more than his predecessor, did not envisage consultation with the allies except in terms of informing them, and not really by way of true cooperation with them[43] and that the new president was inclined to adopt a strategy that France reproved, and which his predecessor had himself opposed. Decidedly, thought Couve de Murville, tripartism belonged to a "bygone era."[44]

BERLIN: ACTS 2 AND 3

Events in the last months of 1961 would confirm this. Returning in the summer and autumn, the Berlin affair would in effect once again put to the test the Alliance's solidarity. Even if the construction of the wall on August 13 marked the end of a crisis lasting nearly three years, its consequences would for a long time hang over the evolution of the Alliance and over the direction of French policy.

From Vienna to Berlin

After his stay in Paris, Kennedy met Khrushchev in Vienna on June 3 and 4. The Soviet leader, who no doubt thought in the light of the Bay of Pigs fiasco that he was dealing with a weak president, or at least an inexperienced one, restarted the crisis by giving Kennedy a note containing the usual demands, combined with a new six-month ultimatum. The confrontation between the two men was tough. Kennedy came out of it shaken and alarmed. Tensions mounted during June under the effect of Khrushchev's threatening declarations.

The American president was counting on French support. He was certain that de Gaulle "shared his concern about the threatening character"[45] of the Soviet note. In 1961 as in 1958, de Gaulle adopted an intransigent attitude to Khrushchev's ultimatum. His motivations were still the same: a conviction that only firmness could make Soviet blackmail fail; a desire to proclaim unfailing support for Adenauer's Germany; and a concern to demonstrate the justness of his positions on the Alliance. He thought the security and cohesion of the West were involved: "What we had better do for the moment," he replied to Kennedy, "is to speak clearly, to take openly military precautions and to show ourselves in total accord."[46] This manifestation of support and firmness was well received by the American president, who noted their "total agreement" on a line of "firmness and solidarity."[47] When on July 25 Kennedy announced to his citizens in a televised speech that he was intending to resist Soviet attempts to end the U.S. presence in Berlin and that, to this effect, he would ask Congress for a supplement of three billion dollars for the defense budget as well as a call-up of reservists, de Gaulle awarded him full marks.[48]

However, behind the apparently common attitude over Berlin could be seen, as during previous episodes, a disparity that would gradually reemerge. Deep down, de Gaulle too thought that Kennedy, in Vienna, had lacked assurance faced with Khrushchev. For de Gaulle, always more convinced that Moscow had neither the means nor the will for a truly bellicose policy, the Soviet leader had handily profited from the American president's inexperience; Kennedy's lack of *sang-froid* had fed the tension.[49] But beyond questions of personality, deeper discord loomed in the background. While Kennedy, once the crisis occurred, tried to exercise unrestricted leadership, de Gaulle would take a distance from U.S. policy, which as the president announced on July 25, had military as well as diplomatic aspects: the management by Washington of a strong reinforcement of American and allied conventional might in Europe; and the hypothesis of negotiation with Moscow over the substance of Berlin, hence the German question. Each of these two issues would go against the French position. If de Gaulle was favorable to a rise in military power to respond to Soviet threats, he did not accept that the crisis became a pretext for a long-lasting modification of NATO strategy. And he was especially opposed in the current situation to talks with the Soviet Union, in which he already saw the outline of an exclusive U.S.–Soviet dialogue over European affairs. In short, the effects of the Berlin affair in the summer and autumn of 1961 represented, once again, a political and strategic contest of prime importance for East-West—and also West-West—relations.

The Military Dimension

When the tension increased at the end of July 1961, the United States contemplated the reinforcement of its conventional potential in Europe and asked the allies to do the same. Kennedy wrote personally to de Gaulle about this.[50] On August 8 Rusk explained in front of the Atlantic Council the measures proposed by Washington and on August 19 SHAPE detailed, country by country, the operational measures to be taken. They included growth in infantry troop levels and equipment, putting at SACEUR's disposal supplementary combat units and increasing the number and capabilities of support and reserve forces.[51]

De Gaulle was not caught short. Even before the American president's move, he had decided at the end of June to return to France one of the divisions stationed in Algeria, and he could announce to Kennedy the probable recall of a second division that summer, as well as a 30 percent increase in infantry and air troops put at NATO's disposal. By the autumn, he estimated that French forces in France and Germany had been strengthened by "about fifty thousand men with corresponding materiel and several squadrons," by displacing them from Algeria.[52] His heartfelt wish was to demonstrate that the French intended to give concrete military substance to the Western solidarity it advocated. This effort produced its effect, particularly on the Americans, and the Pentagon bureaucrats were pleased with the strong French participation in the reinforcement of NATO's posture.[53] Gavin, always inclined to defend French policy, was relieved that de Gaulle had anticipated the problem of the rise in military power over that year and concluded that France is "probably the strongest ally we have in Europe."[54]

But the effort France put into the common defense in summer 1961 did not herald a more favorable attitude to NATO properly speaking. Thanks to the positive change in the Algerian situation and to the Berlin crisis, there was certainly a conjunctural strengthening of France's participation in integrated defense. But de Gaulle saw beyond that. For him, these moves showed that "the reappearance of a real French military power in Europe" would necessarily involve a modification of the integrated military structure.[55] Far from renouncing the idea of disengaging France from NATO's military mechanisms, de Gaulle reaffirmed this all the more clearly since the rise in French power in Central Europe would in time be incompatible with integration. His attitude hardened in the autumn and winter of 1961 when Washington hoped to augment U.S. military presence in France so as to strengthen its logistics. Out of the question, responded de Gaulle, as long as NATO remained as it was. The Americans could strengthen their European logistics from the ports of Anvers and Rotterdam instead. As for an increase in American troops and materiel in France, it would only be acceptable if the forces in question were (as stipulated by the Franco-German agreement of 1960)[56] placed under French control. "This is the practice of any alliance when it is not about integration. We think it necessary not to extend integration any more than it is already," except by transforming the American military presence into an "occupation."[57] This is just what Armed Forces Minister Pierre Messmer shortly afterward told Roswell Gilpatric, the assistant secretary of defense, in more diplomatic terms.[58]

While having himself, in the context of the Berlin crisis, taken important measures to strengthen the posture of French forces in Central Europe, de Gaulle was irritated by the turn taken in the campaign launched by Washington in favor of NATO's conventional buildup. Paris and Washington were drawing opposite strategic lessons from the crisis. The Kennedy team, even before the abrupt rise in tension over the summer, had reached the conclusion that allied strategy (which the Atlantic Council had debated at its request in the spring, without arriving at any conclusions[59]) was unsuited to a possible trial of strength over Berlin, due to too low a nuclear threshold. As a result, it saw the crisis as retrospective confirmation of the indispensable conventional reinforcement of NATO in Central Europe. For Washington, it was actually the rise in allied military power that had given the United States the strategic flexibility to manage the crisis and to avoid confrontation. Once the crisis was passed, the U.S. strategists, capitalizing on their successful military management of it, intended, as a result, to perpetuate the advantages of conventional reinforcement of NATO by imposing a long-lasting change on Western strategy in the direction of the flexible response.[60]

This was exactly what worried French strategists, already alerted by the Council's discussions in May, who did not think that such a reinforcement, while useful at the time in the Berlin situation, could respond if necessary to "a wide-scale action" that would encompass the whole European front.[61] For the French, now very conscious of U.S. strategic intentions, it was a matter of avoiding the Berlin buildup leading to a "modification of the strategic concept" being made "for the benefit of certain theories concerning limited conventional wars."[62] For de Gaulle, who in this crisis behaved in all respects as if France were already an effective atomic power, it was firmness combined with the risk of nuclear confrontation that alone had been able—and would be able in the future—to dissuade the Soviets from an attack. The crisis confirmed his determination to give France an autonomous nuclear strategy and strengthened his idea that the United States would in the future only hesitate more and more to put its atomic firepower in play in cases like Berlin.[63] The crisis was therefore a new and important phase in the strategic divorce between France and the United States.

The Diplomatic Dimension

The divorce also had a diplomatic aspect. In July, as we have seen, Kennedy thought a pure and simple demonstration of Western strength to be insufficient if not dangerous. While he wished to maintain military pressure, he also wanted to avoid appearing trigger-happy. Thus, he was prepared to suggest the possibility of eventual negotiations over Berlin. If at the time this propensity to negotiate remained almost imperceptible behind his firmness of tone, it was very much present in his speech on July 25 in which the president, anxious to take the initiative, said he was determined to search for the conditions for peace "thanks to formal or informal meetings."[64] At the beginning of August, American diplomats tried to give substance to this initiative. The goal was the one Kennedy had suggested in an outline to de Gaulle the preceding month: invite the Soviet Union to participate in a conference of the four foreign ministers. From August 5 to 7 Rusk, Douglas Home, and Couve de Murville met in Paris to discuss this goal, in the presence of German minister Heinrich von Brentano.[65] But the meeting delivered nothing. Disagreements were laid out along the same line as in 1959–1960: at one end, the British, desirous to start negotiations as soon as possible; and at the other end, the French, anxious along with the Germans to avoid spiraling concessions; and between the two, but clearly closer to the former, the Americans, for whom it was indispensable to manage public opinion by not excluding hypothetical negotiations.

Differences did not pertain, though, to the fate of the city and its inhabitants. The construction of the Berlin Wall on August 13, which effectively stifled any hope of freedom in East Germany, was greeted in Western capitals with the same feeling of impotence. There was no question of Washington, London, Paris, or even Bonn resorting to force, and hence risking confrontation to prevent the definitive division of the city. This was the consequence of a simple fact, that is, Soviet domination in its own sphere of influence. The Western nations rapidly reached the conclusion that the construction of the wall, by putting an end to the human hemorrhaging that was bleeding East Germany, would lead to stabilizing the Berlin problem. In effect, for Moscow it was a matter of saving face while consolidating the Berlin and German status quo—and eventually the European one—without there being an actual retreat by the Western nations, whose rights over the city remained.

But the difference in diplomatic approach between Paris and Washington was accentuated. De Gaulle the day after the erection of the wall ruled out any attempt to settle the Berlin question, at least in the current state of things. Kennedy was insistent: It was indispensable that the Big Three propose negotiations over Berlin before the nonaligned summit that was opening in Belgrade on September 1, even if they were really to begin later. He let it be known that Washington would move ahead even if Paris chose to dissociate itself from this initiative. But de Gaulle did not bend; though he understood the importance of public opinion, particularly from the American standpoint, he thought that it should not interfere with the "real responsibilities" of the Big Three. Eventual negotiations would not fail to turn to the benefit of the Soviets, given their advantage on the ground, and would lead fatally, if gradually, to the abandonment of Berlin.[66]

During the fall of 1961, the gap deepened still more between Paris's position and Washington's. The same arguments were ceaselessly repeated by both parties: a French refusal to negotiate under threat, which would be a sign of weakness and might in the end lead to a confrontation that was precisely what was to be avoided; and an American wish to reassure public opinion and not give free rein to a pattern of confrontation over Berlin without knowing the real Soviet intentions. De Gaulle kept France outside the discussions between Rusk and Andrei Gromyko in New York at the end of September, on the margins of the UN General Assembly; he even declined once more the proposal Kennedy made to him in mid-October to get involved in exploratory Soviet–American talks that might take place between the chief Soviet diplomat and the U.S. ambassador to the USSR. And if he could not oppose Washington's pursuing "soundings" with Moscow, at least he deplored the fact that they dangerously resembled real negotiations.[67]

At the end of 1961, French and American disagreements over Berlin were at their height, threatening by the same token to rupture Western solidarity against the USSR. During a Paris meeting between the three foreign ministers on December 11 and 12, Rusk and Couve de Murville opposed each other quite severely over Berlin. Couve de Murville repeated that to negotiate "would only prove to the Russians that we are sensitive to their threats." Rusk rebutted with the necessity of showing public opinion that "everything was being done to avoid war" and insisted on the need to preserve Alliance unity, about which he was "very worried." It took a telephone call from Kennedy to de Gaulle (a means of communication the latter disliked, especially without minimum warning) to achieve a compromise communiqué that did not satisfy the Americans, who were literally worn down by Paris's attitude.[68] Rusk "had had enough of de Gaulle"; France blocked everything and threatened, he thought not without paradox, Western cohesion; if you "really mean business about going to war, the first thing is to have contact with the enemy," know his intentions.[69]

Even if the episode left traces, the argument gradually went away during the first months of 1962. Of course, de Gaulle continued to refuse to participate, from near or far, in the Moscow exploratory talks between Gromyko and the U.S. ambassador Llewelyn Thompson, "unacknowledged but certainly negotiations" that could only lead London and Washington to "espouse Soviet theses little by little."[70] But things remained there. In the course of the spring, despite a lowering military tension, the idea of a political settlement disappeared for good, since the Soviets returned to their initial position: transformation of West Berlin into a free city. But for de Gaulle the diplomatic phase that followed the summer's crisis constituted a warning. It made evident the risk of bilateral Soviet-American dialogue on European security and on the German issue. Such a dialogue could take place only to the detriment of the West, since Moscow did not accept the status quo and it could only hurt the Europeans excluded from the bipolar game. In sum, de Gaulle was afraid that growing détente would result in a new "Yalta."[71] By proclaiming unwavering solidarity with Adenauer (within certain limits, it is true, starting with the wall) and an intransigent position toward Moscow, he tried to strengthen the basis of his Franco-German and Western European policy and to lay the foundations of a policy of détente that would take quite another path than the one, despite his warning, the Americans were exploring at the end of 1961. In this sense, the Berlin crisis and its fallout heralded wider differences over the system of European security as a whole that would pit Paris and Washington against each other three years later. At the start of 1962, the tripartite proposals of 1958 were only a distant memory.

FROM ATHENS TO PHILADELPHIA

The months that followed would accentuate the divorce within the Alliance even more, as well as differences of opinion between the French and Americans. In the spring of 1962, two parallel fault lines clearly appeared within the Western bloc: the first concerned nuclear issues and the second the political and strategic construction of Western Europe and its relations with the United States.

The Lavaud Mission

In winter 1961, then in spring 1962, the nuclear issue was again at the center of transatlantic debates. First the specter of "atomic secrets" reappeared. Some within the American administration, led by Gavin, continued, as a year earlier on the eve of the Kennedy–de Gaulle meeting, to defend a more open approach. France, he maintained, "has accomplished substantial progress" in the military nuclear field, which under the McMahon Act as amended in 1958, ought to give it the right to benefit from American assistance.[72] It must be recognized that France was and would remain a nuclear power, and it would be possible, with some concessions, to bring it within NATO's bosom. In fact, at the start of 1962, Washington still did not completely rule out "softening" the American position if necessary, as Gavin still and always recommended, at the risk of annoying people.[73] And while the French side still held to the principle of nuclear independence, it did not rule out hypothetical cooperation, which would be useful in the realm of ballistic technology (guidance and propulsion systems) and in techniques of enriching uranium (compressors for the isotopic separation and a gas diffusion plant being constructed at Pierrelatte) as well as computer systems. Paris thought that American reluctance to cooperate in these fields that were not specifically nuclear was not justified by the McMahon Act. Accordingly, at the end of February, Michel Debré let it be known that the French government saw in the restrictive attitude of the American administration a serious factor in the deterioration of relations between the two countries; even if de Gaulle demanded nothing officially, Paris expected concessions in the missile domain.[74]

This hardening of tone was largely for tactical reasons. On March 4, General Gaston Lavaud, responsible for arms procurement, arrived in Washington. Paris hoped to obtain from this mission, planned several months before, the possible acquisition of materiel and technologies for its military program, whereas Washington wished for French purchases to contribute to easing its balance of payments deficit, now a primary preoccupation in Washington from the perspective of a more equal sharing with the allies of the cost of defending Europe. The visit was prepared several weeks in advance on both sides, by McNamara and Messmer and their respective departments. However, as Lavaud's arrival approached, ambiguities remained. The American side wanted to limit French purchases to conventional arms, while the French side wanted to extend them to domains more or less directly linked with setting up their *force de frappe*.[75]

The Lavaud mission, as a result, quickly turned into a dialogue of the deaf. The Americans stuck to their reasoning: French purchases should both alleviate the payments deficit that resulted from the U.S. contribution to the defense of Europe, and also strengthen the conventional capability of NATO by improving the equipment of French divisions at its disposal, but should by no means contribute to the French atomic effort. For the French, it seemed a very strange trade that would consist of their acquiring, in the name of U.S. economic equilibrium, arms that did not fit in with their own strategy. Lavaud and his aides, who considered their mission to be technical, could only be astonished that the Americans imposed restrictions as to the materiel they wanted to acquire. So the concrete results were well below the expectations of both.[76]

The failure of the Lavaud mission at least had the effect of clarifying the debate over "atomic secrets." Kennedy, who once again intervened personally on the issue, demanded a note on the French position from Gavin, who wrote him a new plea in favor of a softer policy. The ambassador thought that the McMahon Act was applied too extensively to the French case and feared that this attitude might incite Paris to refuse to cooperate in other areas, including the General Agreement on Tariffs and Trade (GATT), to which the Kennedy administration, justly preoccupied with its commercial balance, attached great importance—in short, that it might compromise the "global" approach of the Alliance that Washington had been trying to get underway for a year. But Kennedy confirmed his position: There was no question of the United States helping independent nuclear forces, and if the restrictions he imposed went beyond the letter of the McMahon Act, it was on purpose. Moreover, there was also the matter of gradually ending nuclear aid to Great Britain so as to set up a "single Atlantic deterrence." In mid-April, Kennedy, preferring the State Department line over that of the Pentagon and other sectors of the administration, formally adopted this resolutely restrictive policy toward the French nuclear effort.[77]

From the French side, the Lavaud mission confirmed—as if that were necessary—that the idea of cooperation with the United States in establishing the *force de frappe* was decidedly at an impasse. The American attitude was even interpreted by Couve de Murville as proof of pure and simple incoherence: the United States had ended up refusing a transaction they had themselves called for in the name of their balance of payments, and of an allied solidarity that ought to extend to economics. This sentiment was shared by the Defense Ministry, where it was pointed out that the list of Lavaud purchases had been drawn up with a concern to avoid any difficulty with U.S. legislation.[78]

The Athens Speech

The month of May 1962 was a high point of Franco-American nuclear antagonism. On May 5, in Athens, on the occasion of NATO's ministerial session, McNamara delivered to the allies the first systematic explanation, at least at this level, of the new U.S. strategy (discussion in the spring of 1961 between permanent representatives, suspended over the summer, having been just preliminary).[79] By doing this, he launched a campaign whose openly declared objective was the Alliance's adoption of the Acheson report's strategic options—in other words, flexible response. The Athens speech was, in substance and form, the pure product of strategic thinking by McNamara and his team of defense intellectuals: intelligent and brilliant, logical and synthetic, but also cold and disembodied— and, more or less consciously, politically maladroit, even though the principal themes of McNamara's speech, whether on strategy or on nuclear consultation and "control," had of course been taken up as a U.S. initiative by the representatives to NATO's Council since the start of the year.[80]

In his speech, McNamara first dealt with the strategic nuclear component of deterrence. According to him, it should henceforth put the accent no longer on the objective of massive destruction by strikes against cities, but on antiforce options, so as to limit the civilian damage of a possible nuclear exchange. If such a strategy were adopted by the Alliance, the Soviets would be persuaded to do the same. And in this case, he explained coldly, a Soviet attack would cause 25 million deaths in the United States and a few less in Europe, as against 75 and 115 million, respectively, in case of strikes against cities. And from the U.S. standpoint, explained McNamara, this calculation could only strengthen the credibility of extended deterrence.

But the counterpart of this strategy of "controlled and flexible response," explained the secretary of defense, was the necessity of centralizing nuclear planning and decision making. It would be absurd to unleash an anticity strike when the Alliance was in a position to effect antiforce strikes that could disarm the enemy and avoid useless destruction in the West. Evidently, the still-not-yet-operational French arsenal was his target, as well as the British nuclear force. And McNamara went on to conclude: "In short, then, weak nuclear capabilities, operating independently, are expensive, prone to obsolescence and lacking in credibility as a deterrent."[81] Nevertheless, as he had indicated during the ministerial meeting in December, the Americans wished to respond to the desire of the allies to participate in the development of strategy, by enlarging nuclear consultation within NATO. This was the point of procedures known as the Athens Guidelines that McNamara got adopted by NATO (but about which France formulated some "reservations"), that called for eventual consultation over recourse to nuclear arms, "time and circumstances permitting."[82] Of course, the real concern was to reassure the allies of the determination of the United States to turn to nuclear weapons to repulse an attack that conventional means alone could not achieve, and to give them the feeling of having a say in American nuclear strategy. But this did not prevent McNamara from stressing that the United States thought that NATO should not depend exclusively on strategic nuclear power to deter the Soviet Union from undertaking the smallest aggression—hence, he insisted, the necessity for the allies to fulfill the objectives for conventional forces defined in 1961 (document MC 26/4), specifically, thirty divisions along the central front. According to McNamara, only this effort to raise conventional power would permit putting an end to NATO's "extreme reliance"[83] on nuclear forces.

The Athens speech (of which McNamara gave a "nonclassified" version the following month at the University of Michigan) was a turning point. The speech was the first official presentation to the allies by such a senior figure of the flexible response strategy, and it also contained the first explicit and public condemnation of France's nuclear effort. French reactions were not surprising. De Gaulle in his press conference on May 15, 1962, declared that "no one can tell today when, how, or why" America (or the USSR) would use atomic weapons, which only confirmed the need for France to have its own. "The efficiency of protecting Europe with American bombs is in question," he declared on May 9 to the Council of Ministers.[84] As for nuclear consultation, Paris held to the "reservations" expressed in Athens by Maurice Couve de Murville:[85] to the extent that the allies had no real control over the decision to use them and that U.S. policy ostensibly intended to raise the nuclear threshold, contrary to European interests. The Athens Guidelines indeed contained nothing new—especially in relation to what Kennedy had proposed to de Gaulle a year previously within a bilateral framework. The Athens speech thus merely strengthened the French conviction that the American nuclear guarantee was more relative, and the French nuclear effort more necessary than ever.

In this first half of 1962, the French, from a strategic standpoint, were far from being isolated within the Alliance. Paris stressed that the Europeans had a common perspective in nuclear affairs, even if the Americans did not understand this. This argument had weight. Adenauer's government, which from the start had limited confidence in Kennedy, welcomed the new U.S. strategy very unfavorably. The Germans saw in it a *fait accompli* and a dangerous strategic slippage that weakened deterrence. This was a risk to which the Germans, on the front line to the East, were and would remain particularly sensitive, which explained in large part, French diplomats thought, the desire expressed by Bonn in the first months of 1962 for a military rapprochement with France. (In fact, Franz-Josef Strauss, the defense minister, who was the most outspoken opponent of flexible response within the federal government—which earned him the label of German "Gaullist"—did not hesitate to reoffer the French the nuclear cooperation that de Gaulle had suspended in 1958.[86]) Paris also intended, naturally, to capitalize in the spring of 1962 on European—and especially German—disquiet by presenting the French nuclear program as a counterweight to flexible response, itself described as a prologue to American strategic disengagement. "Since we are in Europe," stressed de Gaulle, the *force de frappe* is "the beginning of a European force."[87]

Even though Paris affected to consider it a "non-event," the Athens speech did not leave the French indifferent. The charge led by McNamara against the *force de frappe* aroused extreme irritation. In Messmer's entourage, it was thought that Washington was acting like a "master" rather than a "leader."[88] The deterioration of Franco-American relations that followed Athens was even conveyed by a serious misunderstanding. In June, Kennedy in a press conference declared that American participation in the development of the *force de frappe* would be "inimical" to "the common interests of the members of the Alliance." But the turn of phrase lent itself to confusion. In Paris, it was understood that it was the French nuclear effort itself, and not possible American assistance, that was judged "inimical" by Washington.[89] Faced with the breadth of the public disagreement between the two capitals after Athens, both sides quickly tried to calm things down. Washington even broke its habit of nonassistance to the *force de frappe* by agreeing to sell France some KC-135 refueling planes, indispensable for allowing the Mirage IV fighters to reach Soviet territory. In fact, the progress made during Rusk's visit to Paris at the end of June permitted the two governments to correct the image, spread and aggravated by the press, of a profound deterioration in bilateral relations, and perhaps to dissipate certain misunderstandings. No, the French said, the *force de frappe* would not perform the function of a "trigger" to unleash American nuclear fire; yes, it could even be used in coordination with NATO.[90] But this was only a passing improvement. The logic of strategic antagonism that was established between the French and the Americans would resurface in the second half of 1962, all the more so since it was compounded by a political contest whose stake was the construction of Europe.

The Failure of the Fouchet Plan

The spring turning point indeed was not limited to nuclear affairs. Onto the line of strategic division that appeared after Athens was superimposed a line of political division that gradually came to light. Europe and NATO: these were the two terms of the other great debate that then arose. Starting in the summer of 1960, as we have seen, there was interference between the question of NATO and the project for the political union of the Europe of Six that was becoming the major issue of Gaullist diplomacy.[91] For de Gaulle "there could not be a European political personality if Europe did not have a personality from a defense standpoint," and if Europe were made, then "another NATO is necessary," since NATO is "not the defense of Europe by Europe but the defense of Europe by Americans."[92] For him, the constructions of a political and strategic Europe and Alliance reform were really two sides of the same coin.[93]

Throughout 1961, after the Franco-German initiative at Rambouillet and the establishment of the Fouchet Commission,[94] the question of the interaction between Atlantic defense and European defense was not posed with acuity. The Americans were scarcely worried about the possible risk of "conflict between European cooperation and NATO."[95] Things changed in 1962. In early January, de Gaulle became aware of the final version of the treaty project, elaborated by the Quai d'Orsay and negotiated among the Six since October 1961. Thinking no doubt that the text still concealed, behind apparent compromise, fundamental differences, he undertook to "touch up" the text.[96] This was the origin of the second Fouchet Plan that marked a French toughening. Beyond the significant changes in a more confederate or intergovernmental direction, the new version dug a chasm between the future European Union and NATO, the latter not even mentioned directly. While the modifications to the text could not be calmly welcomed by the Five, de Gaulle's goal, however, was not to sink the enterprise, but rather to raise the stakes before the final negotiations.[97]

De Gaulle adopted a more offensive European discourse. He declared that it was a matter of constructing a body that was "the most powerful, prosperous and influential in the world." This discourse reflected the new reality of French power, almost freed of the Algerian burden and ensured of its atomic force: previously an "integrated," meaning eclipsed, nation, France now found again its role and status. And if this causes "astonishment and even bitter feelings," de Gaulle said, "it is a fact that will have to be accepted until the time comes when it is recognized as fortunate."[98] This change of tone worried the Americans: A European Union acting in the defense domain might become a bloc within NATO and consequently contest U.S. leadership. After having met him at the end of February, Gavin was persuaded that the General had a well-developed plan to give the Europe of Six a common defense policy that in time would challenge the structure of the Alliance, and he foresaw that the determining stake in the coming months would be Germany, the real pivot between the Atlantic system and the projected European Union. Instead of trying in vain to bring France back into NATO's bosom, Gavin thought the United States should ensure that the Federal Republic of Germany chose Washington rather than Paris when it was confronted with such a choice.[99]

But after France announced the second Fouchet Plan at the end of January, the European plan stalled. The responsibility was not Paris's alone. In February and March 1962, de Gaulle was ready for compromise on most of the litigious questions, except no doubt for that of supranationality. After a meeting with Adenauer in Baden-Baden on February 15, he accepted that there be "mention somewhere of the Atlantic Alliance."[100] He had the feeling after his meeting in Turin on April 4 with the Italian president of the Council Fanfani and his foreign minister, Antonio Segni, during which he moved closer to Rome's median position, that an agreement was possible. At this stage, de Gaulle had practically abandoned the modifications introduced in January.[101]

Yet, in Paris on April 17, the Six separated with an acknowledgment of failure. London, officially a candidate for entry into the EEC since July 31, 1961, had announced on April 10 through its negotiator Edward Heath that Great Britain was ready to participate in discussion by the Six of political union. Nothing more was needed for The Hague and Brussels, unconditionally favorable to British participation in the European construction, to adopt a dilatory attitude that amounted to making their acceptance of the Union depend on British membership. Simultaneously, the Dutch and the Belgians, followed by the Italians, who were attached to a supranational concept of the European Community, redoubled their intransigence over this, especially when the risk became apparent of a Europe dominated by the Franco-German axis without a British counterweight. From a French standpoint, this was an intrinsically contradictory attitude, since London had an intergovernmental concept of political Europe, near to that of de Gaulle and at the other end of the spectrum from that of Joseph Luns or Paul-Henri Spaak.

Yet, this contradiction had a rationale. The fundamental reason for the Belgian and Dutch refusal, for the Italians' muted support, and for the ambivalent attitude of the Germans—in short, for the failure of the Fouchet Plan—was the question of the U.S. role in Europe. Indeed, French policy with regard to NATO, which as a whole had toughened at the end of 1961 and start of 1962 (Spaak had proved particularly irritated by Paris's intransigence over Berlin at the ministerial meeting of the Atlantic Council in December), worried some of the European allies, starting with the Belgians, in the same way as did France's contesting American nuclear policy increasingly openly. Spaak on April 17 clearly posed the basic problem: There was no question of him accepting the Fouchet Plan as long as he was not certain that French intentions "were really to maintain contact with *les Anglo-Saxons* and to strengthen the Atlantic Alliance."[102]

Each Had a Design

But not everything was over on April 17, since the question of the role and organization of Western Europe was at the heart of the debate over the Alliance. If the growing differences between France and its allies over NATO had been the catalyst of the failure of the Fouchet Plan, this failure acted inversely to reveal these differences. For the United States it was clear that de Gaulle's European policy "cuts directly across U.S. interests, all along the board."[103]

During May, the European question threatened, like the nuclear issue, to become the apple of transatlantic discord. In his press conference on May 15, de Gaulle raised the temperature. "One of France's essential goals," he said, was for Europe to be able to act in the world, to defend itself, participate in development, and to contribute to détente and international balance. The proponents of supranationality, far from working for an autonomous Europe, wished in reality to maintain the American hold: an "integrated" Europe would have no policy and would remain tagging behind America; "there would perhaps be a federator, but the federator would not be European." As for the Alliance, he repeated, it was to be revised because of the irremediable weakening of the U.S. guarantee and the necessary unification of Western Europe. This was why France for its part would continue to modify the modes of its participation in the organization.[104]

This press conference marked a real turning point in French political life. De Gaulle's virulent attack on a supranational Europe ignited sharp reaction among the Europeanists. Five ministers belonging to the Mouvement Républicain Populaire (MRP, the Christian Democratic Party) resigned. This movement sustained a certain parliamentary opposition to de Gaulle's foreign policy, currently limited but which would crystallize after 1965 over European and Atlantic issues. As for the press, the majority of which was pro-European, it adopted frequently sharp criticism of de Gaulle's policy. But the episode, even though badly received by the political and media elites, did not threaten public confidence in this policy, because the French, beyond theological quarrels over the modes of European construction, considered General de Gaulle as a true European. Shortly after the crisis of spring 1962, 49 percent of them saw him as a "decided partisan of European unification" as against only 23 percent who had the opposite opinion.[105] Here lies a durable trait of de Gaulle's foreign policy, in line with his idea of his role as a statesman: it is opinion that follows him and not the reverse. This trait would be verified in years to come during decisive events for the future of his country, Europe, and the Alliance.[106]

The support of the French people strengthened de Gaulle's European policy, which could only worry the Americans even more. The day after the press conference, Gavin came to lunch with de Gaulle. The atmosphere was not good; the ambassador stressed that the General's ideas risked being badly received in Washington. De Gaulle replied that he was used to it and raised his bid. The United States, he said, should not interfere in the problems of Europe. No doubt angry about the U.S. attempts to steer the process of European unification, de Gaulle was particularly frank, to the point that Gavin, while usually understanding, was "almost startled" by the toughness of his ideas on the role of the United States in Europe.[107]

The reaction from Washington came quickly. On May 18, Kennedy, who was aware of the minutes of the conversation, wrote personally to Gavin. His instructions were firm. The ambassador should explain to de Gaulle that it was impossible both to ask the United States to defend Europe in case of war and to remain outside its affairs in peacetime. "If Europe were ever to be organized so as to leave us outside," wrote Kennedy, "it would become most difficult for us to sustain our present guarantee against Soviet aggression." In short, France could not simultaneously count on the "military presence" and the "diplomatic absence" of the United States in Europe. And if France persisted in trying to attract the Germans toward its own position, Washington counted on putting Bonn's back to the wall.[108]

Here we are at the heart of the Franco-American misunderstanding. Despite its rhetoric on the subject since the early 1950s, the interest of the United States consisted in avoiding Europe of the Six being transformed into an autonomous strategic entity that would radically modify the givens of the transatlantic situation and would compromise U.S. preeminence in Europe. This is what Alphand took from a conversation with Walt Rostow, head of the State Department's Policy Planning staff, for whom, if in the long-term "association between Europe and the United States must become an association between equals, without protector or protégé," it remained nevertheless that Washington, "whether its allies wished it or not, must play its role as leader and impose its will when the superior interest of the West required it."[109] It could not be stated more clearly that Washington wanted to take an active role in the Western Europe debate, and that there was rhetoric on the one hand and reality on the other. In fact, on the two key problems, British candidacy and supranationality, the American administration was opposed to Paris. At first, the United States was evidently favorable to the entry of Great Britain into the Common Market, as it insistently reminded the French in the spring of 1962.[110] For Washington, British membership would evidently be a guarantee against the constitution of a continental Europe built around a Franco-German axis, in which its influence would be limited. Moreover, and for the same reason, the Americans were more than ever favorable to a unified Europe on Monnet's model, and not on Fouchet's. George Ball, a longtime friend of Monnet's, was within the American administration the most ardent defender of this approach to European unification. The Americans hoped that by attenuating the unfavorable effects of European "nationalisms," it would reduce the capacity of the Six to be an obstacle to U.S. influence. One Europe with British participation, even confederate, would work as well as a federal Europe, even without British participation, in the interests of the United States.

Despite the definitive failure of the Fouchet Plan and despite a manifest will on both sides to defuse the disagreement over Europe, the Kennedy administration remained worried about the consequences of de Gaulle's European policy. And while the Americans, through Rusk, said they were ready to recognize that France was not seeking, by promoting a "stronger and more independent

Europe," to put an end to the Atlantic Alliance but to "adapt to the new situation," they remained openly concerned about "the evolution of Europe partly because of their commercial interests and partly because of the political and military consequences that might result from European organization."[111] It was in this context that the Kennedy team felt the need for a global concept that would give coherence to its European policy and above all offer a dynamic and convincing presentation of it. Such was the "Grand Design" sketched in a flamboyant speech Kennedy gave on July 4 in Philadelphia in which Monnet's influence was manifest: to fix comprehensively all political, strategic, and economic problems affecting relations between the United States and Western Europe.[112] On this anniversary of the Declaration of Independence, he proposed nothing less than a Euro-American "declaration of interdependence" aiming at an "Atlantic partnership" that would allow Europe and America to "put forward a coordinated policy in all domains" and "on a fully equal basis."[113] It was a notable speech, but without great practical consequence; for despite the brilliant language, the modes of this "association" were not made explicit. On the other hand, Kennedy was precise about its presupposing British membership in the EEC and its being facilitated by the emergence of a federal Europe.[114] In fact, the concept of an Atlantic partnership was designed, at least in part, to mask a contradiction that Kennedy would never resolve between the idea of an Atlantic community and the reality of U.S. leadership.[115]

In Paris, the Philadelphia speech was welcomed by the press and by most commentators, who saw in it an event of historic importance and a clear signal that the United States was not renouncing its presence in Europe.[116] De Gaulle's reaction was undoubtedly quite opposite. Perhaps there is a disillusioned echo of it in a letter addressed some days later to Michel Debré (who on April 14 had been replaced by Georges Pompidou as head of the government): " 'Integration' has just disintegrated. This is true for NATO. It is true for Europe. The unreal character of myths that we have known is more and more evident."[117] But despite last attempts, it was clear in the summer of 1962 that a political Europe as de Gaulle conceived it would not be realized for quite some time either. In the months and years to come, the General, to be sure, would continue to defend his vision of Europe, but without believing it to be in the near future, since the European debates of 1960 to 1962 had ultimately opposed de Gaulle's Europe to that of Monnet, as two "clearly defined, distinct and irreconcilable" concepts.[118] But his Atlantic policy would continue well after 1962 to be largely determined by the prospect of a united and autonomous Europe, which nevertheless remained his long-term objective.

TOWARD THE TRUE TEST

After the heady spring moments, the summer was a calm period in Western diplomatic relations. De Gaulle paused in his challenge to the Alliance established order. No doubt he was somewhat disillusioned by recent developments. "World affairs," he told Alphand, "are blocked and neither Kennedy nor I can change anything about that."[119] Yet behind this disillusion, the basic tendencies of French policy remained constant, as would soon be very clear.

From Six to Two

The very day of the Philadelphia speech, de Gaulle and Adenauer had a decisive meeting in Paris during which they agreed on a European strategy.[120] In case of the failure of the last attempt at saving the Fouchet Plan undertaken by Fanfani, they would organize an agreement between France and Germany that would pre-figure for two a political Europe that was for the time being impractical for six. De Gaulle had no faith in the Italian attempt, which was in fact rapidly getting stuck. In the course of the summer, two years after the Rambouillet meeting, de Gaulle and Adenauer realized the failure of a political Europe and fell back on their two-way union, "while leaving open to the four others the possibility of join-ing at any time."[121] But the situation was quite different from the one prevailing in the summer of 1960 that had led, in Franco-German relations, to a return to the seesaw of the autumn. On the French side, the definitive resolution to the Al-gerian conflict strengthened de Gaulle's hand in his contesting the Atlantic status quo; on the German side, Adenauer (who had only limited confidence in Kennedy) felt more and more disquiet about U.S. leadership, which he judged vacillating in the light of the last months of the Berlin crisis.

The defense of Europe was accordingly at the center of the new phase of Franco-German rapprochement decided upon in the summer of 1962. To de Gaulle's mind, the establishment of a political Europe of Six would lead to re-organizing NATO, and so in the same way would the Franco-German entente lead to "examining the defense of Europe in the strictest sense."[122] Adenauer knew his views on the issue. He knew that, for the General, direct defense of German terri-tory was first and foremost the responsibility of the Bundeswehr, if necessary with the help of American and British allies, with French forces having a role in reserve of this advanced line of defense.[123] This in no way meant that France would not intervene in Germany and that it would stick to the defense of its own territory, since for de Gaulle Europe "forms a strategic whole" and it was "the ground for one and the same battle."[124] In fact, it was essential for de Gaulle to convince Ade-nauer that the distance France was taking from the integrated organization would not lead to inaction, or even to French neutrality in case of aggression against the FRG. At Mourmelon camp, where he attended Franco-German military exercises at Adenauer's side during his visit to France in July 1962, de Gaulle clearly con-firmed this. Hands pressed together and fingers intertwined, he ensured the chan-cellor that France would not leave Germany alone in case of conflict.[125] And dur-ing his triumphant visit to Germany in early September, in front of students at the Führungsakademie of the Bundeswehr, the army academy in Hamburg, he called for, as "essential to the union of our two peoples," Franco-German cooperation "with a view to a single and same defense."[126]

Thus, military solidarity was at the core of the growing Franco-German entente, and the strategic context lent itself to that. German distrust of the new American strategy was far from dissipated, as confirmed by the conversation Adenauer had several days later in his villa at Cadenabbia on Lake Como with the secretary general of NATO, Dirk Stikker, and Norstad, who would soon be leaving his post. The chancellor confided that he was still not "clear" on the American policy, like most Europeans, since American declarations on the defense of Europe were contradictory. At bottom, he said, "this makes it extremely difficult for Europeans to depend wholly on the United States" and this was why de Gaulle wished Europe to possess its own nuclear capability.[127] Adenauer feared American disengagement from the defense of Europe and no longer had the reservations he had previously about the prospect of a more autonomous European defense. As such, he gave credit to the idea advanced by Paris some months before: that the *force de frappe* had a certain European role to play, even if its control should remain essentially national.

Franco-American Prettification, France–NATO Deterioration

The French and Americans, in parallel, after crossing swords in the spring over nuclear issues were now anxious to calm things down. In the autumn, this tendency seemed lasting. The Kennedy team understood that the *force de frappe* was on its way to becoming a reality with which it would have to deal. While there was no questioning of the basics, namely its refusal to foster the French nuclear program, it was felt "that some degree of moderation and flexibility" in presenting the American position would not be misplaced. Best for now to avoid touching on an issue that had fruitlessly poisoned relations between the two countries. It was in this context that General Gavin's resignation occurred and his replacement by a veteran diplomat, Charles (Chip) Bohlen. The true reasons for this departure were known by everyone in Paris (Gavin was considered in Washington much too favorable to the French nuclear effort); yet, paradoxically, it was in line with the desire of the Kennedy administration to start on a new footing, to turn over a new leaf.[128] The French frame of mind was much the same. De Gaulle, always pragmatic, thought that the Americans must sooner or later take account of the existence of a nuclear France. While he envisaged less than ever any kind of actual atomic cooperation, Paris did not reject eventually coordinating the use of the *force de frappe* with the United States.[129] And while all this still appeared rather distant because the French nuclear force was not yet operational, one could speak of a certain détente in Franco-American nuclear affairs.

Yet the prettification was transitory and did not prevent a new deterioration in relations between France and NATO. De Gaulle in the autumn of 1961 (as mentioned earlier) had begun to toughen his stance toward integration and foreign military presence in France, and now went farther. The question of U.S. troops, once technical, became political. De Gaulle was irritated when he realized at the end of September that some months earlier, Michel Debré, then prime minister, had authorized the installation of a NATO wartime headquarters in Vermanton. Only the president of the French republic, he said, was entitled to make such a decision in the Council of Defense.[130] As for Norstad's departure (which the French—correctly—attributed to his declared hostility to a strategy relying too exclusively on conventional means),[131] and his replacement by General Lyman Lemnitzer, decided unilaterally by Washington in the course of the summer, they were an opportunity for de Gaulle to stress again that NATO was an organization of sovereign states. Hence there was no question of accepting this designation without his at least seeing personally the person concerned—though he in no way challenged the principle of an American SACEUR, fully justified by U.S. preponderance within NATO.[132]

In any case, de Gaulle was pursuing French disengagement from integration. As planned, two French divisions (out of four) withdrawn from NATO in 1956 to be transferred to Algeria, now repatriated, were not reassigned to NATO despite the allies' pressing demands. Even though the French permanent representative, François Seydoux, as well as the chief of staff of the armed forces, General Charles Ailleret, explained to the Council on November 7 that the divisions concerned, stationed in metropolitan France under national command, could reinforce if necessary the forces assigned to NATO—the meeting was rough. Seydoux faced the critics but did not try to disguise the fact that the French decision was part of a systematic policy, since NATO's structure no longer corresponded with reality.[133]

In fact, the end of the Algerian War allowed a French military buildup in Central Europe that had been almost constantly prevented since the end of the 1940s by colonial conflicts. It was clear that this buildup would not benefit the integrated military structure, since de Gaulle intended to profoundly change not only the organization of French forces, but also that of commands, notably in wartime. National command would be the rule, and NATO command the exception.[134] The year 1962 thus marked a decisive turning point in the direction of renationalization of French defense, in peacetime as well as wartime. This change, while it did not arouse consensus within the political class, did benefit from public support, which, here too, followed de Gaulle. Between 1958 and 1962, citizens became more hostile to the American military presence in France and to the integrated organization, but without being hostile either to the Alliance itself or to America.[135] In short, the French followed a policy that aimed at national independence in the name of a better Western alliance.

The Cuban Crisis

These tendencies (Franco-German rapprochement, Franco–NATO estrangement) were already at work when the Cuban missile crisis took the whole world "close to war."[136] Informed on October 16 of the installation by the Soviets of IRBM launch pads in Cuba, it was not until October 22 at 7 P.M. Washington time that Kennedy announced his decision to establish a blockade around Cuba. Several hours previously, during the afternoon of October 22, Paris time, de Gaulle received Dean Acheson at the Elysée Palace. Because the Kennedy team had already decided its line of conduct in the preceding days, it was clear that the former secretary of state's approach involved information and not consultation, as he confirmed with de Gaulle from the start.[137] Acheson wanted to show de Gaulle aerial photos that demonstrated Soviet and Cuban preparations, but the General, to illustrate his conception of confidence among allies and to underline that he did not consider himself to be consulted, refused at first to examine the photographs. If the American president took the decisions that Acheson was reporting, he hinted, it was in full knowledge of the cause and foreseen consequences. De Gaulle thus gave unconditional French support to him for measures that he judged appropriate, then looked at the snapshots that confirmed their rationale. This would prove the firmest solidarity among Washington's allies.

After Acheson's visit, the official position of de Gaulle was made public after the Council of Ministers on Wednesday, October 24. France noted the measures taken by the United States, and if it held events in Cuba to be "distinct from the current situation in other regions of the world," it was ready to examine their possible consequences "for the security of Europe," in line with the "reciprocal engagements that constitute the Atlantic Alliance."[138] In fact, this carefully drafted communiqué conveyed between the lines the conception of the Alliance for which de Gaulle had been calling for more than four years. Indeed, it stressed that the United States (as the letter of the Washington Treaty authorized) had not taken account of the fact that this crisis might sooner or later necessarily have repercussions on Europe. Thus, there was U.S. unilateralism in an affair crucial for world and European security. For de Gaulle, the Alliance was an alliance of principle that went beyond the formal arrangements of NATO and even the text of the treaty. This, in turn, implied the unconditional engagement of France alongside the United States, all the more ostensibly so since the United States cared little about consulting France.

Thus beyond the solidarity voluntarily proclaimed in order to distinguish the French concept of the Alliance from American practice, to de Gaulle the crisis confirmed more than ever the rightness of his strategic demands. In the aftermath of the crisis, Washington and London even had the feeling that he would put back on the table the question of tripartite consultation.[139] "Neither you nor us have been consulted by the United States," he wrote to Macmillan, "and nothing has convinced me more of the need to establish between Washington, London and Paris the kind of organized cooperation that I proposed in vain in 1958." However, the opposite occurred: The missile crisis persuaded him of the illusory character of this proposition. He thought that Kennedy had behaved well this time, and that he had proved his self-control and judgment. But beyond the behavior of individuals, he mostly learned from the unfolding of the crisis the fact that the Americans "had been convinced that their security was directly threatened by the existence in Cuba of nuclear arms directed against their territory."[140] To Rusk, who thanked him for French support during the face-off, he replied that this support "did not count for much because it was an essentially American affair"—not without adding that "if a world war had resulted, France would have been alongside the United States."[141] The message was clear: The United States had demonstrated that its main priority was the immediate defense of its essential interests, with those of Europe coming after.[142]

On the other side of the Atlantic, the interpretation of the event was evidently diametrically opposite. The journalist Walter Lippmann, who spoke publicly in Paris at the end of November, echoed the Kennedy team's version: The crisis had illustrated the fact that nuclear power was indivisible and that centralized control of atomic firepower was indispensable. It had also proved that possession of nuclear power should not exclude strong conventional capability, since that was what had permitted the success of the blockade operation and, ultimately, the favorable outcome. In short, the Cuban crisis justified flexible response. Paris did not like this conclusion and drew the opposite one; in essence, the French saw in this speech another manifestation of an increasing American grasp after the Cuban victory.[143] Thus the Cuban crisis, like that of Berlin, both catalyzed and revealed strategic changes. To de Gaulle, it confirmed the basic trend for the United States to fall back on itself and act unilaterally, as well as the emergence of a Soviet-American pattern of management of East-West tensions, which could only persuade Washington to maintain Europeans in a subordinate role. In fact, the Cuban crisis strengthened the bipolar logic that he was determined to combat.

FROM CUBA TO NASSAU

In the weeks following the crisis, this reading of events caused de Gaulle to accentuate the broad outline of his own policy, all the more so since the favorable outcome of the face-off had the immediate, perceptible effect of augmenting Kennedy's personal power and that of the United States as the incontestable leader of the Western alliance. Between the end of October and the end of December 1962, de Gaulle confirmed his strategic choice of an entente with Germany within the perspective of a "European" Europe at the same time as he moved farther away from *les Anglo-Saxons*.

From Rambouillet to Nassau

The missile crisis had the initial effect of strengthening the Franco-German entente. Since the end of September, the two governments examined the draft of the agreement refined after the summer meetings. No sooner had the Cuban alert passed than de Gaulle thought that the crisis should lead to further strengthening of the ties between Germany and France.[144] And on the German side, Adenauer's powerfully unfavorable impression of Kennedy had been in no way modified by the crisis. The chancellor noted that the American administration had not been able to foresee the confrontation, which in his opinion confirmed Kennedy's weakness when faced with the USSR.[145] During a visit to Washington on November 13 and 14, he measured the extent to which Kennedy intended to profit from the prestige he had managed, despite everything, to retain from the crisis in order to take the Alliance in hand and block de Gaulle's European plans, notably by reminding Bonn of its Atlantic duties and by defending the cause of British membership in the EEC. Yet Adenauer was more convinced than ever of the necessity of an entente with France. Politically weakened, he wanted to give it a firm foundation and turned to the idea of a formal Franco-German treaty that would bind his successors.[146] De Gaulle welcomed this view, which was to be confirmed at the very end of the year.

It went differently for Franco-British relations. Things had changed since the meeting between de Gaulle and Macmillan in Champs-sur-Marne on June 2 and 3 during which a Franco-British entente had appeared possible. Macmillan had given the General a lovely profession of European faith. Minimizing the technical problems of his country's possible EEC membership, he had rallied to the prospect of a political Europe along the lines of the Fouchet Plan, which at the time was not definitely defunct. Moreover, the two men had exchanged viewpoints on strategic and defense issues and had found no major incompatibility, even though de Gaulle had not disguised the fact that because of the "special relationship," British participation would totally change the givens of European construction. Yet discussions had remained at a general level over military matters and though the prospect of nuclear cooperation had been mentioned in the press and foreign offices before the meeting, it was certainly not pushed at Champs.[147] The meeting, as a result, had concluded on an optimistic note. On the one hand, de Gaulle had been sincerely impressed by the European protestations of Macmillan; on the other, the latter had left Champs convinced that British membership was close at hand.

In the autumn and particularly after the Cuban crisis, this optimism disappeared.[148] Negotiations for British membership ran into commercial and agricultural problems linked with the Commonwealth. From the political standpoint, the Fouchet Plan, now definitely abandoned, had given way to the Franco-German rapprochement, made urgent by the Cuban crisis. Yet Macmillan, who misperceived this profound change in context over the previous six months, still hoped to be able to concretize the achievements of the Champs meeting and proposed to de Gaulle, once the crisis was passed, a new meeting, which took place at Rambouillet on December 15 and 16.[149] This was a decisive meeting during which two principal topics were covered, Europe and nuclear affairs, which though not formally linked, were increasingly so in strategic realities and therefore in de Gaulle's thinking.[150]

The main discussion was about Europe. But to the proclaimed confidence of Macmillan that British candidacy was on the right road, de Gaulle gave a straight reply. He thought that on the contrary the Brussels negotiation was about to fail. Great Britain had not renounced its requirements, notably commercial, which if they were accepted, would profoundly change the nature of the Common Market and would weaken its cohesion. As for the political Europe prefigured in the Fouchet Plan, it was no longer on the agenda. More than the implied blunt refusal that de Gaulle had conveyed to him over the EEC, it was the latter point that Macmillan had trouble accepting. French refusal, thus already hinted at in Rambouillet, indeed placed Macmillan in a very difficult political situation. During the preceding months, the British government had been convinced, under his own impulse, that Britain must imperatively participate in the construction of Europe to remain a participant in continental equilibria and to maintain its position as arbiter.[151] But, this was precisely what de Gaulle wanted to avoid, because such a configuration, by ratifying a strong Anglo-Saxon influence, would only lead to the failure of the "European" Europe he wanted to build around the Franco-German entente. Thus when Macmillan left Rambouillet on December 16 to meet Kennedy two days later, he had not received definite notification of France's rejection of British candidacy, but he could scarcely have any illusions about it.

The second round of talks covered nuclear questions. For some time, the British had said they were in favor of atomic cooperation with France. In a context of European unification and redefinition of U.S. strategy, they advanced the necessity for the two European nuclear powers to not depend exclusively on the United States in this domain. The French side was not insensitive to this argument, unusual on the part of Great Britain and close to the French line, and they did not doubt the sincere desire of the British to "do something" with France in this area, but they wondered what the real objectives were. Was it payment offered France for Great Britain's entry into the Common Market? Or a way of blackmailing the Americans to obtain more from Washington in the atomic area, at a time when the British program was having difficulties?[152] In both cases, de Gaulle could not consider as a priority any Franco-British nuclear cooperation that might be developed on such a basis, for it did not really belong to the perspective of European strategic autonomy. And if at Rambouillet he did not rule out all possibility of collaboration, especially in missile production and the eventual coordination of nuclear forces, such cooperation did not offer France determining advantages; its program was progressing autonomously and was likely incompatible with the British program, which was more and more tightly linked to the United States. One thing did not escape the French: Great Britain depended in a growing manner on America in the atomic realm, and the latter, through the special nuclear relationship, possessed more "means to bend certain orientations of English policy."[153]

In fact at Rambouillet Macmillan thought he ought to keep de Gaulle informed of the problems Great Britain was encountering in this area. The British nuclear force, which relied essentially on aerial delivery (the "V" bombers), was threatened with obsolescence due to progress in Soviet air defenses. In 1960, London had chosen to remedy this temporarily by acquiring from the United States the Skybolt device, releasable at a secure distance by plane. But for budgetary reasons Washington had given up the Skybolt program.[154] Yet Great Britain was counting on maintaining a credible deterrent, explained Macmillan to de Gaulle, and was therefore constrained to procure from the United States Polaris ballistic missiles that it would adapt for submarines. He would discuss the matter with Kennedy, whom he was meeting in a few days in Nassau, in the Bahamas. But Macmillan insisted that London would acquire Polaris freely and properly and would keep an entirely independent nuclear force. De Gaulle noted these details and was pleased with British concern to maintain a credible national deterrent force, since he considered the existence of a British nuclear force wholly in line with European security interests in the same way as the forthcoming existence of the French deterrent force.[155] But the nuclear issue had only been touched on in a minor and rather inconclusive way during the Rambouillet meeting, whose dominant stake was the European issue, which from the British viewpoint had been sliding in the wrong direction since the summer.

In Nassau, where Macmillan and Kennedy met from December 18 to 21, the nuclear issue, however, was central. As he had explained to de Gaulle at Rambouillet, the prime minister had a vital political interest in obtaining from Kennedy the delivery of Polaris missiles. And on the American side, the conclusion had been reached that, whatever the wishes of the administration to see Great Britain abandon or at least reduce its nuclear ambitions, the United States could not ignore the British request, except by putting the Macmillan government in peril and facilitating the victory of a Labour government that would undoubtedly be less favorable to U.S. interests. Even if Kennedy arrived in Nassau unfamiliar with the dossier and miscalculating the stakes, an outline for a U.S. agreement on the delivery of missiles no doubt existed before the meeting.[156] But one problem remained: How to reconcile the transfer of Polaris to Great Britain with the U.S. policy of nonassistance to national nuclear forces? How to present the transaction to the allies without contravening the postulate of the indivisibility of the nuclear within the Alliance? This was the difficulty that Kennedy and his advisors—especially influenced by Ball's anxiety about the impact on other Europeans of new atomic cooperation with London—would attempt to resolve by relaunching in a spectacular way the idea of a multilateral nuclear force, which no longer seemed to loom large, even if in the spring of 1961 Kennedy had once appeared to adopt this idea, initially floated by the Eisenhower administration at the end of 1960.

This explains the ambiguity of the agreements signed by Macmillan and Kennedy, who aimed to reconcile the maintenance of a British nuclear capability with its integration into the MLF. The Nassau agreements carried both the prospect of a *multinational* nuclear force, in fact arising from the simple coordination of national forces within the NATO framework, and thus leaving British autonomy untouched, and the prospect of a *multilateral* force, proposed eighteen months previously by Washington, which would integrate the Polaris delivered to Great Britain without any possibility of their withdrawal, except—in the extreme case—if "supreme national interests [were] at stake."[157] In fact, the Americans, who continued to want to reduce British nuclear autonomy, counted on the second prospect prevailing over the first, and, for the price of Polaris delivery, "making London reverse its long-standing opposition to the creation of a NATO strategic missile force going beyond the national contributions of the U.S. and the U.K."[158] As de Gaulle was expecting, and whatever Macmillan said about it, Anglo-American atomic cooperation, as it went along, tended to whittle down British nuclear autonomy.

From Nassau to Paris

If the Americans were quite conscious that reviving the nuclear "Special Relationship" risked raising the French problem again, it was because they feared that the Nassau Accords would give de Gaulle an argument to demand more strongly U.S. assistance for the *force de frappe*. While a *modus vivendi* had been established between Paris and Washington regarding nuclear questions during the months preceding Nassau, the Anglo–U.S. agreement could light another match. Kennedy wanted to avoid a new confrontation with de Gaulle. At the same time, ignoring the tenor of the Rambouillet meetings, he wanted to facilitate the entry of Great Britain into the EEC.[159] So he decided to seize the chance to try to normalize his relations with de Gaulle and overcome nuclear antagonisms. By offering to extend the Nassau Accords to France when he had categorically ruled out some months earlier any atomic cooperation with France, he hoped—reviving a strategy that had already shown its limits several times—to bring de Gaulle into the Atlantic nuclear bosom (and incidentally facilitating the concluding of a nuclear test ban treaty that Khrushchev, after the Cuban crisis, had floated) and also foster British candidacy. Though the affair was evidently improvised in the course of his meeting with Macmillan, Kennedy was still anxious to look after de Gaulle's susceptibilities and took great care to inform him of the proposal before making it public.

Kennedy thus wrote to de Gaulle after Nassau to make him party to his offer. On December 21, the Elysée chief of staff, Etienne Burin des Roziers, received the missive from Peter Lyon, Bohlen's deputy (since the ambassador was in the Bahamas). De Gaulle, he told him, was "impressed" by Kennedy's message, but wanted to think about it. Burin, who gave no major indication, recognized that the affair was important, but added that there was no hurry. Couve de Murville made the same point to Peter Lyon the next day: the American proposal required long study, and a number of points had to be clarified. In any event, de Gaulle would be at his home in Colombey until December 30, which postponed any discussion with him until New Year's Day.[160]

The Quai d'Orsay was more eager to know more about the proposal. Charles Lucet, the director of political affairs, and Jean de La Granville, head of Pacts, found the proposal very interesting. But they confided to Lyon on December 22 that it did not seem, at least in the current state, to satisfy the requirements made by de Gaulle; in point of fact, it posed the problem of nuclear warheads, without which the Polaris would be useless. The U.S. diplomat nevertheless had the feeling after these talks that the French would proceed to a serious examination of the American offer before making a decision. On December 24, things were clarified, but rather unfavorably. In the course of a golf game, Couve de Murville warned Lyon that the Nassau Accords made more politically difficult Great Britain's entry into the EEC, since it demonstrated that Britain "had not yet decided that she wanted to be really European."[161] (This was also the opinion of Adenauer, who let the French know of his "extreme distrust" of the Nassau Accords, in which he saw a sign of "British decadence" and proof of the correctness of de Gaulle's views.[162]) As for the proposal made to France, Couve de Murville noted that it raised the question of nuclear warheads for ballistic missiles, which France did not possess—miniaturized thermonuclear charges were required—unlike Great Britain.[163] (This decisive point was clear in Washington; Rusk noted, correctly, that while the agreement with London followed on from several years of atomic cooperation, it was not the same with Paris.[164])

The administration was split as usual: Should it do everything so that France accepted the Nassau proposals? This was the opinion of McNamara and the Pentagon. Or should it fear that such a scenario would harm the prospect of a Europe integrated and linked to the United States—for a start, by reawakening Germany's nuclear longings? This is what the State Department feared. As for the president, he did not seem to have a well-developed opinion on the matter. And the French, during the very last days of the year, were increasingly skeptical. In the absence of de Gaulle, it was Couve de Murville who set the tone: the Nassau proposal, it seemed to him, aimed to sap the independence of the *force de frappe*. How could one reconcile, he asked, the financial effort of such an arrangement with the pursuit of the national program, itself lagging behind the Anglo-Saxons? And who would have control of the whole thing?[165]

These questions were broached on December 30 during a sailing trip by Alphand and Kennedy, who were both staying in Palm Beach. On this occasion, the president did not open the key subject of nuclear warheads, rather, he was content to say in very general terms that his December 21 proposal was open for discussion.[166] When at the start of January Bohlen was finally received by Couve de Murville and then by de Gaulle, he apparently brought nothing new. He did not formulate any "special offer" that would take account of the French case in relation to the British case—clearly he did not have a concrete proposal about nuclear warheads.[167] His main mission was, on the contrary, to specify that while after the Nassau Accords the British insisted (for domestic policy reasons) on the idea of a multinational nuclear force that could gather and co-ordinate national contributions, the U.S. objectives were to set up an integrated multilateral force.[168]

If Washington had wanted to provoke a negative response from Paris, American diplomats would not have done otherwise. In any case it seems established that on the American side, even if they did not categorically rule out a form of nuclear cooperation properly speaking to accompany an eventual Polaris delivery and offset the French lag in nuclear warheads and submarines,[169] such a transaction, complicated anyway by the McMahon Act, was neither firmly envisaged nor explicitly proposed to France after Nassau. Kennedy did not appear to be personally committed in this direction, which is not surprising, given his principled hostility to nuclear cooperation with France up until Nassau. In early January, it was the State Department's approach that seemed to have carried the day in Washington, an approach oscillating between two goals: to obtain a radical change in French policy toward NATO and the MLF in exchange for atomic cooperation bought very dearly, in effect at the price of French strategic autonomy; and to make discussions of this subject last long enough to gain time to benefit British candidacy, assuming that Paris would not oppose it before having explored the Nassau offer.[170]

De Gaulle, after deliberation by the Council of Ministers, decided to reject the American proposal.[171] For him, the Nassau offer was unacceptable for technical, strategic, and especially political reasons. He would explain this publicly in his press conference of January 14, 1963, during which he officially—and spectacularly—declined the offer. Technical reasons were that France did not possess either the missile-launching submarines or the corresponding nuclear warheads, and would not have them for several years. The United States after Nassau had not given him a clear signal of its eventual inclination to cooperate with France on the same footing as with Great Britain to produce nuclear warheads and submarines, which to him merely confirmed American policy of recent years.[172]

Strategic reasons included the fact that accepting the Nassau offer would amount, as he told the Council of Ministers in early January 1963, to accepting, behind a screen of independence, placing the future French nuclear force under American supervision.[173] He declared on January 14: "To turn over our weapons to a multilateral force, under a foreign command, would be to act contrary to that principle of our defense and our policy." De Gaulle doubted the efficacy of the safeguard clause stipulated in the Nassau Accords for cases involving "vital interests," since "this multilateral force entails necessarily a web of liaisons, transmissions, and interferences within itself, and on the outside a ring of obligations"[174] in such a way as to doom any vague impulse toward national use "in the unheard-of moments of atomic apocalypse." For him, Great Britain at Nassau had quite simply renounced really independent deterrence.

Political reasons included the fact that the preceding was in contradiction with the requirement of national independence on which de Gaulle was determined, and also with the idea of a "European" Europe. To accept the MLF meant to renounce real strategic autonomy from Washington. "Between a nuclear force integrated within NATO and a national nuclear force," added Couve de Murville, there lies "the whole difference existing between an Atlantic Europe and a European Europe."[175] The Nassau affair justified de Gaulle's idea that Great Britain could not join the Europe of Six without pushing them in the first direction. While at Rambouillet, Macmillan had ensured him of his intention to maintain British nuclear independence and suggested that Great Britain could, in concert with France, contribute to the strategic autonomy of Europe, the prime minister had demonstrated in Nassau how little this commitment counted due to the British attachment to the special relationship with the United States.[176]

"Naturally, what happened changed the tone of my press conference on January 14,"[177] confided de Gaulle some days afterward. It changed the tone but not the substance: If on January 14, de Gaulle announced conjointly both the French veto of British candidacy and his rejection of the Nassau proposal, each of the two decisions had its own logic, at work for months in the first case and for years in the second. By implicitly linking the two issues, de Gaulle was doing nothing more than acting on the reality of the link that had been established between the nuclear issue and the European issue throughout 1962. Of course, in doing this, he chose to give a major political resonance to his double refusal.[178] By preventing Great Britain's entry into Europe and by declining the Nassau offer, de Gaulle openly and spectacularly defied Washington's whole Atlantic policy. In this, 1962 was truly a "decisive year."

NOTES

1. Stanley Hoffmann, *Decline or Renewal? France since the 1930's,* New York, Viking, 1974, ch. 10.

2. In the expression of Alfred Grosser in *The Western Alliance: European-American Relations since 1945,* trans. Michael Shaw, London, Macmillan, 1980.

3. Thomas G. Paterson, ed., *Kennedy's Quest for Victory: American Foreign Policy, 1961–1963,* New York, Oxford University Press, 1989, p. 11.

4. "A Review of North Atlantic Problems for the Future," secret, March 1961, John F. Kennedy Library (JFKL), National Security File (NSF), Regional Security (RS), NATO, box 220.

5. "A Review of North Atlantic Problems for the Future."

6. "A Review of North Atlantic Problems for the Future."

7. See Frank Costigliola, "The Pursuit of Atlantic Community: Nuclear Arms, Dollars and Berlin," in Paterson, *Kennedy's Quest for Victory.*

8. "A New Approach to France," 21 April 1961, JFKL, NSF, Country File, France, box 70.

9. Memorandum to the President, "Luncheon with Jean Monnet," 3 March 1961, JFKL, NSF, Country File, France, box 70.

10. DEPTEL #4770, Paris, Rusk to Gavin, 5 May 1961, JFKL, NSF, Country File, France, box 70.

11. "A New Approach to France," 21 April 1961.

12. "A New Approach to France," second version of 3 May 1961, JFKL, NSF, Country File, France, box 70.

13. Projet d'instruction pour l'ambassadeur de France à Washington (n.d., end of January 1961), in Charles de Gaulle, *Lettres, notes et carnets (LNC) (janvier 1961–décembre 1963)*, Paris, Plon, 1986, pp. 29 ff.; and Cyrus L. Sulzberger, *The Last of the Giants*, New York, Macmillan, 1970.

14. Quoted by Jean Lacouture, *De Gaulle*, vol. 2, "The Ruler," trans. Alan Sheridan, New York, Morton, 1990–1992, p. 371.

15. Telegram, Washington to Paris, #317–34, 23 January 1961 and #519–24, 21 February 1961, MAE, Amérique 1952–1963, États-Unis 9.5.3.

16. Memorandum of Conversation, "Tripartite Consultations between France, the U.S. and the U.K." Kennedy–Chaban Delmas, 10 March 1961, JFKL, NSF, Country File, France, box 70; see also telegram from Washington to Paris, 10 March 1961, MAE, America 1952–1963, États-Unis 9.4.1.

17. EMBTEL, #4522, Paris, "For President and Secretary from Dean Acheson," 2/2, secret, 20 April 1961, JFKL, NSF, France, box 70.

18. "For President and Secretary from Dean Acheson."

19. Press Conference of 21 April 1961, in Charles de Gaulle, *Discours et Messages (DM)*, vol. 3, "Avec le renouveau" (mai 1958–juillet 1962), Paris, Plon 1970, p. 286.

20. EMBTEL #1991, Brussels, 29 May 1961, JFKL, NSF, France, box 70.

21. Note du Service des Pactes, "Coopération atlantique—Consultations à trois," 23 May 1961, MAE, Pactes 1961–1970, box 408.

22. Telegram Washington to Paris #2553–68, 17 May 1961, MAE, Amérique 1952–1963, États-Unis 9.5.3.

23. Note de l'EMGDN, "Evolution du concept stratégique de l'Europe," 23 May 1961, MAE, Pactes 1961–1970, box 408.

24. Note pour le ministre, "Développement à l'OTAN de la question de l'emploi des armes atomiques," 12 April 1962, MAE, Pactes 1961–1970, box 266.

25. McGeorge Bundy, *Danger and Survival: Choices about the Bomb in the First Fifty Years,* New York, Vintage, 1988, pp. 484–85.

26. EMBTEL #1991, Brussels, 29 May 1961, JFKL, NSF, France, box 70.

27. DEPTEL #4770, 5 May 1961.

28. Memorandum of Conversation, Alphand, de Rose, Nitze, 8 May 1961, secret, addressed to Bundy, JFKL, NSF, France, box 70.

29. Memorandum for the President, "Specific Answers to your Questions of March [sic] 29, top secret, 29 May 1961, JFKL, NSF, France, box 70.

30. Maurice Couve de Murville, *Une Politique étrangère, 1958–1969*, Paris, Plon, 1971, p. 99. See the American minutes partially reconstructed by Bernard Ledwidge, *De Gaulle et les Américains. Conversations avec Dulles, Eisenhower, Kennedy et Rusk*, Paris, Flammarion, 1984, p. 100; and by Arthur M. Schlesinger, *A Thousand Days: John F. Kennedy in the White House,* New York, Fawcett Premier, 1965, pp. 325 ff.

31. Outgoing telegram, Paris, 3 June 1961, de Gaulle–Kennedy meetings, MAE, Amérique 1952–1963, États-Unis 9.5.3.

32. Outgoing telegram, Paris, 3 June 1961.

33. Memorandum for the President, "Specific Answers to your Questions"; memorandum, H. Owen to McGeorge Bundy, 9 June 1961, JFKL, NSF, France, box 70; and Couve de Murville, *Une Politique étrangère*, pp. 56–57.

34. Outgoing telegram, Paris, 5 June 1961, de Gaulle–Kennedy Meetings, MAE, America 1952–1963, États-Unis 9.4.1.

35. Minutes of conversation, Kennedy–de Gaulle, 31 May 1961, Paris, in Ledwidge, *De Gaulle et les Américains*, pp. 100 ff.; and Schlesinger, *A Thousand Days*, pp. 326 ff.

36. Schlesinger, *A Thousand Days*, pp. 332–33; outgoing telegram, Paris, 3 June 1961.

37. Telegram, Washington to Paris #2717–20, 10 June 1961, MAE, Pactes 1961–1970, box 261.

38. Note au sujet d'un projet américain de consultations tripartites à MM. Debré et Couve de Murville, 13 June 1961, in de Gaulle, *LNC (1961–1963)*, p. 96.

39. Telegram, Paris to Washington #9506–08, 20 June 1961, MAE, Pactes 1961–1970, box 261.

40. Note au sujet d'un projet américain . . . 13 June 1961.

41. Suggested Covering Letter to General de Gaulle (no date); and DEPTEL (no number), Paris, 30 June 1961, JFKL, NSF, France, box 73; letter from de Gaulle to Kennedy, 6 July 1961, in de Gaulle, *LNC (1961–1963)*, pp. 101–2.

42. See "A New Approach to France," 3 May 1961.

43. See Frank Costigliola, "Kennedy, De Gaulle et la consultation entre alliés," in *De Gaulle en son siècle*, vol. 4, "La sécurité et l'indépendance de la France," Institut Charles de Gaulle, Paris, Plon, 1992.

44. Couve de Murville, *Une Politique étrangère*, p. 58.

45. Suggested Covering Letter to General de Gaulle (no date), and DEPTEL (no number) Paris, 30 June 1961.

46. Letter to Kennedy, 6 July 1961, in de Gaulle, *LNC (1961–1963)*, pp. 102–3.

47. DEPTEL, Paris, 20 July 1961 (no number), letter from Kennedy to de Gaulle, JFKL, NSF, France, box 73.

48. Letter to Kennedy, 27 July 1961, in de Gaulle, *LNC (1961–1963)*, pp. 116–17.

49. De Gaulle, *MH,* p. 259.

50. Letter from Kennedy to de Gaulle, 20 July 1961, DEPTEL, Paris (no number).

51. Paul Nitze, Memorandum for the Vice-President, "Briefing Notes for your Paris Discussion," 27 September 1961, LBJL, NSF, Vice-Presidential Security File (VPSF), box 2.

52. *Le Monde,* 29 June; 30 June; 2–3 July 1961; letter to Kennedy, 27 July 1961; letter to Kennedy, 21 October 1961, in de Gaulle, *LNC (1961–1963)*, pp. 155–58.

53. Memorandum for Col. Howard Burris, Office of the Vice-President, "NATO Country Progress Toward Berlin Buildup," Maj. Gen. F. H. Miller; and "Country Progress Toward Berlin Buildup: France," 20 September 1961, LBJL, NSF, VPSF, box 2.

54. Memorandum of Conversation between Vice-President Lyndon Johnson, Ambassador Gavin, Ambassador Finletter and General Norstad at the U.S. Embassy, Paris, 30 September 1961, LBJL, NSF, VPSF, box 2.

55. Letter to Kennedy, 21 October 1961.

56. See chapter 2, p. 52.

57. Note au sujet de la présence américaine en France, 18 September 1961; note à Michel Debré et Maurice Couve de Murville au sujet des forces américaines en France, 4 October 1961; note au Premier ministre au sujet des effectifs américains en France, 26 October 1961, in de Gaulle, *LNC (1961–1963)*, pp. 142, 147, 159.

58. EMBTEL, Paris, #2287, 27 October 1961, JFKL, NSF, France, box 70.

59. Note pour le Ministre, "Développement à l'OTAN de la question de l'emploi des armes atomiques," 12 April 1962; see above, p. 65.

60. Memorandum for the President, Robert McNamara, 5 May 1961, JFKL, NSF, Germany-Berlin, box 81; see Jane E. Stromseth, *The Origins of Flexible Response: NATO's Debate over Strategy in the 1960s*, London, Macmillan, 1988, pp. 39–41.

61. "Note sur le document américain relatif au *buildup* (draft du 1 août)," EMGDN, 2 August 1961, MAE, Pactes 1961–1970, box 408.

62. "Projet d'instructions pour l'ambassadeur de France à Washington," 9 August 1961.

63. See Meeting between de Gaulle and Alphand, 21 December 1961, in Hervé Alphand, *L'étonnement d'être. Journal 1939–1973*, Paris, Fayard, 1977, pp. 366 ff.

64. Quoted by Schlesinger, *A Thousand Days*, p. 364.

65. Letter from Kennedy to de Gaulle, 20 July 1961; Couve de Murville, *Une Politique étrangère*, pp. 183–84; and Schlesinger, *A Thousand Days*, p. 366.

66. Letter from de Gaulle to Kennedy, 18 August 1961; text proposed for the declaration by the Three, in de Gaulle, *LNC (1961–1963)*, pp. 126–27; letter from Kennedy to de Gaulle 24 August 1961, JFKL, NSF, de Gaulle correspondence 27 July–2 September 1961; letter from de Gaulle to Kennedy, 26 August 1961, in de Gaulle, *LNC (1961–1963)*, pp. 129–31.

67. Letter to Kennedy, 21 October 1961.

68. "Réunion des ministres des Affaires étrangères le 12 décembre 1961 à 16 heures," MAE, Pactes 1961–1970, box 409.

69. Sulzberger, *Last of the Giants*, p. 826.

70. Note pour Maurice Couve de Murville et Pierre Maillard, 5 January 1962; note pour Maurice Couve de Murville, 14 April 1962, in de Gaulle, *LNC (1961–1963)*, pp. 189–90 and 230.

71. DEPTEL, Paris, #6319, JFKL, NSF, France, box 71A.

72. On this point, see chapter 1, p. 5.

73. EMBTEL #2542, Paris, 14 November 1961; letter from Bundy to Gavin, 17 November 1961; memorandum for the President, Ambassador Gavin's Visit, 28 February 1962, JFKL, NSF, France, box 71.

74. EMBTEL, Paris, #4041, 27 February 1962; EMBTEL, Paris, #4052, 28 February 1962; EMBTEL, Paris, #4097, 2 March 1962; and DEPTEL, Paris #4508, 20 February 1962, JFKL, NSF, France, box 71.

75. EMBTEL, Paris, #4508, 20 February 1962; and DEPTEL, Paris, #4072, 1 March 1962, JFKL, NSF, France, box 71.

76. Memorandum of Conversation, General Lavaud, Mr. Nitze, 13 March 1962, Washington, JFKL, NSF, France, box 71.

77. Letter from Gavin to Kennedy, 9 March 1962; memorandum "Balance Sheet of U.S. and French Requests in Military Field," 5 March 1962; draft of a letter from Kennedy to Gavin (n.d.) JFKL, NSF, France, box 71. See also Sulzberger, *Last of the Giants*. p. 859; John Newhouse, *De Gaulle and the Anglo-Saxons*, New York, Viking, 1970, pp. 158–60; and Bundy, *Danger and Survival*, pp. 484–86.

78. Couve de Murville to Sulzberger, 8 June 1962, in Sulzberger, *Last of the Giants*, pp. 881–82; airgram A-2140 Paris, 18 May 1962, JFKL, NSF, France, box 71A.

79. See the presentation by Jane Stromseth, who relies on original documentation, in Stromseth, *Origins of Flexible Response*, pp. 42–48.

80. Note pour le ministre, "Développement à l'OTAN de la question de l'emploi des armes atomiques," 22 April 1962.

81. Quoted by Stromseth, *Origins of Flexible Response*, p. 44.

82. Remarks by Secretary McNamara, Defense Ministers' Meeting, Paris, 31 May 1965, LBJL, NSF, Agency File, DoD, box 11; EMA, "Réunion du comité spécial des ministres de la Défense, 26–27 novembre 1965," 15 November 1965, MAE, Pactes 1961–1970, box 267.

83. Quoted by Stromseth, *Origins of Flexible Response*, p. 47.

84. *Major Addresses, Statements and Press Conferences of General Charles de Gaulle (MA)*, New York, French Embassy, n.d., p. 180; and Alain Peyrefitte, *C'était de Gaulle,* vol. 1, "La France redevient la France," Paris, de Fallois/Fayard, 1994, p. 288.

85. "Intervention de M. Couve de Murville à Athènes le 5 mai 1962," MAE, Pactes 1961–1970, box 267; airgram Paris A-2098, 12 May 1962, JFKL, NSF, France, box 71A.

86. Telegram, Bonn to Paris, #1569–76, 20 March 1962, meeting between Strauss and Messmer on 23 January 1962, MAE, Pactes 1961–1970, box 266.

87. Airgram Paris A-2140, 18 May 1962, JFKL, NSF, France, box 71A; and Sulzberger, *Last of the Giants*.

88. Airgram Paris A-2140.

89. Bundy, *Danger and Survival*, p. 486; and Alphand, *L'étonnement d'être*, p. 379.

90. EMBTEL, Paris #6020, 14 June 1962; EMBTEL, Paris #6219, 23 June 1962, JFKL, NSF, France, box 71A; meeting between Rusk and Couve de Murville, 20 June 1962, MAE, Pactes 1961–1970, box 409.

91. See chapter 2, pp. 50 ff.

92. Note au sujet de l'Europe, in de Gaulle, *LNC (1961–1963)*, pp. 107–8.

93. See Georges-Henri Soutou's demonstration, "Le général de Gaulle et le plan Fouchet," in *De Gaulle en son siècle*, vol. 5, "L'Europe," Paris, Plon, 1992.

94. See chapter 2, pp. 52 ff.

95. Telegram, Washington to Paris #519–524, 23 February 1961, MAE, Amérique 1952–1963, États-Unis 9.5.3.

96. Etienne Burin des Roziers, *Retour aux sources. 1962, l'année décisive,* Paris, Plon, 1986, pp. 47, 53.

97. See Soutou, "Le général de Gaulle et le plan Fouchet."

98. Speech of 5 February, 1962, in *MA*, p. 159.

99. EMBTEL, Paris #3764, 14 February 1962; EMBTEL, Paris #3973, 21 February 1962, JFKL, NSF, France, box 71.

100. Note pour Maurice Couve de Murville, 16 February 1962, in de Gaulle, *LNC (1961–1963)*, p. 209.

101. Burin des Roziers, *Retour aux sources*, p. 48; see also Soutou, "Le général de Gaulle et le plan Fouchet."

102. Couve de Murville, *Une Politique étrangère*, pp. 368–69; quote from Soutou, "Le général de Gaulle et le plan Fouchet."

103. Memorandum, "Thoughts on Reading the Morning Papers," 9 May 1962, JFKL, NSF, France, box 71A.

104. Press conference of 15 May 1962, *MA*, pp. 170–84.

105. Poll by IFOP 4–8 June 1962, quoted in Jean Charlot, *Les Français et de Gaulle*, Paris, Plon, 1971, p. 276.

106. See on this point Serge Berstein, *La France de l'expansion*, vol. 1, "La République gaullienne 1958–1969," Paris, Le Seuil, in the series "Nouvelle histoire de la France contemporaine," no. 17, 1989, p. 146; and Danielle Bahu-Leyser, *De Gaulle, les Français et l'Europe*, Paris, Presses Universitaires de France, 1981, pp. 104 ff., 202 ff.

107. EMBTEL, Paris, #5424, 16 May 1962, JFKL, NSF, France, box 71A.

108. Letter from Kennedy to Gavin, 18 May 1962, JFKL, NSF, France, box 71A.

109. Alphand to Couve de Murville, 9 May 1962, "La stratégie américaine d'après M. Walt Rostow," MAE, Amérique 1952–1963, États-Unis 9.5.6.

110. Memorandum of Conversation, Ball, Couve de Murville, Gavin, 21 May 1962; DEPTEL, Paris #6412, 31 May 1962, JFKL, NSF, France, box 71A.

111. Telegram, Washington to Paris, #3317–30, 9 June 1962, MAE, Amérique 1952–1963, États-Unis 9.4.1.

112. André Kaspi, "Unité européenne, *partnership* atlantique," *Relations internationales*, no. 11, 1977, pp. 231–48. See also Denise Artaud, "Le Grand Dessein de J. F. Kennedy: proposition mythique ou occasion manquée?" *Revue d'histoire moderne et contemporaine*, vol. XXIX, April–June 1982, pp. 235–66.

113. Quoted in Pierre Melandri, *L'Alliance atlantique*, Paris, Gallimard/Juillard, 1979, pp. 154–55.

114. Artaud, "Le Grand Dessein de J. F. Kennedy"; and Melandri, *L'Alliance atlantique*.

115. See Costigliola, "The Pursuit of Atlantic Community."

116. EMBTEL, Paris #109, 6 July 1962; airgram Paris A-51, 7 July 1962, JFKL, NSF, France, box 71A.

117. Lettre à Michel Debré, 25 July 1962, in de Gaulle, *LNC (1961–1963)*, pp. 253–54.

118. Burin des Roziers, *Retour aux sources*, p. 49.

119. Meeting on 30 August, in Alphand, *L'étonnement d'être*, p. 384.

120. For what follows, see Hans-Peter Schwarz, "Le président de Gaulle, le chancelier fédéral Adenauer et la genèse du traité de l'Elysée," in *De Gaulle en son siècle*, vol. 4, "La sécurité et l'indépendance de la France," Institut Charles de Gaulle, Paris, Plon, 1992; Georges-Henri Soutou, "Les problèmes de sécurité dans les rapports franco-allemands de 1956 à 1963," *Relations internationales*, no. 58, Summer 1989, pp. 227–51, and "Le général de Gaulle et le plan Fouchet," paper cited; Pierre Maillard, *De Gaulle et l'Allemagne. Le rêve inachevé*, Paris, Plon, 1990, pp. 20 ff.; and Burin des Roziers, *Retour aux sources*, pp. 138 ff.

121. Lettre à Fanfani, 10 July 1962; note à Etienne Burin des Roziers, 26 July 1962; and lettre à Konrad Adenauer, 15 July 1962 (quoted) in de Gaulle, *LNC (1961–1963)*, p. 246 ff.

122. Quoted by Georges-Henri Soutou, "Les problèmes de sécurité dans les rapports franco-allemands de 1956 à 1963."

123. See chapter 2, p. 38.

124. Note au sujet de l'Europe, 17 July 1961, in de Gaulle, *LNC (1961–1963)*, pp. 107–8.

125. Personal interview.

126. Speech given before the officers of the German War academy, 7 September 1962, in de Gaulle, *DM,* vol. 4, "Pour l'effort" (août 1962–décembre 1965), Paris, Plon, 1970, pp. 12–13.

127. EMBTEL, Paris #1406, 20 September 1962, JFKL, NSF, France, box 71A.

128. Instruction for Ambassador Bohlen (n.d., end October 1962); memorandum, "Relations with De Gaulle," David Klein to McGeorge Bundy, 7 November 1962; airgram Paris, A-286, 5 August 1962, JFKL, NSF, France, box 71A.

129. Alphand, *L'étonnement d'être*, pp. 379, 385. See also CIA, Information Report, "Differences between President De Gaulle and Prime Minister Pompidou," 20 July 1962; and airgram Paris, A-251, 2 August 1962, JFKL, NSF, France, box 71A.

130. Note pour MM. Pompidou, Messmer et Couve de Murville, 10 September 1962, in de Gaulle, *LNC (1961–1963)*, p. 261.

131. Telegram REPAN, 20 July 1962, MAE, Pactes 1961–1970, box 267.

132. Note au sujet de la nomination du commandant suprême de l'Organisation du Traité de l'Atlantique Nord, 19 July 1962; communiqué de la présidence de la République au sujet du général Lauris Norstad, 21 July 1962, in de Gaulle, *LNC (1961–1963)*, pp. 250–52.

133. Memorandum for Mr. Bundy, "French NATO Deficiencies," 9 October 1962, Colonel L. J. Legere; Paris, Polto #539, 8 November 1962, Finletter to Rusk, JFKL, NSF, France, box 71A.

134. Note sur l'organisation du commandement en temps de guerre, 12 November 1962, in de Gaulle, *LNC (1961–1963)*, pp. 273–74.

135. See François Poher, *Présence militaire américaine en France et opinion publique française de 1958 à 1967*, M.A. thesis, Université Paris X, 1991.

136. Broadcast address, 31 December 1962, in *MA*, p. 206.

137. For what follows, see the interview with Dean Acheson, Oral History Series, JFKL, and Burin des Roziers, *Retour aux sources*, pp. 135 ff.; see also Maurice Vaïsse, "Une hirondelle ne fait pas le printemps. La France et la crise de Cuba," in Maurice Vaïsse, ed., *L'Europe et la crise de Cuba*, Paris, A. Colin, 1993.

138. See Déclaration au sujet de Cuba à l'issue du Conseil des ministres du 24 octobre 1962, in de Gaulle, *LNC (1961–1963)*, p. 270, clarified by the letter to Adenauer, 26 October 1962, in de Gaulle, *LNC (1961–1963)*, pp. 270–71, and Burin des Roziers, *Retour aux sources*, p. 136.

139. See Memorandum of Conversation, "Political Consultation," W. W. Rostow and H. Alphand, 9 November 1962; airgram Paris A-1170, 15 November 1962, JFKL, NSF, France, box 71A.

140. Lettre à Harold Macmillan, 6 November 1962, in de Gaulle, *LNC (1961–1963)*, p. 272.

141. Telegram SECTO #8, Paris-Washington, 13 December 1962, in Ledwidge, *De Gaulle et les Américains*, p. 132.

142. Personal interview.

143. Walter Lippmann's speech before the English-speaking press, 29 November 1962, EMBTEL, Paris #2313, 1 December 1962, JFKL, NSF, France, box 71A.

144. Lettre à Konrad Adenauer, 26 October 1962.

145. Hans-Peter Schwarz, "Adenauer et la crise de Cuba," in *L'Europe et la crise de Cuba*, edited by Maurice Vaïsse, Paris, A. Colin, 1993.

146. See Maillard, *De Gaulle et l'Allemagne*, pp. 208–9; handwritten note, Legere to Bundy, 10 November 1962, JFKL, NSF, France, box 71A.

147. Meetings between de Gaulle and Macmillan, Telegram Paris to Washington #10054–66, MAE, Pactes 1961–1970, box 409; "Thoughts on Reading the Morning

Papers," 9 May 1962; see also Burin des Roziers, *Retour aux sources*, p. 151, and Peyrefitte, *C'était de Gaulle*, p. 299.

148. Personal interview.

149. Lettre à Harold Macmillan, 23 November 1962, in de Gaulle, *LNC (1961–1963)*, pp. 275–76.

150. The French and British minutes are discordant on certain points, notably nuclear questions, and the polemic following de Gaulle's press conference on January 14 was fed by these discrepancies. See the French viewpoint in Burin des Roziers (who drafted the French minutes from the interpreter's notes), *Retour aux sources*, pp. 152 ff., confirmed by Peyrefitte, *C'était de Gaulle*, pp. 332 ff.; for the British version, see Newhouse, *De Gaulle and the Anglo-Saxons*, pp. 205 ff.

151. Ledwidge, *De Gaulle et les Américains*, pp. 304–5; Burin des Roziers, *Retour aux sources*, p. 158.

152. Geoffroy de Courcel to M. Couve de Murville, 3 December 1962; note, "Programme de défense britannique—Coopération avec d'autres pays," 10 December 1962, MAE, Pactes 1961–1970, box 409.

153. Hervé Alphand to Couve de Murville, "Considérations sur l'accord de coopération atomique anglo-américain à des fins de défense mutuelle du 3 juillet 1958," MAE, Amérique, 1952–1963, États-Unis 9.5.3.

154. Telegram, London to Paris, #4708–10, 4 December 1962, MAE, Pactes 1961–1970, box 409; "Proposed US–UK Agreement for a Substitute Weapon Incident to Skybolt Cancellation," 17 December 1962, LBJL, NSF, VPSF, box 9, "Kennedy-Macmillan Meeting"; "The Multilateral Force—Where it comes from—What it is—and what it is not," LBJL, NSF, Subject File, MLF, box 25, "MLF Bundy Paper," pp. 17–24.

155. Burin des Roziers, *Retour aux sources*; Peyrefitte, *C'était de Gaulle*, p. 363; Newhouse, *De Gaulle and the Anglo-Saxons*, pp. 207–8.

156. Sec "Proposed US–UK Agreement . . . ," and "The Multilateral Force . . ."

157. Text of Nassau Agreement in *Documents on American Foreign Relations 1962*, New York, Council on Foreign Relations, 1963, pp. 244–45.

158. "The Multilateral Force . . . ," p. 20.

159. See Newhouse, *De Gaulle and the Anglo-Saxons*, pp. 222–23.

160. EMBTEL, Paris, #2582, 21 December 1962; EMBTEL, Paris #2594, 22 December 1962, JFKL, NSF, France, box 71A.

161. EMBTEL, Paris #2594, 22 December; EMBTEL, Paris #2595, 24 December 1962, JFKL, NSF, France, box 71A; "Conséquences de l'accord anglo-américain des Bahamas," 22 December 1962, MAE, Pactes 1961–1970, box 267.

162. Telegram #6619–35, Bonn to Paris, 27 December 1962, MAE, Amérique 1952–1963, États-Unis 9.5.3.A.

163. EMBTEL, Paris #2594, 22 December; EMBTEL, Paris #2595, 24 December; "Conséquences de l'accord anglo-américain des Bahamas," 22 December 1962.

164. Letter, Rusk to Kennedy, 24 December 1962, JFKL, NSF, France, box 71A.

165. Memorandum for the President, "Hervé Alphand," 29 December 1962, JFKL, NSF, France, box 71A; Alphand, *L'étonnement d'être*, pp. 390–91.

166. Memorandum for the President, "Hervé Alphand"; Alphand, *L'étonnement d'être*, p. 391.

167. Memorandum of Conversation, 28 February 1963, Rusk–Alphand, 6 March 1963, JFKL, NSF, France, box 72.

168. DEPTEL, Paris #3235, 3 January 1963, JFKL, NSF, France, box 72; memorandum for the President, "Hervé Alphand."

169. "The Multilateral Force . . . ," p. 22.

170. Cf. "Skybolt and Nassau," 15 November 1963, report by Richard Neustadt to Kennedy, pp. 103–5, JFKL, NSF, France, box 319–324, quoted by Frank Costigliola, "Kennedy, de Gaulle et la consultation entre alliés."

171. Burin des Roziers, *Retour aux sources*, p. 159, and Peyrefitte, *C'était de Gaulle*, pp. 339 ff.

172. Press Conference held at the Elysée Palace, 14 January 1963, in *MA*, p. 219.

173. Quoted by André Passeron, *De Gaulle parle, tome II (1962–1966),* Paris, Fayard, 1966, p. 200.

174. Press conference of 14 January 1963, in *MA*, p. 219.

175. Couve de Murville, *Une Politique étrangère*, p. 411.

176. See Passeron, *De Gaulle parle*, p. 199.

177. Passeron, *De Gaulle parle*, p. 199.

178. See Peyrefitte, *C'était de Gaulle*, pp. 334–35.

Chapter Four

The Power to Say No (1963–1964)

The double French "No" on January 14, 1963, represented an unprecedented challenge to the Atlantic leadership of the United States as well as to its strategy toward Europe. "The scandal was enormous,"[1] notes Alain Peyrefitte. On that day Kennedy's "Grand Design" was demolished. To be sure, de Gaulle did not manage with the Elysée Treaty to lay a firm Franco-German foundation for the "European" Europe he had wanted to establish with the Fouchet Plan; yet he still intended to prevent the emergence of a Euro-Atlantic ensemble increasingly integrated under U.S. direction. In the emerging struggle of influence between Paris and Washington, in which Germany was the principal stake, France's ability to maneuver, as it recovered its power, was far from negligible; but it was also true that its principal partners, starting with the FRG, were not ready to follow its logic of independence to the end. France did possess in these two years, however, the power to block U.S. policy. Without giving up his own long-term vision of European security organization, de Gaulle was in a position to obstruct this policy over the principal issue of the times, the nuclear question. This explains his opposition to the plan for a multilateral force proposed in Nassau, with respect to which he moved from neutrality to open hostility, as well as his rejection of flexible response, which Washington was trying to impose on the allies. In parallel, he continued to modify the nature of military relations between France and NATO. Sticking to the policy announced in 1958, he reduced French participation in the integrated organization even more, while embarking on a fundamental reform of the structures and strategy of the French military, now reorganized around a nuclear deterrent capability that became truly operational in 1964.

Thus, two strategies for Europe confronted each other against the background of a transformation in the Franco–U.S. and Euro–U.S. power relations. And if the transatlantic quarrel was amplified in 1963, it was because Europe was consolidating its prosperity and searching for a political existence, while America was beginning to feel the limits of its power—yet wanting to maintain its leadership.

"EUROPEAN" EUROPE VERSUS ATLANTIC COMMUNITY

In denouncing on January 14, 1963, the prospect of "a colossal Atlantic Community under U.S. dependence and leadership that would soon completely swallow
up the European Community,"[2] de Gaulle, six months after the Philadelphia
speech, finally gave his reply to Kennedy's proposal for an Atlantic partnership,
a reply that in effect smashed the "Grand Design" of the U.S. president and hit
the United States like a bombshell. The General's press conference, cabled Alph-
and, provoked "profound upheaval inside the administration and in political circles," since "for the first time in fifteen years," the Americans had the impression
"of seeing the edifice of their foreign policy crumble." It was as if de Gaulle's
press conference had suddenly revealed the limits of the power of the United
States, which was "brutally thanked" for everything it had done for Europe since
the Marshall Plan by a gesture of "unbearable defiance" from an ally. Alphand
noted that this would only encourage among Americans certain isolationist tendencies with respect to a "Europe that wanted no more of them."[3]

Alphand, during these months, could observe the breadth of the misunderstandings. Kennedy and his team constantly asked him the same question:
"[W]hat does General de Gaulle want?" And despite his efforts to explain the
Gaullist policy (which he summed up as "Alliance and independence"), the ambassador was inclined to think that the U.S. president "still imagines that the principal objective of our policy consists of excluding the United States from Europe
on the economic plane as well as on the defense plane."[4] He concluded the same
about Congress, which had a "narrow," even "neo-isolationist mind,"[5] in which
there were numerous attacks against France, accused of risking "a dislocation of
the Alliance." The attacks were even sharper because, against the background of
the Kennedy Round launched in May 1963, commercial contentions (such as the
"frozen chicken war" in the autumn) were now piled on top of political and strategic disagreements.[6] The climate until the autumn remained quite rough, thought
Alphand, due to "the systematic desire to report with malice and even to distort
French views."[7] For Maurice Couve de Murville, it was one of the gravest crises
of the decade in Franco–U.S. relations, a crisis that went to "the bottom of
things," he added, in that it bore on "the very nature of relations" between America and Europe.[8]

The Battle for Germany

Federal Germany, the pivot of the Atlantic system and cornerstone of a "European" Europe that remained the long-term objective of Gaullist policy, was the
prime stake in this crisis. The General's double "No" to *les Anglo-Saxons* a few
days before the date forecast for the conclusion of the Franco-German Treaty, evidently complicated things. The chancellor had to face open dissidence, notably
on the part of Minister of Foreign Affairs Gerhard Schröder, who was favorable

to the entry of Great Britain into the EEC, but also from within his Bundestag majority, highly Atlanticist in leaning. Support rose in Germany in favor of postponing signing the treaty as long as the British case was not settled. Adenauer also had to face personal pressure from Jean Monnet and Walter Hallstein, as well as from Dean Acheson and John McCloy, who gave him the same advice.[9] However, the chancellor, who after the Cuban crisis admired de Gaulle more and trusted Kennedy less, was more convinced than ever of the need for a Franco-German entente, and so he did not yield. On January 22, at the Elysée, de Gaulle and Adenauer signed a treaty on Franco-German cooperation, a treaty that set up close cooperation between the two countries (calling for a biannual summit at the level of president and chancellor and trimesterly meetings of foreign ministers), and aimed in particular to strengthen coordination of their defense policies (quarterly meetings of ministers, bimonthly of military chiefs, and the creation of institutes of operational research). The goal was to reach common strategic ideas, to increase exchanges of personnel between the armies, and to harmonize armament policies.

Although the Elysée Treaty did not include anything that might directly hurt the functioning of the Alliance, it left no doubt (seen from Washington — where it was obviously interpreted in light of the January press conference) that it ran against U.S. and Atlantic interests. Kennedy wondered if de Gaulle was trying to systematically reduce U.S. influence and presence on the Continent. No, he was told by Bohlen, whose analysis was temperate, de Gaulle was not "systematically" anti–United States, but thought that France and its European partners should be prepared for a U.S. withdrawal from Europe, which was according to him inevitable in the long run.[10] The ambassador insisted on what he rightly thought was at the heart of the Franco–U.S. difficulties: de Gaulle had a habit of speaking without distinguishing clearly between the present, the near future, and the distant future, which lent itself to misunderstanding.[11]

Washington chose to react aggressively to the Elysée Treaty, and starting in February U.S. diplomats orchestrated a vast maneuver aiming to annul its effects. The French saw the Americans exercising strong pressure on the Germans by insinuating that Gaullist diplomacy enjoined the latter, in effect, to "choose between Paris and Washington." Despite French denials and refutations of this interpretation of their policy, the U.S. offensive really consisted of putting Bonn's back against the wall. The Germans did not conceal from the French that they could not "pronounce themselves in favor of Paris" as long as the FRG depended on the United States for its defense.[12] Moreover, Adenauer's position was weakened by several things: his advanced age; his approaching retirement; the rise in opposition to his policy even within his own party; the strong current, especially in economic circles, favorable to a Europe that was open and based on free trade; and finally the priority attached to an alliance with the United States — all this led him to climb down.[13] At the start of April, he ended up accepting the principle of a preamble to the treaty, inspired by Monnet, which was voted upon by the Bundestag on May 16 at the same time as it ratified the treaty and which would substantially diminish its scope. The text of this preamble solemnly restated "the principal aims that the Federal Republic of Germany had pursued for years," particularly strengthening "the common defense within the framework of the North Atlantic Alliance and the integration of the forces of the Pact's member-states," and also "the unification of Europe . . . by admitting Great Britain into it."

The addition of such a preamble marked a political defeat for Adenauer and gave a red light to de Gaulle's plans; it conveyed a net reequilibration of Bonn's European and Atlantic policy in favor of Washington. But this was not sufficient to quiet U.S. suspicion of a Franco-German axis, nor concerns about French policy as a whole. By making a visit to Germany (June 23 to 26), Kennedy intended to achieve this U.S. countermove in person. While the sympathy he won in West Germany and in Berlin, speaking the historic words *"Ich bin ein Berliner,"* was not necessarily stronger than the emotion that de Gaulle had aroused during his state visit in September 1962, it could not escape French notice that the president's tour, which put in evidence the priority for Germans of relations with the United States, was an uncontested success for U.S. diplomacy.[14] So it is not surprising that the first Franco-German summit to be held after the treaty was signed, in Bonn on July 4 and 5, 1963, produced no concrete progress in the realms of defense and security.[15]

De Gaulle was not mistaken that the Franco-German impetus was broken. "It remains for us both," he concluded at the end of the summit, "to demonstrate to our respective countries, to Europe, and the world, that this treaty is fertile."[16] In the fall, Washington gave a fresh blow to Franco-German military cooperation by concluding important agreements with Bonn for arms cooperation (coproduction of tanks, cooperation in logistics, and so on), a domain that had been privileged in the Elysée Treaty.[17] Franco–U.S. disagreement over Germany was at a peak. Passing through Washington in October, Couve de Murville spoke bitterly of the U.S. policy, which he complained to Rusk, aimed to force the Germans to choose between Paris and Washington.[18] When he was received at the White House, Kennedy reproached him that the Elysée Treaty was directed against NATO and against the United States.[19] It was a pointless dialogue but it clearly turned to Washington's advantage in the autumn.

The arrival of Ludwig Erhard as successor to Adenauer on October 16 further decreased any prospect of realizing the terms of the Elysée Treaty with respect to defense and security. Adenauer's successor, who did not share his personal suspicions against Kennedy, was clearly more Atlanticist in orientation; moreover, he had neither the interest in nor the taste for Franco-German relations as did the man from Ronsdorf. To the Americans, who thought they had won "the fight for Germany's friendship," de Gaulle at the end of 1963 seemed at an impasse: the Franco-German treaty was dead and the MLF project, in which Bonn was now firmly involved, was on its way. The situation appeared so unfavorable to de Gaulle that some people in Washington feared a counteroffensive by him on the German issue—while concluding that it was bound to fail.[20] U.S. diplomacy could boast of having obliged the Germans to choose Washington over Paris, while imputing this choice to Gaullist diplomacy. Seen from Paris, it was obviously a low blow, a "bad joke."[21] Nevertheless, de Gaulle was resigned, at least for the moment, to the relative failure of the Franco-German enterprise, even if he deplored this: "One could not say that Germany and France are yet agreed on formulating policy together and one could not deny that this results from the fact that Bonn has not up until now believed that this policy should be European and independent."[22]

France and NATO: "Never Mention It"

The collapse of cooperation between Paris and Bonn during 1963 naturally made de Gaulle skeptical about the possibility of pushing the Alliance in the direction of European autonomy. Of course, this remained a long-term goal of French diplomacy, as Couve de Murville reminded Kennedy during a trip to Washington at the end of May.[23] But it was now clear that this distant prospect, which was not shared by his European partners, was not by its nature going to hasten the transformation of the Alliance that de Gaulle was demanding. Washington concluded that the question of reforming NATO quite simply no longer interested de Gaulle. Had he made the slightest proposal about it since the failure of the tripartite memorandum?[24] During a fresh visit to Washington in the autumn, Couve de Murville found himself being asked by his U.S. counterpart why France did not make constructive proposals about NATO, instead of taking unilateral initiatives such as the withdrawal of its fleet from the Atlantic naval command.[25] The answer was very simple, explained the chief French diplomat: Paris alone was in favor a profound reform of the Alliance that aimed at giving Europeans greater responsibility. All the other countries were against such a reform, at least for the time being. So why raise the issue as long as there was no united European position?[26] With the loss of impetus of the Franco-German dynamic and the relative isolation of Paris, French leaders were aware of their slender influence over NATO affairs, which Couve de Murville this time recognized implicitly in talks with Kennedy. Thus there would be no more French proposals about a total reform of the Alliance; the best thing for the French and Americans to do was to "leave things as they were and never speak about them," he explained. As for the unilateral measures taken by France in military matters, far from hurting the Alliance, they could only strengthen it.[27]

The political context was indeed less favorable than ever for French proposals about NATO. The German rapprochement with America was confirmed by a mutual understanding between Erhard and Lyndon Johnson. Moreover, Adenauer was not the only one to exit the scene in the fall of 1963. In October, a weakened Harold Macmillan resigned after a political scandal, the Profumo affair; he was replaced as head of the Conservative government by Alec Douglas Home, who would nevertheless cede less than a year later to Labour prime minister Harold Wilson. With Macmillan's departure, de Gaulle lost (whatever the vicissitudes of Franco-British relations) another choice colleague, and one whose successors would prove less preoccupied by continental affairs and more Atlanticist. Then on November 22, 1963, Kennedy was assassinated. "It's a tragedy," said de Gaulle when he arrived in Washington for the funeral, where he met Johnson, who was anxious to establish good relations and told him that France was an unfailing ally, as the Cuban crisis had proved to him.[28] Despite the politeness, a mistake in protocol (the unilateral announcement by Washington of the forthcoming visit by de Gaulle to the United States, previously negotiated with Kennedy[29]) would quickly set the tone for relations between the two men. De Gaulle and Kennedy had been able to appreciate each other despite their disagreements; de Gaulle and Johnson (who would only meet one more time, on the occasion of Adenauer's funeral in 1967) would disagree without appreciating each other at all, particularly since Johnson's arrival in the White House accentuated a basic tendency that had been detectable in Kennedy's last months: A relative falling back on itself on the part of an America taken up with domestic problems and increasingly with its involvement in Southeast Asia, and thus more and more inclined to unilateralism. All this led de Gaulle in the coming months toward an Atlantic policy that was even less active and less constructive. The United States had no other response to this policy than to try to reassert its own leadership.

In Search of Leadership

After Kennedy's assassination, Americans sought to reassert their managing role in NATO in order to dissipate an atmosphere of uncertainty that they attributed to de Gaulle's policy, considered "more clearly than ever" as directed against Atlantic integration. To be sure, the reasons for discord were numerous: East-West relations and disarmament, the MLF, military integration, and the problem of nuclear responsibilities and doctrine. However, the U.S. administration tried to avoid a direct confrontation over any of these issues with Paris, in order to preserve the unity and good functioning of NATO as much as possible.[30] Thus, the final communiqué of the Council's ministerial session in December 1963 papered over these dissensions and stressed Atlantic cohesion as the best guarantee of East-West stability. Naturally, this solved nothing: throughout 1964 French policy within the Alliance remained unchanged. With the approach of the spring ministerial session, to be held in The Hague in May 1964, the Johnson administration saw in this policy "a threat of disintegration," since it consisted of benefiting from NATO protection without accepting "the system of force commitments and integrated commands on which the defense of the Alliance is based." While proclaiming the need for radical changes in the structure of the Alliance, the French, moreover, were refusing to put forth their own proposals on the excuse that they would not obtain the necessary support.

Yet the U.S. administration considered France's position within the Alliance as "too strategically located, too much the geographical center of NATO" to run the risk of a confrontation with Paris; only a calm but firm demonstration of U.S. leadership could overcome the French problem without opening a serious crisis within the Alliance.[31] This, however, did not prevent Rusk from making his customary protests in The Hague, nor his Belgian counterpart Spaak from deploring de Gaulle's hostility to *les Anglo-Saxons* and to NATO's military organization and his opposition to European political integration.[32] These criticisms were badly received by the French, who sent a simple message: The more the allies attacked his policy, the more de Gaulle was likely to strengthen it. But they also made it clear that the questioning of integration would take a back seat, at least for a while: because de Gaulle wanted to maintain the two French divisions in Germany so as not to hurt Franco-German relations, and because he did not want to challenge the Alliance before the presidential election. The message, then, was neither to wait for French proposals for reorganizing NATO, nor require France to make them.[33]

Integration, however, was not the only issue of Atlantic discord. In the spring of 1964, the question of the Alliance's political cohesion resurfaced, but inversely to the way it had in 1958. Whereas de Gaulle in his memorandum had demanded in vain an assertion and organization of allied solidarity beyond the North Atlantic zone, it was now Washington that made itself the champion of Atlantic cohesion on a global scale. Now the stakes largely turned on the problems of the Far East, on which France and the United States had increasingly diverging perspectives. Washington saw in the French attitude to this region's problems (de Gaulle's recognition of the People's Republic of China on January 27, and his declared hostility to growing U.S. engagement in Vietnam) a lack of Atlantic solidarity. The Alliance's viability, insisted the Americans, grew out of "more effective consultation within NATO on outstanding political problems," consultations that would not be "limited to matters restricted to the North Atlantic area" and that should "cover East-West problems arising anywhere."[34]

Yet de Gaulle, in the months that followed, was inclined neither to approve of U.S. policy in Southeast Asia nor to foster its reassertion of Atlantic leadership. During his press conference on July 23, he developed his ideas about European security. Three themes stood out. The first was not new: the conditions that in 1949 has justified a NATO dominated by the United States no longer existed; instead, there must be an alliance between the United States and a responsible and autonomous Europe. The second theme was also familiar: two years after the failure of the Fouchet Plan, a "European" Europe—even one restricted to France and Germany—remained a French goal, prime though remote. This was why it pursued in its own way what "could and should be a European and independent policy," deriving principally from an independent nuclear program. It was the third theme that was the most innovative. "The division of the world into two camps," stated de Gaulle, "less and less corresponds to the real situation," since "the monolith of the totalitarian world is being dislocated": China had broken with the Soviet Union; its European satellites were distancing themselves from Moscow; and the Communist economic and social model was about to fail in the USSR itself.[35] In short, de Gaulle prophesied the overcoming of blocs, and he now situated French policy toward the Western alliance within this perspective.

This perspective was naturally rejected in Washington, not without caricaturing it: What was remembered from the press conference was that de Gaulle considered the Atlantic Alliance as an arrangement improvised at the end of the 1940s to oppose the Soviet threat and that it must be ended now that this threat was reduced.[36] This was an approximate interpretation that neglected the Gaullist distinction between NATO and the Alliance, but it does explain why at the end of 1964 the Americans "thought it less and less likely that the French would continue to be bound by the North Atlantic Treaty."[37] With NATO's ministerial session approaching in Paris on December 15, the U.S. diagnosis of the French "problem" was the same as the previous year but more somber: French opposition to an Alliance resting on military integration and political cooperation was "increasingly clear," with de Gaulle's goal being to "restructure" Europe and the Alliance so as to "undercut NATO's role in the defense of the West." Faced with all that, the U.S. line of action should remain unchanged: to reassert the leadership of the United States in European eyes while avoiding a direct confrontation with France.[38]

MLF: STRATEGIC ARRANGEMENT AND POLITICAL GAMBLE

During 1963 and 1964, transatlantic misunderstanding revolved around the plan for the multilateral force (MLF). Launched by the Eisenhower administration at the end of his term in 1960, taken up with little conviction by Kennedy in the spring of 1961, and received since then by the allies with only moderate enthusiasm, the MLF had been revived in Nassau in the hope of solving the British and French nuclear problem.[39] A veritable strategic hydra, from the start the MLF had assumed a variety of forms. At the end of 1962 and start of 1963, when the MLF entered a phase of active negotiation among the allies, the project called for the establishment of a fleet of twenty-five surface ships, each equipped with eight Polaris missiles with megaton nuclear warheads. Each ship had a multinational crew and the whole arrangement would be financed pro rata by member countries, depending on their participation. The MLF would be placed under SACEUR orders in peacetime, but the decision to use nuclear fire would belong collectively and unanimously to member states. While the United States thus reserved the right of veto, the Americans dangled the possibility of renouncing it someday in the event of the development of a unified European mechanism of decision making. This last point was obviously critical and would remain at the heart of the debate.[40]

The MLF, even more than a strategic arrangement set up to solve the problem of atomic responsibilities within the Alliance, represented a political gamble. For Paris, it was an illusion: Behind an exceedingly complex military project, the MLF (coming after the Cuban crisis) confirmed the U.S. rejection of any real nuclear sharing and any real European strategic autonomy; as a matter of fact, Kennedy, in January 1963, declared to the National Security Council that the MLF had the advantage of "increasing the dependence of Europeans vis-à-vis the United States."[41] Hence the nickname "multilateral farce" invented by the French, who saw the MLF as a nuclear extension of the concept of the "Atlantic community," a project rather designed to undermine the strategic foundations of a "European" Europe. At the same time, lurking behind the illusion of nuclear sharing they denounced, the French were worried to find a prospect that was evidently unacceptable to Paris: the accession by Germany to nuclear power, thanks to the MLF. After January 1963, the major stake in the Franco–U.S. debate over the MLF—as over other Alliance problems—therefore concerned Germany and its nuclear status. A complex triangular relationship was set up over the MLF among Paris, Bonn, and Washington.

A Triangle of Nuclear Desire

With de Gaulle having rejected the Nassau offer and declined any French participation in the project, at the start of 1963 the MLF problem was now recentered on the German problem. Subsequent to the French "No," relieving German nuclear "itching" became the Americans' principal motivation—not to say obsession. Throughout 1962, Bonn had given out disturbing signals: Adenauer let it be understood that the FRG needed "compensation" to balance the nuclear status of France and Great Britain; and Franz-Josef Strauss (who resigned at the end of the year after the *Spiegel* scandal) demanded increased German control over NATO's nuclear weapons on its territory. The Kennedy team saw in these demands a more or less remote threat of German insistence on acquiring nothing less than an independent nuclear deterrent. At the close of a particularly difficult year for relations between Bonn and Washington, the prospect of a German nuclear Gaullist-type policy haunted certain sectors of the U.S. administration.[42] The State Department, on the initiative of George Ball, now made itself the champion of an MLF, considering that the sole means of annulling this risk was by giving the Germans the feeling of having a finger on the nuclear button. On the contrary, McNamara and his team were by no means convinced of the military advantage of sharing atomic hardware through an MLF–type arrangement. The defense secretary thought that the proposals for consultation that he had made in Athens in 1962 and renewed in Ottawa in May 1963 were sufficient—in short, that the sharing of nuclear *soft*ware was satisfactory, even from the German viewpoint. But despite these reservations, the Pentagon did not try to hinder moves by the partisans of the MLF. Kennedy, also skeptical about military aspects of the project, was sensitive to the German nuclear problem and so let its proponents go ahead. At the end of January 1963, Ambassador Livingston Merchant undertook an exploratory mission on the MLF with the Europeans.[43]

Meanwhile, George Ball was received by Adenauer (on the very day of de Gaulle's press conference) and convinced the chancellor to support the project. Concerned to reassure the Americans of German loyalty to the Alliance at the very time de Gaulle was shaking its cohesion, Adenauer wanted above all to increase German influence over nuclear affairs. Perhaps too, while he was preparing to sign the cooperation treaty with de Gaulle, he wanted to quieten U.S. fears (never truly dissipated since the Strauss–Chaban agreements of 1958) regarding hypothetical nuclear cooperation between France and Germany.[44] Though the Elysée Treaty did not call for a reinstatement of the nuclear cooperation that de Gaulle had ended in 1958, the subject had been previously more than mentioned, notably at Rambouillet in the summer of 1960, in terms that, while vague, left open a possibility. De Gaulle, sensitive to the importance Adenauer attached to the issue, perhaps tried again to raise the issue with him in early 1963. At least this is what the Americans suspected.[45]

It is true that de Gaulle seemed pleased to keep doubts alive. In early January, with Bohlen, he mentioned the "inevitability" in the long term of the Germans acquiring the nuclear bomb,[46] a prophecy he repeated to Dean Rusk in early April. And despite the evaporation of Franco-German cooperation in the first months of 1963, some people in Washington continued to fear French nuclear advances to Germany. Even though the administration generally considered that Bonn could only refuse such an offer, the perceived danger was of seeing the Germans use Paris's hypothetical nuclear proposals to raise the stakes over the MLF,[47] the goal of which was precisely to moderate German nuclear ambitions. But if the Americans suspected the French of dangling possible nuclear cooperation in front of the Germans, the distrust was reciprocal. In the very first months of 1963, Paris, to be sure, did announce a neutral position on the MLF: although France refused to participate in it, France did not intend to hinder it. But the French had a major objection: the MLF, far from moderating it, risked precisely strengthening German nuclear yearning. In the spring, Couve de Murville warned the Americans that as soon as the Germans had achieved their rise in conventional power, they would also demand their own nuclear capability. The MLF was for them only the first step toward a real German nuclear force.[48]

Couve de Murville's trip to Washington in the spring of 1963 was the occasion to review disagreements over the MLF. The Americans suspected the French of doing everything to oppose the MLF behind which, Kennedy said, Washington was rallying "in the hope of solving the German problem." Couve de Murville replied that France had nothing against the U.S. proposals but considered them simply unrealizable. Given the way negotiations evolved, he argued, there was a risk of "being faced with a force that was no longer multilateral but bilateral," meaning German and American. The Germans, added Couve de Murville, would ask even more of the Americans, who would only have succeeded in developing "their appetite for things atomic." To which Kennedy retorted that the future French *force de frappe* was itself an "invitation" to the Germans to do the same, since it could only arouse a feeling of inequality that it would be difficult to dissipate.[49] Thus, while both men agreed that a German national nuclear capability would have catastrophic consequences, as much in the East as in the West, the mutual suspicions would not go away.

Undoubtedly, these reciprocal insinuations by the French and Americans over nuclear cooperation with Germany were somewhat forced and implausible, since the prospect of such cooperation appeared to each side as both dangerous and unlikely. The core of the debate was really political: it was about the way to avoid Germany's demanding parity status with its allies and aspiring to end the discrimination to which the country had been subjected in nuclear matters. In this, this debate converged with the more general one over the organization of the Western alliance: the MLF, through the German nuclear problem, was related to the fundamental political debate between the French and the Americans. Thus, Couve de Murville held that the Elysée Treaty aimed to allow France to steer German ambitions and that in the longer term, as the political unification of Europe progressed, these ambitions would be absorbed into a European nuclear deterrent, linked with that of the United States, in which the Germans would be involved. Finally, he added, the German nuclear problem would only be solved when there existed "a European political power enabled to make decisions."[50] But George Ball retorted that a "Europe of nations," borrowing de Gaulle's designation, was simply incompatible with a sole political authority that was indispensable for European deterrence. On the contrary, with the Gaullist conception of Europe, which privileged the role of states, how would the Germans, too, not consider a national deterrent as the only solution to their nuclear problem? The experience of history, added Ball, proved that the Germans would not accept their discriminatory situation forever. This was why the United States supported the idea of a multilateral force. "While the MLF was admittedly not perfect," he concluded, "it was the best that can be done, given the realities of present institutional progress."[51]

Nonproliferation or Nuclear Sharing?

In reality, the Kennedy administration had been actively considering since 1962 another way of handling the problem of dissemination in general and the German nuclear question in particular, which would take the form of a nuclear nonproliferation treaty (NPT).[52] In the first months of 1963, Washington discreetly approached the allies on this subject. France was not hostile to the project, but, as in the case of the MLF, did not think itself directly concerned. Paris moreover felt there was incompatibility between the MLF and the NPT. To the extent that the former aimed to associate Germany and other nonnuclear states more closely with the management of military atomic affairs, it was *ipso facto,* thought Paris, in contradiction with the latter. (This was a position that the USSR shared; in a memo sent to Washington in the spring of 1963, Moscow judged as incompatible with the very idea of nonproliferation any "double key" procedure concerning U.S. tactical nuclear weapons in Germany, and most of all the MLF.) Simultaneously, and despite major differences between Soviets and Americans on this point, the French, in the context of the post-Cuba détente, were worried that the project could consecrate the nuclear duopoly on the backs of Europeans.[53] "It is a fact," Couve de Murville told Dean Rusk, "that you are more or less formally discussing a certain number of things with the Russians."[54]

Nevertheless, the NPT was not yet "ripe." At the time, the spring and summer of 1963, another treaty was the order of the day. Under negotiation for years and now benefiting from the favorable post-Cuba climate, it concerned a partial limitation of nuclear tests. The Nuclear Test Ban (NTB) Treaty, aiming to prevent nuclear explosions in the atmosphere, in space, and underwater, permitted only underground tests. De Gaulle's position was clear: For him, the NTB tended to consecrate the nuclear monopoly of *les Anglo-Saxons* and the Soviets. France, which had not yet mastered the technique of underground tests, naturally should be able to pursue its campaign of open-air tests unless it wanted to compromise its atomic independence. But Washington attached great importance to the NTB, which also fit into the logic of nonproliferation. So it was in the hope of obtaining France's adherence that the Kennedy team partially reopened the issue of Franco–U.S. atomic cooperation that had been closed after Nassau.

At the end of July, Bohlen discussed the subject with de Gaulle. In exchange for his adherence to the test ban treaty, France, he suggested, might benefit from some form of U.S. nuclear assistance.[55] The General's response was negative — even if he did not reject once and for all adhering to the NTB, there was no question of it for the time being. And he did not believe in hypothetical U.S. assistance — even if Kennedy wanted it, which he strongly doubted, there remained the obstacle of U.S. legislation. And even in the event of nuclear cooperation with the United States, France would need to proceed with its own tests.[56] The same day, de Gaulle confirmed to former vice president Nixon, received at the Elysée, that he had kissed good-bye to Franco–U.S. atomic cooperation. For the time being all that could be envisaged was coordination of targets among the French, British, and Americans in case of conflict. The United States, he added, should understand "that it was essential that France should be independent and that this in effect lay at the root of the difficulties" between the two countries.[57]

On August 5, 1963, a treaty limiting tests was signed in Moscow by the Americans, British, and Soviets. The episode had exacerbated misunderstanding between Paris and Washington even more, first because the thorny issue of nuclear cooperation had been reopened — uselessly, since the proposal for U.S. aid that had been formulated at the end of July was confined in effect to the technology of underground nuclear experiments, excluding weapons properly speaking,[58] which limited its attraction for the French. It was now finally clear to the Americans that de Gaulle would not compromise over nuclear independence, which effectively limited the possibility of future cooperation to coordinating targets.[59] Washington's policy was fixed, this time definitively: it was pointless to mention the possibility of U.S. assistance that de Gaulle was not asking for and that would create problems with Germany.[60] The case of Franco–U.S. cooperation would be definitively closed in April 1964 when Johnson signed a directive (NSAM #294) solemnly restating the policy of nuclear nonassistance to France or any other country aspiring to an atomic military capability.[61] But while the NTB affair was punctually reviving nuclear misunderstandings between France and the United States, it was above all de Gaulle's denunciation of the bipolar logic of arms control, pointedly expressed by him at the end of September 1963, that gave rise to a new phase of tension between Paris and Washington.[62] Going beyond the problem of limiting tests, this disagreement in fact concerned the whole organization of European security. After the Moscow Treaty was signed, the White House did not know how to renew the dialogue.[63] How could it convince de Gaulle that Washington's policy was not aiming at "the maintenance of U.S. influence or control of Europe"?[64]

French Deterrence and European Deterrence

This question was even more difficult because in the autumn of 1963 the MLF issue had begun to get more venomous. Discussions inside a Paris working group on the MLF set up by the Americans at the beginning of the year, and interrupted in the spring by Italian and British political crises, started up again in October.[65] Although France refused to participate, it had abandoned the neutrality pronounced at the year's start; Paris was now worried about the dynamic the Americans had succeeded in generating. Hence, there was an attempted counteroffer aimed at attenuating the MLF's attraction by publicly proclaiming the prospect of a European nuclear deterrent. Michel Habib-Deloncle, France's secretary of state for foreign affairs, declared at the end of September that "when Europe has strengthened its political structures, it will be necessary to define how the effort undertaken by France could be used by all European nations for common defense." The Americans thought his statements had been authorized; de Gaulle was indeed aware of them in advance.[66] And it was not the first time that the European dimension of the French nuclear effort had been publicly advanced by a senior government figure: Pierre Messmer, in the spring of 1963, had already declared that "possession by France of nuclear weapons will be a cornerstone of European construction."[67] But this public speech was especially aimed, as the Americans could tell, at breaking the momentum of the MLF. For Bohlen, de Gaulle was leaning on London's policy by suggesting that France would prove more open to British membership in the EEC if Great Britain held itself apart from the MLF.[68] And Washington thought that it was Germany that was really targeted: Paris was trying to seduce Bonn by holding out German participation (but not necessarily in the form of "outright French aid to a national German nuclear weapons program") in a hypothetical European deterrent.[69]

But French and U.S. rivalry for the role of nuclear protector of Europe was an unequal battle. De Gaulle possessed a not-yet-operational deterrent capability, hence one with no real outside credibility. Moreover, as McGeorge Bundy remarked to Hervé Alphand, the hypothesis of a "political unity" such that "Europe might have nuclear weapons" was a "seductive" formula, but would take "a long time to bring about."[70] And in the fall of 1963 the whole political context was scarcely favorable to it, notably due to the failure of the Elysée Treaty. The Germans, while formally saying they were favorable to "a European nuclear force at a later stage in the creation of a political Europe," did not hide the fact that, for the time being, it was really the MLF in which they placed their hopes of having a real influence over nuclear deterrence.[71] The Americans were hardly worried: the French move risked the repercussion of having the inverse effect of strengthening the impetus of the MLF and the entente between Germany and America.[72]

This is indeed what occurred during 1964. The nuclear triangle—France, Germany, and the United States—functioned to Bonn's advantage. During Erhard's visit to Paris in mid-February, the nuclear issue was raised. De Gaulle assured the chancellor that in case of a Soviet attack against the FRG, the French atomic force would be employed. The Germans took note of this, but they quickly pointed out to the Americans that this engagement was "a little vague as to the precise time at which the force would be employed."[73] This confidential remark evidently aimed to reassure Washington of the relative value that Bonn granted to French deterrence, while forcing the United States to be more precise about its own conditions for the recourse to nuclear weapons in case of an attack on Germany. Meanwhile, Bonn was still far from having definitively accepted the logic of flexible response, which Germany considered (on this point following, if less openly, de Gaulle's line of argument) contrary to its interests.

The same scenario took place during de Gaulle's visit to Bonn in July 1964. According to rumor in the German and U.S. press, de Gaulle was asking Erhard for a German "contribution" to the French nuclear effort. But Paris denied this: the information was likely given to the press, in distorted form, by Erhard himself. And Couve de Murville made it plain that if de Gaulle had actually mentioned the eventual possibility of a European deterrent, he had only suggested an interim arrangement of a political nature between France and Germany over nuclear matters. As for proper atomic cooperation between France and Germany, there had been no question of it since 1958, even if the Germans tended to imply the contrary.[74] The reality, however, was certainly halfway between. In the context of intense discussion over the MLF (reopened as we shall see during Erhard's trip to Washington the preceding month), de Gaulle may have proved forthcoming when he mentioned Franco-German nuclear relations to the chancellor—in the hope of attenuating the Germans' enthusiasm for the MLF; on his side, Erhard had every interest in exaggerating the General's overtures when speaking with the

Americans, so as to raise the stakes over the MLF. The Germans, who found themselves placed — or pretending to be so — by Paris in front of a choice between the latter and the *force de frappe*, naturally leaned toward the MLF.[75]

1964: The Year of the MLF

Nineteen sixty-four was the year of the MLF and it ended with a European and Atlantic crisis in which the MLF was at the stake. Starting in the spring, it became "the central objective of U.S. policy."[76] MLF proponents, mostly in the State Department, were more than ever persuaded that it would solve the nuclear problem of NATO and strengthen its cohesion as a "tight alliance with a closely integrated military power," while causing de Gaulle and his "old-fashioned" and dangerous concept of NATO to fail. The MLF, by avoiding the proliferation of national forces, would offer in effect a formula for nuclear sharing, without which the FRG would feel doomed to an inferior status and so would redouble its nuclear demands. Three and a half years after having launched the idea, the Americans had to understand, according to its zealots, that there was evidently no better solution than the MLF.[77]

However, the intrinsic contradictions of the MLF were increasingly patent. Whereas the United States wanted to avoid independent nuclear powers appearing within the Alliance, Germany (and also Italy) wanted the MLF in time to be transformed into a European force autonomous from the United States — as the latter had been suggesting since the beginning in an ambiguous way — that is, without a U.S. veto (this was the object of the "European clause" requested by Bonn and Rome).[78] And both of these demands, difficult to reconcile with each other, were increasingly asserted in the spring of 1964: the former because the NPT, once the Moscow Treaty was signed, moved to the foreground of U.S. preoccupations; and the latter because the Germans, by means of the MLF, aspired more than ever to a major role in nuclear affairs. But the multilateralist lobby in the State Department thought this contradiction could be overcome by convincing the USSR that the MLF did not by nature favor proliferation, and, though not formally promising the Germans a European clause, by not excluding the possibility that in the long term the MLF might effectively become a nuclear force autonomous from the United States, hence without a U.S. veto.[79] A real diplomatic and strategic chasm was in prospect.

Other threats weighed over the MLF during the spring of 1964, apart from the French position and the active hostility of the USSR. Great Britain had an increasingly less favorable attitude: in the run-up to a general election, positions were more polarized. The Conservative Party in power, attached to a national nuclear force recommended in the 1964 Defense White Paper, did not want to back the MLF. As for the Labour Party, it continued to oppose the MLF as likely to encourage German nuclear aspirations.[80] Most importantly, the U.S. administration was itself divided. If George Ball still thought there existed a "substantial possibility" of agreement among the allies concerned, the Pentagon, as much in the person of McNamara himself as among the chiefs of staff, continued to have "serious reservations" about the MLF. Between the two poles, the president's immediate entourage adopted a cautious position. For McGeorge Bundy, it was urgent not to rush and not to try to impose the MLF on the British as elections approached. As for Johnson himself, he was lukewarm about a complex project inherited from his predecessor.

However, the president saw in the MLF a means of opposing the Gaullist conception of a "French organized Europe" that could rely on "German support for the *force de frappe*." He feared that a failure of the MLF might considerably increase de Gaulle's "chances of success."[81] During a White House meeting on April 10, 1964, Johnson stated his position in these terms: the Europeans should be told that he thought the MLF "the best way to proceed," and if possible try to obtain allied agreement before the end of the year.[82] Ball and the "multilateralists" carried the day: Johnson and Erhard reopened the MLF issue during the chancellor's visit to Washington in June, and the final communiqué stated their intention to come to an agreement before the end of the year.[83]

The reopening of the MLF issue merely hastened the moment of truth. Already in the summer of 1964, some feared a new crisis on the scale of the one over the European Defense Community.[84] In front of the growing difficulties encountered by the MLF in Great Britain, in Italy, and especially in Germany, where Erhard felt the increasing influence of "Gaullists" who wanted to strengthen Franco-German ties and threatened to make this theme an electoral issue (encouraged in this by de Gaulle's European nuclear discourse), Ball tried again to speed things up. On his advice, Erhard, emphasizing to the Bundestag the risk of the MLF's failure if negotiations were prolonged, suggested to Johnson that the FRG and the United States come to an agreement with each other before the end of the year, if necessary without the other interested Europeans. By the end of the summer, however, the new secretary general of the Alliance, the Italian Manlio Brosio, complained that this revival of German–U.S. activism had the predictable effect of pushing France "from indifference to hostility."[85]

French opposition to the MLF indeed was now out in the open. De Gaulle, who until then had not taken it seriously, seemed to fear that the project would actually be realized. He warned Erhard that Germany's participation in the MLF could have grave consequences for Franco-German cooperation.[86] In the course of the autumn, Paris strengthened its tone and aired its refusal publicly. For the French government, the MLF was potentially "destructive for Europe, provocative to certain other countries, and in the end directed more or less against France," declared Prime Minister Georges Pompidou. And because it was contrary to the spirit of the Elysée Treaty, he added, pursuing the project could lead to a serious deterioration in relations between France and Germany.[87] Pompidou made these statements, which amounted to a barrage against the MLF, against the backdrop of a Franco-German crisis over the Common Agricultural Policy

(CAP), which was being attacked by the Americans within the context of the Kennedy Round of trade negotiations and over which de Gaulle, who had made the CAP a priority objective, also threatened to break with Bonn and his other European partners. Once more, strategic disputes, coming on top of contentious economic issues threatened to degenerate into a major transatlantic and European crisis.

At the end of October, Maurice Couve de Murville confirmed to the Americans the strengthening of the French position. France, he told Bohlen, thought that including Germany in the MLF could only "whet their appetite for nuclear matters" and that, on this matter, France "shared the Soviet point of view."[88] Seen from Paris, the Americans, with their MLF offer, had wholly created the problem of full possession by Germany of nuclear weapons; until the recent intensification of the campaign for the MLF, the French noted, Germany had made no demands for them. Considering which, added General Michel Fourquet, secretary general for national defense, the United States could congratulate itself on having raised the serious difficulties that were now appearing between France and Germany.[89] For French diplomats, these difficulties were summarized by the real question raised by the MLF: Was West Germany going to remain European or transform itself into a state "tied to the U.S. orbit"?[90] This question was all the more pressing because major defense agreements, signed on November 14 by McNamara and his German colleague Kai-Uwe von Hassel, seemed to consecrate the new German–U.S. axis.[91]

The recriminations were reciprocal. As with the question of NATO, the Americans reproached the French for their nonconstructive opposition to the MLF. But the French response did not vary: What good were concrete proposals as long as there was no plan for a united Western Europe?[92] In the very important speech he gave in Strasbourg at the end of November, de Gaulle put the finishing touches to the French countermove, insisting that "in these times of threats and nuclear 'escalation,'" there was no other route than "the organization of a Europe in and of itself" for its own defense.[93] This was an implicit criticism of the MLF and it was interpreted as such in Washington; but it was not accompanied by any concrete proposal.[94]

The MLF Crisis

While France, despite the distant prospect of a united Europe with its own nuclear deterrent, had no alternative solution to propose, it did possess a real power of preventing the MLF. In Germany, the debate between Gaullists and Atlanticists was raging; Erhard no longer appeared able to make the MLF acceptable to the Bundestag, where the majority of the CDU–CSU Party coalition refused to take the risk of a break between Germany and France over the MLF. In October, Washington realized that Paris's intransigent opposition was starting to undermine the already fragile support of other countries.[95] While most of them were not disposed to let France weaken transatlantic ties by causing the MLF to fail, they also saw the project as a U.S. provocation that could only push de Gaulle to persevere in his critique of NATO and of the EEC, a prospect that most Europeans wanted to avoid at all costs. Moreover, the MLF, many Europeans thought, might complicate the bettering of East-West relations and the policy of arms control.[96] At the end of 1964, Soviet opposition to the MLF clearly intensified to the point of becoming a major obstacle to the plan.[97]

The French refusal, the German strife, the European reticence, and the Soviet opposition all had the effect of raising serious questions within the Johnson administration. Returning from Europe in mid-October, Walt Rostow had the feeling that "a major turning point" was approaching, and that beyond the particular question of the MLF, it was European security as a whole that was at stake: Would the West evolve in the direction of increased integration within the Alliance or, on the contrary, toward a dismantling of the latter?[98]

In the final months of 1964, the United States began a rethinking of the MLF that would quickly lead to its being shelved. This move was less strong in the State Department, where it was considered that renouncing the MLF would have grave consequences, particularly on relations between America and Germany,[99] than in the White House, where it was suggested without hesitation that the United States do "a turn around," in other words that it renounce the MLF once and for all.[100] Yet the need to reexamine the project was admitted everywhere in the administration, including among unconditional supporters of the MLF who were hoping to shift de Gaulle's attitude by convincing him that the MLF was not contrary to his vision of Europe. At a time when the *force de frappe* was becoming operational, this might call for a concession that the United States had until then refused to make: recognizing the major role of France in nuclear affairs.[101] The State Department in mid-November attempted a vague overture in this direction, trying to convince the French that "the [MLF] enterprise [was] not directed against them" and that in the event it became concrete, the United States, while understanding the refusal of France to participate in it, would wish to discuss "cooperation and coordination" between the MLF and the *force de frappe*.[102] Paris was not demonstrably opposed in principle to a coordination of targets between the French force and the different Anglo–U.S. nuclear components; but it appeared difficult to go beyond that as long as de Gaulle remained hostile to the MLF.[103]

The nuclear issue thus continued in essence to divide France and the United States. Dean Rusk's visit to de Gaulle, on the margins of the Atlantic Council in mid-December 1964, concluded with a frank statement of disagreement over the NPT, a prime concern of the Johnson administration and about which de Gaulle did not mince words. For him, nuclear proliferation was inevitable unless prevented by force, which nobody was disposed to use. In addition, a treaty was superfluous, since neither France nor the United States—or for that matter any other nuclear power—was "about to give the bomb to anyone."[104] As for the MLF, it would at a minimum (despite the U.S. right of veto) give the impression "of German participation," for example with regard to targeting, which would have "a bad effect in Eastern Europe," and "a not too good [effect] in the West." In short, concluded de Gaulle, if everything acted to guarantee that the Germans forever renounced a national nuclear capacity, these disadvantages would be secondary; but the MLF "will not eliminate the German appetite but will, in all probability, increase it," which might have "disastrous" consequences for the Alliance.[105]

De Gaulle's admonitions were superfluous: the MLF at this stage was already failing. Considering the damages caused within the Alliance by a project that originally aimed to strengthen its political and strategic cohesion, Johnson, in the very last days of the year, decided to abandon it *de facto*.[106] The MLF would still remain for another year more or less formally on the agenda; its promoters did not easily give up, despite the presidential decision. But Couve de Murville could note during a trip to the U.S. capital in early 1965 that "it seems that the idea of a multilateral force, even if some contacts continue, has been practically abandoned by Washington."[107] This was a result to which de Gaulle would, in the end, have largely contributed.

NUCLEAR STRATEGIES

Parallel to the controversy over the MLF, then at its height, differences between French and U.S. ideas about strategic issues, which in recent years had become clearer, were transformed during 1963–1964 into sharp opposition. While Washington was resolved to obtain from its allies a drastic modification of NATO doctrine in the direction of flexible response, Paris intended to quite obstruct this shift.

The Great Debate

What up until then had been just a growing difference of opinion over Alliance doctrine became, with the political rupture of January 1963, a strategic rupture. For de Gaulle, who had been tending toward this conclusion for years and had been repeating it in public for months, "U.S. nuclear power does not respond, necessarily and immediately, to all eventualities concerning Europe and France." What was new in what he announced at his press conference of January 14 was that France was now intent on contesting the U.S. strategic "monopoly," even if it was aware of the limits of its own capabilities. "Since when is it proved that a nation should remain deprived of the most effective weapons for the reason that its eventual principal adversary and its principal friend have means very superior to its own?"[108] For de Gaulle, not only should France have its own nuclear capability, but it should also have its own strategy, and this without raising a contradiction with the principle of the Alliance.[109]

With 1963 began a new phase of activity in the promotion of flexible response by Washington among its allies. After the crises of Berlin and Cuba, the Americans were more convinced than ever of the double necessity of strengthening nuclear control and centralization within the Alliance and of increasing the conventional defense capacity of NATO in Europe; this was the only way for the United States to overcome the dilemma of capitulation versus annihilation in which the balance of terror had locked it. The Americans thought that NATO would be perfectly able, given sustained effort in this direction, to contest Soviet conventional superiority, judged to be "mythic" by the Pentagon (an almost mathematical demonstration of this was performed by Pentagon officials like Alain Enthoven and Paul Nitze).[110] The strategic debate within the Alliance was not new: opened during the Eisenhower administration and again in 1961 with Kennedy's arrival in office, it had taken off and been made public in 1962, after the Athens and Ann Arbor speeches.[111] But in 1963, the French well understood that for Washington it was a matter of undertaking a proper modification of allied strategy and of getting NATO to officially adopt flexible response, a prospect unacceptable to Paris.[112] Hence this debate became the Alliance's great debate. And even if France was not the only one to contest flexible response (criticism from some German politicians, notably Franz-Josef Strauss, during the last months of 1962 had been particularly nurtured), the debate was above all between France and the United States.

It was also a debate within France. General Pierre Gallois, often considered to be "authorized," labeled himself the foremost scourge of flexible response in France. In a series of virulent articles published in 1962 and 1963, he criticized the idea of centralizing nuclear decision making and the concept of antiforce strategy. Above all, he rejected the conventional rationale of flexible response by pushing to its extreme the argument that the new U.S. strategy was both the sign and the mode of its inevitable nuclear disengagement from Europe.[113] At the opposite end, Raymond Aron presented himself as a nuanced defender of flexible response. In publishing in book form (*Le Grand Débat* [1963]) the course on nuclear strategy that he had given at the Institut d'Etudes Politiques in 1962–1963, he thought, as he put it in the preface to the U.S. edition (1965), that "it was of primary importance that the policy makers and the public on either side of the Atlantic gain a greater understanding of the positions held on the other side."[114] Taking up again practically the same arguments as McNamara in Athens, he sharply criticized de Gaulle's nuclear ideas, deploring notably the refusal of the Nassau offer. Finally, between the two extreme positions in the French strategic debate, incarnated respectively by Gallois and Aron, other people such as General André Beaufre sought an intermediate stance.[115] Thus opened in 1962–1963, the French strategic debate would not quiet down for a long time as it closely followed the vicissitudes of flexible response.

De Gaulle remained essentially pragmatic. Aron, despite his fundamental disagreement, recognized this himself: the General was not doctrinal about deterrence, he proposed no theory or system for the French nuclear effort.[116] And de Gaulle confirmed this, not without a certain irony, in thanking Aron for having addressed his book to him: "Basically, everything . . . comes down to a single quarrel: yes or no, should France still be France? This was already the issue at the time of the Resistance. You know what I have chosen, but I know there is no rest for theologians."[117] Similarly, in thanking the same day General Beaufre for his *Introduction to Strategy*, de Gaulle recalled that "in this matter, the only practice that is worthwhile is by virtue of men and according to circumstances."[118] Such was truly the Gaullist philosophy of strategy, whether in debates among allies or in the elaboration of French doctrine. For de Gaulle, debates over nuclear strategy posed both political problems (the role of France, the role of NATO, the role of Europe, and so on) and military problems, that is, questions of means. All the rest belonged to abstract speculation. This would be confirmed by his attitude in the months and years to come.

Conventional Defense and Nuclear Threshold

From the U.S. viewpoint, making allied strategy evolve in the direction of flexible response meant above all strengthening NATO's capability for conventional defense in Central Europe. To do this, as McNamara had announced to the Atlantic Council in December 1962, one had to start by "closing the gap between NATO's military requirements and national force programs."[119] In fact, the force objectives announced by NATO in 1961 for the central front in the document MC 26/4 were still far from being attained.[120] Therefore, Washington wanted to obtain from the allies some firm commitments in this direction, starting in the first months of 1963, by means of a long-term plan for increasing the conventional power of allied forces. Washington's intention was thereby to achieve "a *de facto* modification of NATO strategic doctrine."[121]

In January 1963, the first steps were taken by the Alliance's secretary general, Dirk Stikker, encouraged by Washington. He proposed starting a process for defense planning with a time horizon of the end of the 1960s. His proposal was examined by the Atlantic Council during the spring ministerial session in Ottawa from May 22 to 24. According to Stikker, the goal of defense plans (NATO Force Planning Exercise) was to reconcile "military, technical and financial factors, leading to attainment of a balanced relationship between NATO strategy, military forces, and military budgets and plans." By strengthening "integrated planning within the NATO framework,"[122] integrated defense properly speaking would in time be strengthened. This was why such a proposal could not be calmly welcomed in Paris, where it was understood as no less a matter than modifying Alliance strategy, which the French categorically refused to envisage.[123] De Gaulle was opposed to "NATO's embarking on some sort of plan in the medium or long term." He instructed Couve de Murville not to associate France with the exercise and not to communicate to NATO any long-range data on French defense.[124] In fact, during a meeting of the Military Committee at the level of chiefs of staff on June 25, 1963, the French delegate expressed his country's disagreement. And on July 25, the permanent French representative attacked the exercise, pointing out that long-term defense planning presupposed prior agreement on strategy. But such an agreement did not exist.[125]

In the autumn of 1963, the allies nevertheless tried for a compromise. Acting on a proposal offered jointly by the French representative and the secretary general, they decided to create a new body, the Defense Planning Committee (DPC). In setting up the DPC, which was nothing other than the Atlantic Council deliberating defense plans, the allies thought they could satisfy France, whose minimum requirement was that these issues be approached as a priority on the political level. Under the DPC's direction, military authorities were to agree on a strategic concept and define force objectives accordingly.[126] But strategic differences remained and they crystallized over the development within the military committee and the Standing Group of document MC 100/1, which aimed to evaluate "the military situation and its impact on NATO in the prospect of 1970" so as to adapt the strategic concept of the Alliance defined in December 1956 in the document MC 14/2. In fact, the discussion of MC 100/1, voted upon in December 1961 and effectively launched in 1963, was blocked after October 1963 by the French.[127] De Gaulle thought that France "should not support" a document whose ideas were fundamentally different from those of France, in short, that the Americans should choose between modifying the project of MC 100/1 and trying to get the new strategic directives adopted at the highest political level in the Alliance, that is, by the Atlantic Council itself, at the risk of a head-on confrontation with France. For de Gaulle, "the question was serious enough for us to play straight."[128]

The document in question was opposed to French strategic ideas on two key points. The first was about the level of aggression beyond which NATO should have recourse to nuclear weapons, that is, the nuclear threshold. On this point, MC 100/1 insisted on the necessity of reducing dependence by NATO on nuclear weapons to counter "limited" aggression, this thanks to the growth in the efficacy and volume of conventional forces.[129] But France considered that MC 14/2, which should remain the reference document on strategic issues, precisely excluded any idea of a limited conventional war, even if it called for conventional response to "infiltrations, incursions or localized hostile actions"[130] — in short, to frontier incidents. The second point concerned the modes of possible recourse to atomic fire, especially whether to use mainly tactical or strategic strikes. MC 100/1 postulated that in case of limited aggression, escalation to strategic nuclear strikes should be avoided. This really meant rejecting the "trip wire" strategy that had been at the heart of the doctrine of massive retaliation since the second half of the 1950s.[131]

The French therefore saw in these tendencies "the index of too much hesitation over the recourse to nuclear weapons to defend Europe."[132] The United States intended not to use these weapons except in case Soviet aggression caused everything to crumble in the European theater, noted de Gaulle. Thus, there was an "essential difference of opinion over strategy between America and Europe," since U.S. policy aimed to strengthen conventional defenses through allies—in order to avoid a situation where an attack the United States considered "limited" in Europe might drag them into a "nuclear escalation" that would run the risk of Soviet reprisals on their own territory. While de Gaulle understood that there was a strategic logic to this in line with U.S. interests, he thought that European interests lay elsewhere. Europe could not be defended "without a complete nuclear deterrent" and inasmuch as it was impossible for it to increase indefinitely its conventional forces (which in any case could not attain Soviet troop levels), then "nuclear weapons should be used immediately for its defense."[133]

Two Ideas of Deterrence

Thus, strategic differences that were spotlighted in the autumn of 1963 mainly sprang from a disagreement over the nature of deterrence. The Europeans, explained Maurice Couve de Murville that fall, thought that in order to be effectively able to deter any kind of aggression, the West had to "make it clear" that it was prepared to respond "through nuclear weapons." Thus the Europeans conceived of nuclear weapons "primarily as a deterrent."[134] But with flexible response, the effect of deterrence would be "seriously hurt," since the USSR would see it as hesitation to use nuclear weapons. As a result, the problem was "much more political than military."[135] This was why the French insisted on keeping the strategy of an immediate nuclearization of conflict, one that NATO had adopted in 1956. Faced with this line of argument, Dean Rusk summed up the U.S. concept: In order to be in a position to deter, the strategy's credibility was "of the utmost importance," such that the maintenance of powerful and effective conventional forces was still the best way of preventing an attack.[136]

In Washington, France's discussion was seen largely as a pretext for contesting U.S. policy. But some were not insensitive to French arguments. Ambassador Thomas Finletter advised Washington not to present the rise in NATO's conventional power that was being demanded by the United States as serving "to re-fight World War II." Even if the reevaluation of the balance of forces in Central Europe might lead one to think that it would be possible to successfully wage a large-scale conventional fight, such a presentation, he argued, would only "raise serious questions about the future U.S. commitment" to the defense of Europe.[137] But Bohlen thought that de Gaulle was mainly trying to profit from the new presentation of U.S. strategy in order to "promulgate the theory that the U.S. could not be relied on to use nuclear weapons in Europe." He recommended avoiding such expressions as "pause" so as not to give ammunition to a policy that aimed to discredit the U.S. guarantee.[138]

France's strategic ideas were, on the other hand, well understood and even shared by the principal European allies. As the Council's ministerial session approached in December 1963, Paris's position on MC 100/1 and on the possible revision of MC 14/2 appeared relatively close to those of London and Bonn. Washington recognized that "the French, U.K. and German views on strategy are closer together than to the U.S. view."[139] Paris reached the same conclusion, that it could count on "some support or at least intermediate stances between the U.S. theses and ours"[140]—hence U.S. "uncertainty" before NATO's ministerial session.[141] De Gaulle, who had decided to clearly pose the question of Alliance strategy, refused any prior bilateral discussion with the Americans on this matter, over which he thought no agreement possible as long as there remained a "U.S. strategic monopoly." Authorizing conversations between "second order military people or bureaucrats on the subject of NATO's 'strategic ideas' could only lead to equivocations," he thought.[142]

Faced with French intransigence, Washington tried once more to avoid confrontation while attempting to end the deadlock. The Americans thought that "the last thing needed now is a debate on strategy" and that it was better for NATO to concentrate "on specific shortcomings of forces and the cost of fixing them up."[143] A discussion "in a public forum" of Alliance strategy was "totally useless and possibly dangerous," Bundy told Alphand, since "for years now, the question of knowing when, where and who would unleash an atomic attack had been the subject of numerous studies that concluded that it was impossible to answer this kind of question logically and that the final decision rested, for a period impossible to determine, in the hands of the United States."[144] At the same time, Washington wished to avoid isolating the French. Therefore, it had to avoid a fundamental debate, "work" the British and the Germans bilaterally, and try to make progress with the defense planning process. It also had to remain content to "secure French approval for moving ahead in the DPC without their participation,"[145] while trying to secure France's involvement in some aspect or other of the exercise, such as the examination of resources.[146] The U.S. line was clear by the end of 1963: ensuring the conventional reinforcement of NATO *de facto* without openly raising at the highest level the question of the Alliance's strategy, which meant making progress pragmatically on the process of integrated defense planning.

Flexible Response or Nuclear Escalation?

During 1964, disagreements between Paris and Washington continued, as France's nuclear military capacity became operational. In July, the first atomic bombers of the French deterrent force, the Mirage IVs, entered into service. In this context, de Gaulle made the contours of French nuclear strategy more precise. In a Defense Council meeting on March 7, he clearly reasserted the prime role of nuclear weapons and the necessity of having immediate recourse to them in case of attack from the East.[147] He rejected any idea of a pause or controlled escalation. For him, any Soviet attack in Europe was answerable by nuclear reprisals: this was the opposite of flexible response.

French opposition to the latter did not spring, though, from a rejection of the role of classic forces or tactical nuclear weapons, but rather from a fear of seeing the Americans retrench behind flexible response and tailor their engagement to their own interests, whereas the Europeans would have to defend their very existence.[148] As the army chief of staff made plain, it was not a question of renouncing all conventional defense, but of understanding that it was not a matter of preparing a classic "great war." For General Ailleret, a conflict in Europe would probably arise from a conventional war that escalated fatally into tactical and then strategic nuclear strikes. Thus, there was unity and continuity between nuclear and conventional weapons, and the critical point of the strategic debate was the "relationship" between conventional forces and nuclear forces, and not a choice between one or the other.[149] France was therefore not "totally" opposed to flexible response, but it rejected the premise of the possibility of an exclusively conventional defense of Europe. Thanks to the effect of surprise and the geostrategic advantage the Soviet Union possessed, it would be in a position to defeat any arrangement for classical defense along the Iron Curtain, which would be breached whatever its robustness. For France, the strategy of flexible response came down to establishing a static defense inherited from the "Maginot Line"; it was a strategy that undermined deterrence and could even be an invitation to aggression. Only a nuclear threat was effective protection against a Soviet offensive in Europe. And Ailleret concluded that it would be necessary in time, in the East as in the West, to reduce classic forces, since they were costly and scarcely useful.[150]

French opposition to flexible response in 1963–1964 was thus less related to operational strategy than to the Alliance's grand strategy. It was in these terms that de Gaulle several times posed the problem publicly at the end of 1964. For the General, there existed between the United States and the USSR "a sort of automatic balance of deterrence" that "really only covered themselves and not the other countries of the world," not even their respective allies, who were reduced to "having to accept strategic dependence . . . on whichever of the two giants does not threaten them."[151] It was precisely this geostrategic situation that flexible response reflected, hence the need for Europe to be in a position to fill in for the deficient nuclear guarantee of the United States—thanks in the first instance to the French atomic force.[152] The latter had a *de facto* European value, he pointed out to the president of the Bundestag, since "we are in Europe, whereas the Americans are not. If Germany were destroyed, France would be equally and reciprocally so. But Germany and France can perfectly well be destroyed without the United States being so."[153] It was above all in the name of Europe that de Gaulle rejected the logic of flexible response.

A Recognition of Discord

At the end of 1964, the differences between allies were more evident than ever. The Americans had to bow to the evidence: within the Alliance, views ranged across the whole strategic spectrum. At one extreme were the unconditional supporters of nuclear weapons, for whom a solely conventional defense was not viable and, at the other extreme, those who recommended a nonnuclear defense on a large scale and concluded that a tactical nuclear option could not be substituted for it.[154] The French view, which claimed to be faithful to NATO's official doctrine as adopted in 1956 but wanted to add even more insistence on strategic nuclear strikes than in MC 14/2, was close to the former approach. The British view recommended a capacity for conventional resistance for a few days, followed if necessary by "selective" use of nuclear weapons (to mark the link to a "general" use of nuclear weapons). The Germans were in favor of rapid recourse to low-yield tactical nuclear weapons as a substitute for a purely conventional defense, followed if necessary by massive nuclear strikes.[155] The American view obviously corresponded to the other approach. It consisted of promoting a strong conventional defense and rejected the possibility of substituting tactical nuclear weapons (TNWs) for conventional ones, while recognizing that it was preferable to keep a limited number of TNWs to reassure the Europeans.[156] Its premises remained unchanged, meaning that the balance of forces in Central Europe was not really so unfavorable to NATO, making it possible to envisage a solid classic defense, which by diminishing the risk of escalation to a general nuclear war offered hope of overcoming the capitulation versus annihilation dilemma, while minimizing, in the event of conflict, the collateral damage and military uncertainty that were inextricably linked to the use of nuclear weapons.[157]

The French side stuck to a position that was endlessly repeated in public and to NATO bodies throughout 1964, especially by Ailleret. But with no illusions: If they thought they had for a year succeeded, by defeating MC 100/1, in putting "a provisional end to the offensive" unleashed by the United States "to get new strategic ideas adopted by the Alliance," they knew very well that behind "the fiction of the validity of the 1956 directives," NATO military authorities were in the process of choosing flexible response.[158] The Americans, despite officially maintaining MC 14/2, in fact imposed "a defensive strategy in which nuclear weapons would only be used as a last resort, meaning probably too late for an important stake not to be already lost in Europe."[159] But the French knew that apart from denouncing it, they could do little against this modification to allied strategy, since, as de Gaulle reminded Rusk before the Council meeting, only the United States could ultimately decide on the timing and circumstances of using nuclear weapons.[160] He could not do much, he confided to Cyrus L. Sulzberger the following week, if not "look ahead to the future," in other words, prepare Europe for the disappearance of American nuclear protection.[161]

Indeed, the Americans did not intend to abandon their policy in favor of a NATO military posture that was both more effective and more flexible, or to give up their efforts to obtain from the allies a more equitable sharing of the "burden" of defense. On the contrary, "but without provoking a confrontation with the French," they intended to take advantage of the ministerial session of December 1964 to unveil to the allies an updated presentation of the U.S. approach to the Alliance's military and strategic problems. And to encourage the Europeans to accept a modification of strategy in due course, Washington considered it useful, in line with promises given in Athens in 1962 and in Ottawa in 1963, to "educate" them about the eventual effects of a nuclear war. In fact, Washington was less on the defensive with respect to Paris than a year previously. For despite French opposition to the exercise, the process of defense planning, the Pentagon thought, had begun to have results, if only because it had led allied ministers to ask the fundamental question concerning the adequacy of existing strategic directives (MC 14/2) to the current situation.[162] And in a concern to take the sting out of a U.S. policy that for more than three years had been hammering the need for a stronger conventional defense and a raised nuclear threshold, McNamara declared that "the present force structure is broadly adequate," and that "except for a few countries, large increases in defense budgets are not needed."[163] Washington played the card of strategic appeasement and so the ministerial session took place without any major upset. Nevertheless, by the end of 1964, while the dialogue between France and the United States on NATO strategy appeared less tense than a year before, nothing was solved. It was patent that in the strategic realm as in the political, the split within NATO was durable.

IN THE REAR OF THE FORWARD LINE: FRANCE AND INTEGRATED DEFENSE

In 1963 and 1964, de Gaulle pursued the withdrawal of France from integrated defense. Acting upon the allies' refusal to see the Alliance change and taking into account the desire of the Americans to impose unilaterally a new NATO strategy, he intended to manage military relations between France and NATO as a function of a radical restructuring of French forces and strategy upon which the country, freed from the Algerian burden and about to possess an operational nuclear weapon, was intending to proceed. Yet if major decisions were taken that modified France's role in the Central European theater during these two years, France's distancing itself from military integration did not signify, contrary to the general perception of the allies, less military solidarity.

From the Atlantic to the Iron Curtain

In June 1963, de Gaulle took a new decision to withdraw French integrated forces. This time it concerned naval units under the Atlantic command (ACLANT) and the Channel command (ACCHAN), specifically an aircraft carrier and twenty other ships that as of January 1, 1964, would pass under national command in peacetime as in wartime. This decision was the logical consequence of one taken in 1959 over the Mediterranean Fleet; since the end of the Algerian conflict, a majority of its ships had indeed been reassigned to the Atlantic theater, *ipso facto* returning to a status of being "earmarked" for assignment to NATO. This regrouping accomplished, Paris now proposed to apply the same regime of strictly national command to them as in the Mediterranean, so as to homogenize the status of the French fleet as a whole.[164] The decision sprang from a tardy awareness (and a fortuitous one: de Gaulle realized the considerable importance of the French fleet now under SACLANT after a visit by its commander to the Elysée) that the integration situation was being maintained in the Atlantic and the English Channel unlike in the Mediterranean.[165] For de Gaulle, it meant remedying an oversight by putting an end to the "bad farce" consisting of France declaring itself ready to place "almost our entire fleet" under NATO orders in wartime.[166]

But the decision also was part of a long-term strategy: After the Algerian conflict, which had mobilized the Mediterranean Fleet, and with the prospect (though still distant) of a submarine-based nuclear force, France was redesigning its navy to benefit the Atlantic and reasserting national control over it. Moreover, the decision was not neutral, politically speaking. Following up on 1959 decisions about the Mediterranean, the 1960 ones about air defense, and the 1962 ones about the two divisions repatriated from Algeria, it obviously aimed to reassert the overall direction of French policy. But like the 1959 decision (which gave way to a cooperation between France and NATO in the Mediterranean considered "excellent"[167] by the integrated commands and hence transferable to the Atlantic), the 1963 decision did not actually have any military impact on NATO, as the U.S. officers concerned themselves admitted.[168] French military authorities accordingly were authorized to make contact with allied commands to organize cooperation between French national forces and those of NATO in the Atlantic and in the Channel.[169] By 1964, two agreements for formal cooperation in naval affairs were concluded between France and NATO, one for the North Atlantic (the Barthélemy-Smith agreement), the other for the Channel (Barthélemy-Woods).[170] Of course, these agreements responded to the requirement clearly formulated by de Gaulle that there be "neither in the Mediterranean nor in the Atlantic or Channel any kind of subordination, nor any kind of membership, of any French command in any foreign command."[171]

After 1963, a more important change took place in Central Europe, the principal theater of NATO operations since it included German territory. This change confirmed a long-term tendency. At the beginning of the 1950s, the era when Germany was only a glacis, the allies planned to contain a Soviet attack along the Rhine. Then, with Germany's entry into NATO and the buildup of the Bundeswehr after 1955, it was a question of defending the Central European theater along a north-south line crossing the middle of the FRG. Finally, at the beginning of the 1960s, NATO began to consider implementing a strategy of "Forward Defense,"[172] so as to take account of the full operational capacity of the Bundeswehr, but also with the goal of reinforcing the Alliance's conventional defense, now a key U.S. priority. "We have to understand," Norstad argued, that "victory in the battle must be achieved along the Iron Curtain itself."[173] Hence a more advanced organization of NATO's defensive system, foreseeing a series of well-defined "layers" that would be assigned to different allied army corps stationed in the FRG, each charged with defending its advanced position along the inter-German or German-Czech border, with the whole thing under the operational command of CINCENT.[174]

Forward Defense was in principle effective starting on September 1, 1963.[175] But since the decision not to assign the two "NATO" divisions repatriated from Algeria, which had been announced in the fall of 1962, it was probable that France would have at best a minor role in the new forward arrangement.[176] At the end of 1963, Paris refused to take responsibility for a whole "layer" situated along the German-Czech border.[177] France's military role in Central Europe was thus situated in the rear of the forward defense that was being set in place. SHAPE's operational planning envisaged that in case of conflict, French forces in Germany (the Second Army Corps, composed of two divisions and assigned to the Central Europe command, itself held by a French general) would act in tandem with the Second German Army Corps. The whole would form an army under French command, but the French corps would be in the rear, less advanced and less exposed than the German corps, with the latter responsible for the German-Czech frontier.[178]

This choice confirmed the gradual distancing of France from NATO. A fully fledged participation in Forward Defense would have meant a major involvement in the increasingly integrated military organization that Washington was trying to promote. But the choice also reflected the reality of French means then available for the Central Europe theater, which, barely a year after the end of Algerian operations, were too limited to permit an appreciable French contribution to the new defense arrangement.[179] The logistics of French forces in Germany did not permit envisaging their engagement so far from their base (essentially the Rhineland-Palatinate and Baden-Wurtemberg) as the German-Czech border; and displacement further east of French garrison zones in Germany would have caused more than negligible difficulties.[180] But the position of quasi retreat in relation to integrated forward defense, as adopted by France after 1963, was also an extension of previous developments. Under the combined effect of displacement toward the east of the allied line of defense and the diminution of its military means in Central Europe, France had progressively come to occupy only a marginal position in NATO's forward line. The French air and land units still assigned to the integrated organization now constituted, it was increasingly clear, a reserve force for the Americans and especially for the Germans, more present in forward positions in the CENTAG (southern Germany) zone. This tendency was not totally condemned by the allies, even if many saw it as the sign of lessened French solidarity. For several years, certain military leaders, including U.S. ones, had even considered it desirable that NATO plans grant more importance to such a reserve role as strategically useful for an advanced defense that was more and more static, and a role for which the French forces appeared eminently designed. And when the German general Graf Kielmansegg, the new LANDCENT ("land" adjunct to the French CINCENT) assumed his functions in September 1963, at the same time as Forward Defense became effective, he perfectly accommodated the French position in the rear of it. For him, Forward Defense needed a designated reserve, and the French forces could fill this role.[181]

Toward a National Strategy

The shift of the French position toward the rear of the integrated defense, though, arose first and foremost from a national strategy that was being developed. De Gaulle himself had for several years considered that geography and strategy imposed such a role on France.[182] After 1963, he thought it was time to undertake the overhaul of the military. This was the main aim of an important Defense Council meeting he conducted in July 1963, during which conflict scenarios were examined and general troop restructuring, particularly land and air, was accordingly decided upon.[183]

These choices reflect first of all a well-defined idea of the role of conventional forces. France's fight within NATO bodies against the adoption of flexible response was translated into the reality of French military planning, which after Algeria tended to diminish the importance of classic defense. This option resulted from budgetary constraints due to the nuclear priority, but also from an idea of deterrence that rejected the raising of the nuclear threshold that would result from setting up a conventional defense in conformity with U.S. requirements, considered excessive by France.

The choice of a reserve position also responded to an equally well-defined idea of the role of the French battle corps in the Central European theater. De Gaulle as the author of *Vers l'armée de métier* (*The Army of the Future* [1934]) naturally had a mobile and offensive conception of the role of French air and land forces assigned to the defense of Europe and of France. No doubt he thought, along with Ailleret, that an essentially static and linear forward defense belonged to a new "Maginot Line," and that French forces ought not to be locked within this concept. For the General, these forces, which should possess French-made TNWs and should no longer depend on those of the United States (the decision to develop a short-range nuclear missile as well as a tactical nuclear bomb was taken in June 1963), would thus have the mission of a massive counteroffensive, with eventual recourse to TNWs.[184]

In March 1964, General de Gaulle officially ratified within the Defense Council this concept of air and land operations in Europe: French forces should be in a position to "conduct offensive action, all elements gathered, with all the support of classic and atomic firepower."[185] He foresaw that "if it is the East that attacks Europe, we will counter-attack immediately, straight away on Russian soil with atomic weapons, in Germany if we have the time, or in France."[186]

This conception of France's role in the defense of Europe was therefore now manifestly at odds with NATO's concept of defense: to increased integration it opposed the principle of national command; to a linear and static defense it opposed mobility starting from a rear position; and to a capability for prolonged conventional resistance it opposed the prospect of early use of tactical and strategic nuclear firepower.[187] But in de Gaulle's mind there was no question of overturning the principle of military solidarity between France and its allies. True, some people imputed to him the idea that it was now a priority to prepare to defend French territory exclusively by leaving to the allies the responsibility for defending Germany. They held that de Gaulle thought that a conflict in Europe, following from a Soviet attack, would unfold in two successive and perhaps disjointed battles: a battle for Germany, from which France could stand aside, and a battle for France, for which it must be ready as a priority.[188]

Yet nothing indicates that the idea of "two battles" was at the heart of the defense doctrine put in place by de Gaulle in 1963–1964. In his important speech at the École Militaire in February 1963, he indicated that "if the battle for Germany, the first battle of the war, turns out badly, whether it has been more or less atomic or not at all, it would be instantaneously followed by the destruction or invasion of France."[189] To be sure, this statement, if one overinterprets the text, could give credit to the idea of two battles, yet it is clear on the essential point: If the first battle were lost, the second *ipso facto* would be, too. In reality, de Gaulle knew perfectly well that the defense of France was to be played out in Germany and that the two countries, in the era of atomic missiles and bombs, belonged in face of the Soviet threat to one and the same strategic space.[190] And although the declaratory policy might sometimes lend itself to accentuating the national dimension of French defense, there was no question for him of decoupling the defense of the French Hexagon from that of Germany. Had he not stated, fifteen years previously, that the Red Army was only two stages of the Tour de France away? The defense policy put in place after 1963, despite the growing distance separating France from Atlantic military integration and the shift of its military role in Central Europe toward the rear of NATO's defense, remained solidly oriented to this prime geostrategic given fact for French defense.

A Coherent Military

De Gaulle's goal in adapting the French military to the new strategic circumstances was thus certainly not to challenge the military solidarity between France and its allies in Europe. On the contrary, he explained, France, "while combining its defense with that of its allies, intended to keep control over it and, if required, bring to the common effort something quite other than the soulless and impotent assistance of a people who were no longer responsible for themselves."[191] Such was the General's goal in getting underway with a profound transformation of the military that would break with its colonial past and finally adapt it to the nuclear era. But while there is no doubt that this effort should, from de Gaulle's perspective, contribute to the strengthening of the Alliance, it could not be accommodated by its current structures and organization, that is to say, integration with the NATO framework.

It was during the Defense Council of July 1963 that de Gaulle announced the major outline that would govern the reorganization of the French forces.[192] In place of the traditional vertical separation among the land army, the air force, and the navy, the forces would be articulated around their three major missions: forces of deterrence (and air defense), forces of maneuver (or intervention), and operational defense of territory.[193] It was naturally as a function of the first of these missions, the deterrence strategy, that the three groups of forces were organized; their coherence was guaranteed by the principle of national command—hence the creation of a single joint command for the French Metropolis-Mediterranean zone, to which all nonnuclear forces would report.

From the standpoint of relations between France and NATO, what mattered were the forces of maneuver. These had the mission of manifesting France's solidarity with its allies in Europe, while the forces of deterrence (in the beginning, the strategic air force) and the forces of operational defense of territory were to respond to a uniquely national logic. But for de Gaulle, the nuclear priority and the need to reassert the national character of the military did not mean that the air and land forces of maneuver were to be neglected.[194] It is true he proceeded to a considerable reduction in the size of the land army that, after the Algerian conflict, still had surplus troops. But these reductions were accompanied by a significant effort at modernization and reequipment, with the goal of adapting these forces to the Central European theater from which they had until then remained distanced. More compact but also more powerful and mobile, and equipped with TNWs, they would be able to play a greater role on the Continent, according to the strategy developed at the same time. During the Defense Council of July 1963, the General announced the model for a land battle corps for 1970 that would possess five armored divisions and a light division, with a full complement of men and equipment. As for the operational defense of the territory, it would have six brigades.[195]

At the end of 1964, the general orientation of de Gaulle's defense policy and Atlantic policy was clear. After the crisis of October and November over the MLF, there was no doubt that the relations between France and NATO would continue to be strained and that French participation in the integrated military organization would be reduced still more. Although Washington did not think that the General would go so far as to break with the Alliance, people were waiting for a "major confrontation" with de Gaulle over NATO and particularly over nuclear questions.[196] In fact, the General announced his intentions a little more precisely: Before 1969, the date planned for the renewal of the Washington Treaty, the Alliance, while evidently still necessary, ought to have established another organization. In any case, France would not accept maintaining "the kind of machinery that now exists" beyond that date.[197] On December 31, he predicted that 1965 would see France continue to break free of "all systems that under cover of the 'supranational' or else 'integration' or even 'Atlanticism,' in reality would keep us under the hegemony we know."[198]

NOTES

1. Alain Peyrefitte, *C'était de Gaulle*, vol. 1, "La France redevient la France," Paris de Fallois/Fayard, 1994, p. 351.
2. Press Conference of 14 January 1963, in *Major Addresses, Statements and Press Conferences of General Charles de Gaulle (MA)*, New York, French Embassy, n.d., p. 214.
3. Telegram #651–59, Washington to Paris, 28 January 1963, MAE, Amérique 1952–1963, États-Unis 9.4.1.
4. Telegram #2137–41, Washington to Paris, 9 April 1963, MAE, Amérique 1952–1963, États-Unis 9.4.1.
5. Telegram #3599–605, Washington to Paris, 14 June 1963, MAE, Amérique 1952–1963, États-Unis 9.4.1.
6. Telegram #6226–26, Washington to Paris, 30 October 1963, MAE, Amérique 1952–1963, États-Unis 9.4.1.
7. Telegram #5452–56, Washington to Paris, 25 September 1963, MAE, Amérique 1952–1963, États-Unis 9.4.1.
8. Maurice Couve de Murville, *Une Politique étrangère 1958–1969*, Paris, Plon, 1971, p. 106.
9. On this point, see Pierre Maillard, *De Gaulle et l'Allemagne. Le rêve inanchevé*, Paris, Plon, 1990, p. 211.
10. EMBTEL, Paris #3293, 16 February 1963, JFKL, NSF, France, box 72A.
11. Letter, Bohlen to Bundy, Paris, 2 March 1963, JBJL, NSF, Bundy Files, boxes 15–16.
12. Telegram #1190–1209, Bonn to Paris, MAE, Amérique 1952–1963, États-Unis 9.4.1.
13. Maillard, *De Gaulle et l'Allemagne*, p. 215.
14. Telegram #4653–4667, Bonn to Paris, 27 June 1963, MAE, Amérique 1952–1963, États-Unis 9.4.1.
15. See Maillard, op. cit. *De Gaulle et l'Allemagne*, p. 217.
16. Toast given by de Gaulle on the occasion of the dinner of honor given by the Chancellor, 4 July 1963, in Charles de Gaulle, *Lettres, notes et carnets (LNC) (janvier 1961–décembre 1963)*, Paris, Plon, 1986, pp. 347–49.
17. "De Gaulle Backed into a Corner?" CIA, Office of National Estimates, Memorandum #73-63, 10 October 1963, JFKL, NSF, France, box 72A.
18. David Klein, Memorandum to the President, "Couve de Murville's Meeting with the Secretary of State," 7 October 1963, JFKL, NSF, France, box 72A.

19. Memorandum of Conversation, Kennedy–Couve de Murville, 7 October 1963, JFKL, NSF, France, box 72A.

20. "De Gaulle Backed into a Corner?" CIA, 10 October 1963.

21. Couve de Murville, op. cit. *Une Politique étrangère*, p. 264.

22. Press Conference, 23 July 1964, in Charles de Gaulle, *Discours et Messages (DM)*, vol. 4, "Pour l'effort" (août 1962–décembre 1965), Paris, Plon, 1970, pp. 222 ff.

23. Telegram #3146–63, Washington to Paris, 26 May 1963, MAE, Amérique 1952–1963, États-Unis 9.4.1.

24. Airgram A2924, Paris (n.d., May 1963), "Notes on General de Gaulle," JFKL, NSF, France, box 72.

25. See pp. 129–30.

26. Memorandum of Conversation, Rusk–Couve de Murville, 8 October 1963, JFKL, NSF, France, box 72A; telegram #5672–5701, 7 October 1963, MAE, Pactes 1961–1970, box 409.

27. Department of State, Memorandum of Conversation, Kennedy–Couve de Murville, "Franco–U.S. Relations and Europe," 7 October 1963, JFKL, NSF, France, box 72A; see also telegram #5702–21, 7 October 1963, MAE, Pactes 1962–1970, box 409.

28. Telegram, Department of State to U.S. Embassy, Paris, 3 December 1963, "Summary of Conversation between President and De Gaulle, Evening of Nov. 25," LBJL, NSF, France, box 169, vol. 1, memos.

29. Cf. Bernard Ledwidge, *De Gaulle*, New York, St. Martin's Press, 1982, p. 316.

30. "Scope Paper," NATO Ministerial Meeting, Paris, 16–18 December 1963, Draft, 30 November 1963, LBJL, NSF, International Meetings and Travels File (IMTF), box 34, "NATO Defense Policy Conference," p. 1.

31. "Scope Paper," NATO Ministerial Meeting, The Hague, 11–14 May 1964, LBJL, NSF, IMTF, box 34.

32. EMBTEL, Brussels, #217, 11 May 1964, LBJL, NSF, IMTF, box 34.

33. EMBTEL, The Hague, #36, 13 May 1964, LBJL, NSF, IMTF, box 34.

34. "Scope Paper," NATO Ministerial Meeting, The Hague, 11–14 May 1964.

35. Press Conference of 23 July 1964, in *DM*, vol. 4, pp. 223 ff.

36. Memorandum, David Klein to McGeorge Bundy, "De Gaulle's Press Conference," 23 July 1964, LBJL, NSF, France, box 170.

37. "Scope Paper," NATO Ministerial Meeting, Paris, 15–17 December 1964, LBJL, NSF, IMTF, box 34.

38. "Scope Paper."

39. See chapter 2, p. 53, and chapter 3, pp. 91–94. On the MLF, see Colette Barbier, "La force multilatérale," *Relations Internationales*, no. 69, Spring 1992, pp. 3–18.

40. Note du Directeur politique, 6 December 1962, MAE, Pactes 1961–1970, box 267.

41. Quoted by Marc Trachtenberg, "L'ouverture des archives américaines," in Maurice Vaïsse, ed., *L'Europe et la crise de Cuba*, Paris, A. Colin, 1993, p. 33.

42. Cf. "The Coming Crisis on the MLF," A. Buchan, 23 June 1964, LBJL, NSF, Subject File, MTF, box 23.

43. Cf. Jane Stromseth, *The Origins of Flexible Response: NATO's Debate over Strategy in the 1960s,* London, Macmillan, 1988, pp. 75 ff.

44. Stromseth, *Origins of Flexible Response*, p. 83.

45. See chapter 2, p. 50 and also Maillard, *De Gaulle et l'Allemagne*, pp. 218–19.

46. Letter, Bohlen to Bundy, 2 March 1963.

47. EMBTEL, Secto 9, Paris, 8 April 1963, JFKL, NSF, France, box 72; see also CIA, "De Gaulle Backed into a Corner?" 10 October 1963.

48. EMBTEL, Paris, #3752, 19 March 1963; EMBTEL, Paris, #3864, 26 March 1963, and "Brief of President's talk with Couve de Murville on May 25," JFKL, NSF, France, box 72.

49. Telegram # 3146–63, 26 May 1963, see also "Brief of President's talk with Couve de Murville on May 25."

50. Telegram # 3146–63, see also "Brief of President's talk with Couve de Murville on May 25."

51. Memorandum of Conversation, Ball–Couve de Murville, 25 May 1963, JFKL, NSF, France, box 72.

52. See "The Non-Proliferation Treaty," Spurgeon A. Keeny, Jr., 24 December 1968, LBJL, NSF, NSC History, boxes 55–56.

53. Memorandum of Conversation, Rusk–Alphand, 28 February 1963, EMBTEL Paris #4697, 16 May 1963; briefing paper, "The President's Meeting with French Foreign Minister Couve de Murville," 25 May 1963, JFKL, NSF, France, box 72.

54. Couve de Murville–Rusk Meeting, 7 April 1963, MAE, Pactes 1961–1970, box 409.

55. EMBTEL Paris #475, 30 July 1963, JFKL, NSF, France, box 72.

56. EMBTEL Paris #475.

57. EMBTEL Paris #475; DEPTEL Paris #596, 31 July 1963, and EMBTEL Paris #515, 1 August 1963, JFKL, NSF, France, box 72.

58. Memorandum, Bundy to De Zulueta (aide to Macmillan), 25 September 1963, JFKL, NSF, France, box 72A.

59. "Continuing Elements of De Gaulle's Foreign Policy," Charles E. Bohlen, 7 August 1963, JFKL, NSF, France, box 72A.

60. Memorandum to the Secretary of State, Charles E. Bohlen, Paris, 13 December 1963; memorandum, Ball to President, 24 November 1963, LBJL, NSF, France, box 169.

61. "Department of State," vol. 1, ch. 3, "Europe," section D, "France" (n.d., end 1968), LBJL, Administrative Histories.

62. Speech given in Lyon, 28 September 1963, in de Gaulle, *DM*, vol. 4, pp. 134 ff.

63. Memorandum for McGeorge Bundy, "Bohlen's Think-Piece on De Gaulle," David Klein, 19 August 1963, JFKL, NSF, France, box 72A .

64. DEPTEL, Paris #1507, 25 September 1963, JFKL, NSF, France, box 72A.

65. "Outline for Congressional Committee Briefings," Foreign Relations (n.d., June 1964), LBJL, NSF, MLF, box 22, pp. 4–5; *Revue de défense nationale*, October 1963.

66. *Le Monde,* 25 September 1963; EMBTEL Paris #1441, 24 September 1963, JFKL, NSF, France, box 72A.

67. Pierre Messmer, "Notre politique militaire," *Revue de défense nationale*, May 1963, pp. 746–61.

68. EMBTEL Paris #1430, 24 September 1963, JFKL, NSF, France, box 72A.

69. "France Offers Nuclear Tie to Europe," State Department, Thomas L. Hughes, 24 September 1963, JFKL, NSF, France, box 72A.

70. Telegram #6983–93, Washington to Paris, 9 December 1963, MAE, Amérique 1952–1963, États-Unis 9.4.1.

71. Telegram #7786–88, Bonn to Paris, 19 October 1963, MAE, Amérique 1952–1963, États-Unis 9.4.1.

72. See CIA, "De Gaulle Backed into a Corner?"

73. EMBTEL, Bonn #2939, 18 February 1964, LBJL, NSF, France, box 169.

74. Cf. Eckart Conze, "La coopération franco-germano-italienne dans le domaine nucléaire dans les années 1957–1958," *Revue d'histoire diplomatique,* 104th year, nos. 1 & 2, 1990, pp. 115–32; EMBTEL Paris #518, 29 July 1964, EMBTEL, Bonn #380, 30 July 1964 and EMBTEL Paris #1132, 28 August 1963, LBJL, NSF, France, box 170.

75. EMBTEL Bonn #380, 30 July 1964, EMBTEL Bonn, #395, 31 July 1964, LBJL, NSF, France, box 170.

76. "The Coming Crisis on the MLF," A. Buchan, 23 June 1964.

77. "Outline for Congressional Committee Briefings," Foreign Relations (n.d., June 1964).

78. Telegram #7786–88, Bonn to Paris, 19 October 1963.

79. "Outline for Congressional Committee Briefings."

80. "United Kingdom," appendix to the previous document.

81. "Memorandum of Discussion of the MLF at the White House at 5:30 P.M. on Friday April 10, 1964," 11 April 1964; and "Briefing for the President. Notes on the MLF: Status and Needed Decisions," LBJL, NSF, MLF, box 22.

82. "Memorandum of Discussion of the MLF at the White House," LBJL, NSF, MLF, box 22.

83. Barbier, "La force multilatérale."

84. "The Coming Crisis on the MLF," A. Buchan.

85. Memorandum to the Secretary from William R. Tyler, "Highlights of my Discussion with Brosio, September 28, 1964," LBJL, NSF, MLF, box 22.

86. André Fontaine, "Histoire de la force multilatérale," *Le Monde*, 19 November 1964; EMBTEL Paris #3107, 19 November 1964, LBJL, NSF, MLF, box 24.

87. Statements to the parliamentary press on 5 November 1964, *Le Monde,* 7 November 1964; EMBTEL, Paris #2808, LBJL, NSF, MLF, box 24.

88. EMBTEL, Paris #2384, 23 October 1964, LBJL, NSF, MLF, box 24.

89. EMBTEL, Paris #2791, 6 November 1964, LBJL, NSF, MLF, box 24.

90. EMBTEL, Paris #2638, 31 October 1964, LBJL, NSF, MLF, box 24.

91. *Le Monde,* 18 November 1964.

92. EMBTEL, Paris 3105, 19 November 1964, LBJL, NSF, MLF, box 24.

93. Speech given in Strasbourg, 22 November 1964, in de Gaulle, *DM*, vol. 4 (1962–1965), pp. 312–16.

94. EMBTEL Paris #3505, 11 December 1964, LBJL, NSF, MLF, box 24; and Passeron, *De Gaulle parle*, p. 243.

95. Memorandum, David Klein to McGeorge Bundy, "The MLF," 10 October 1964, LBJL, NSF, MLF, box 23.

96. "Review of Possible Modifications in the MLF to Take Account of West European Problems Revealed during the MLF Negotiations," Memorandum to the Secretary, DOS, Director of Intelligence and Research, Thomas L. Hughes, 28 October 1964, LBJL, NSF, MLF, box 23.

97. "Soviet Opposition to Multilateral Force is Intensified," Memorandum to the Acting Secretary, DOS, Director of Intelligence and Research, Thomas L. Hughes, 16 December 1964, LBJL, NSF, MLF, box 23.

98. Memorandum to the Secretary from W.W. Rostow, "The Coming Crunch in European Security," 12 October 1964, LBJL, NSF, MLF, box 23.

99. "Review of Possible Modifications in the MLF."

100. Memorandum, David Klein to McGeorge Bundy, "The MLF," 10 October 1964.

101. "Considerations Involving Germany and France which are Pertinent to Modifications of the U.S. Position on MLF," D. E. Mark, 4 November 1964, LBJL, NSF, MLF, box 23.

102. DEPTEL, Paris #2765, 12 November 1964, for Bohlen and Finletter, LBJL, NSF, MLF, box 24.

103. EMBTEL Paris #3105, 19 November 1964, doc. cit.; EMBTEL Paris #3505, 11 December 1964; SECTO #26, Paris 2/3, 16 December 1964, LBJL, NSF, MLF, box 24.

104. EMBTEL, Paris SECTO 26, 1/3, 16 December 1964, LBJL, NSF, MLF, box 24.

105. EMBTEL, Paris SECTO 12, 3/3, 15 December 1964, LBJL, NSF, MLF, box 25.

106. *New York Herald Tribune,* 21 December 1964.

107. Telegram, Washington to Paris, 19 February 1965, #43, MAE, Pactes 1961–1970, box 409.

108. Press Conference of 14 January 1963, in de Gaulle, *DM*, vol. 4 (1962–1965), pp. 61 ff.

109. See the speech at the École Militaire, 15 February 1963, in de Gaulle, *DM*, vol. 4, pp. 84 ff.

110. See Stromseth, *Origins of Flexible Response*, pp. 50–51.

111. See chapter 3, p. 75 ff.

112. Telegram REPAN #7, 10 January 1963, MAE, Pactes 1961–1970, box 267.

113. See especially "Deux budgets militaires, une politique de sécurité," *Revue de défense nationale,* June 1962; "Les sophismes de M. McNamara et le départ du général Norstad," *Revue de défense nationale,* October 1962; and "La nouvelle politique extérieure des États-Unis et la sécurité de l'Europe," *Revue de défense nationale,* April 1963. If de Gaulle thought that Gallois "had very good ideas," the latter was by no means his advisor. See Peyrefitte, *C'était de Gaulle*, p. 422.

114. Raymond Aron, *The Great Debate,* trans. Ernst Pawel, New York, Doubleday, 1965, p. viii.

115. General André Beaufre, *Introduction à la Stratégie,* Paris, Armand Colin, 1963; *Dissuasion et stratégie*, Paris, Armand Colin, 1964.

116. Aron, *Great Debate*, p. 121.

117. Lettre à Raymond Aron, 9 December 1963, in de Gaulle, *LNC (1961–1963)*, p. 400.

118. Lettre au général d'Armée (CR) André Beaufre, 9 December 1963, in de Gaulle, *LNC (1961–1963)*, p. 401.

119. "The Troop Problem and Burden-Sharing" (n.d.), LBJL, Administrative Histories (AH), Dept. of State (DoS), vol. 1, ch. 3 (Europe). On long-term defense plans, see Stromseth, *Origins of Flexible Response*, pp. 51 ff.

120. The objectives of MC 26/4 were for 28 1/3 divisions aligned on the central front in 1966, of which 4 French divisions in principle were to be assigned to Central European command. Details are in Frédéric Bozo, *La France et l'OTAN. De la guerre froide au nouvel ordre européen,* Paris, Masson, in series "Travaux et recherches de l'IFRI," 1991, p. 49; and in Stromseth, *Origins of Flexible Response*, pp. 46–47.

121. "Scope Paper," NATO Ministerial Meeting, Paris, December 15–17, 1964, LBJL, NSF, International Meetings and Travels File (IMTF), box 34.

122. Chronology of Actions in NATO on NFP Exercise, LBJL, NSF, IMTF, box 34. "NATO's Defense Policy Conference," 2 December 1963.

123. Telegram REPAN #7, 10 January 1963; "Examen du concept stratégique de l'OTAN," EMA, 20 April 1963, MAE, Pactes 1961–1970, box 267.

124. Lettre à Maurice Couve de Murville au sujet de l'organisation (militaire) du Traité de l'Atlantique Nord, 7 June 1963, in de Gaulle, *LNC (1961–1963)*, p. 339.

125. Chronology of Action in NATO on NFP Exercise, pp. 2–3.

126. Chronology of Action in NATO on NFP Exercise, p. 4.

127. Chronology of Actions by Military Committee/Standing Group Concerning NATO Long Term and Force Planning (Background Paper), LBJL, NSF, IMTF, box 34; "NATO Defense Policy Conference," 2 December 1963; Chronology of Actions in NATO on NFP Exercise.

128. Note pour MM. Pompidou, Messmer, Couve de Murville et le général de division aérienne Gauthier, 25 October 1963, in de Gaulle, *LNC (1961–1963)*, p. 381.

129. Most Important Points of MC 100/1, Appendix 1, Chronology of Actions by Military Committee/Standing Group Concerning NATO Long Term and Force Planning (Background Paper), p. 2.

130. "Examen du concept stratégique de l'OTAN," 20 April 1963.

131. Most Important Points of MC 100/1, pp. 2–3.

132. "Nouveau projet d'analyse de la situation militaire quant à ses incidences sur l'OTAN jusqu'en 1970," MAE, Pactes 1961–1970, box 267.

133. Note pour MM. Pompidou and Couve de Murville au sujet des directives stratégiques de l'OTAN, 27 October 1963, in de Gaulle, *LNC (1961–1963)*, pp. 382–83.

134. Memorandum of Conversation, Rusk–Couve de Murville, 8 October 1963, JFKL, NSF, France, box 72A.

135. Minutes of a luncheon given on 30 November 1963 by Couve de Murville, 3 December 1963, MAE, Pactes 1961–1970, box 267.

136. Memorandum of Conversation, Rusk–Couve de Murville, 8 October 1963.

137. Paris, POLTO #713, 26 November 1963, LBJL, NSF, IMTF, box 34.

138. Memorandum to the Secretary of State, Charles E. Bohlen, Paris, 13 December 1963, LBJL, NSF, France, box 169, Vol. 1, Memos.

139. "NATO Force Planning" (n.d.), LBJL, NSF, IMTF, box 34, "NATO Defense Policy Conference," 2 December 1963.

140. Note du service des Pactes, 22 November 1963, MAE, Pactes 1961–1970, box 267.

141. "Scope Paper," NATO Ministerial Meeting, Paris, December 16–18, 1963, Draft; 30 November 1963, LBJL, NSF, IMTF, box 34.

142. Note à MM. Pompidou et Couve de Murville au sujet de conversations bilatérales sur l'Organisation du Traité de l'Atlantique Nord, 8 November 1963, in de Gaulle, *LNC (1961–1963)*, p. 389.

143. "NATO Forces Planning" (n.d.), LBJL, NSF, IMTF, box 34, "NATO Defense Policy Conference," 2 December 1963, p. 1.

144. Telegram #6983–93, Washington to Paris, 9 December 1963.

145. "NATO Force Planning," p. 2.

146. TOPOL, Paris #693, 26 November 1963, LBJL, NSF, IMTF, box 34, "NATO Defense Policy Conference," 2 December 1963.

147. Brouillon avant le Conseil de Défense du 7 mars 1964, in de Gaulle, *LNC (janvier 1964–juin 196)*, Paris, Plon, 1986, p. 44.

148. General François Valentin, "La dissuasion et les armements classiques," in *L'Aventure de la bombe*: *De Gaulle et la dissuasion nucléaire (1958–1969)*, Institut Charles de Gaulle, Paris, Plon, 1985.

149. Général d'Armée Ailleret: "Unité fondamentale des armements nucléaires et conventionnels," *Revue de Défense Nationale,* April 1964, pp. 565–77.

150. "Opinions sur la théorie stratégique de la *flexible response*," *Revue de Défense Nationale*, Aug./Sept. 1964, pp. 1823–40.

151. Press conference at the Elysée Palace, 23 July 1964, in de Gaulle, *DM*, vol. 4, pp. 222 ff.

152. Speech in Strasbourg, 22 November 1964, in de Gaulle, *DM*, vol. 4, pp. 312 ff.

153. Interview with M. Gerstenmeier, Bundestag president, end of October 1964, MAE, Pactes 1961–1970, box 261.

154. "The Role of Tactical Nuclear Forces in NATO Strategy," Defense Background Brief, NATO Ministerial Meeting, Paris December 1964, Top Secret, LBJL, NSF, Committee Files (CF), Committee on Nuclear Proliferation, box 4, p. 1.

155. "The Role of Tactical Nuclear Forces," pp. 1–2.

156. "The Role of Tactical Nuclear Forces," p. 3.

157. "The Role of Tactical Nuclear Forces."

158. Conseil de Défense, Annexe 1, "Concept stratégique," 30 October 1964, MAE, Pactes 1961–1970, box 267.

159. Lettre du ministre des Armées au Général, chef de la délégation française au Groupe Permanent, 6 November 1964, MAE, Pactes 1961–1970, box 267.

160. Telegram SEC to 12, Paris, 2/3, 15 December 1964, LBJL, NSF, MLF, box 24.

161. De Gaulle to Sulzberger, 21 December 1964, in Cyrus L. Sulzberger, *An Age of Mediocrity, Memoirs and Diaries 1963–1972,* New York, Macmillan, 1973, p. 143.

162. "Scope Paper," NATO Ministerial Meeting, Paris, 15–17 December 1964, p. 2.

163. "The Troop Problem and Burden Sharing."

164. Memorandum, "Analysis of French and Belgian Force Changes in NATO," 28 July 1963; EMBTEL Paris, Polto #1612, 19 June 1963; EMBTEL Paris, Polto #1634, 26 June 1963, JFKL, NSF, France, box 72A; *Revue de Défense Nationale,* July 1963; see also chapter 2, p. 45, for the difference between "assignment" and "earmarked for assignment."

165. EMBTEL, Paris #5243, 19 June 1963, JFKL, NSF, France, box 72A; interview.

166. Note au suject du commandement suprême allié en Atlantique, 21 March 1963, in de Gaulle, *LNC (1961–1963)*, p. 324.

167. EMBTEL Paris #808, 20 August 1963, JFKL, NSF, France, box 72A.

168. EMBTEL Paris #4842, 24 May 1973, JFKL, NSF, France, box 72A

169. EMBTEL Paris, Polto #1634, 26 June 1963.

170. French admiral Barthélemy was commander-in-chief (of French naval forces) in the Atlantic (CECLANT); American admiral Smith was SACLANT; and British admiral Woods was CINCHAN. A similar agreement would not occur for the Mediterranean until 1972. Cf. Diego A. Ruiz-Palmer, "France," in Jeffrey Simon, ed., *European Security Policy after the Revolutions of 1989*, Washington, National Defense University Press, 1991.

171. Note pour Georges Pompidou au suject du retrait de l'OTAN des forces navales françaises, 4 March 1964, in de Gaulle, *LNC (1964–1966)*, p. 43.

172. For what follows, see details in Bozo, *La France et l'OTAN*, pp. 87 ff.

173. "Exposé du général Norstad sur la stratégie de l'avant," 23 February 1962, MAE, Pactes 1961–1970, box 266.

174. Cf. Général de Maizière, *Rationalisation du déploiement des forces sur le front central,* Study for the Commission on Defense and Arms Questions, WEU Assembly, 2 April 1975, pp. 16 ff.; and Philip Karber, "In Defense of Forward Defense," *Armed Forces Journal,* May 1984.

175. Personal Interview.

176. EMBTEL Paris, Polto #539, 8 November 1962, JFKL, NSF, France, box 72A.

177. *New York Herald Tribune*, 28 April 1964.

178. Personal Interviews; details in Bozo, *La France et l'OTAN*, p. 88.

179. Personal Interview.

180. *New York Herald Tribune*, 28 April 1964; memorandum of Conversation, Rusk–Couve de Murville, 8 October 1963, JFKL, NSF, France, box 72A.

181. Personal Interviews.

182. See chapter 2, p. 50, and chapter 3, p. 83.

183. Brouillon de notes pour un Conseil de Défense, 11 July 1963, in de Gaulle, *LNC (1961–1963)*, pp. 61–63. See also Valentin, "La dissuasion et les armements classiques,"—the author has consulted the Defense Council minutes.

184. See Valentin, "La Dissuasion et les armements classiques," p. 191.

185. See Valentin, "La dissuasion et les armements classiques."

186. Brouillon avant le Conseil de Défense du 7 mars 1964, in de Gaulle, *LNC (1964–1966)*, p. 44.

187. "Examen du concept stratégique de l'OTAN," MAE, 20 April 1963.

188. Personal interview; see also Lothar Rühl, *La Politique militaire de la Véme République*, Paris, Presses de la F.N.S.P., 1976, pp. 184–85.

189. Speech given at the École Militaire, 15 February 1963, in de Gaulle, *DM*, vol. 4, pp. 84 ff.

190. See chapter 3, pp. 83-84.

191. Radio and television broadcast, 19 April, 1963, in de Gaulle, *DM*, vol. 4, pp. 92–96.

192. Valentin, "La dissuasion et les armements classiques," p. 190.

193. Jean Planchais, "l'Armée après l'Algérie," *Le Monde,* 22 June 1963; *La défense: la politique Française et ses réalisations,* Paris, La Documentation Française, 1966, pp. 10 ff.

194. Valentin, "La dissuasion et les armements classiques."

195. Brouillon avant le Conseil de Défense du 7 mars 1964, de Gaulle, *LNC (1961–1963)*, p. 351. Details in Lothar Rühl, *La Politique militaire.*

196. *The Guardian,* 23 November 1964.

197. De Gaulle to Sulzberger, 21 December 1964, in C. Sulzberger, *Age of Mediocrity,* p. 143.

198. Radio and television broadcast from the Elysée, 31 December 1964, in de Gaulle, *DM*, vol. 4, pp. 317–19.

Chapter Five

The End of Subordination
(1965–June 1966)

Previously springing from an essentially West-West problematic (relations between Europe and the United States), starting in 1965 France's policy toward the Atlantic Alliance more clearly pertained to an East-West problematic: pan-European relations. It was a Europe from the Atlantic to the Urals that de Gaulle now took as the scope of his actions. His policy of "détente, entente and cooperation" aimed at a radical transformation of the European system and called more urgently for a modification of relations between France and the Alliance. By putting an end in March 1966 to the kind of "subordination known as integration" within NATO, de Gaulle intended not only to restore France's "free hand" but also to break with the logic of the Cold War. But if the decision of March 1966 truly marked a turning point with considerable military, strategic, and political consequences, it did not thereby constitute a rupture between France and the Alliance. The withdrawal from the integrated military organization consecrated a redefinition, undertaken some years previously, of the relations between France and NATO, which de Gaulle was increasingly trying to incorporate into a scheme of global dimensions.

This activist, if not revisionist, international policy benefited from the domestic stability of the Fifth Republic. It especially relied on the recognized renewal of French power, whose economic foundation appeared particularly solid in the middle of the decade: the rate of growth (an average of 5.8 percent a year in the 1960s) placed the country far in front of the United Kingdom (2.9 percent), the United States (3.9 percent), and even Germany (4.9 percent); the French economy was opening to the outside world and increasing its competitiveness; and research and investment efforts, the modernization of the production apparatus, and technological development all were spectacular.[1] De Gaulle really now had the means to back up a policy of independence and transformation of the international order.

FROM ONE EUROPE TO ANOTHER

The European context in the first half of 1965 lent itself to this reorientation of French policy. The cornerstone of European construction, the Franco-German entente, sank to its low point. The Elysée Treaty remained a dead letter and the Germans were less inclined than ever to contest U.S. leadership in Europe. The main problems in the EEC (supranationality, British candidacy, external tariffs, agricultural policy) and in the Alliance (MLF, military integration) had for several months fed the discord between Paris and Bonn. The Americans at the start of 1965 could be reassured that France and Germany had European and Atlantic policies that were diametrically opposed, which in the near or medium-term future prevented a rapprochement between the two countries, and even more so, any resurgence of European political unification that would take place to the detriment of U.S. interests.[2]

In fact, European construction in the first half of 1965 entered an unprecedented political crisis. Once the autumn crisis over CAP was surmounted, the European Commission in Brussels tried to increase its prerogatives. For Walter Hallstein, the president of the commission, and his deputy, Sicco Mansholt, it was a matter of obtaining from France concessions regarding supranationality in exchange for concessions on its agricultural requirements, which for de Gaulle was a flagrant "provocation." The General refused to give in over the essential thing—accepting supranational power, even in embryo—and thought that his partners did not want to clarify the situation. On June 30, 1965, the French government thus decided to break off discussions by adopting "a position of total reserve": the policy of the empty chair.[3] It was the start of a crisis that would last more than six months. "Western Europe" was less a reality than ever.

Yalta, Twenty Years Later

The priority for de Gaulle was now pan-European. For several months he had been mentioning Europe "from the Atlantic to the Urals" and announcing a slackening of the Soviet bloc "monolith," and he was now trying to give concrete content to these phrases. The press conference of February 4, 1965, held twenty years to the day after the opening of the Yalta Conference, provided the occasion. His geopolitical postulate was simple: "The German problem is the European problem *par excellence*," but it remained unsolved because Germany was still divided, with the West having failed in a strategy that since the end of the early 1950s aimed to make "Moscow pull back" and to "give Germany back its unity" by "powerfully strengthening NATO."[4] The policy of "roll back," explained de Gaulle, could only result in a general conflict for which no one in the West was prepared. As for the Soviets, they could not hope to impose their system on the whole of Germany. In short, the Cold War's system could not provide a definitive answer to the German and European problem, and only an overcoming of the logic of blocs could free Germany and Europe from the impasse of division. Such a process, to be sure, could not be developed except over a long period, and under certain conditions: the effective slackening of the Soviet domination of Eastern Europe; the definitive renunciation by Germany of nuclear weapons and its acceptance of its current frontiers; and the political and military organization of the Europe of the Six. But it was time now "to get underway and choose" this framework for a settlement of the German question: It was up to the countries most interested in the fate of Germany, that is to say the European countries, to get it started and then guarantee it.[5]

It was thus, in outline, a German and a European settlement that de Gaulle was sketching: "Such is the only way that can lead to a rebirth, the only link that can maintain Europe in a state of equilibrium, peace, and cooperation from one end to the other of the territory that Nature gave it."[6] But if the stated, long term ambition was to get beyond Yalta, the General was also trying, in the short term, to take the initiative in East-West relations, because a Soviet–U.S. détente was underway that might leave Europe and France in a secondary role, or even witness it being forged to their detriment. He hoped, at the same time, to augment the European role of France from the standpoint of Bonn and other Europeans by outlining what in time might be a solution to the German question. Yet the General thus opened the most ambitious phase of his strategy: according to Stanley Hoffmann, he was trying "on his own," to "realize a prophecy."[7] In 1965, the European system indeed appeared frozen in its Cold War logic, even though that logic was now more pacific: for in Washington, as in Bonn and Moscow, the status quo, despite the rhetoric, seemed long-lasting and even desirable to the extent that it guaranteed stability.

Hence the reaction of the main interested parties to de Gaulle's press conference. In Washington, the "European" approach to the German problem he outlined was interpreted as aimed at nothing less than excluding the United States from an eventual pan-European settlement. Hadn't he tried in 1962 to keep the United States out of the political construction of Western Europe? This was obviously an unacceptable prospect, if only because the United States was one of the four guarantors of Germany's status. Couve de Murville, passing through Washington at the end of February, had to tell Rusk that France totally recognized the involvement of the United States in any European settlement of the German question.[8] De Gaulle himself repeated this to Manlio Brosio, stating that such a settlement would only be possible in the event of a profound change in the regimes of Eastern Europe and the Soviet Union.[9] The reactions were still more virulent in West Germany, since de Gaulle's statement appeared to question the official doctrine that reunification could only result from Western firmness and the pure and simple application of the principle of self-determination. This ruled out any recognition, even provisional, of the reality of the division of Germany, and any "*droit de regard*" by European countries other than the four guarantor powers about the ways and means of reunification.[10] Hence the attitude of

Schröder, who was very critical of the idea of Europeanizing the German question, which he chose to see, like a large portion of the German press, as a means of excluding the United States.[11]

Between the Superpowers

In the weeks that followed, de Gaulle made his position more precise. It indeed differed from that of the FRG and the United States on two important points: First, he did not flinch from saying that the solution to the German problem would not take place for a long time, perhaps a generation, whereas West German doctrine maintained the possibility of immediate reunification. Second, he foresaw (he had said so since 1959) that the prerequisite was an agreement between Germany and its neighbors over its borders (whereas Bonn officially refused to recognize the Oder-Neisse Line) and also over its weapons, with nuclear ones remaining prohibited.[12]

But essentially, it was not a matter, as the General repeated again to Bohlen in early May 1965, of envisaging a European settlement that excluded the United States, but on the contrary, of enabling such a settlement of the German question to flow from the evolution of East-West relations in Europe.[13] And it was even less a matter of France wanting to come to an understanding with the USSR behind Germany's back. Though Paris and Moscow shared the same viewpoint on the issue of borders and the nuclear status of Germany, and though de Gaulle's "European" approach did not seem too removed from the Soviet idea of a pan-European conference on security, there was no question for the General of accepting, as Moscow wished, the *fait accompli* of the division, meaning recognizing the GDR.[14] De Gaulle made it a point to show himself clearly in favor of German unification. And if the Bonn government distrusted what it interpreted as a return to a Franco-Russian policy of balancing Germany, the former chancellor Adenauer, for his part, had total confidence in the General. De Gaulle, he told Henry Kissinger in June 1965, knew that Germany's destiny and that of France were inextricably linked, and so he would not sell German interests short.[15]

It remains true, however, that de Gaulle situated his policy of détente in a balancing game between the United States and the USSR. In the first months of 1965, he loudly reacted against U.S. hegemony. During the February 4 press conference, his virulent contestation of the U.S. dollar as the reserve currency was resented in the United States as a veritable "assault on the dollar" and as a new attempt to injure "the prestige and influence of the United States in the world." Then in May, his criticism of the U.S. intervention in the Dominican Republic (in the wake of a tour of Latin America in the fall of 1964 during which he had tried to reintroduce French influence into the "backyard" of the United States) fed the feeling across the Atlantic that the General "was systematically taking a position counter to American interests."[16] But it was foremost the problem of Vietnam that poisoned relations between France and the United States. For months, de Gaulle had been warning the Americans against the logic of military intervention on which they were embarking. Since February 1965, there had been a definite escalation and now the United States was bombing North Vietnam. So de Gaulle began a no-holds-barred condemnation of American involvement; as a result, a growing proportion of Americans now perceived his policy as essentially anti-American.

This was all the more so because the first months of 1965 were marked by an overture to the East, where the General judged that, once the parenthesis of Khrushchev's "adventurism" was closed, France should put itself in the forefront. In March an agreement about SECAM, the French color television system, was signed and in April the Soviet foreign affairs minister Andrei Gromyko came to visit. Although there was no political agreement between Paris and Moscow, the French insisted there was a real desire for rapprochement, as they told the Americans.[17] In the spring of 1965, French policy took a decisive turn. To be sure, one could not speak of a search for a "third way," for de Gaulle was trying to question power blocs; yet he was contesting the established order based on the balance between the superpowers. France, he said, having "been able to resist the sirens of abandonment and having chosen independence," intended, without denying "American friendship," to reestablish on the Old Continent an "equilibrium founded on agreement and cooperation," and beyond Europe, to sustain the aspirations of other peoples to national liberation. He acknowledged that if all this "seems sometimes to inconvenience a nation that might think itself, by virtue of its power, invested with supreme and universal responsibility," it nevertheless remained true that France, "a nation with a free hand," certainly intended—by upsetting the world game of "two hegemonies"—to make "the liberty, equality, and fraternity of peoples" the foundation of "another order."[18] Not for a century and a half had France pretended to stand for universality to this degree.

NATO as a Bloc

For de Gaulle, getting beyond Yalta first of all meant breaking with the logic of blocs within the Atlantic Alliance and consequently modifying France's situation in relation to NATO, all the way to its logical conclusion. This perspective did not go unnoticed by Bohlen, for whom the General was aiming at the pure and simple suppression of the integrated organization, of SHAPE, the command structure, troop assignments, and infrastructures—"in short, any aspect of NATO which contained elements of integration."[19] De Gaulle, he thought, considered that a diminution in the Soviet threat to Europe was probable and thus he envisaged an alliance relying on cooperation among national general staffs in peacetime. He intended to keep French participation to a strict minimum, before proceeding to a more radical modification of relations between France and NATO. But this would not happen before 1969, when the French nuclear force would have attained a respectable level and when, moreover, the question of renewing the Washington Treaty would be raised, at least theoretically.[20]

Bohlen was correct, as de Gaulle confirmed to Alphand in early January 1965. Between that moment and 1969, France would detach itself from "NATO," even if the Alliance should continue. Integration would be replaced by cooperation among national forces, including nuclear, and neither commands and troops, nor foreign means of communication "that we do not control"[21] would remain in France. Brosio took from a visit to the Elysée some weeks later the idea that the General wanted to establish an alliance "of a classic type," which would not prevent the United States from maintaining troops in Germany, or U.S. facilities in France. The secretary general even "hoped that NATO had several years without tragedy in store," although he was aware that he should "concern himself with the future" of the integrated organization, which he acknowledged should be effectively adapted.[22]

At the start of 1965, things appeared clear in outline, but de Gaulle still wanted to maintain some uncertainty about his plans. Thus at the end of February, he examined the possibility of a "bilateral alliance treaty between France and the U.S." that would succeed NATO—a project that seemed to go beyond his previously stated position. Although the project did not necessarily postulate that the Washington Treaty was null and void, it did question not only NATO but, at least partially, the multilateral character of the Alliance properly speaking.[23] By all accounts, de Gaulle in the spring of 1965 was impatient and seemed to want to hurry things along. The ambitious East-West prospect that he now defended could not be accommodated within the NATO status quo. Learning at the end of April about a plan to renovate SHAPE installations in Rocquencourt, he ordered his prime minister to put a stop to the operation, judging "that such an installation would be totally contradictory with the idea that we have of NATO."[24] This signal did not go unnoticed in Alliance circles.

Contradictory Signals

During the month of May 1965, de Gaulle went farther. Receiving Bohlen early in the month, he confirmed to him that he still thought an alliance among France, the United States, Great Britain, and Germany was indispensable, but not necessarily in the current form of the Atlantic Pact, that is to say, an alliance among fifteen countries. Between then and 1969, integration should cease and foreign forces in France should pass under exclusively French command; and Bohlen remarked that he heard de Gaulle mention "flatly" for the first time the possibility of foreign forces leaving.[25] The General confided several days later to Alphand no less squarely that "NATO will disappear as far as we are concerned in 1969." The decision would be announced at the start of 1966. The Atlantic Pact, he continued, to the great surprise of his ambassador, would also disappear and would be replaced, "if our partners so wish, with bilateral agreements."[26]

All this, however, was just a trial balloon. On May 19, Couve de Murville reassured Alphand that the Atlantic Pact would indeed be maintained, and in 1966 it would be a matter of negotiating a restructuring of NATO alone.[27] The following month, the minister confirmed to Sulzberger that France wanted to keep the Alliance and its current functioning, including the Atlantic Council and that there was no question of negotiating bilateral treaties. Only a reform of the organization was envisaged, for which Paris, moreover, had no plans at the moment.[28] The General himself confirmed this to Sulzberger and then to Alphand: The Alliance could continue in the form of the 1949 treaty, at least if the United States accepted it in the absence of integration; the bilateral arrangements mentioned previously would concern only military structures.[29]

In the spring of 1965 de Gaulle did not seriously plan to challenge the Alliance properly speaking. Although during May the Service des Pactes produced a series of notes bearing on the Washington Treaty and the conditions for its eventual revision,[30] and although the secrétariat général de la défense nationale made a "review of NATO's civil and military bodies in France,"[31] it was more a matter of studying to what extent a reform of NATO implied a modification of the treaty, rather than planning a repudiation of the latter.[32] But the General, at a time of sharp tension between France and the United States, particularly over Vietnam, was content to entertain a certain ambiguity, fed by his distinction between the Alliance and NATO, which was often badly understood in Washington. Paul-Henri Spaak was not wrong in seeing in his statements a way of raising "the worst fears," designed to produce in future "a sigh of relief" among those who had taken him at his word.[33]

The Americans nevertheless had a conviction that de Gaulle, while not intending to quit the Alliance, was planning to withdraw France from integration and oblige NATO to get out of France in 1966, right after his likely reelection. Thus Bohlen advised Washington to proceed with studies of the relocation of U.S. forces stationed in France and of the military arrangements to be concluded in case of forced departure.[34] The problem from the American standpoint was delicate, since only de Gaulle was master of the time-scale. This presented a dilemma: Should the Americans take "pre-emptive" steps to reassume the initiative, or rather let the General "nibble" at the U.S. position, "possibly leading eventually to larger bites"? The first option, which might take the form of a unilateral U.S. decision on withdrawal, offered the advantage for the United States of emphasizing its disapproval of de Gaulle's policy; but several months before the French presidential elections, this could rebound against Washington, especially if "Gaullist propaganda" made use of it. As for the second option, it obviously risked ending in a French *fait accompli* that would reduce, if not nullify, the U.S. margin of maneuver.[35]

Finally, the most reasonable option from the U.S. standpoint seemed to be "keeping readiness" for the end of 1965, content to dot the "i's" after the election by firmly reasserting its attachment to the current functioning of the Alliance.[36] Six months into 1965, reflection on ways of dealing with the possibility of a French decision to break with NATO was thus well underway in the United

States. At the end of June, George Ball decided to have talks soon in Paris with the other allies about the Alliance's future. These consultations, insisted Bohlen, should be very discreet, so as to avoid the French being informed about them.[37] In any event, the Americans were less ready than ever to envisage a reform of NATO along French lines. At this stage, one could say that the idea of NATO without France was beginning to take shape.

Strategic Toughening

In the first months of 1965, the nuclear and strategic issue was not immune from the Gaullist hard line. The General now insisted less on the need for palliating the inevitable erosion of U.S. deterrence against the Soviet threat than on the guarantee of independence conferred by atomic weapons in relation to any potential aggressor.[38] Under the combined effect of the effective entry into service of its own deterrent forces and the new political orientation de Gaulle had adopted, French strategic discourse was becoming systematized. A body created in 1964 by Pierre Messmer within the Ministry of Defense to participate in the planning of arms policy, the Centre de Prospective et d'Evaluation (CPE), after 1965 became interested in nuclear strategy problems, under the influence of Colonel Lucien Poirier. France, he thought, "should be aware of what the singularity of its position implied" and define a national strategy appropriate to a medium nuclear power. In June 1965, the CPE sent the defense minister an initial study titled "Missions and Tasks of the Armed Forces for the Prospective Future." Messmer gave it to the Elysée and de Gaulle expressed his approval of the document, at least in its thrust. This document would be followed in March 1966 by a more elaborate study, titled "Logical Study of a Strategic Model Conceivable for France."[39]

The work of the CPE was a theoretical application of the general orientation established by de Gaulle. It stressed the "invariables" of French deterrent strategy, in the forefront of which was decision-making autonomy. But the influence of the CPE was limited by two factors: the attitude of the military staffs, who thought that it was up to them to define the concept of deterrence; and the pragmatism of General de Gaulle, little inclined to strategic theorizing and no doubt perplexed by the idea of "virtual" use of deterrent forces, which was at the core of Poirier's and the CPE's thinking.[40] But they certainly contributed to the radicalization of the official presentation of French strategy, which from 1965 on increasingly stressed the massive use of strategic nuclear weapons and the opportunity to confine classic forces to the "role of covering, exploiting, and concluding nuclear actions"[41] (knowing that it was only in November 1966 that a firm decision would be taken to build a national tactical nuclear weapon[42]).

This amounted to a patent incompatibility between French and American strategic discourses. While in December 1964 the possibility of coordination among American, British, and French nuclear forces was still mentioned, there was now no question of it. Bohlen thought that the French would not accept the prospect of a strategic rapprochement with the U.S. that was incompatible with the proclaimed necessity of nuclear independence but also with the overture to the East wanted by de Gaulle.[43] In the spring of 1965, the disagreements between France and the United States grew sharper. The French position remained unchanged: Flexible response rested on the idea that it was possible to confront with conventional forces "limited enemy action in Europe"; but given the lack of depth to the European theater, even a "limited" action would soon lead to losses of territory considered prime by the Europeans; moreover, the document MC 14/2, which remained "the only strategic concept accepted by the Alliance and which there was no question of challenging," precisely ruled out any idea of limited conflict.[44] Moreover, the French placed the nuclear threshold very low, since they considered that a Soviet attack superior in volume to a brigade or a division would amount to "characterized aggression" and would therefore be answerable by a nuclear response.[45]

In fact, de Gaulle held to an intransigent line. As the Council's spring ministerial session approached, to be held in Paris from May 31 to June 2, 1965, he instructed Messmer, in case of a challenge to NATO's current strategic plans, to take note of the fact that "NATO in its current state no longer responds to its objective which is to assure the defense of Europe." A modification of NATO's strategy in the direction of flexible response could lead France to reconsider its participation in the organization.[46] This instruction was even leaked to the principal allies, as if to demonstrate Paris's firmness on the strategic issue.[47] At the same time, the French announced that they were refusing to participate in the "Fallex 66" exercise, for which NATO's military authorities had begun planning the scenario, since this project had not taken account of the observations made by the French during the preceding exercise "Fallex 64" and therefore reflected a "conventional strategy sprinkled with the selective use of nuclear arms." Fallex 66 would thus become the vehicle of a "debatable exploitation" tending to prove that flexible response might be applied usefully in the defense of Europe.[48] To be sure, Brosio tried to get Messmer to agree that France would reconsider its decision not to participate. But the defense minister gave a blunt refusal: the exercise was in total contradiction with French doctrine and, for that matter, with NATO's.[49]

McNamara's Offer

The 1965 spring ministerial session would nevertheless mark a turning point in the evolution of the Alliance's nuclear problems. Some in Paris had for several weeks thought they were observing "a noticeable change" in U.S. discourse, even foreseeing "abandonment of anti-force strategies and especially abandonment of the concept of a pause."[50] In fact, McNamara sounded a new note. Though he reiterated his usual argument (the nature of the threat had changed and justified a sustained conventional effort), he was quick to add that the United States "strongly supports the view that if it appears that forward defense by conventional means cannot protect the integrity of NATO territory, the Alliance will not hesitate to use battlefield or tactical nuclear weapons." What was needed was both expanded conventional forces and powerful nuclear forces. The number of U.S. nuclear warheads in Europe had been steadily increasing, he observed, and this simple fact ought to silence those (he was of course targeting the French) who were spreading the rumor that "the United States is planning to de-nuclearize Europe."[51]

These statements testify to the fact that U.S. policy, whose objective was still to raise the nuclear threshold, had to deal not only with the uneasiness of Europeans, but also with military and budgetary realities. As it was now admitted in Washington, these made it difficult to put an end to the "nuclear dependency" of NATO.[52] The aim was clear: By giving a less radical formulation to flexible response, the Americans were trying to reestablish a strategic consensus within NATO by taking as much account as possible of European reservations, so as to isolate France. These reservations (aside from those of France) indeed happened to be less strong than in 1962, when Paris spoke up for European strategic interests in face of the new U.S. approach. Yet it was also and at the same time a matter of preparing the ground for an important U.S. initiative regarding nuclear consultation. This subject was not new: since 1961, McNamara had mentioned the need for closer nuclear consultation within NATO; in May 1962 the Athens guidelines had introduced conditional procedures for consultation before recourse to nuclear arms; finally, in May 1963 it had been decided to establish a deputy SACEUR for nuclear affairs, to be reserved for a non-American.[53] But McNamara wanted to go further. He proposed the creation of a select committee of "four or five ministers of defense" that would be responsible for studying the possibility of increased allied participation in nuclear (including strategic) planning and the improvement of prenuclear communication and consultation procedures.[54]

Although McNamara asserted that his proposal was complementary to it, it was clear that it was a substitute for the MLF, whose failure by then was obvious though not official.[55] In fact, this move ratified the victory of those like McNamara who had thought for several years that the Alliance's nuclear problems should be solved by consultation rather than by a hypothetical sharing of decision making on the type of the MLF.[56] In effect, the "software" advocates had defeated the "hardware" proponents. But the McNamara proposal also wanted to respond to French strategic dissidence: By rallying the allies to an improved consultative process for which there was a strongly felt need, the Americans hoped to solder NATO together, even without France, around their own nuclear concepts.

The day after McNamara's speech, Messmer took note of the proposal for a select nuclear committee. He indicated that it would be closely examined by the French government, "such a study perhaps leading to better understanding in the realm of nuclear cooperation."[57] Nevertheless, most observers thought that the French response would be negative. The U.S. initiative responded in a certain manner to the demand expressed by de Gaulle in 1958 to establish systematic strategic consultation among Western powers. But it was much too late: France was embarked on a political and strategic path that scarcely left any room for such arrangements; besides, Paris did not wish for Germany or Italy to be associated with such a structure, for the same reasons as with the MLF; and finally, the U.S. proposal appeared too much as a counterblast to French policy, if not a move to isolate Paris in the strategic debate within the Alliance.[58]

In the days that followed the Council meeting, uncertainty reigned on the fate of the McNamara proposal. While the British were enthusiastic, the Germans, who were interested in increasing their influence on nuclear issues, were still reserved about an initiative that appeared to confirm the definitive abandonment of the MLF. As for other countries, starting with Italy, they feared not being members of the committee.[59] Thus much would depend on France's attitude, since it could block the process at the level of the Council; in which case, suggested Brosio, it would be necessary to pursue it informally. In any case, the problem arose of the composition of the committee; it would be difficult to refuse participation to those who wanted to sit on it, as Canada was already implying.[60]

During the month of June, the French position became more precise. Pierre de Leusse, the representative on the Council, explained to Brosio and his colleagues the reasons for French reticence, principally the fact that nuclear planning was a political matter that went beyond the scope of defense ministers. Thomas Finletter, the U.S. representative, thought this was a specious argument; for him the select committee would only be responsible for making proposals that would then be taken up by foreign ministers.[61] Then what use, replied the French, were procedures for nuclear planning and consultation in the absence of a consensus on strategy itself?[62] In fact, from the French standpoint the problem was essentially political: the U.S. proposal reinforced a whole conception of NATO with which France now disagreed quasi-systematically. It remained to be seen to what extent, while abstaining from participating in it, Paris would try or not try to make the McNamara committee fail.[63]

THE WAIT

During the second half of 1965, de Gaulle's policies appeared less active, or at least less demonstrative. The crisis of the empty chair, not always understood by the French electorate, no doubt contributed, as the presidential election of December 1965 approached, to a moderation in the expression of an Atlantic policy that remained essentially uncompromising. But the process of disengagement continued, and in parallel, the Americans intensified political and military preparations to cope with the French withdrawal.

"The Most Drastic Action"

With the summer of 1965, the overt preoccupation of the Americans became to prepare NATO for such a possibility. As he had decided the preceding month, Ball held a series of bilateral talks in Paris on July 12 and 13 about the future of the Alliance with Brosio and British, German, Dutch, Italian, and Belgian officials. The purpose was to show that the United States was taking care to consult its faithful allies before announcing a final policy.[64] But in fact the general outline of this policy had already been determined, and consultation consisted instead, as often is the case, of informing the allies. It was clear, explained Ball, that France was sooner or later going to take new measures that might weaken NATO. But the United States had no interest in "old-fashioned bilateral alliances" that, without an integrated military structure, did not mean anything. The main message that Ball wanted to give was that NATO could perfectly well remain effective despite a possible French withdrawal. The United States had undertaken technical studies along these lines, which showed that the displacement of installations currently in France could be compensated by new arrangements with the United Kingdom, the Netherlands, Belgium, and Germany. Ball, conscious that the European allies dreaded a showdown with France, insisted that Washington wished as much as possible to avoid a French withdrawal. But the French must understand that in a climate of uncertainty, their allies were really obliged to consider possible options.[65]

Ball returned to Washington with a feeling that the allies, while wanting to avoid a confrontation with Paris, wished to prepare to cope with a hypothetical French withdrawal—in short that they were following the U.S. line.[66] During the summer, U.S. preparations steamed ahead. In August, the White House issued a directive (NSAM #36) inviting the State Department, the Pentagon, the Central Intelligence Agency, and the U.S. Information Agency, as well as the Atomic Energy Commission, to undertake the necessary studies with a view to the decisions the United States might have to take in such an eventuality. These studies would be supervised by the secretary of state and lead to a report that would be submitted by September 1.[67]

Meetings held during the summer proceeded to exhaustive examination of the problem. A wide range of options was envisaged, including establishing formal French command over U.S. forces, maintaining the option of operational integration of the French Forces in Germany (FFA), and so on. With the State Department represented by George Ball, the Pentagon by Cyrus Vance, and the Chiefs of Staff by General Earl Wheeler, all agreed on the main objective: to assure NATO that it would function no matter what happened, but not on the political approach to take. The State Department was more in favor of a hard line (explaining to de Gaulle that he could not have the advantages of NATO without the disadvantages) than were either the Pentagon or the Chiefs of Staff, which were both more pragmatic.[68]

Apart from this internal split, the U.S. approach to the French problem remained as a whole fundamentally conservative. Ruling out any restructuring of NATO, it aimed at making a possible French withdrawal have the least possible impact on its efficacy and cohesion. If de Gaulle distinguished between the Alliance and NATO, the Americans thought the two things were "inextricably tied together" and that only keeping integration would permit NATO to be kept, and hence maintain a U.S. military presence in Europe.[69] The idea that its functioning should be overhauled was only advocated by people outside the administration, such as former president Eisenhower, who let it be known that he "had been giving a good deal of thought to the problem." The former SACEUR did not believe it possible to return to a classic type of alliance, but he thought that a possible solution would be for France and Germany to be jointly given the most important military responsibilities in Central Europe. The overall command would be given to France and operational command of advanced forces to Germany.[70] Despite his reputation as a conservative, General Eisenhower proved not only more innovative than the current administration, but in fact rather close to the French position.

De Gaulle continued to foment uncertainty. During his September 9 press conference, he declared that "by 1969 at the latest, the subordination called 'integration' that NATO entails and which puts our destiny under foreign authority, will cease as far as we are concerned."[71] This sibylline sentence purposefully confused his challenges to military integration, NATO, and the Alliance itself by mentioning the date set in the treaty for possible withdrawal by a member-state. At the Quai d'Orsay, whose departments scarcely seemed informed of the General's intentions, all hypotheses were being studied, using the notes prepared in the spring.[72] As for the Americans, they thought it prudent to prepare the Alliance "for the most drastic action at the earliest time without assuming that this is inevitable"[73]—or even the most probable. The best analysts of the General's policy felt that he could not push "disintegration" too far except at the risk of leaving Germany much freer in its moves. Thus, it should be foreseen that although de Gaulle might try to take France out of Atlantic integration, he would also wish to keep the FRG integrated, and this despite his "doctrinaire" statements against NATO.[74] This was perhaps reassuring from the military standpoint but left the political problem untouched, particularly in the eyes of the State Department, whose Europeanists were always concerned with sparing Germany. Rusk warned there was no question of "subjecting the FRG to special discrimination (such as the retention of integrated forces in Germany only)."[75] More than ever, Germany was at the core of the European and Atlantic problematic of French policy.

"Getting the Alliance Moving Again"

Meanwhile, forward planning for the French withdrawal went ahead. In the first fortnight of October 1965, the Pentagon organized a war game aimed at studying the problems that might arise from French policy and involving U.S. officials

posted to Paris, Bonn, and London, as well as White House and military bureaucrats.[76] The exercise put the previous studies to the test, and one thing was already
clear. It appeared that the end of the U.S. military presence in France would have
mostly logistical consequences. The vast majority of the troops and installations
involved the U.S. Army's communications system in Europe: networks of depots,
bases, and supply centers of the Seventh Army; and the rest were more negligible (air force bases in Evreux, Laon, Châteauroux, and Toul, and some navy installations in Villefranche). The impact of measures that de Gaulle might take
would be relatively limited, since the West-East logistical route across France in
support of U.S. forces in Germany had, for economic reasons, been abandoned in
recent years (except for hydrocarbons that continued to be transported through
the Donges complex). It was the ports on the North Sea that were now being used;
depots and other installations situated on the Atlantic had been closed or placed
in reserve. The U.S. presence in France, all forces combined, had already been reduced by half since 1962, from 57,400 to 28,700 men, largely because of the
growing difficulty of concluding agreements with France.[77]

   In late autumn, Couve de Murville warned Rusk that France would make its
position known in the spring of 1966, probably in March.[78] Secrecy over de
Gaulle's exact intentions still remained, however: even Director of Political Affairs Charles Lucet (who was readying to take the Washington ambassadorship
that Hervé Alphand was leaving to become secretary general at the Quai d'Orsay)
still did not appear informed at the end of October.[79] And the Americans noted
that the relevant departments of the Quai d'Orsay and the secrétariat général de
la défense nationale (SGDN) that were preparing notes about the different possible options were truly ignorant about which one the General would adopt.[80]

   The first round of the presidential elections was set for December 5. De Gaulle
was aware that his policy toward the Alliance and the United States was not a
winning theme in public opinion and that, on the other hand, the European crisis
could make his position fragile. His principal opponents campaigned against his
European policy, starting with Jean Lecanuet, who represented in the tradition of
the Mouvement Républicain Populaire (MRP) the advocates of a supranational
Europe (and hence of Atlanticism). The candidate of the left, François Mitterrand,
defended ideas close to Lecanuet's but less assertively, if only because his candidacy had the implicit support of the Communist Party. The General remained discreet about his intentions concerning NATO,[81] since the Atlantic issue represented a limited electoral stake due to the relative lack of interest by a public that
largely accepted his policy on the Alliance.[82]

   With the approach of the 1965 autumn ministerial session of the Council, to be
held in Paris from December 14 to 16, the situation was quite clear. The United
States acted more than ever as if it were now necessary to reckon without France
in moving the Alliance forward. It wanted to avoid any confrontation and ensure
the smooth functioning of NATO while demonstrating its utility in the new international context.[83] In fact, Washington succeeded during the ministerial session

in "getting the Alliance moving again": adopting a system of force planning over five years; starting to think about relations between military planning and arms control; and advancing the work of the nuclear select committee. On all these subjects, the apparent firmness shown by Couve de Murville in fact concealed a retreat, which Washington attributed to the French concern to avoid a confrontation with the United States on the eve of the second round of the presidential elections, but also to the fact that France was now isolated, with the majority of the allies having decided to move along without it if necessary.[84]

From the Select Committee . . .

This isolation was clear in the nuclear area, where the United States succeeded, in the aftermath of the previous spring's initiative, in taking affairs in hand while closing down the MLF issue for good. While practically abandoned at the end of 1964 by Johnson, it had continued to complicate relationships among the allies, especially between Bonn and Washington. Johnson had asked a special committee presided over by Roswell Gilpatric to think about the problem of nuclear proliferation;[85] it had concluded by the start of 1965 that the signature of a nonproliferation treaty should be a prime objective, even if this contradicted plans for nuclear sharing on which the United States was embarked.[86] But it was only in the summer of 1965 that this objective prevailed, despite the opposition of multilateralists in the State Department. The MLF, whose clinical death was confirmed in August, was buried once and for all at the end of December during a new visit by Erhard to Washington. The administration's prime objective was now to obtain the adherence of the USSR to the NPT, over which negotiations had begun in the summer.[87] And though the Germans at first did not react well to the prospect of a definite abandonment of a project—the MLF—in which they had invested so much, the Americans at the end of the year thought they would be able to retake the initiative and try a "new approach" by concentrating on nuclear consultation, as they had already begun doing at the spring ministerial session. The White House thought it was possible to convince the Germans that the feeling of security they were seeking depended more on their active role in nuclear planning than on "participation in nuclear weapons systems" like the MLF.[88]

Meanwhile, the French refusal to participate in the select committee was confirmed during the summer of 1965. The decision was made by de Gaulle himself on July 5, 1965. The McNamara proposal, he thought, changed nothing fundamental, meaning America's determination to impose flexible response. Worse, it "tended to introduce Germany into the front rank of powers to discuss the issue," which was dangerous, at least politically.[89] On July 7, Paris signaled its negative decision to NATO through the intermediary of the permanent representative Pierre de Leusse.[90] The French position was simply "no approval of the McNamara offer, but no opposition if the others want to act without our participation."[91]

At the end of July, the composition of the select committee appeared final: while initially the three nuclear powers were to sit with three nonnuclear ones, the Committee in France's absence would consist of the United States, Great Britain, Germany, Italy, the Netherlands, and Canada (with the latter two taking turns if France reversed its policy of abstention).[92]

The French "empty chair" had the effect of increasing the isolation of Paris within the Alliance in general and over nuclear affairs in particular. During the fall, the McNamara initiative went ahead. Since the idea of a select committee of five or six members clashed with the desire of most of the member states to participate in it, McNamara proposed in October substituting a "special committee" open to all interested countries, with the same mandate.[93] In November, this mandate was made precise: It involved studying the nuclear aspects of measures to take in crisis situations as well as ways of allied participation in nuclear planning—to the great regret of the French, for whom the project of a special committee went beyond the consultative and technical role initially discussed.[94] While Paris could conceive that Germany might be associated by this means with nuclear consultation, it could not accept its participating in nuclear planning.[95] But it was really too late to oppose a process that was advancing pragmatically without France. On November 27, the defense ministers of ten countries in the Alliance (Belgium, Canada, Denmark, Germany, Greece, Italy, the Netherlands, Turkey, the United Kingdom, and the United States) decided formally to establish a Special Committee, which remained in principle an *ad hoc* body. Three working groups were created within it, on communications, information exchange, and nuclear planning properly speaking. The third working group was obviously the most important, and the United States, Great Britain, Germany, and Italy sat on it as well as a representative drawn by lot from the other Alliance countries.[96] The French were not only isolated, but kept in ignorance of the workings of the Special Committee whose working documents were reserved to participating countries only, as the U.S. Congress required.[97]

If the McNamara initiative acquired such dynamism, it was because the Germans fully supported it, which the French appeared at first to have underestimated. At the end of November, Couve de Murville indeed remained persuaded that the affair would precipitate a confrontation between Bonn and Washington and that the Germans would not agree to the McNamara Committee being substituted for the MLF.[98] But Bonn, putting on a brave face, tried to grasp the influence over nuclear consultation being offered by Washington. The FRG had remained until then completely outside operational nuclear problems, though it was of vital interest to it. This is what McNamara skillfully stressed after the creation of the Special Committee. McNamara explained to his German colleague that there had not existed until then any rational plans for using nuclear weapons in Europe. The only use planned for these weapons was to be in conjunction with those of the Strategic Air Command and Polaris missiles assigned to the European theater. But apart from this apocalyptic scenario, nothing was planned at the moment regarding their selective use, with the allies having not even yet decided where and how nuclear weapons would be used in Germany.[99] McNamara's interest was obviously in drawing as disturbing a picture as possible of the nuclear unpreparedness of NATO and the United States in case of war in Europe so as to rally the Germans to the planning and consultation process that he was proposing, and at the same time to make them forget about the MLF. It was also a means of consigning to the back burner of German worries the fear of a denuclearized defense of Germany; McNamara indeed had no trouble showing that the opposite ought to disturb the Germans: the risk of uncontrolled recourse to nuclear weapons in the event of conflict on their territory, especially since, as he had recalled in May during the Council's spring session, the U.S tactical nuclear arsenal in Europe was steadily growing.

The effect of these statements on the German minister was immediate. Von Hassel was very surprised by what he heard, persuaded as he had been that SACEUR had a plan for the nuclear defense of German territory. It was quite clear that neither von Hassel nor Wilhelm Grewe, ambassador to NATO, possessed basic knowledge about nuclear operations.[100] How in these conditions could they reject the principle of nuclear consultation and planning within NATO?

... to the Special Committee

The Atlantic Council of December 1965 confirmed, from the U.S. standpoint, that "the prospect of nuclear consultations in the Special Committee of defense ministers obviously is developing a good deal of interest."[101] The French no longer had much control over the idea's momentum. It was largely to make an impact, after a progress report presented by Brosio on December 14, that Couve de Murville sounded the charge against the Special Committee and went back on the tacit green light given by Paris some weeks previously. He recalled that it was supposed to be "a working group created provisionally under the authority of certain member-states," which could not have the status of a "permanent body" of the Council that Washington was trying to confer on it.[102] This sally provoked an immediate response from British minister Dennis Healey and from Schröder, as well as a long procedural quarrel, and precipitated a frank exchange between Couve de Murville and Harlan Cleveland, the new permanent U.S. representative. Brosio, angered by the French position, declared abruptly that France could choose to participate or not in the work of NATO, but that it could not prevent others from going ahead.[103] As for Rusk, he raised the stakes the next day: "No one member can prevent a group of other members [from] getting together to advance the purposes of the Alliance."

The whole day was spent in negotiations between the French and the Americans, and secondarily the Germans and British, over the final communiqué of the ministerial session. An agreement was reached with the greatest difficulty; the communiqué barely mentioned discussions of the Special Committee and its work.[104] This day marked an important stage in what clearly appeared as the prelude to a strategic divorce between France and the rest of NATO. On the key question of nuclear relations among the allies, Paris did not even try any longer to wield its strategic argument, which was the gulf between the French conception of deterrence and flexible response. This was secondary in relation to the institutional aspects: France now systematically opposed any project that might lead to a strengthening of NATO. The main reason for the French refusal was in fact fundamentally political. On the one hand, it was a matter of rejecting anything that might lead to a perception of a strategic alignment alongside the United States as well as a loss of autonomy in relation to NATO. On the other hand, it was a way of adopting a position compatible with the French policy of détente, for Moscow was totally opposed to the McNamara Committee.[105]

As a result, the unanimity that had been the rule in the Alliance was impossible, and a simple consensus more and more difficult. It was clear that this situation could not last. Although France formerly could pretend to represent a European point of view within NATO on nuclear and strategic problems, this was manifestly no longer the case. It found itself isolated thanks to the firmness of the positions adopted and the success of U.S. policy, which had succeeded in overcoming the concerns of the other Europeans regarding strategy and also in giving an institutional start to this emerging nuclear consensus, from which France held itself apart. France appeared to be practicing systematic and procedural obstruction. In this, it "only strengthened the determination of the United States, Great Britain, and Germany."[106]

Détente and Alliance

In the second half of 1965, the theme of overcoming the system of blocs was confirmed as the major axis of Gaullist policy. De Gaulle became more precise about his February 1965 initiative and his ideas for a European and world order that might succeed that of Yalta: "A set of facts of immense bearing is currently working to reshape the universe," he stated in his September press conference. France must now free itself from "obedience to Moscow" as well as from the "preponderant" actions of the United States. "A nation on the rise," demographically, economically, culturally, and militarily, it must have a policy that is its own and "steer clear of any dependency." Thus, France could act in favor of cooperation and the settling of conflicts in the world, by virtue of "the opinion held of her historically, which opens up to her a sort of latent credit when it comes to the universal." Hence the active cooperation it was setting up in Africa, Latin America, and the Middle East. Hence its disapproval of the "current combat" in Asia, meaning the war waged in Vietnam by the United States and its support for "the effective end of any foreign intervention." As for Europe, it must organize itself with a view to a "constructive entente from the Atlantic to the Urals" so as to resolve by "general agreement" all its problems, starting with the central one of Germany. This was what France was trying to work toward through "the new course" of its relations with "Russia," but also through rapprochement with the formerly friendly countries of Rumania and Poland.[107]

The overture to the East was indeed becoming concrete. From October 28 to November 2, Maurice Couve de Murville was in Moscow. The U.S. side was closely interested in a visit that would consolidate a dialogue already well underway, and which de Gaulle made use of in his dealings with the United States and with the Alliance. But as Washington observed, the exercise had its limits. Several weeks prior to the presidential election, de Gaulle did not want to arouse concern in public opinion, even if he was perhaps tempted to profit from his overture to the East as far as leftist voters were concerned, the communists especially. Moreover, relations between France and Germany remained rather bad and Paris wanted to avoid any misunderstanding with Bonn over de Gaulle's Eastern Europe policy, which the Germans naturally had a tendency to see as a policy of balancing Germany.[108] Yet while the Americans thought there was no common vision between France and the Soviets of what a German or overall European solution might be (de Gaulle could not change his position regarding the GDR, which there was no question of recognizing), there did exist on both sides the same concern to limit the political and military influence of Germany, notably in the nuclear area, and to obtain a recognition of the Oder-Neisse border.[109]

De Gaulle certainly was not dreaming of a "counteralliance" with Moscow (1944 was long past) but he did place relations between France and the Soviet Union within a pan-European perspective of détente and cooperation.[110] Couve de Murville's visit to Moscow, the Americans noted, did not give rise to any agreement liable to prejudice German or Western interests, and it concluded with a communiqué faithful to the Gaullist thesis that an eventual reunification of Germany could only be made under terms favorable to the interests of both East and West.[111] But the visit confirmed de Gaulle's wish to strengthen the dialogue with Moscow and to recognize the existence of "many natural affinities and many common interests."[112]

At the end of 1965, the German question remained at the heart of French preoccupations. In early December, Couve de Murville confided to U.S. journalists that in his opinion reunification might happen within five years, for the Soviet Union was ready to envisage this prospect so as to prevent the implementation of agreements on nuclear sharing within the Alliance. Senior figures at the Quai d'Orsay expressed themselves in similar terms: West German participation in formulas for nuclear sharing could only postpone until much later a European arrangement and put the brake on East-West rapprochement by contributing to "freeze" the Cold War dividing line.[113] De Gaulle said the same thing to Erhard during the Franco-German summit at Rambouillet on December 20 when he underlined the dangers that German nuclear policy might "create with regard to the possibilities of a reunification of Germany."[114] Such statements invited interrogation. Since his February press conference, had not de Gaulle seemed to hint that the solution to the German question was a matter of a generation or less? And was not the USSR more firmly than ever attached to the division of Germany and its political and legal consecration? In fact, one had to read between the lines. These statements were a reminder of France's position on several problems: its hostility to any participation by Germany in nuclear arrangements within the Alliance; and its conviction that the prospect opened by de Gaulle on February 4, 1965, was the only one that could actually result in the overcoming of the logic of blocs and consequently the division of Germany. In sum, he was loudly asserting an original idea of détente that differed from the idea that Paris's principal allies continued to have of East-West relations and of the German question.

At the end of 1965, the Americans thus came to realize that the Gaullist policy of détente was perhaps the most serious challenge made to NATO, whose very *raison d'être* it profoundly questioned. And the Johnson administration began to be convinced that to be able to answer this challenge, it had to pose the issue of the Alliance's role in fundamentally political terms. This is why, as the December ministerial session approached, Washington hoped to strengthen political consultation within NATO by proposing to its allies two themes for deliberation. The first concerned East-West relations. The initial hypothesis was simple: "NATO's problems are [the] consequence of [its] full success,"[115] since it had been able to deter the USSR and persuade it that cooperation was better than aggression. As a result, the Alliance had to know how to manage this success, in other words, be in a position to adapt to a real détente—always on condition that the USSR itself was sincerely ready to put a brake on its militarist policy and especially its arms program. While waiting, NATO should pursue its effort: it was only when the Soviet Union would give clear signs of its new attitude that NATO should review its own strategy and its own military planning, and eventually engage in arms control. As for the second theme for deliberation, it was less novel: to work toward strengthening the cohesion of NATO outside the area spelled out in the treaty, in a new era when the threat (most obviously Vietnam) was no longer confined to Europe.[116] The United States thus came around, timidly to be sure, to posing the basic question of the Alliance's role. It even did so, paradoxically, in terms that recalled at least in part the approach used by de Gaulle from the beginning. In the months that followed, this approach became clearer. It would eventually result in a new "concept" of the Alliance and East-West relations.

For France, it was too little too late. After having been put to a second ballot by François Mitterrand, General de Gaulle was reelected on December 19 with 54.5 percent of the votes. While the election results and the very fact that a second round had been necessary might disappoint the Gaullists, the General's actions were legitimated. Analysis of the vote made it appear that his foreign policy had not been sanctioned by the electorate. Opposition to his European policy had played only a marginal role in the election, and opposition to his Atlantic policy even less.[117] At the end of 1965, the rupture between France and NATO approached its logical conclusion.

THE WITHDRAWAL

The principal mystery remaining at the start of 1966 with regard to de Gaulle's intentions toward NATO concerned the precise moment he would choose to announce his decisions. Even if the moment seemed imminent, de Gaulle more than ever was master of the calendar and, as so often, he played his cards close to his chest.[118]

Master of the Calendar

At the end of January 1966, the relevant French ministries were still ignorant about the deadlines that de Gaulle had already fixed. The bureaucrats in the Ministry of Foreign Affairs in charge of the matter were reduced to gleaning from the General's entourage scraps of information gathered by third parties, including foreign figures like Brosio or Bohlen.[119] The head of the Service des Pactes, Jean de La Granville, nevertheless thought the General would stick to the schedule announced in broad outline some months earlier, and that he would "raise the issue of NATO" at the end of February or early March.[120] Couve de Murville was of course informed of de Gaulle's intentions, but he revealed nothing, even to his main associates.[121] But he had asked Pactes to study what the definitive French position on NATO might be and what decisions would need to be taken.[122]

In the note he wrote on this occasion, La Granville adopted the hypothesis that these decisions would above all aim at strengthening French control over operations undertaken within the NATO framework on French territory, while trying to gradually lessen the foreign military presence. One possible solution would be the transfer to French command of all the U.S. forces present on national territory; these forces would receive from French authorities a permanent delegation of command regarding ordinary operations, but an express agreement from French authorities would be necessary in case of nonroutine operations. In parallel, while maintaining French participation in SHAPE and AFCENT, it would be necessary to modify the current conditions of integration. SACEUR, in the actual state of things, could not automatically have access to French forces (any more than to other national forces assigned to his command) without a firm decision by the government, but once the decision was taken, he could use these forces where and however he wanted to on NATO territory without referring back to the French government. To remedy this, one solution would consist of excluding French soil from the zone of Allied Command Europe (as was the case with Great Britain), in such a way that SACEUR operations could not take place there without the consent of the French government. And La Granville insisted on the fact that nothing in all this "requires an amendment of the North Atlantic Treaty or even prevents us from participating in SACEUR's staff."[123]

If the viewpoint of the Quai bureaucracy was not in basic contradiction with Gaullist ideas, it was clearly a retreat from the General's plans, since by all the evidence, he intended to go beyond a simple adjustment of French participation in the integrated military system. The Quai d'Orsay's hierarchy was generally inclined to moderation in relations with the Alliance and concerned to limit the damage to a "minimum." The ministry bureaucrats were worried about an intransigent policy that they feared would lead to the isolation of France and to a rupture with Germany.[124] Indeed, de Gaulle blew hot and cold: on January 20, he let it drop to Brosio that he intended to challenge the Atlantic Pact;[125] but on February 20, he ensured Bohlen that "he would not touch the Treaty itself but only the Organization."[126] French officials no longer knew what to think: did de Gaulle want to quit the Alliance or NATO? In fact, as in 1965, the first option was not really envisaged; at the Elysée, they were working on the second. These contradictory signals aimed to maintain the suspense before the February 21 press conference, in the course of which de Gaulle intended to announce his decision to withdraw from the integrated military organization and to keep France in the Alliance.[127]

The Decision

The General thought the moment had finally come to clarify the relations between France and NATO. He considered his international moves legitimated by the French election. The Luxembourg compromise on January 29, 1966, had put an end to the European crisis. While the United States was stuck in the Vietnam War, the USSR was confirming its interest in détente in Europe.[128] Germany was more than ever aligned with Washington's positions, using the Atlantic Alliance and U.S. protection, thought de Gaulle, as support for its "new ambitions," notably nuclear; in the East this policy could only be perceived as aggressive or *revanchiste*, and hence incompatible with a German or European settlement. France in this context felt itself becoming a world power once more, and it was incumbent upon France, in de Gaulle's eyes, to gradually rally all parties interested in such an overall solution by taking the lead in a détente with the East.[129] In this situation, nothing prevented it from taking action. On February 21, 1966, he outlined the general thrust: the continued validity of the Washington Treaty, but the unsuitability to "new conditions" of "arrangements" taken since then, meaning NATO; their unsuitability first of all to a situation in Europe characterized by the diminution of the Soviet threat and by the erosion of the U.S. guarantee; unsuitability also to the situation outside Europe, with the Vietnam conflict carrying a risk of involvement for U.S. allies; and finally unsuitability to the situation in France, now determined to "dispose of her own destiny."[130] As a result, he announced, the partial measures of withdrawal taken since 1959 would be completed and extended to units still integrated (essentially French forces in Germany), which would be subject to procedures for practical cooperation in the event of a conflict. As for foreign forces in France, they should report to French authority alone, which—given that the allies and especially the United States were not disposed to accept French command over their own forces—meant the departure of those forces, so as to "reestablish a normal situation of sovereignty." De Gaulle concluded that "it was by no means a matter of a rupture, but of a necessary adaptation," which France intended to gradually put into effect so that "its allies would not be suddenly inconvenienced by this move."[131]

It remained to make the ways and means and schedule more precise, which de Gaulle did on February 24. The foreign military presence in France would end within a year. French forces in Germany (with the exception of those present in Berlin that were part of the occupied status of the city) would be withdrawn from integration in peacetime. "Practical bilateral arrangements" could be concluded, however, so as to prepare for the possibility that the United States might have access to "certain facilities that might be agreed upon" on French territory (air bases, communications infrastructure, and so on) "under the hypothesis that in time of war we would decide to act in common." The same was true for French forces in Germany, whose "possible participation" in a "common Allied military action" might be planned in advance by an "agreement among chiefs of staff."[132]

The General intended to proceed with the allies in the most courteous manner possible. On March 7 he notified the principal party of his decisions; his letter to Johnson, handwritten as if to "cloak" the content,[133] was followed on March 9 by individual messages addressed to Wilson, Erhard, and the Italian president Giuseppe Saragat. Then, on March 11 and 29, the French government sent to the fourteen other Alliance members aide-mémoires detailing the content of the decisions taken.[134] France envisaged "remaining, as of the present and for the time being, a party to the treaty signed in Washington on 4 April, 1949."[135] On the other hand, it intended to modify its participation in the "organization," meaning "all the agreements, arrangements, and decisions taken ulterior to the signature of the treaty, either in a multinational form or in a bilateral form," since the current modes of operation of NATO no longer corresponded to the new course of East-West relations and to the imperatives of French defense. As for the unilateral character of this decision, it had resulted from the impossibility of modifying the organization of the Alliance by "common accord" with France's allies, "all supporters of maintaining the status quo, if not the strengthening of everything that, from the French viewpoint, appears now to be unacceptable."[136]

The cessation of the foreign military presence in France was to be effective on April 1, 1967, affecting the headquarters, units, and installations conceded to the United States (or Canada) bilaterally as well as to, *a priori*, facilities benefiting the FRG under the agreement of October 25, 1960. Also implicated were the interallied commands (AFCENT at Fontainebleau, SHAPE at Rocquencourt, and the NATO Defense College among others) established according to NATO arrangements and which were to leave national territory by the same date. Subsequently, agreements might be reached about the use of these facilities in case of conflict and French military missions to allied commands established after their transfer. On the other hand, assignment to NATO of French air and land forces in Germany would cease on July 1, 1966. The possible conditions for their engagement alongside the allies in case of conflict might be discussed; accordingly it was proposed to maintain the FFA on FRG territory despite their withdrawal from integration.[137]

Reactions in France

In France, the surprise effect was achieved. The statements of February 21 had been relatively vague about deadlines. As a result, the press, largely pro-Europe and pro–NATO, with the exception of the communist press, condemned the decision all the more outspokenly, indignant about the absence of consultation within the government and with the allies. Then indignation gave way to worry: A good number of newspapers feared the isolation of France and wondered about the future of the U.S. security guarantee once the withdrawal took effect.[138] The attitude of the political class was more varied. The socialist party (SFIO) and the MRP decided on April 13 after a general policy speech by Georges Pompidou to present a motion of censure condemning the "withdrawal from NATO." Presented by fifty-some centrist and Socialist deputies and defended by François Mitterrand, but opposed by René Pleven and Gaston Defferre, it received only 137 votes. This parliamentary episode showed both the division among politicians and the gradual erosion of the opposition to the General's defense policy. New and importantly, the communists did not take part in the condemnation of de Gaulle's Atlantic policy—since they basically approved of it. On the right, support was obviously unanimous on the part of the Union pour la Nouvelle République (UNR), but it extended as far as independent republicans, who overcame their reservations. In the center, only the Socialists formed a bloc, since the centrists, though now in the opposition, were divided over the European and Atlantic issue.[139]

In this situation, the government had no trouble defending its policy in Parliament, especially since public opinion was behind de Gaulle. In March 1966, 48 percent of the French thought the Atlantic Alliance had an important role. The Gaullist policy even strengthened this conviction, since it had been only 47 percent in October 1964 and would be 51 percent in October 1967.[140] But this attachment to the Alliance did not spring from an unconditional Atlanticism, since the French simultaneously ratified the decision to quit the integrated organization:if at the end of March, only 22 percent approved and 38 percent disapproved of this decision, one month later the figures were 39 percent approving and only 27 percent disapproving.[141] So, with support for the principle of the Atlantic Alliance and rejection of integration within NATO, French opinion, as far as can be discerned, faithfully reflected de Gaulle's position and supported his policy of independence.

It is true that the presentation of France's position within the Alliance was both simple and designed to promote adherence. In the public debate that followed de Gaulle's decision, this official presentation was organized in effect around three key ideas. The first was that there was a "clear and essential" distinction (that de Gaulle had indeed been making for years) between the Alliance and NATO, with France remaining in the first and leaving the second.[142] The second was that military integration constituted a hindrance to sovereignty and might have involved France in a conflict in which she would not have chosen to participate: by "withdrawing from NATO," France reestablished its "decision-making autonomy" and broke with "the automaticity" of the integrated system. The third idea was that the U.S. nuclear doctrine not only no longer ensured the security of Europe, but that it was also a warlike doctrine, in contrast to a French doctrine that addressed "not the organization of war, but of deterrence."[143] Now, each of these three statements contained, if not a distortion of the truth, then at least a simplification. Though France was leaving the integrated military structure, it was not leaving NATO properly speaking;[144] and though this structure was an intricate one, especially in Central Europe, it did not in principle automatically engage the forces concerned; and finally, though the doctrine of flexible response stressed (more than did French doctrine) effective conventional and nuclear operations, it was no less a doctrine of deterrence.

The object of this presentation was in fact to elicit the consent of the French people (hence a nuclear strategy that was being presented as a way of avoiding war), but also to increase France's diplomatic influence, as much in Europe and the Alliance as in relation to the East and the Third World (hence the systematization of the break between France and NATO and the dramatization of the disagreement between Paris and Washington). The French people learned their lesson well: asked about the subject in the autumn of 1967, a large majority thought that France did not belong to NATO but that it belonged to the Alliance.[145] From March 1966 onward, there was thus a declaratory presentation of the relations between France and NATO that tended to be dissociated from operational reality, which meant that the 1966 rupture was above all a political rupture. This trait would for many years be an essential aspect of relations between France and the rest of the Alliance.

Reactions within the Alliance

But for the time being, this partly explained the very negative tone of allied reactions to the announcement of the French withdrawal, especially in the United States. It was, in the opinion of Roger Vaurs, press and information officer at the French embassy, one of the most severe crises in Franco-American relations since the EDC. On top of all those crises that had preceded it in recent years (the MLF, attack on the dollar, the Vietnam War, and so on), it threatened to generate, he thought, "a climate of incomprehension," not only between governments, but also in public opinion, which was more serious.[146]

The commentaries were not unanimously disapproving, however. Walter Lippmann, among others, thought that de Gaulle's decision would allow an evolution in NATO that had been pending for a long time. In Congress, those like Democratic senators Mike Mansfield and William Fulbright, who were increasingly critical of U.S. military overengagement, whether in Asia or in Europe, thought that de Gaulle was doing the United States a favor by making it think about a way of giving the Europeans more responsibility for their own defense. After the French withdrawal, the theme of "burden sharing" logically moved to the center of the U.S. debate over the Alliance. But for the majority of Americans, de Gaulle, by withdrawing France from the military organization of the Alliance, the symbol of U.S. engagement in the defense of the free world, was showing ingratitude and incarnating the tendency of Europeans to abuse their generosity. And in denouncing U.S. hegemony, he directly challenged the ideal image the United States had of its international mission.

In a first phase, the reactions of U.S. officials were full of ill-concealed anger. Bohlen, summoned on March 7 by Couve de Murville to give him de Gaulle's letter to Johnson, declared that "the effect produced in the United States will be considerable" and that "Franco-American relations will be hurt for a long time."[147] George Ball was outraged by the fact that de Gaulle was playing with impunity on the geographic situation of France, which whatever happened "would be protected by American power." But surprise alone does not explain these reactions: The Americans had been warned throughout 1965 of the probability of such a decision, as Couve de Murville reminded Bohlen, adding that "the fact is simply that the problem has reached maturity." Hence, American irritation is also to be explained by the style of the decision, taken without consultation, about which the United States ambassador complained.

Though the French stressed that they had tried for years to convince their allies to transform NATO, as seen from the United States their decision indeed fundamentally undermined the multilateralism of the Atlantic Alliance; in short, said Bohlen, it "emptied the Alliance of its content" and "violated the treaty of 1949."[148] From the French point of view, these recriminations of course only betrayed the hypocrisy of a dominant power that disguised behind a multilateralist discourse a scrupulous defense of its own interests. The General was therefore not surprised by the first U.S. reaction to his decisions. To Konrad Adenauer, who on March 10 deplored the Americans' "overhasty response," de Gaulle replied: "I understand they are vexed. In their place, I would be as well. America has all the means and has never suffered. It envisages an alliance only on condition that it controls it."[149]

In the rest of the Alliance the first reactions were generally of the same kind. Inside NATO, the bureaucrats, both civil and military, reacted all the more harshly because the French decisions directly challenged their actions. Though

Brosio, diplomat and Francophile, proved anxious to calm things down, there were still in NATO "excited people who would willingly punish France, without really knowing how." Faced with that, French diplomats and military personnel were keen to limit the damage by preserving as much as possible the quality of their contacts and personal relationships within NATO. In the Atlantic Council, the first reactions among national representatives were unsurprising. After "silent consternation," everyone spoke up.[150] U.S. permanent representative Harlan Cleveland, backed up by SACEUR General Lyman Lemnitzer, hammered that the maintenance of the integrated system was the condition *sine qua non* of the maintenance of the U.S. military presence in Europe. Grewe, the German ambassador to NATO, defended unconditionally Atlantic military integration as guarantor of solidarity and hence of security faced with the Soviet menace, but also as a reassuring arrangement for the allies, who had allowed the German army to be reconstituted and the FRG to return to sovereignty.[151] The British representative proved particularly "harsh" and deplored "the grave situation" created by the French decision.[152] Finally, the "small powers" in the Alliance were divided. Some adopted a firm line toward France, such as the Netherlands, which followed Great Britain. Others such as Canada, Denmark, and Norway were concerned both to preserve the cohesion of the Alliance and to maintain good relations with France and so adopted a moderate position.[153]

The most striking aspect of the allied reactions to de Gaulle's decisions was their incomprehension, most interpreting the French withdrawal as a decision governed by purely national interest. In the best of cases, the allies — like Cleveland — saw it as a measure designed only to flatter the chauvinism of the French and to feed the myth of France's "grandeur."[154] In the worst of cases, they discerned (in light of the General's Eastern Europe policy) the outlines of French neutrality, if not a reversal of alliances. The fact that the Gaullist policy also belonged to a dynamic vision of East-West and West-West relations did not generally occur to the allies. Here no doubt lies a form of de Gaulle's failure, since despite years of explaining his policy he had not managed to make himself heard. This failure culminated in the decision of March 1966; but de Gaulle was resigned to an allied incomprehension that ironically threw his grand policy into even sharper relief.

A FREE HAND

Once the first reactions were over, the allies appeared concerned to limit the impact of the French decision on Alliance cohesion and on relations between France and NATO. The United States, following the line adopted several years before and in line with personal instructions from Johnson, sought appeasement. Negotiations between France and the United States opened in the spring of 1966, on which depended in turn the future of relations between France and NATO.

Negotiation

In this negotiation, France had the advantage. In its geostrategic situation, the disadvantages of a profound break with the rest of NATO would basically be fewer for itself than its allies. Moreover, the French had a well-defined idea of the type of relations they wished to establish with NATO: France, "gradually retiring from NATO, a supplementary organization added three years after the North Atlantic Treaty, will remain a member of this treaty and will continue to assume its engagement. Canadian and American installations in France will remain in place and might be used in case of war. French forces will have cooperation agreements with Allied forces, the American in particular."[155]

The U.S. situation was less favorable. Washington's interest lay in obtaining the maximum cooperation with France after its withdrawal, which placed the United States in the situation of petitioner. Moreover, uncertainty about French intentions remained, which the White House situated somewhere between "a neutralist position" (France withdrawing its troops from Germany, leaving NATO, and not establishing any defense arrangement at all with the United States or other allies) and a "diluted NATO" (in which France would maintain its troops in Germany, remain within allied bodies for planning and alert, and would permit allied overflight and keep the Atlantic Council based in Paris).[156]

At the end of March, the Americans appeared determined, though, despite this uncertainty, to face up to the French challenge. Dean Acheson was put at the head of an interdepartmental task force asked to make recommendations on policy after the French decision, so as to adapt NATO to this new situation and especially to strengthen Alliance organization beyond the current crisis. Acheson's personality, as in 1961, set the tone: Washington was choosing both the continuity of Atlantic policy, but also the reaffirmation of American leadership. The former secretary of state submitted his conclusions in a series of secret notes, addressed personally to Johnson between March and June 1966.[157]

However, there existed within the administration serious differences in approach to the French problem that reproduced the splits that had existed for several years. On one side, the State Department defended a hard line. Rusk, and especially Ball and Acheson, thought that the United States should denounce "the serious consequences of de Gaulle's unilateral decisions," without which public opinion and the various European parliaments, as well as the U.S. Congress, would stop taking the Alliance seriously.[158] This intransigent attitude was the product of Atlanticist and Europeanist "ideologues," concerned to avoid the disintegration of the "Atlantic community," but also of those who, like John McCloy, were preoccupied with the evolution of Germany and feared the impact de Gaulle's decision might have on it. McCloy, present in Bonn during April, seemed to his German hosts extremely virulent about France, imputing to de Gaulle the aim of "destroying NATO" and maintaining the FRG in a state of perpetual inferiority.[159]

On the other side, the Defense Department, led by McNamara, was much more pragmatic and defended a more subtle approach. The Pentagon wanted to avoid any polemic with de Gaulle so as to continue, as calmly as possible, to strengthen integrated defense without France.[160] While Ball went so far as to suggest that the United States drag its feet in withdrawing from French territory, McNamara saw in the French decision an opportunity to rationalize NATO's structure, to improve its efficiency, and cut its costs. The White House occupied an intermediate position. Johnson's entourage thought that while a minimum of debate on the French position was inevitable, in Congress especially, it should be as moderate as possible, since the prime objective was to allow NATO to continue functioning without France. This was an aim that, given the power and leadership of the United States within the Alliance, could be attained without a confrontation with Paris, conditional on making the allies feel the crucial importance of choosing multilateralism and integration over bilateralism and fragmentation; on avoiding putting the United States in the position of petitioner, while endeavoring to obtain from de Gaulle a minimum necessary for allied defense; and finally, on effecting the withdrawal of U.S. forces and installations promptly.[161]

It was this attitude that Johnson ended up imposing, so that ideas nearer to the Pentagon's than the State Department's prevailed. The president saw "no benefit to ourselves or to our allies in debating the position of the French government" since the priority was "to rebuild NATO outside of France as promptly, as economically, and effectively as possible."[162] This approach was formally adopted in a presidential directive on May 4, 1966 (NSAM #345), asking the different departments concerned to issue constructive proposals to strengthen the Alliance. This document was addressed to the relevant agencies, starting with the Pentagon and the State Department, as well as to the U.S. military hierarchy in France.[163]

Foreign Presence in France

The moderate line adopted by Johnson allowed broaching in favorable conditions the two issues of U.S. troop withdrawal and of future relations between French forces and NATO. The first question was less problematic. The Pentagon scrupulously applied the presidential directives. On May 25, Robert McNamara could confirm to Johnson that, without prejudice to the diplomatic and legal discussions then underway between Paris and Washington, the withdrawal of U.S. troops and installations in France could begin.[164] The Pentagon intended to profit from the opportunity to improve its military deployment in Europe. Depots would essentially be transferred to Germany, along with a portion of the ten thousand men involved, with the other portion being repatriated to the United States; the principal U.S. national commands (USCINCEUR, USAREUR) would be reorganized and transferred to Belgium or Germany; and air forces would be evacuated before September 1—two air transport squadrons (thirty-two C-130s) to Great Britain and six tactical reconnaissance squadrons (ninety-six aircraft) to

the United States in the first instance and later to other European countries—
everything according to an overall redeployment plan by the U.S. Air Force. The
remainder, notably communications lines (including the pipeline), would have to
wait until the French government announced its intentions toward their possible
use by the United States in case of war.[165]

While the departure of U.S. forces did not pose a major problem, it remained
to be determined to what extent these forces could in the future count on using
French territory and airspace, which had until then constituted the bulk of the
French contribution to allied defense. To be sure, the French Hexagon would not
be directly implicated in combat operations, since the line of allied defense was
located along the Iron Curtain. Yet, even if the Americans managed to depend on
it less, France remained the logistic key to NATO, and the unavailability of its territory would represent an uncertainty for American reinforcements in case of conflict. Moreover, it would create discontinuity between the Central European and
Southern European theaters, due to the fact of Swiss and Austrian neutrality. As
for French airspace, it had great operational and logistical importance in wartime
as in peacetime.[166]

Thus the administration wished—as Paris had suggested—to negotiate on all
points and, by demonstrating American goodwill (rapid evacuation of French territory, willingness to conclude new arrangements), to try to obtain the best possible conditions.[167] At the end of May, Bohlen got instructions to make contact with
Couve de Murville to define the nature of the negotiations between Paris and
Washington on the whole set of questions pertaining to the facilities granted by
France to the United States. The ambassador was to point out that the intention
manifested by France to remain part of the treaty implied, from Washington's
viewpoint, that the United States could continue to enjoy indispensable facilities
so as to allow them to fulfill their engagement in mutual assistance. Hence the
specifics that Bohlen was supposed to obtain: Could the United States continue
to use the Donges-Metz pipeline in peacetime and wartime? What were French
intentions regarding the possible use of bases by the U.S. Air Force? Would the
agreements for overflight of French territory be kept? These were subjects about
which Bohlen was to let it be known that the U.S. government "earnestly hoped"
that the French government would prove cooperative.[168]

The Problem of French Forces in Germany

The problem of French forces in Germany, which were no longer integrated as of
July 1, 1966, was equally delicate, but not so much for military reasons. The two
divisions concerned, already posted to the rear of the allied lines, could not in any
case, integrated or not, play a major role in forward defense; as for the attack air
forces stationed in the FRG (in particular the two F-100 squadrons with nuclear
capability), even if their withdrawal was potentially more contentious because it
reduced the strike capability available to SACEUR, it also had limited impact be-

cause their availability to NATO had already been reduced for some years.[169] The problem with the FFA was really political. It was even considered by the White House in the spring of 1966 as "the hottest near-term issue."[170] The German government indeed thought that the presence of French forces in the FRG was tied to their role in NATO's integrated defense. For Bonn, the maintenance of the FFA outside NATO was unacceptable, since it would amount to restoring a regime of occupation and ratifying a difference in status between France, absolved of any military subordination, and Germany, entirely integrated within NATO. But Paris considered that the right to station the FFA in the FRG grew out of agreements prior to the entry of Germany into NATO, and was not called into question by the withdrawal decision. France thus proposed to maintain them after July 1.[171]

Washington firmly supported Bonn's position, at least at first. The administration indeed feared that de Gaulle's policy would only have the consequence of destabilizing the Western anchorage of Germany: "The Germans [might] over time feel that they have been cast adrift. A growing sense of uncertainty and insecurity on their part could lead to a fragmentation of European and Atlantic relations, which would be tragic."[172] Moreover, the question of the FFA was not immaterial to the United States itself, to the extent that it might affect, more or less directly, the situation of their own forces in Germany as well as the application of German-American agreements on their stationing.[173] This was at a time when, in the middle of the Vietnam War, the U.S. military presence in Europe began to be seriously contested by a whole segment of public and political opinion. For Washington as for Bonn, things were very simple: the question should be resolved in terms acceptable for NATO, or French troops ought to leave. John McCloy, sent to Bonn to develop a common position with Germany and Britain, was very keen on the link between the United States and the FRG; an Atlanticist by conviction, he was irreducibly hostile to de Gaulle's policy, and so encouraged a hard line from Erhard and Schröder. Hammering home that de Gaulle was trying to dominate Europe and to contest Germany's status and rights, he confirmed to Bonn's rulers the support of Johnson for a strong German position.[174]

However, U.S. support for a maximalist position on the FFA faded rapidly during May, with Johnson adopting a flexible line regarding Paris. In any case, it was clear that de Gaulle would not accept any agreement that automatically prescribed the passing of the FFA to NATO command in the event of conflict, as Bonn demanded. The White House thought that the McCloy line was untenable, and that it should prepare a fallback position.[175] Paris let it be widely known that France was no "*demandeur*" and that if Bonn so wished, it would repatriate its forces. De Gaulle confirmed during June to Bohlen that, to the extent that the two divisions in question could militarily play the same role while remaining stationed in France, he wished to maintain them on the other side of the Rhine only if, for "symbolic" or "political" reasons, Bonn expressly desired it (but whatever happened, the air force would be repatriated).[176] As a result, the Germans softened their position. Despite Schröder's intransigence, Erhard compromised. Like most German politicians, he wanted to maintain a French military presence in the FRG.[177] Bonn now accepted the principle of keeping the FFA even without NATO integration. The French position was on the way to prevailing, leading the United States to adjust its own attitude.[178]

It was the same concerning the future role of French forces in relation to the common defense, a problem closely linked to the preceding one. At first, the Fourteen, led by the United States, insisted on the need to define a clear political framework for discussion of this subject between SACEUR and the French CEMA, General Ailleret, the aim being to obtain firm engagements from Paris as to the role of the FFA in the event of conflict. De Gaulle proved intransigent on this point. For him, such discussions should be strictly technical and not question the principle of the decisions taken in March. Faced with the General's firmness, the allies had to reverse course and accept the principle of exploratory discussions between Ailleret and Lemnitzer, with no prior political directive.[179] In June 1966, in fact, the aims of these discussions remained unchanged, from de Gaulle's viewpoint: to find an agreement with Germany on the maintenance of the FFA and to define their relation to the integrated military organization in the event of conflict ("liaisons," "automatic exchange of information, especially on respective actions, projected or resolved").[180]

Faced with this determination, the allies had to bend. On June 7 and 8, the Atlantic Council met at the ministerial level for the first time since the announcement of the French decisions and determined, in a compromise formula, the procedures for negotiations between France and the Fourteen. On this occasion, the "integrated" allies took a series of measures to rearrange the military organization and to strengthen the system of integration: replacing the Standing Group with an international military staff placed under the authority of the Military Committee; and unifying land, air, and naval commands in Central Europe. These measures aimed to take account of the French withdrawal and to rationalize the integrated structure so as to improve efficiency and strengthen NATO cohesion.[181]

Three months after the announcement of the decisions taken by de Gaulle, nothing was yet really solved regarding future relations between France and NATO, with proper discussions not having begun. Nevertheless, two points were already clear. First, France's allies, led by the United States, had managed to reassert their unity. In this sense, the idea of a NATO "without France" (though it remained in the Alliance), which had been taking shape for several months, was now becoming concrete. The U.S. approach—avoiding confrontation with Paris while circumscribing the risk of Gaullist ideas being propagated—had born fruit. But second, the allies had not been able to prevent French "unilateralism." Not only was there no question of making de Gaulle "pay" for his decisions, as some wished at first, but it appeared very difficult, in the face of the General's determination, to impose on future relations between France and NATO anything that would tend to limit the scope of these decisions. At most it would be possible to bargain over some practical aspect of future cooperation on a case-by-case basis.

In this sense, one could say that de Gaulle at the start of the summer of 1966 had attained his goal: in the absence of obtaining an overall reform of the Alliance, he had definitively imposed the redefinition of the relations between France and NATO embarked upon in 1959.

Such was the situation when the first effects of French decisions were felt. On July 1 the assignment of French forces in Germany to SACEUR command ended. Simultaneously, the last French CINCENT, General Jean Crépin, transferred his command to General Graf Kielmansegg, previously his "land" aide. (The fact that AFCENT now reported to a German general was in the order of things: after the French withdrawal, the Bundeswehr was incontestably the principal military force assigned to NATO.) Finally, as it had formally announced to the French government in its aide-mémoire of April 12, the United States ended on the same date the arrangements for the eventual use by French forces in Germany of U.S. tactical nuclear warheads, judging that these arrangements presupposed integration into NATO of the forces concerned.[182]

Integration, "Offspring of the Cold War"

After the decision to withdraw, de Gaulle's policy toward NATO appeared more clearly than ever to be linked to his idea of East-West relations. As we have seen, the General justified his decisions to a great extent by the attenuation of the Soviet threat and the lowering of tension that after the crises of the Cold War resulted in the prolongation of the status quo — a status quo that the Russians "now sought" and that the Americans "had very well accommodated," it was thought in Paris.[183] But in the spring of 1966 de Gaulle went further. The withdrawal from NATO was not merely a result of a new course in East-West relations; he wanted it to be the driving force. In breaking with the logic of integration, France hoped to promote an overcoming of the monolithic blocs "in the East as in the West." In fact, it was thought in Paris, "the Socialist camp is also evolving from the notion of a bloc to that of an alliance." Thus, "Romania was using the French policy to resist attempts at integration pursued by Moscow within the Warsaw Pact," and this movement could extend to other satellites, which, "far from playing Moscow's game," would oblige the USSR to "a growing relaxation of its grip on the countries of the East."[184] As Georges Pompidou summed it up, it was a matter in the East and West of doing away with integration, which, since it "foresaw in peacetime the establishment of a mechanism for collective war," was "an offspring of the Cold War and contributed to perpetuating it."[185]

The spring of 1966 was a high point in the French policy of détente, one that rejected both passive acceptance of the status quo and the bellicose roll-back, and that postulated the existence of a "chance to put an end to the division of Europe," which ought to be "seized by undertaking a far-sighted policy that would gradually rally all interested parties, i.e., all European peoples, starting with the Germans."[186] His policy toward NATO indeed gave de Gaulle arguments to denounce the Yalta order and to defend a pan-European perspective first sketched on February 4, 1965. This was noted by Democratic senator Frank Church, who had been received for a long visit at the Elysée in early May 1966. Postulating that the East-West confrontation could not be the basis of a European settlement, de Gaulle defended a pragmatic approach to détente that, relying on "cooperation in certain practical areas," then favoring "better political relations between East and West" in Europe, would one day result in a "general negotiation," including the German question.[187] The conditions were that the FRG from the outset accepted the minimal conditions for eventual reunification (borders, nuclear arms, and so on), since "as long as Germany, in the Alliance, remains what it is, or what it appears to be, i.e. a country that has others alongside to support its ambitions and its demands," real and lasting détente would be impossible. This is why East-West rapprochement must proceed via a radical transformation of NATO, an organization that perpetuates the Cold War and freezes the German question, since it encourages the approach of the rulers in Bonn, for whom "the German problem and reunification should be solved first and that then there would be an entente between East and West," whereas in reality "détente must be made first," with reunification coming "afterward, but on certain conditions."[188]

This obviously posed the problem of the role and presence of the United States in Europe. Talking with Church, personally in favor of a reduction in U.S. military presence, de Gaulle made an important point in this regard: any settlement of the German and European question, he explained, even if it occurred within a framework that was primarily European, would involve the United States. France certainly was not seeking the departure of U.S. troops in Europe, since the time "had not yet come." European equilibrium depended on that, because the Soviet threat, while reduced, had not disappeared, and because the U.S. presence (but also British and French) in Germany ensured, while waiting for a definite settlement that would prevent it from becoming "threatening" again, a guarantee against this possibility. This was why, he insisted, the departure of U.S. troops from France by no means meant that the same thing should happen, at least in the foreseeable future, on the other side of the Rhine. If the presence of American troops "is justified in Germany, it is not justified in France." No doubt, in the longer term, de Gaulle thought, like Church, that the indefinite maintenance of an American military presence did not coincide with history.[189] It was even conceivable that at the end of the day the overall European solution that he imagined would involve a withdrawal of U.S. forces from Germany in exchange for a Soviet withdrawal from the GDR and Eastern Europe.[190] But this possibility was not on the horizon in 1966.

The Voyage to Moscow

As de Gaulle's trip to the USSR at the end of June approached, Franco-Soviet relations were at the heart of allied perplexity about a French policy interpreted at one extreme as the outline of an *"alliance de revers,"* even if this analysis was not dominant. However, though the trip to Moscow was to be the occasion for a brilliant demonstration of independence, de Gaulle saw the limits of rapprochement. To former chancellor Adenauer (who among German politicians was undoubtedly the least worried by the General's Eastern European policy), he confided before his departure that he would not make a "fundamental agreement" with the Soviets. And even if, in Moscow, European security and hence Germany came up, de Gaulle had no illusions: "The European entente that will be the key to reunification" was not imminent. "But it is important that the question be posed and that it is France that does so in this sense."[191] Erhard was much more distrustful than his predecessor, and on the eve of his voyage to Moscow, de Gaulle tried to reassure him: "Germany has nothing to fear, on the contrary," since it amounted to favoring "an evolution and finally a solution to the German problem."[192] And although it was clear, he told Bohlen, that the USSR hoped to obtain a sort of consecration of the status quo (i.e., a recognition of the GDR), he would do nothing that might suggest he was ready to move in that direction. On the other hand, German reunification was promising to be a long process, and he hoped to obtain from the Soviets an admission that it was at least a distant goal.[193]

The Gaullist approach remained, though very removed from the U.S. vision of things. Détente with Russia was "desirable," explained Bohlen, but German reunification, from the U.S. standpoint, was the precondition. This is precisely what de Gaulle was refuting: today, Germany does not represent a danger to anyone; but if reunification, "for which the French stood in principle," should happen "suddenly," it would only lead to the consolidation of the Soviet hold over Eastern Europe (whose countries were seeking Moscow's protection) as well as strong apprehension in Western Europe.[194]

The General was received in the USSR with exceptional consideration from June 20 to 30, 1966. He obviously enjoyed the prestige given by his break with NATO, which perhaps raised among the Soviets a hope for a more radical distancing in the future.[195] But the fundamental discussions, largely with Leonid Brezhnev, brought no surprises. De Gaulle explained his idea of the triad "détente, entente and cooperation," with the problems of Europe being solved within a European framework and not by a tête-à-tête between the USSR and the United States. Brezhnev answered him by mentioning the Soviet plan for a European conference on security without U.S. participation. De Gaulle did not reject such a conference, but he noted that the United States could not be excluded from the solution to the German question, and that its eventual departure could not be a precondition for it.[196] And though there was Franco-Soviet agreement on the issue of borders and the nonnuclear status of Germany, there remained a central disagreement over its eventual unity. De Gaulle certainly stressed that France "is neither very ardent nor very much in a hurry"[197] to see this come about, but he defended its historical necessity in time, which precluded recognition of the GDR. Taking away any German hope of unification would indeed lead to dangerous frustrations for Europe as a whole. The General, as he had promised Adenauer three months earlier, thus defended the Germans' cause. It was really a matter of "removing the German problem from the contest between the USSR and the United States"[198] and more generally, from bipolar confrontation.

There was indeed a chasm between this vision and that of the Soviet leaders, for whom German reunification was unthinkable in the foreseeable future, and recognition of the existence of the GDR indispensable.[199] Yet though he made no progress on the German issue, the voyage to the USSR was a success. Without at all marking a reversal of alliances, it confirmed the autonomy and dynamism of French foreign policy. The United States was aware of this, and the importance of the event appeared clearly: the General had demonstrated that détente could be taken in hand by the Europeans.[200] Thus, de Gaulle's East-West strategy, closely linked to his approach to Alliance issues, represented in the wake of the French withdrawal from the integrated organization a fundamentally political challenge. To respond to this challenge by using and adapting NATO so as to retake the initiative in European security affairs, was now—beyond the problem of the military and strategic consequences of the French withdrawal—the principal objective of the Atlantic policy of the United States.

NOTES

1. Figures quoted in Serge Berstein, *La France de l'expansion*, vol. 1, "La République gaullienne 1958–1969," Paris, Le Seuil, 1989, p. 151.
2. EMBTEL, Paris #3893, 8 January 1965, LBJL, NSF, France, box 170.
3. Maurice Couve de Murville, *Une Politique étrangère 1958–1969*, Paris, Plon, 1971, pp. 330–34.
4. Press conference of 4 February 1965, in Charles de Gaulle, *Discours et Messages (DM)*, vol. 4 "Pour l'effort" (août 1962–décembre 1965), Paris, Plon, 1970, pp. 325 ff.
5. De Gaulle, *DM*.
6. De Gaulle, *DM*.
7. See Stanley Hoffmann, *Decline or Renewal? France since the 1930's*, New York, Viking, 1974, p. 304.
8. Memorandum of Conversation, Rusk–Couve de Murville, Washington, 18 February 1965, LBJL, NSF, France, box 171.
9. Note by J. Schricke, 13 March 1965, MAE, Pactes 1961–1970, box 259; EMBTEL, Paris, Polto #1247, 1 March 1965, LBJL, NSF, France, box 171.
10. Renata Fritsch-Bournazel, *L'Union soviétique et les Allemagnes,* Paris, Presses de la F.N.S.P., 1979, pp. 130–31.
11. Couve de Murville, *Une Politique étrangère*, p. 269.
12. EMBTEL, Paris, #3893, 8 January 1965, box 170; EMBTEL, Paris #6236, 4 May 1965; EMBTEL, Paris #6237, 4 May 1965, LBJL, NSF, France, box 171.
13. EMBTEL, Paris, #6237, 4 May 1965.
14. EMBTEL, Paris #6181, 1 May 1965, LBJL, NSF, France, box 171.

15. "Conversation with former Chancellor Adenauer," Henry Kissinger, 22 June 1965, LBJL, NSF, Files of McGeorge Bundy, boxes 15–16.

16. "Rapport de gestion 1952–1966," Roger Vaurs, director of the press and information service of the French Embassy, to Couve de Murville, New York, 13 April 1966, pp. 26–27 (document received from the author).

17. EMBTEL, Paris #6236, 4 May 1965; memorandum of conversation, Rusk–Couve de Murville, Washington, 19 February 1965, LBJL, NSF, France, box 171.

18. Broadcast speech from the Elysée Palace, 27 April 1965, in de Gaulle, *DM*, vol. 4, pp. 354–58.

19. EMBTEL, Paris #3798, 5 January 1965, LBJL, NSF, France, box 170.

20. EMBTEL, Paris #3798.

21. Hervé Alphand, *L'Etonnement d'être. Journal 1939–1973*, Paris, Fayard, 1977, p. 444.

22. Note by J. Schricke, 13 March 1965.

23. Note sans destinataire au sujet d'un projet de traité militaire franco-américain, 23 February 1965, in Charles de Gaulle, *Lettres, notes et carnets (LNC) (janvier 1964–juin 1966)*, Paris, Plon, 1987, p. 134.

24. Lettre à Georges Pompidou au sujet d'un QG de l'OTAN, 27 April 1965, in de Gaulle, *LNC (1964–1966)*, p. 153.

25. EMBTEL, Paris #6238, 4 May 1965, LBJL, NSF, France, box 171.

26. Alphand, *L'Etonnement d'être*, pp. 452–53.

27. Alphand, *L'Etonnement d'être*, p. 454.

28. EMBTEL, Paris #7065, 14 June 1965, LBJL, NSF, France, box 171; and Cyrus L. Sulzberger, *An Age of Mediocrity: Memoirs and Diaries, 1963–1972,* New York, Macmillan, 1973, p. 182.

29. Alphand, *L'Etonnement d'être*, p. 461; EMBTEL, Paris #51, 2 July 1965, LBJL, NSF, France, box 171, and Sulzberger, *Age of Mediocrity*, p. 185.

30. Note pour le ministre,12 March 1965, MAE, Pactes 1961–1970, box 261.

31. Note, "Présence de l'OTAN en France," 17 March 1965, MAE, Pactes 1961–1970, box 261.

32. Jean Lacouture, *De Gaulle,* "The Ruler 1945–1970," trans. Alan Sheridan, New York, Norton, 1992, pp. 382–83; personal interview.

33. Quoted by Pierre Melandri, *L'Alliance atlantique,* Paris, Gallimard/Julliard, 1979, p. 187.

34. Sulzberger, *Age of Mediocrity*, p. 180; EMBTEL, Paris #6843, 3 June 1965, LBJL, NSF, France, box 171.

35. EMBTEL, Paris #6904, 1/2, 5 June 1965, LBJL, NSF, France, box 171.

36. EMBTEL, Paris #6904, 2/2, 5 June 1965, LBJL, NSF, France, box 171.

37. EMBTEL, Paris #7218, 21 June 1965, LBJL, NSF, France, box 171.

38. See for example the broadcast speech of 27 April 1965, already cited, and General Charles Ailleret, "Evolution nécessaire de nos structures militaires," *Revue de Défense Nationale*, June 1965, pp. 947–55.

39. Lucien Poirier, *Des Stratégies nucléaires,* Paris, Hachette, 1977, pp. 317–18; and Marcel Duval and Yves Le Baut, *L'Arme nucléaire française. Pourquoi et comment?,* Paris, S.P.M./Kronos, 1992, p. 51 footnote.

40. Interviews; Duval and Le Baut, *L'Arme nucléaire française,* p. 52; Lacouture, *De Gaulle*, p. 431; Poirier, *Des Stratégies nucléaires*, p. 321.

41. Ailleret, "Evolution nécessaire de nos structures militaires."

42. General François Valentin, "La dissuasion et les armements classiques," in *L'Aventure de la bombe. De Gaulle et la dissuasion nucléaire (1958–1969)*, Institut Charles de Gaulle, Paris, Plon, 1985.

43. EMBTEL, Paris #5745, 9 April 1965, LBJL, NSF, France, box 171.

44. Note de l'EMA à l'attention du ministre des Armées, "Questions éventuellement abordées à la réunion des ministres de la Défense de l'OTAN (31 mai–2 juin 1965)," MAE, Pactes 1961–1970, box 261.

45. EMBTEL, Paris, Polto #1634, 11 May 1965, LBJL, NSF, France, box 171.

46. Note pour Pierre Messmer au sujet de la prochaine réunion de l'OTAN, in de Gaulle, *LNC (1964–1966)*, p. 154.

47. It is transcribed word for word in EMBTEL, Paris, Polto #1634, 11 May 1965.

48. Projet de déclaration du ministre des Armées sur la non-participation de la France à l'exercice "Fallex 66," EMA, 25 May 1965, MAE, Pactes 1961–1970, box 261.

49. EMBTEL, Paris, Polto #1711, 26 May 1965, LBJL, NSF, France, box 171.

50. SGDN, note du Général Fourquet, 16 March 1965, box 267.

51. "Remarks by Secretary McNamara, Defense Ministers' Meeting, Paris, France," 31 May 1965, LBJL, NSF, Agency File, box 11, DoD.

52. See Jane Stromseth, *The Origins of Flexible Response: NATO's Debate over Strategy in the 1960s*, London, Macmillan, 1988, pp. 91 ff.

53. "Remarks by Secretary McNamara, Defense Ministers' Meeting, Paris, France," 31 May 1965, pp. 11–12.

54. "Remarks by Secretary McNamara, Defense Ministers' Meeting, Paris, France," 31 May 1965, p. 12.

55. "Remarks by Secretary McNamara, Defense Ministers' Meeting, Paris, France," 31 May 1965, p. 13.

56. See chapter 4, p. 111; see also David N. Schwartz, *NATO's Nuclear Dilemmas*, Washington, Brookings, 1983, pp. 179 ff.

57. Note, "Déclarations françaises concernant le comité McNamara," 29 November 1965, MAE, Pactes 1961–1970, box 267.

58. *New York Times,* 1, 2, and 6 June 1965.

59. Schwartz, *NATO's Nuclear Dilemmas*, p. 182.

60. EMBTEL, Paris, Polto #1770, 5 June 1965; DEPTEL, Paris, Polto #6713, 29 June 1965, LBJL, NSF, France, box 171.

61. EMBTEL, Paris, Polto #1883, 30 June 1965, LBJL, NSF, France, box 171.

62. Couve de Murville, *Une Politique étrangère*, p. 72.

63. EMBTEL, Paris, Polto #1883, 30 June 1965.

64. EMBTEL, Paris, Polto #63, 13 July 1965, 1/3, LBJL, NSF, France, box 171.

65. EMBTEL, Paris, Polto #63.

66. Memorandum of Conversation, Ball, Vance, Wheeler, 26 August 1965, LBJL, NSF, France, box 171.

67. DEPTEL, Paris #738, 14 August 1965, LBJL, NSF, France, box 171.

68. Memorandum of Conversation, Ball, Vance, Wheeler, 26 August, 1965.

69. DEPTEL, Paris #1153, 13 September 1965, LBJL, NSF, France, box 171.

70. Memorandum, "Meeting with General Eisenhower," General Goodpaster, 14 September 1965, LBJL, NSF, Memos to the President, box 7.

71. Press conference held at the Elysée, 9 September 1965, in de Gaulle, *DM*, vol. 4, pp. 372 ff. For a detailed account of the French decision based on recently released material, see Frédéric Bozo, "Chronique d'une décision annoncée: le retrait de l'organisation militaire," in Maurice Vaïsse, Pierre Melandri, and Frédéric Bozo, eds., *La France et l'OTAN, 1949–1996*, Brussels, Complexe, 1996.

72. Note non datée sur la France et l'Alliance (fin oct.–début nov.); note "Révision des accords bilatéraux franco-américains," MAE, Pactes 1961–1970, box 261.

73. Memorandum, "France and NATO," 25 September 1965, LBJL, NSF, France, box 172.

74. Research Memorandum, "De Gaulle's 'Attack' on the Atlantic Alliance," Thomas L. Hughes, 30 November 1965, LBJL, NSF, France, box 172.

75. DEPTEL, Paris #1711, 19 October 1965, LBJL, NSF, France, box 172.

76. Memorandum, R. C. Bowman to McGeorge Bundy, "Senior review of Epsilon I-65," 18 October 1965; and memorandum, Admiral C. J. Van Arsdall, head of the Joint War Games Agency, 1 October 1965, LBJL, NSF, Agency File, boxes 31–33.

77. Airgram Paris A-784, 19 October 1965, "Annual Review of U.S. Military Installations in France," LBJL, NSF, France, box 172.

78. Couve de Murville, *Une Politique étrangère*, p. 78.

79. EMBTEL, Paris #2300, 27 October 1965, LBJL, NSF, France, box 172.

80. EMBTEL, Paris #2847, 23 November 1965, LBJL, NSF, France, box 172.

81. See the broadcast speech of 30 November 1965, de Gaulle, *DM*, vol. 4, pp. 403 ff.

82. Cf. Danielle Bahu-Leyser, *De Gaulle, les Français et l'Europe*, Paris, Presses Universitaires de France, 1981.

83. EMBTEL, Paris #3060, 2 December 1965, LBJL, NSF, France, box 172.

84. EMBTEL, Paris #3491, 18 December 1965, LBJL, NSF, France, box 172.

85. "The Non-Proliferation Treaty," Spurgeon A. Keeny, Jr., 24 December 1968, LBJL, NSF, NSC History, boxes 55–56.

86. "A Report to the President by the Committee on Nuclear Proliferation," 21 January 1965, LBJL, NSF, NSC History, boxes 55–56.

87. *New York Times*, 1 July 1965, 17 October 1965; and 22 December 1965; see also Schwartz, *NATO's Nuclear Dilemmas*, p. 122.

88. "The Case for a Fresh Start on Atlantic Nuclear Defense (with no Mixed Manned Forces or Plans for such Forces)," McGeorge Bundy, 18 October 1965, LBJL, NSF, Memos to the President, box 5.

89. Note du Général de Gaulle, 5 July 1965, MAE, Pactes 1961–1970, box 267.

90. Telegram, Paris to Washington #11872–76, 11 July 1965, MAE, Pactes 1961–1970, box 267.

91. J. Schricke à H. Ruffin, 9 July 1965, MAE, Pactes 1961–1970, box 267.

92. Telegram, REPAN #265, 23 July 1965, MAE, Pactes 1961–1970, box 267.

93. Telegram REPAN #329, 12 October 1965, MAE, Pactes 1961–1970, box 267.

94. Note, "Comité spécial et plans de défense de l'OTAN," 15 November 1965, MAE, Pactes 1961–1970, box 267.

95. Note de Henri Ruffin, 23 November 1965, MAE, Pactes 1961–1970, box 267.

96. Telegram, REPAN #368, 27 November 1965, MAE, Pactes 1961–1970, box 267; Paul Buteux, *The Politics of Nuclear Consultation in NATO, 1965–1980*, Cambridge, Cambridge University Press, 1983, pp. 44–45.

97. REPAN Telegram #375, 30 November 1965, MAE, Pactes 1961–1970, box 267.

98. "Réactions du ministre sur la note concernant le Comité spécial des ministres de la Défense, 19 November 1965, MAE, Pactes 1961–1970, box 267.

99. EMBTEL, Paris, Polto #918, 29 November 1965, LBJL, NSF, France, box 172.

100. EMBTEL, Paris, Polto #918, 29 November 1965.

101. EMBTEL, Paris #3491, 18 December 1965, 1/2.

102. "Intervention de M. Couve de Murville au Conseil de l'OTAN le 14 décembre 1965," 15 December 1965, MAE, Pactes 1961–1970, box 267; EMBTEL, Paris #3444, 16 December 1965, 1/2.

103. EMBTEL, Paris #3444, 16 December 1965, 1/2.

104. EMBTEL, Paris #3444.

105. Note, "L'URSS et le comité McNamara," 16 February 1966, MAE, Pactes 1961–1970, box 267; Henry A. Kissinger, interview with La Granville, 23 January 1966, "Personal and Confidential," LBJL, White House Central File, box 8, p. 5.

106. EMBTEL, Paris #3444, 16 December 1965, 1/2.

107. Press conference at the Elysée, 9 September 1965.

108. Cf. EMBTEL, Paris #2327, 28 October 1965, LBJL, NSF, France, box 172, 1/2; and Couve de Murville, *Une Politique étrangère*, p. 209.

109. EMBTEL, Paris #2327, 28 October 1965, LBJL, NSF, France, box 172, 2/2.

110. On this point see Pierre Maillard, *De Gaulle et l'Allemagne. Le rêve inachevé*, Paris, Plon, 1990, pp. 247–48.

111. EMBTEL, Paris #2604, 10 November 1965, LBJL, NSF, France, box 172.

112. Quoted by Marie-Pierre Rey, *La Tentation du rapprochement. France et URSS à l'heure de la détente 1964–1974*, Paris, Publications de la Sorbonne, 1991, p. 39.

113. Airgram Paris A-1127, 11 December 1965, LBJL, NSF, France, box 172.

114. "La République fédérale et le problème nucléaire de l'Alliance atlantique en 1965," 24 January 1966, MAE, Pactes 1961–1970, box 267.

115. EMBTEL, Paris #3060, 2 December 1965, LBJL, NSF, France, box 172.

116. EMBTEL, Paris #3060, 2 December 1965.

117. See the analysis by François Goguel, "L'élection présidentielle française de décembre 1965," *Révue française de science politique,*" vol. 16, no. 2, April 1966, pp. 244 ff., taken up in Bahu-Leyser, *De Gaulle, les Français et l'Europe*, p. 76.

118. Personal interview. On what follows, see Bozo, "Chronique d'une décision annoncée."

119. See especially Note pour le Ministre, 21 January 1966, Service des Pactes; "Note de M. De Leusse en date du 21 janvier"; Lettre à Charles Lucet, 15 February 1966, MAE, Pactes 1961–1970, box 261.

120. Henry Kissinger, interview with La Granville, 23 January 1966, "Personal and Confidential," LBJL, White House Central File, Confidential File, box 8.

121. Personal interview; Lettre à Charles Lucet, 26 January 1966, MAE, Pactes 1961–1970, box 261.

122. Henry Kissinger, interview with La Granville, 23 January 1966.

123. Note, "L'Alliance atlantique," 17 January 1966, MAE, Pactes 1961–1970, box 261; see also the La Granville–Kissinger meeting, 23 January 1966.

124. La Granville–Kissinger meeting, 23 January 1966.

125. Note pour le Ministre, 21 January 1966.

126. Note de Jean de La Granville, 11 February 1966, MAE, Pactes 1961–1970, box 261.

127. Note de Henri Ruffin pour Etienne Burin des Roziers, 31 January 1966; Lettre à Charles Lucet, 15 February 1966, MAE, Pactes 1961–1970, box 261.

128. Couve de Murville, *Une Politique étrangère*, p. 78.

129. Exposé au Conseil des Affaires Étrangères sur l'Allemagne, 4 February 1966, in de Gaulle, *LNC (1964–1966)*, pp. 246–48.

130. Press conference held at the Elysée, 21 February1966, in de Gaulle, *DM*, vol. 5, "Vers le terme" (janvier 1966–avril 1969), Paris, Plon, 1970, pp. 6 ff.

131. Press conference held at the Elysée, 21 February 1966.

132. "Note au sujet du retour à la souveraineté nationale de notre défense," 24 February 1966, in de Gaulle, *LNC (1964–1966)*, pp. 256–57.

133. Personal Interview.

134. Letters to Johnson, Erhard, Wilson, and Saragat in de Gaulle, *LNC (1964–1966)*, pp. 261–67; aide-mémoires of 11 and 29 March in L. Radoux, *La France et l'OTAN,* Assemblée de l'UEO, June 1967, pp. 48–50, 53–55.

135. Letter to Johnson.

136. Aide-mémoire of 11 March 1966.

137. Details in the aide-mémoires of 11 and 29 March.

138. Bahu-Leyser, *De Gaulle, les Français et l'Europe*, pp. 160 ff.

139. Bahu-Leyser, *De Gaulle, les Français et l'Europe*, pp. 63 ff.

140. Bahu-Leyser, *De Gaulle, les Français et l'Europe*, p. 214.

141. IFOP polls on 25 March/12 April 1966 and 1/10 May 1966, quoted in Jean Charlot, *Les Français et de Gaulle*, Paris, Plon, 1971, p. 269.

142. Quoted in Lothar Rühl, *La Politique militaire de la Vème République*, Paris, Presses de la F.N.S.P., 1976, p. 145; and Ministère des Affaires étrangères, *La Politique étrangère de la France en 1966,* La Documentation Française, 1966, p. 47.

143. Quoted in Rühl, *La Politique militaire*, pp. 144–45.

144. On this point, see the evidence offered by François de Rose, *La France et la défense de l'Europe*, Paris, Le Seuil, 1976, pp. 25 ff.

145. See the poll done on 25 September and 2 October 1967, quoted in Charlot, *Les Français et de Gaulle*, p. 270.

146. "Rapport de gestion 1952–1966," pp. 28–30.

147. Telegram Paris to Washington, 8 March 1966, top secret, Bohlen–Couve de Murville meeting, MAE, Pactes 1961–1970, box 261.

148. Telegram, Paris to Washington, 8 March 1966, top secret, Bohlen–Couve de Murville meeting.

149. Tête-à-tête entre le général de Gaulle et l'ancien chancelier allemand Konrad Adenauer, 10 March 1966, in de Gaulle, *LNC (1964–1966)*, pp. 267 ff.

150. Gerd Schmückle, "Le général de Gaulle quitte l'organisation militaire de l'OTAN. Réactions et actions au Conseil de l'OTAN," in *De Gaulle en son siècle*, vol. 4, "La sécurité et l'indépendance de la France," Institut Charles de Gaulle, Paris, Plon, 1992.

151. Rühl, *La Politique militaire*, pp. 125–27.

152. Telegram REPAN, 9 March 1966, MAE, Pactes 1961–1970, box 261.

153. Olav Riste, "Le Général de Gaulle, les alliances et les petites puissance d'Europe," in *De Gaulle en son siècle*, vol. 4, "La sécurité et l'indépendance de la France," Institut Charles de Gaulle, Paris, Plon, 1992.

154. Harlan Cleveland, *NATO: The Transatlantic Bargain*, New York, Harper & Row, 1970, p. 104.

155. MAE, note sur les relations franco-américaines, 21 March 1966, published in Jean-Raymond Tournoux, *La Tragédie du Général,* Paris, Plon, 1967. On what follows, see Bozo, "Chronique d'une décision annoncée."

156. Memorandum for the President, "NATO," 18 May 1966, Walt W. Rostow and Francis M. Bator, LBJL, NSF, Memos to the President, box 7, p. 3.

157. Administrative Histories, Department of State, vol. 1, ch. 3, Europe, "French Withdrawal and NATO Countermeasures," p. 6, LBJL, Administrative Histories.

158. Memorandum for the President, "NATO," 18 May 1966, p. 4.

159. EMBTEL, Bonn #3305, 15 April 1966, LBJL, NSF, Subject File, box 21. On McCloy's mission to Bonn, see p. 173.

160. Memorandum for the President, "NATO," 18 May 1966, p. 4.

161. Memorandum for the President, "NATO," 18 May 1966, pp. 4, 6.

162. Administrative Histories, Department of State, vol. 1, ch. 3, Europe, "France," pp. 5–6, LBJL, Administrative Histories.

163. Administrative Histories, Department of State, vol. 1, ch. 3, Europe, "France"; and memorandum to the Secretary of State; memorandum to the Secretary of Defense, Lyndon B. Johnson, 5 May 1966, LBJL, NSF, Memos to the President, box 7.

164. Robert S. McNamara, Memorandum for the President, "Disposition of U.S. Facilities and Forces in France," 25 May 1966, LBJL, NSF, France, box 172.

165. Robert S. McNamara, Memorandum for the President.

166. Details in Frédéric Bozo, *La France et l'OTAN. De la guerre froide au nouvel ordre européen*, Paris, Masson, in series "Travaux et recherches de l'IFRI," 1991, pp. 97 ff.

167. Memorandum for the President, "NATO," 18 May 1966, p. 6.

168. DEPTEL, Paris #4307, 23 May 1966, Rusk to Bohlen, LBJL, NSF, Memos to the President, box 7.

169. See Brigadier Kenneth Hunt, *NATO without France: The Military Implications*, Adelphi Paper no. 32, London, I.I.S.S., 1966; and Carl H. Amme, Jr., *NATO without France: A Strategic Appraisal*, Stanford, CA, Hoover Institute, 1967; details in Bozo, *La France et l'OTAN.*

170. Memorandum for the President, "NATO," 18 May 1966, p. 1.

171. Memorandum for Mr. McCloy in his Discussion of French Forces in Germany, 9 April 1966, LBJL, NSF, Subject File, box 21.

172. "Draft Letter to Prime Minister Wilson," Lyndon B. Johnson (n.d. or addressee), LBJL, NSF, Memos to the President, box 7.

173. Memorandum for McCloy . . . , 9 April 1966.

174. Memorandum for McCloy . . . , 9 April 1966; EMBTEL, Bonn #3305, 15 April 1966; EMBTEL, Bonn #3318, 16 April 1966, and EMBTL, Bonn #3321, 17 April 1966, LBJL, NSF, Subject File, box 21.

175. Memorandum for the President, "NATO," 18 May 1966, p. 5.

176. Text of Cable from Ambassador Bohlen (Paris, 8672), 13 June 1966, LBJL, NSF, Memos to the President, box 8, p. 3.

177. Michael M. Harrison, *The Reluctant Ally: France and Atlantic Security*, Baltimore, Johns Hopkins University Press, 1981, p. 155.

178. Administrative Histories, Department of State, vol. 1, ch. 3, Europe, "French Withdrawal and NATO Countermeasures."

179. Administrative Histories, Department of State, vol. 1, ch. 3, Europe, "French Withdrawal and NATO Countermeasures."

180. "Brouillon de note au sujet des troupes françaises en Allemagne et américaines en France," 2 June 1966, in de Gaulle, *LNC (1964–1966)*, p. 304.

181. Cf. Rühl, *La Politique militaire*, pp. 140–41.

182. Memorandum for the President, 27 June 1966, Francis M. Bator, LBJL, NSF, Memos to the President, box 7.

183. Projet de circulaire (n.d., mid-March 1966), François Puaux, MAE, Pactes 1961–1970, box 261.

184. Projet de circulaire.

185. Déclaration du gouvernment à l'Assemblée Nationale, 13 April 1966, quoted in *Revue de Défense Nationale*, June 1966.

186. Projet de circulaire.

187. Procès-verbal de l'audience à l'Elysée de M. Church, sénateur des États-Unis d'Amérique, 4 May 1966, in de Gaulle, *LNC (1964–1966)*, pp. 292 ff.

188. Procès-verbal de l'audience à l'Elysée de M. Church.

189. Procès-verbal de l'audience à l'Elysée de M. Church.

190. Maillard, *De Gaulle et l'Allemagne*, pp. 249–50.

191. Tête-à-tête entre le général de Gaulle et l'ancien chancelier allemand Konrad Adenauer.

192. Lettre à Erhard, 16 June 1966, in de Gaulle, *LNC (1964–1966)*, pp. 306–7.

193. Text of Cable from Ambassador Bohlen (Paris #8672), 13 June 1966.

194. Text of Cable from Ambassador Bohlen.

195. On de Gaulle's trip to the USSR and its results, see Maillard, *De Gaulle et l'Allemagne*, pp. 249 ff.; François Puaux, "L'originalité de la politique française de détente," in *De Gaulle en son siècle*, vol. 5, "L'Europe," Paris, Plon, 1992; and Rey, *La Tentation du rapprochement*.

196. Puaux, "L'originalité de la politique française de détente"; Maillard, *De Gaulle et l'Allemagne*.

197. Puaux, "L'originalité de la politique française de détente."

198. Puaux, "L'originalité de la politique française de détente."

199. Maillard, *De Gaulle et l'Allemagne*, p. 250.

200. CIA, Intelligence Memorandum #1590/66, 20 July 1966, "France, the USSR and European Security (De Gaulle's Visit to the USSR)," LBJL, NSF, France, box 172.

Chapter Six

One Alliance, Two Strategies (July 1966–1967)

Between the summer of 1966 and the end of 1967, de Gaulle's quarrel with the United States took the form of an all-out confrontation. With the United States enmeshed in Vietnam, the General on September 1, 1966, denounced in Phnom Penh the murderous "illusions" of recourse to force and prophesied the ultimate powerlessness of the U.S. war machine in the face of nationalisms that it was merely exacerbating. As for a France resolved to keep "a free hand," it saw itself as the natural spokesperson for those who aspired to peace and, as with Cambodia, advocated neutrality.[1] As a source of unprecedented influence and prestige, especially in the Third World, de Gaulle's condemnation of the war in Vietnam cannot, however, be reduced to an expression of anti-Americanism; rather it sprang, against the background of a denunciation of the logic of blocs, from disapproval of the United States as a superpower gone astray. Meanwhile, the United States, still blinded by the "arrogance of power" but less convinced than before of waging a just war, was stung by these criticisms, which questioned both the morality and the efficacy of its actions.

De Gaulle went further during the Six-Day War in the spring of 1967 when he insinuated that the problem of Vietnam and that of the Middle East were linked ("one conflict contributes to igniting another one"[2]) and that the United States could only make any solution to the Arab-Israeli conflict more difficult by taking Israel's side. Yet it was in July 1967 that the General pushed his quarrel with the Americans to extreme language. In Montreal, his celebrated *"Vive le Québec libre"* was his way of putting *les Anglo-Saxons* on trial before the bar of history. It was the apogee of the rhetorical and political confrontation between France and the United States. In the United States, the Montreal speech unleashed a furious reaction, and even in France a real malaise beset politicians, including those in the majority; in denouncing in August 1967 "the solitary exercise of power," Valéry Giscard d'Estaing was already announcing the final phase of the Gaullist presidency.

187

The French, however, still supported de Gaulle in his defiance of the United States. In 1967, ratings for the United States were at their lowest since the end of the Fourth Republic, with only 29 percent of the French thinking that the two countries had related interests, as opposed to 46 percent who thought they had different interests.[3] And yet, despite this difficult Franco-American context, relations between France and NATO were redefined during these months in a relatively calm manner, whether at the political, strategic, or military level. On the one side, thanks to the French decision, the United States reaffirmed its Atlantic leadership so as to consolidate the cohesion and legitimacy of NATO, but without breaking off relations with France. On the other side, while having quit integration for good, France intended to remain a committed member of the Alliance. Thus the 1966 decision would lead not to a rupture, but to a new *modus vivendi* between France and NATO within an Alliance that was now at "14 + 1."

A RELEGITIMATED ALLIANCE

In the eighteen months following the French withdrawal, the allies, propelled by the United States, would try to bring long-term responses to the double challenge thrown down by de Gaulle. By taking the decision to break with integration, the General had raised both the question of the Alliance's functioning and that of its missions, its very *raison d'être*. In 1966–1967, NATO managed to arrive at long-lasting solutions to both of these problems, with de Gaulle's policy acting to expose the Alliance's difficulties but also to facilitate their solution.

The Functioning of the Alliance

In 1966, the question of the Alliance's functioning had become urgent for the United States. Since 1963, the risk of NATO's paralysis had grown due to the French policy. Paris had for four years prevented the adoption of flexible response and for a year had opposed the establishment of a body for nuclear consultation. From the U.S. standpoint, this policy sprang from a systematic obstructionism, and Washington had to restore the organization's functioning to allow U.S. leadership to be exercised without Paris being able to hinder it.

But this goal was balanced by another imperative, that of attenuating as much as possible the impact of the break between France and the allies, first, to permit militarily effective cooperation between France and NATO, and second, so as not to contradict the principle of an alliance among "equals" that was at the basis of the Atlantic window-dressing of U.S. hegemony (even if its application was at least debatable). Allowing France to play too ostensibly on a special status within the Alliance—profiting from the security that it offered without accepting its constraints, such as integration—would be precisely to undermine this principle and risk seeing France being emulated, by Germany to start with, thereby compromising U.S. leadership and Alliance unity. If France should be allowed to "participate in Alliance activities to the extent she wishes," on the other hand the United States could not accept France being able to "block or delay any progress in fields or activities to which she does not contribute," nor give the impression that it could continue "to obtain full benefits" from NATO "while refusing to participate in the integrated military defense."[4]

The affair was settled quietly in autumn 1966. It was France who proposed a compromise formula: enlarge the scope of the Defense Planning Committee (DPC; created in 1963 to supervise force planning) that, now sitting without France, would be concerned with all questions of a military nature in which it was not involved. This solution was accepted by the Fourteen and ratified on November 2 by the Atlantic Council, which met for the first time as a fourteen-member DPC two days later.[5] Without formally consecrating the duality of the Council (which would have posed problems with regard to the treaty), the formula amounted to just that, since from the beginning the DPC was nothing other than the Council, in other words the supreme body of the Alliance, but deliberating on defense questions. The Alliance would thus function with fifteen members at the political level within the North Atlantic Council, and with fourteen at the military level within the DPC. Thus was instituted *de facto* an Alliance of "14 + 1" of which France remained a full member, but in which it essentially held itself apart from common military activities. This compromise satisfied Washington even though the United States thereby came to ratify implicitly the French distinction between NATO and the Alliance that until then it had ceaselessly contested.

De Gaulle would have wished for the Council to be kept in Paris.[6] The presence on French territory of the Alliance's supreme political body (called into existence in Article 9 of the Washington Treaty) would indeed have consecrated his idea of the Alliance by demonstrating that France remained essentially a fully fledged ally. But, from the U.S. point of view, this would have handed too much to the General, "in light of the reduced participation" of France in NATO. Moreover, the Americans hoped that the Council would be located near SHAPE, itself transferred to Belgium. Only some countries like Denmark and Canada were hesitant to see the Council leave France, fearing that Paris might react negatively to this move; but the decision to transfer it to Brussels was finally taken without difficulty. In the wake of this, the Fourteen decided that the Military Committee to which France no longer belonged (while remaining represented by a liaison body, the head of which had observer status) would be itself transferred from Washington to Brussels. An international military staff, also without French participation, was created to assist it.[7] It replaced the Standing Group, the only institution in the Alliance that partook, albeit only formally, of the tripartism that France had promoted in vain. This gave satisfaction to the "small" countries by ending a kind of discrimination.

The autumn ministerial session, held in Paris from December 14 to 16, 1966, (while the transfer of SHAPE, AFCENT, and the Defense College was underway and the last major decisions on relocating had just been taken, concerning the Military Committee and the Council) ratified these new institutional arrangements. "For the first time in NATO history," the DPC, composed of the fourteen defense ministers, dealt with military matters and the North Atlantic Council, composed of fifteen foreign ministers, with the Alliance's political matters. In short, Washington thought that "NATO is leaving France" without creating tensions; from then on, it would be able to cooperate with Paris "to the extent that this does not damage essential interests," but it should continue to be modernized and adapted by the Fourteen to the new political, strategic, and military situations. In sum, not only had the Alliance "met de Gaulle's challenge," by solving, from an institutional viewpoint, the question of "the France–NATO relationship," but the Atlantic organization found itself improved, rationalized (by the regrouping of SHAPE, the Council, and the Military Committee), and even "democratized" (by the suppression of the Standing Group).[8]

The Alliance's *Raison d'Être*

Yet from the U.S. viewpoint, at the end of 1966 there remained grave uncertainties to dissipate, in both the military area, where most of the allied countries, starting with the United States itself, were subject to pressures to lower their defense effort, and in the strategic area, where NATO's new doctrine remained to be refined. But for the Johnson administration, the principal challenge was political in nature. The Americans fully realized that the atmosphere of détente settling over Europe and between the two Great Powers could not avoid having an impact on an Alliance created at the climax of the Cold War to confront the Soviet threat. This threat had not disappeared, but perception of it was becoming blurred. The United States should therefore demonstrate that "in spite of the reduced probability of a war in Europe, the nature of the Soviet threat still calls for an effective NATO" and that inversely, "a strong Alliance is an essential prerequisite to the attainment of a genuine détente and an equitable settlement in Europe."[9] In short, as de Gaulle had been hammering for years, the political and strategic conditions that had given birth to the Alliance had radically changed, and it became of primary concern for Washington to convince the Europeans that NATO remained indispensable in the context of détente.

De Gaulle's policy was at least indirectly responsible for the move to redefine the objectives and political legitimation of the Atlantic Alliance that occurred during the second half of 1966, under U.S. impetus. In a few months, the problematic of East-West relations in Europe was indeed totally changed. After de Gaulle's trip to Moscow, the idea of détente had made progress in the East, with the Soviet Union and its satellites solemnly declaring themselves in favor of it in a document that they adopted in July 1966 in Bucharest, which formally proposed a conference on European security, thus echoing the Gaullist triad. In the West, the change came first from Washington, where the administration after long demarcating itself from them, now professed on East-West relations views that were closer to those of de Gaulle. On October 7, 1966, in an important speech given in New York, Johnson launched a U.S. policy of détente in Europe, which according to him should go hand in hand with modernizing NATO and strengthening European integration (two points on which he obviously differed from the General) and would eventually allow Germany to be unified. The Americans were now convinced, in large part under pressure from de Gaulle's East-West activism, that maintaining their Atlantic leadership meant abandoning a status quo policy that could no longer satisfy their European allies. However, Vietnam was obviously not absent from Johnson's preoccupations: détente with the USSR aimed also at obtaining, thanks to Moscow's influence, greater moderation on the part of Ho Chi Minh and North Vietnam.

Things were also changing in Germany. The Erhard–Schröder tandem had since the spring been manifesting a very cautious change in attitude on détente and on the issue of relations with the FRG's eastern neighbors (this was the subject of the "peace note" of March 25, 1966). The advent of a "grand coalition" government in the fall, with the Christian Democrat Kurt Georg Kiesinger as chancellor and the Social Democrat Willy Brandt as foreign minister, seemed to herald a profound change. Less dependent on the United States, more attentive to Franco-German relations, the Kiesinger–Brandt tandem seemed determined to work toward a decisive improvement in relations between West Germany and the communist countries.[10]

In this context, at the end of 1966 the Americans thought the moment had come for the Alliance to tackle the question of détente. Their worry was the overly wide spectrum of views that they thought existed among the allies on the subject of East-West relations, and the concomitant risk, in a climate of détente, of seeing some of them negotiate at any cost an East-West rapprochement without care for Alliance interests as a whole. It was preferable, from Washington's point of view, to put some order into all that and to arrive at a common approach, in some way to "NATO-ize" détente. Preferable and also manageable, since, as the Americans told themselves, the allies basically aspired for the most part to an East-West rapprochement, and all of them also recognized the indispensable character of NATO "as long as the basic problems of peace and of European security and German reunification have not been resolved."[11] The United States, like most of its allies, to sum things up, "sees a need to articulate an up-to-date role for the Alliance," to ensure its "continued relevance to efforts to improve East-West relations," and finally, to ensure "continued governmental and public support for the goals of Western cohesion and the Alliance's deterrent strength."[12] Hence the idea of expressing and collectively applying these ideas among the allies.

The exercise was not entirely new. The problem of political consultation was almost as old as the Alliance. In 1956, with the three "wise men's" report on nonmilitary cooperation (in the context of the first East-West "thaw"), the allies had pledged to intensify consultation within NATO so as to agree on overall political perspectives, but this pledge had remained a dead letter. While since then the need for coordination among the allies (demanded by de Gaulle in his own way in 1958) had figured ritually in their communiqués without any concrete result, by 1966 the context had completely changed: the U.S. administration was now decided upon taking the initiative to obtain results, quite simply because it was totally in its interest to do so.[13]

The "Future Tasks" of the Alliance

It was Belgian diplomacy that supplied the opportunity. Noting the wish of most of the member-states to strengthen the political dimension of the Alliance after the French withdrawal, Pierre Harmel, the Belgian foreign minister, proposed in the autumn of 1966 to undertake a study of the "future tasks of the Alliance." The proposal, still only vague, tied in with the preoccupations of the Americans, to whom the Belgians transmitted at the end of November, in a bilateral way, a memorandum laying out their initiative. The State Department indeed saw in a collective examination of Alliance functions a way of answering the issues of the moment: the increased power and role of Western Europe, as well as the balance to be established in Alliance strategy between defense and détente. Even more important, the exercise would reassert the validity of the Washington Treaty beyond 1969 and explain the need for the Alliance to "younger generations." In sum, it would offer a "constructive" approach to Alliance affairs after the French withdrawal.[14]

The Harmel proposal was put on the agenda of the ministerial session of December 1966. Washington could well see the advantage of letting a European country take the initiative; on the other hand, the United States had decided to be the driving force in the exercise, so as to orient it to the U.S. perspective. The Americans already had definite ideas about the project; in particular, they thought that it should be exclusively political in nature, because the military and strategic problems should be handled elsewhere. Moreover, this was the condition for French participation in the study—one they sorely wanted, seeking to "neutralize" de Gaulle's Eastern European policy. Washington wanted East-West relations, the problems of European security and the German question, internal relations in the Alliance and European unification, and political consultation and the organization of NATO to be the principal subjects tackled.[15]

On the eve of the ministerial session, allied reactions to the Belgian project, pushed by the United States, remained uncertain.[16] In fact, the debates within the Council highlighted the skepticism of some allies about the usefulness and nature of the exercise. Nevertheless the Harmel project was adopted unanimously without major difficulty, not even on France's part. In a resolution appended to the communiqué, the Fifteen decided "to study the future tasks which face the Alliance, and its procedure for fulfilling them, in order to strengthen the Alliance as a factor for a durable peace."[17] This led Rusk, cabling Johnson the results of the ministerial session of December 16, to report that "the NATO meeting has gone well."[18]

Discussions within the Council confirmed that Bonn was finally accepting the principle of an East-West rapprochement that would be not the end result but rather the precondition of a settlement of the German question. This is what Rusk realized in listening to Willy Brandt's speech: the new German government, he wrote to Johnson, did not intend to remain "bound by the rigid theology of the Adenauer period," and appeared "prepared to probe the possibilities of better relations with Eastern Europe, including the East Germans." Had the secretary of state forgotten that the United States had acquiesced to that theology until very recently? Be that as it may, Rusk now recommended letting the West Germans get involved in rapprochement with the East: "this may not move us forward, but twenty years of hostile confrontation has not done so."[19] Meanwhile, the Kiesinger–Brandt tandem, in its governmental declaration on December 13, had confirmed the evolution begun in the spring regarding Bonn's position on détente and the German question.[20] Seen from Paris, this marked the start of a rallying to de Gaulle's position, and the Quai d'Orsay congratulated itself that the Kiesinger government now recognized in détente the means of resolving the German problem and arriving at a European arrangement.[21] A meeting between de Gaulle and Kiesinger in January 1967 would confirm a certain convergence between France and Germany, notably over relations with the East.[22]

Nevertheless, French diplomacy found itself in a sort of dilemma. Washington, Bonn, and NATO itself were now implicitly recognizing the correctness of French ideas, particularly on the key point of détente as a process rather than as a result. As Maurice Couve de Murville noted with a certain irony, as soon as it was "recommended by Washington," détente became "respectable."[23] But this new fact posed certain problems for French diplomacy. No longer the only one proposing a coherent approach to détente, it lost *ipso facto* part of its originality, hence its impact on East-West relations. Moreover, the emergence of a U.S. policy of détente increased the risk, still felt in Paris, of a Soviet-American rapprochement that might be made to the detriment of Europeans. Finally and perhaps more seriously, the launch of a dynamic and autonomous *Ostpolitik* could well carry in time the threat of the political emancipation of West Germany in Europe, if not of a rapprochement between Germany and the Soviet Union.

The Harmel Report

Therefore, though France took part in elaborating the Harmel report throughout 1967, its participation was not exempt from difficulty. To Paris it appeared more and more clearly that the exercise was really aimed at reconsolidating the Alliance and reasserting U.S. leadership, while acting as a riposte to de Gaulle. By associating with it unreservedly, France might risk endorsing the U.S. approach and thereby blunting its own Atlantic "difference." And yet, the Harmel exercise adopted, at least partially, the Gaullist approach to détente; by demarcating from it, Paris would risk contradicting its own policy.

During the first months of 1967, this dilemma was scarcely apparent, with the basic questions not really yet broached. At the end of February, the Council created a working group under the chairmanship of Manlio Brosio. This "special group" split its work into four rubrics, each given to a subgroup, with activities being coordinated by *rapporteurs*. The first subgroup, cochaired by German and British diplomats, would deal with East-West relations; the second, chaired by Paul-Henri Spaak, with relations among the allies; the third, under the American Foy Kohler, with the general defense policy of the Alliance; and the fourth, under a Dutch university professor, with issues outside the NATO area. Although a participant in the exercise, France did not play a major role.[24] American diplomacy, while giving the major roles to its best European allies (the German and British cochairmanship of the "East-West" subgroup was in this respect characteristic), was strongly involved, notably via close bilateral contacts with the Belgians.

During the ministerial session of June 13 to 15, 1967, in Luxembourg, the foreign ministers of the Fifteen examined an interim report prepared by the special group. At this stage, the content of the Harmel report was merely sketched, and the most politically sensitive questions remained to be treated, notably in the subgroup on East-West relations, which had not yet touched the German question and the problematic of an eventual European settlement.[25] While the French representative during the spring had uttered certain reservations about the work of the fourth and especially the second subgroup,[26] seen from Washington, the exercise was unfolding in a satisfactory manner. The discussions begun at the start of the year were judged to be "frank" by the U.S. administration and augured "valuable conclusions," all the more because NATO was also making strides in the military and strategic areas, notably after the establishment of the nuclear planning group (see below).

The fact that the Harmel exercise had progressed to that point without real friction even on France's part (although France was expected to be less keen when it came to adopting definitive conclusions[27]) strongly contributed, from the U.S. viewpoint, to giving the Alliance a "new sense of purpose," stimulated as it had been by the period "of intense and constructive activity" since the French withdrawal—and even thanks to it. The Alliance was on its way to resolving the principal practical questions linked to de Gaulle's decision, but also to facing the political challenge the General had made.[28] To be sure, in the spring of 1967, important subjects still threatened to divide the allies, such as the Vietnam War and the Arab-Israeli conflict. But overall, the Americans thought, "the state of the Alliance is definitely better than many officials and journalists thought possible one year ago."[29]

In the fall, though, as could have been predicted, the Harmel exercise ran into fundamental difficulties. But it was not the result of the work of the subgroup on East-West relations that gave rise to the most controversy—even from Paris, where it was observed that it "bore the mark of French ideas;"[30] nor even the "defense policy" group, which did not concern France directly and which, by affirming that defense and deterrence were compatible with détente, scarcely aroused argument. As for the "out of area" group, which prescribed better coordination of global policies among the allies, its content was rather watered-down, even though Paris proved very critical of the idea that the Alliance might contribute to the maintenance of international order beyond the geographic scope of the treaty.[31] It was therefore mostly over the work of the subgroup on relations among allies that things went badly. The report written by Paul-Henri Spaak was (even from the U.S. viewpoint) particularly severe toward France's European and Atlantic policy, "targeted from one end of the report to the other," it was thought in Paris. As a result, the report was purely and simply rejected by the French representative, who considered the document unacceptable and not even suitable for discussion.[32] Couve de Murville and de Gaulle took the matter to Brosio, evoking the possibility that France would dissociate itself totally from the study's conclusions on the future tasks of the Alliance.[33]

This crisis around the Harmel report, which approached its climax in the fall of 1967, did expose growing French frustration with the turn taken by the exercise as a whole. The Harmel report in effect had the main objective of giving NATO a predominant role in the conduct of East-West détente, which, despite the basically limited bearing of the document's content, was contrary to the principle of independence of French foreign policy espoused by de Gaulle. For Paris, the Harmel study should have been merely an exchange of views within the Council, and not be transformed into a system of obligations or commitments on the part of member-states, nor carry "formulas for coordination tending to result in a "single" Alliance policy."[34] France therefore vigorously refused "instituting even the appearance of a policy of blocs that, under the pretext of strengthening and harmonizing the initiatives of allied countries, would only perpetuate a Cold War situation."[35]

In comparison to 1958 and de Gaulle's memorandum, the situation was reversed. France now rejected any Western political coordination that would bind the members of the Alliance too strongly. It is true that the international situation and the givens of the Alliance had radically changed since then. Moreover, the French hard line, very clear in the fall of 1967, went hand in hand with the particularly sharp tensions that resulted from de Gaulle's policy toward *les Anglo-Saxons* in other areas: Vietnam, the Middle East, and Quebec. The idea that the General's policy might lead between then and 1969 to a pure and simple rupture between France and the Alliance was even rumored by some figures close to power like Louis Vallon, whose article, published in September, caused a "wave of disquiet" in NATO.[36] Seen from Washington, the risk had to be taken seriously. The CIA thought that de Gaulle might hope to draw advantages from a French withdrawal from the Alliance, notably vis-à-vis the East, without suffering grave consequences; indeed, U.S. protection would be maintained no matter what happened, especially if France managed to conclude a bilateral military alliance with the United States.[37]

Yet nothing leads one to believe that de Gaulle seriously dreamed in the fall of 1967 of leaving the Alliance, any more than in 1965 or in 1966. On the other hand, Paris wanted to react to the operation of relegitimating NATO that the United States was leading with success and of which the Harmel report was the master stroke. The U.S. administration feared the consequences of confrontation over this; Washington had an interest in Paris being associated with the conclusions of the Harmel report, even if its content was diluted by this. During the final discussions in November, U.S. diplomats accordingly doubled their efforts to avoid a stalemate. In fact, the French recognized the evolution of their partners toward "more realism" and grudgingly moved toward accepting the Harmel report.[38]

The "Report on the Future Tasks of the Alliance" was formally and unanimously adopted on December 14, 1967, by the Atlantic Council, which appended it to its final communiqué. This brief document, whose argument is hardly developed (this was the price of compromise), nevertheless marks an important stage in the history of the Alliance, since it contributed to ending a period of uncertainty, in which the French withdrawal was the apogee. The Fifteen recognized that "the Alliance is a dynamic and vigorous organization which is constantly adapting itself to changing conditions," and particularly to the fact that the international situation "has changed significantly" since 1949. In the new context, the Alliance had two "main functions": to maintain the military power and political cohesion necessary to balance Soviet potential, which remained considerable; and to contribute to détente, which was not in contradiction with "military security." These two functions were closely linked; it is through the maintenance of the military and political cohesion of NATO that the allies were promoting détente, including through a process of balanced disarmament between East and West, in such a way that "the ultimate political purpose of the Alliance is to achieve a just and lasting peaceful order in Europe, accompanied by appropriate security guarantees," obviously including the settlement of the German question. In short, the Fifteen agreed on the "importance of the role which the Alliance is called upon to play in the coming years in the promotion of détente and the strengthening of peace."[39]

From the U.S. viewpoint, the Harmel report was an incontestable success: it consecrated the viability of the Alliance and of United States leadership in Europe at a moment when, on the strategic and military levels, NATO was managing to strengthen its unity.[40] Hence the measured enthusiasm with which Paris welcomed the Harmel report, eighteen months after leaving "integration" and at the close of a year marked by an unprecedented cooling of Franco-American relations. But there was more. To be sure, the Harmel report confirmed (and this was really why France could not dissociate from it) that the Alliance "after several years, is making French policy its own."[41] But to what extent? In consecrating the pursuit of East-West rapprochement as an "essential function" of the Alliance, the United States succeeded at the same time in "NATO-izing" détente. Doing this, they imposed on their allies a concept (and soon a practice) of East-West relations that was antithetical to that developed by de Gaulle since 1965. This concept postulated the strengthening of Western political and military integration as the precondition for East-West rapprochement, whereas for the General only the dissolution of the logic of blocs would permit not only détente, but also entente and cooperation. And this was at the very moment when de Gaulle, after a trip to Poland in September, began to see how rigid and durable the Soviet hold over Eastern Europe really was. The fearful risk since the 1961–1962 crises became concrete: before producing a hypothetical European settlement that would spell the end of blocs, détente in Europe might well, and for a long time, strengthen their existence. In the meantime, the Atlantic Alliance found itself, at the end of 1967, recharged in its *raison d'être* and strengthened in its unity, despite the French withdrawal. Paradoxically, de Gaulle's policy had contributed to this.

FLEXIBLE RESPONSE AND "STRATÉGIE TOUS AZIMUTS"

The French withdrawal totally modified the strategic problematic within the Alliance. The institutional compromise of the autumn of 1966 cleared the way for adopting a new strategy and new procedures for nuclear consultation by the "integrated" allies. Flexible response thus became NATO's strategic doctrine in 1967, while France asserted its own autonomous nuclear strategy.

Nonproliferation (Continued)

The adoption of flexible response by the Fourteen was made possible by the gradual calming of the debate over nuclear sharing. In the fall of 1965 the Germans, as seen above, had agreed, reluctantly, to Washington's abandonment of the MLF.[42] But the delicate problem of the nonproliferation treaty (NPT), actively negotiated by the Americans and Soviets since 1966, remained. For Moscow, the NPT was to prevent any future measure of effective nuclear sharing among Western powers. The Americans had their backs to the wall: they had to either give up the NPT or accept a formulation that made a new version of the MLF impossible, even in the distant future and if European political unification had made some decisive progress.[43] The difficulty would then be to obtain agreement from the Germans (and Italians) to a treaty that not only would put a definite end to any nuclear ambition on their part but would also risk preventing the emergence of a European nuclear identity. In fact, many Europeans (like the secretary general of the Alliance himself) feared that the NPT would put Western Europe in a "second-class category," isolate Germany, and in the end weaken the Atlantic Alliance as a whole.[44] In 1966, the NPT had replaced the MLF as the number one problem in relations between Germany and the United States.[45]

Nevertheless, the Americans were more and more firmly attached to the NPT and were now convinced that the Soviets also wished to sign the treaty. More importantly, it appeared clear at the end of the summer of 1966 that although the USSR still held to the NPT's prohibiting any future return to the MLF, it nevertheless appeared disposed to accept compatibility between the NPT and the existing nuclear arrangements within NATO, that is, double-key nuclear weapons, as well as arrangements discussed under McNamara's initiative, that is, pertaining to nuclear consultation and planning.[46] For the Americans, who had thought until then that Moscow wanted to use the NPT to prevent any nuclear arrangements within NATO, even those put in place after 1957, it was a window of opportunity they did not want to lose at any price.

In early October 1966, Johnson gathered his principal advisers and took a position in favor of the NPT. It was an opportunity for him to try to clarify things in the realm of nuclear sharing: "We are opposed to the proliferation of nuclear weapons. We are not going to turn our nuclear weapons over to any other countries. The responsibility for firing U.S. nuclear weapons rests with the President of the U.S. . . . But we cannot undertake a treaty obligation which commits us to act as if there were no Alliance. . . . We cannot say to our allies that these matters are none of their business."[47] However diversely interpreted within the administration, the president's position seemed to come down to this: yes to a nonproliferation treaty, provided that it authorizes the existing nuclear arrangements within NATO as well as nuclear consultation among allies; and yes to nuclear arrangements among allies, provided they are compatible with the nonproliferation requirement. In any case, the president's will to achieve the NPT gave a decisive impulse to negotiations with the USSR.[48] At the end of October, the U.S. representative, Harlan Cleveland, could declare to the Atlantic Council that the desire to achieve this was great on both sides.[49]

Meanwhile, the German attitude was changing.[50] In 1965–1966, the FRG had proved extremely reticent about the NPT project, not only because it signified the death of the MLF, but also and especially because it was perceived as singling out Germany for a discriminatory nonnuclear status. In the fall of 1966, Bonn proved more disposed to accept the fact that the NPT prohibited any actual nuclear sharing among allies. At the end of September, Erhard and Schröder formally confirmed this to Johnson and Rusk and expressed their attachment to nonproliferation. This was confirmed by the grand coalition government that succeeded Erhard's a few days later. At the Atlantic Council of December 1966, Willy Brandt declared that Bonn was ready to let drop any idea of actual nuclear sharing of the MLF type; he also stated that Germany was giving up the "European clause" under which the United States might transfer to a united Europe a nuclear capability (Brandt thought that a united Europe, in any case a remote prospect, would in any event be recognized as a nuclear power by the simple devolution of France's and Great Britain's nuclear status and that the NPT could in any case be renegotiated at that time). For Rusk, who saw this as a decisive change, the Germans were now ready to accept the NPT.[51]

The secretary of state was overly optimistic. Although the interdiction of any sharing of the MLF type under the NPT was almost accepted in Bonn, there remained the issue of the discriminatory character of the treaty project, which the right (Kiesinger and the CDU) refused; a clear commitment from Germany on the NPT was still far away, and it would not be until 1969 that Germany, with Brandt now chancellor, after a long internal debate would adhere to the treaty. Yet, after years of nuclear ambiguity fed by the debate over the MLF, Bonn did adopt in 1966 a more flexible approach to the question of nuclear sharing.

This change went along with a modification in the German attitude toward détente. Its renunciation of its nuclear pretensions was indeed, from the Soviet viewpoint, the *sine qua non* condition of rapprochement. In this sense, in the nuclear area as in the political area, Bonn little by little came closer to the Gaullist perspective: the General had indicated since 1959 that Germany's definite renunciation of nuclear weapons was the indispensable step toward solving the German question. Thus, Paris welcomed with satisfaction the position expressed by Brandt to the Council in December 1966.[52]

Nevertheless, France dissociated itself more than ever from the NPT project. From the start, de Gaulle had expressed his reservations.[53] Now that the general outline of the future treaty was known, French opposition became categorical. Certainly, France under the NPT was a nuclear state and consequently would not see its status as an atomic power called into question by the treaty (on the contrary, it would be recognized), whereas the nonnuclear status of Germany would be consecrated. Certainly, Paris did not intend to encourage proliferation and clearly considered it desirable to limit nuclear dissemination.[54] In fact, the French opposition was in essence political. The requirement of nuclear independence was hardly compatible with a treaty whose spirit was fundamentally discriminatory toward nonnuclear countries. France, which had experienced a discriminatory nuclear policy (that of the United States), could only state its reservations about the spirit of the NPT.[55] Worse yet, the NPT project was from the French viewpoint the very type of an essentially Soviet-American arrangement that tended to ratify East-West partition and the bloc system, even if in the name of disarmament—and consequently it was entirely contrary to the French idea of détente.

At a time in 1966–1967 when de Gaulle was pushing his denunciation of the double hegemony of the United States and USSR to an extreme, the NPT thus appeared incompatible with French foreign policy and security as a whole. In early 1967, the United States had no illusions about the possibility of bringing France on board.[56] But Washington's principal partners were more or less favorable to the NPT, even if in Germany (and Italy) this was not totally settled. In July 1968 the NPT would therefore be signed without France. But France henceforth would act as if it had ratified the treaty, which demonstrated to what extent its position was essentially political and principled.[57]

Nuclear Planning

Clarification of the double debate between the United States and the USSR and the United States and Germany over nuclear sharing and nonproliferation made possible the logical completion of the initiative taken by McNamara in 1965: the establishment of a procedure for nuclear consultation and, in its wake, the adoption of flexible response by NATO. After the French withdrawal, the Americans were indeed particularly determined to surmount the institutional blockage provoked by de Gaulle's policy in the nuclear domain so as to consolidate the consensus that occurred after the McNamara proposals and, in so doing, neutralize France's strategic dissidence. The institutionalization of nuclear consultation and the adoption of flexible response clearly went hand in hand. It was the new functioning of the "14 + 1" Alliance that would permit this double advance that was both institutional and strategic.

Let us consider the institutional advance first. After the creation of the Special Committee in November 1965 and the three ad hoc working groups, there was progress in setting up bodies and procedures for nuclear consultation.[58] During the first months of 1966, the Americans led by McNamara made a serious information effort about operational nuclear issues, notably within the working group on planning, limited to five countries: the United States, Great Britain, West Germany, Italy, and Turkey. The French withdrawal in March 1966 could only facilitate the process. Paris could no longer obstruct the exercise and realized the European allies' interest in it, especially the Germans, who were satisfied to be able to participate actively in nuclear planning.[59]

In the summer of 1966 (as Moscow no longer sought to oppose it), there was a clear trend toward institutionalizing the working group on nuclear planning. The working group made proposals in this direction at the end of September 1966, which the Americans intended to have ratified by their integrated allies during the Alliance's ministerial session in December 1966. Accordingly, it was at Fourteen within the DPC that the allies formally approved the Special Committee's report proposing its own transformation, as well as that of the working group on nuclear planning, into permanent NATO institutions.[60] For Washington this was proof that the allies "are moving to give substance to their common interests in the nuclear area—in spite of past French objections."[61]

The December 1966 ministerial session resulted in the definitive creation of two bodies on which would sit the defense ministers or their representatives: a plenary body, the Nuclear Defense Affairs Committee (NDAC), open to all interested allies; and a restricted body, the Nuclear Planning Group (NPG), limited to seven members, four permanent (United States, Great Britain, West Germany, and Italy) and three rotating members. Formally, the NPG was subject to the NDAC. But it was the NPG that would do most of the planning and consultation. This dual structure gave the "small" countries in the Alliance the feeling of being fully involved in the process, while allowing, as McNamara wanted from the start, effective work within a restricted setup.[62] On the eve of the NPG's first meeting in April 1967 in Washington, McNamara declared that the new body would allow the allies to have more influence over "assessing the nuclear threat," over "determining what forces were required to meet that threat," and over the "conditions [in which] those nuclear forces would be employed." The NPG had before it an important task: to establish the plans for selective use of nuclear weapons in Europe and to define the role of these forces in the flexible response strategy. This was a difficult task, knowing that until then no systematic study of the role of tactical nuclear weapons in Europe (whose number had been growing steadily since the early 1960s) had been undertaken, nor any coordination of different national viewpoints on this subject.[63]

The setting up of the NPG was obviously a U.S. success. It consolidated the nuclear consensus that the United States had finally obtained from its "integrated" allies, putting an end to a period of several years during which the question of the relation between the nuclear and nonnuclear states had been at the heart of transatlantic problems, particularly through the debate over the MLF. Germany, as pivot of the Alliance, opted for active participation in NATO deterrence, but it renounced nuclear aspirations that had been formerly less modest. Implicitly accepted by Moscow, the creation of the NPG, in parallel with the maturing of the NPT, seemed able to solve the German nuclear problem.

This success had a price, since it consecrated the special status of France and the nuclear division within the Alliance. In fact, it was in the nuclear domain that the divorce between France and NATO was the most evident: Paris refused, in the name of its nuclear independence, any participation in NATO activities in this area; and the United States wanted to avoid France's having any control over the nuclear debates of the integrated allies. Of course, this evolution spelled a defeat for France, which had not been able to promote a European approach to deterrence and offer a credible alternative to the U.S. guarantee. But at the same time, the NPG, complemented by the immanent NPT project, offered a framework able to contain German nuclear ambitions, not a negligible advantage for France.

The Adoption of Flexible Response

In these conditions, the formal adoption by NATO of flexible response was no more than a formality for the Americans. It was on May 9, 1967, that NATO, without France of course, officially ratified the strategic concept of flexible response, almost five years to the day after the Athens speech. At the close of 1967, the integrated allies gave the new strategy a more detailed operational content in the document MC 14/3, titled "Overall Strategic Concept for the Defense of the NATO Area," which replaced the old MC 14/2. Developed within the military committee in the fall of 1967, MC 14/3 (dated January16, 1968) was also adopted at the political level by the DPC.[64]

The new strategic concept was founded on a range "of appropriate responses, conventional and nuclear, to all levels of aggression or threats of aggression." The aim was "first to deter aggression and thus preserve peace," and in the event an act of aggression had taken place, "to maintain the security and integrity" of Alliance territory.[65] To do this, MC 14/3 called for a defense according to three successive phases: a phase of direct defense, at the level of force (conventional or nuclear) adapted to the nature of the aggression; then a phase of deliberate escalation in case direct defense failed; and finally a phase of general nuclear response in case of a major nuclear attack.[66]

In fact, the military and strategic impact of the formal adoption of flexible response by NATO was limited. In 1964–1965, McNamara had begun to moderate his initial ideas by taking account of European views, notably on the nuclear threshold.[67] The strategic document adopted in 1967 was thus remote from the 1961–1962 concept of flexible response. In the face of negative reactions of the Europeans (and not only the French), but also for financial reasons, the Americans had had to come back to a more realistic concept, halfway between the initial maximalist approach of the Pentagon and the idea of a trip wire. MC 14/3 called for a phase of prolonged conventional resistance, but the document did not specify its length. In other words, flexible response in its 1967 version left the key issue of nuclear threshold ambiguous.[68]

The new strategy was thus a political compromise between the U.S. idea and the European idea of deterrence of which France had been until 1965 the champion. For example, after its adoption, the Americans thought that under flexible response a conventional resistance of ninety days should be envisaged; but the Europeans thought that the new strategy required a resistance capability of only a week.[69] Thus, the adoption of the new doctrine was only, for the United States, halfway successful from the military standpoint. In reality, it ratified an existing situation: the level of NATO's conventional defense as it existed in 1967 — a more satisfactory level than in 1961, but insufficient to resolve definitively the fundamental problem of extended deterrence, the dilemma between capitulation and annihilation that flexible response was supposed to bypass.

The adoption of flexible response, on the other hand, was a fully fledged political success for Washington since it represented a "major step toward resolving Alliance disagreements on strategy."[70] It put a stop to almost ten years of debates that had destabilized NATO, and to five years of French nuclear dissidence. Of course, the price of this success was the formal strategic partition of the Alliance and a sort of consecration of this dissidence. But the United States could only congratulate itself on the strategic compromise attained by the integrated allies. The adoption of MC 14/3 after the French withdrawal largely contributed to strengthen NATO unity and U.S. leadership in the Alliance. Moreover, in the months and years to come, the game of nuclear consultations and the functioning of the NPG would gradually consolidate what at the start was only a shaky compromise. Even if the strategic consensus remained fragile, Americans and Europeans got to know each other's perspectives, between which there had not been any real interaction until then. The paradox was that France, yet again, had powerfully contributed.

A Nonevent?

The French side was not mistaken about the significance of the adoption of flexible response. Since 1965 at least, the stakes of the strategic debates between France and the United States within NATO had a political import greater than their military import. For de Gaulle, the adoption of flexible response was therefore, from a military viewpoint, a nonevent. "NATO," he explained a few days after the adoption of MC 14/3, "just echoed what had already been a fact for years," since the United States, thanks to its dominant position in NATO, had already modified *de facto* its strategy, hence that of the Alliance. France, which had unsuccessfully tried to oppose it, was thus not concerned by "the decision taken by NATO." For the General, the basic problem remained the same: the adoption of flexible response merely confirmed the erosion of the U.S. nuclear guarantee.[71]

But MC 14/3 did contribute to radicalizing French dissent, or at least its declaratory expression. Already, before the 1966 rupture, notions of "decision-making autonomy," "vital interests," and "absolute deterrence" had been more and more systematically opposed to concepts of "escalation" and "extended deterrence."[72] After the adoption of flexible response, this differentiation became systematic. It accentuated the tendency, clear after 1965, to present French deterrence in the absence of any reference to the Soviet threat so as to make it more compatible with détente and to demarcate it from U.S. deterrence.

At the start of 1967, de Gaulle wrote a directive laying out the basis of French policy on deterrence until 1980. It relied on "a planetary system" composed of thermonuclear bombs carried by bombers (the first French "H" bomb would explode in 1968), and of intercontinental ballistic and submarine-launched missiles, capable of "striking wherever necessary on the surface of the earth."[73] At the end of 1967, General Ailleret published in the *Revue de Défense Nationale* an article that took up these ideas. The French deterrent force, wrote Ailleret, should not be "pointed in a single direction, that of some a priori enemy, but be capable of intervening everywhere, be therefore what we call, in our military jargon, *all-round*."[74] This expression not only faithfully translated de Gaulle's thought, but he had knowledge of it before the appearance of Ailleret's text, whose content he had approved.[75]

The notion of "all round" deterrence (*tous azimuts* in artillery terms, multidirectional) in any case conforms to a number of de Gaulle's declarations on the subject in years past, even if they did not stress it.[76] Ailleret's article had a major impact and the General endorsed it unequivocally to the audience at the Centre des Hautes Études Militaires (CHEM) in January 1968: "Our atomic weapons system must be all-round. You must know this, you must see this and your studies and your outlook must adapt to it."[77] In fact, the radicalization of the French declaratory strategy, willed by de Gaulle, aimed perhaps above all to make the army chiefs admit the decisive character of the rupture stemming from the nuclearization of French defense, while turning them away from Atlantic conformity.[78] From this viewpoint, the "all-round" deterrent posture underlined, almost to the point of caricature, the primacy of independence regarding military weapons at a time when, more than ever, de Gaulle was stressing the necessity of independence in general. In short, the "non-directed" presentation of French deterrence transposed to the strategic domain the rejection of the logic of blocs and belonged to a prospective vision of an international order that in the long term would privilege threats other than that of the USSR.[79]

But in the wake of the adoption by its allies of flexible response, the "all-round" discourse aimed especially to show French difference within NATO and to act in such a way that the *force de frappe* was not reduced to "a force complementary to that of the principal member" of the Alliance.[80] This objective was fully attained: the "all-round" doctrine was generally received in the United States and in Alliance circles at best as a provocation, at worse as a threat. In France, even in circles close to power, the malaise was real.[81] At the extreme, Ailleret's formula was interpreted as meaning that the United States itself might one day figure among the potential targets of the *force de frappe;* more subtly, it was received as an equivocal declaration of armed neutrality, which would be the logical end product of de Gaulle's policy with respect to the United States and the Alliance.

The first interpretation was absurd: when Ailleret wondered about the United States and its power "in twenty years' time," it was not to suggest that it might end up in the camp of France's enemies, but to question whether it would still be capable of "deterring any risk of major war." The second interpretation is simply erroneous. If the *tous azimuts* doctrine was opposed in principle to flexible response, Ailleret nevertheless emphasized that it did not prohibit "our incorporating in an alliance adapted to the danger to be confronted: it would even allow us to incorporate ourselves for the best, as a member remaining free in the last resort to conduct its own actions, within the common framework of the Alliance."[82]

Beyond the declaratory aspect, the two strategies were indeed not necessarily antithetical or irreconcilable from an operational standpoint. Certainly, "evaluation of the moment of recourse to nuclear weapons" remained the heart of the problem.[83] But though France proclaimed a low nuclear threshold and NATO an elevated one, the operational reality was more nuanced. The United States, as we have seen, had been unable to sufficiently strengthen NATO's conventional defense, and so one could foresee a more immediate resort to tactical nuclear weapons than might be wished. Conversely, on the French side, there was no question of a systematic escalation to a general nuclear response. To be sure, the priority of de Gaulle's defense policy was strategic nuclear capability; yet he considered it indispensable to strengthen the forces of maneuver designed to participate in the common defense of Central Europe alongside the allies. Moreover, he intended to give these forces a national tactical nuclear capability.[84] In November 1966, with the United States having terminated after the French withdrawal the "double key" arrangements that benefited French forces, a firm decision to construct the Pluton short-range missile and the tactical nuclear bomb AN-52 was taken in the defense council.[85] De Gaulle's concept, essentially a pragmatic one, was thus by no means "all or nothing"; even after the withdrawal, it conceived of French strategy in Central Europe alongside the allies as complementary with NATO strategy.[86]

Between the French and American conceptions, there existed in fact, from an operational viewpoint, a difference of degree more than a difference of principle, even if on both sides "the spotlight had been put on this difference for political reasons"[87] (after 1967, and still more after de Gaulle's departure from power, the gap between the declaratory presentation and the operational reality would keep growing). Moreover, in the last analysis, the question of operational articulation between French deterrence and NATO strategy would be played out in the military relations between France and NATO as they had been redefined in 1966–1967, and these relations would be characterized by a concern to ensure a real military complementarity between France and NATO in Central Europe.

FROM INTEGRATION TO COOPERATION

After the French withdrawal, many uncertainties remained about the future of integrated defense. For Washington, it was at least as urgent to tackle the military problems of the Fourteen as to solve the issue of relations between France and NATO in this area, since it was the survival of the Atlantic defense system that was at stake.

Burden-sharing

For the Americans, the future of integrated defense required "burden-sharing," which had become a major theme of transatlantic relations.[88] But it was not a new theme: since the Eisenhower administration the deterioration in the balance of payments, in large part due to the U.S. military presence in Europe, had alerted the Americans to the heavy liability caused by their participation in the defense of Europe and the serious consequences that this might eventually have for transatlantic relations.[89] Particularly sensitive to this issue, the Kennedy administration had obtained from the allies, especially the Germans, measures aiming to offset the outflow of dollars to maintain three hundred thousand American troops in Europe, through the purchase of U.S. military equipment. But, in 1965–1966, the financial difficulties of West Germany upset these arrangements. The U.S. deficit of payments — and also the British one — was aggravated as the U.S. engagement in Vietnam was increasing and as Great Britain was hit by a serious economic crisis.[90] In the fall of 1966, the risk of a withdrawal of U.S. troops from Western Europe became serious, consequent on Senator Mike Mansfield's introducing into the Senate (on August 31) a resolution calling for a "substantial" reduction in U.S. forces permanently stationed in Europe.[91] (McNamara was not against some reduction in troops, which he thought compatible with maintaining the level of military efficiency, on condition that the United States seized the opportunity of the French withdrawal to rationalize their deployment of forces in Europe.[92]) As for Great Britain, its disagreement with Bonn over offsets for the stationing of its forces in Germany threatened, also in the fall of 1966, to end in a drastic reduction of troops in the British army of the Rhine (BAOR).[93]

Burden-sharing, an economic and financial problem for the Americans and the British, had really become a political problem for NATO as a whole. A significant reduction in the U.S. military presence on the Continent could in effect be seen by the Europeans as a weakening of U.S. commitment to the defense of Europe and as a confirmation of the Gaullist analysis of the ineluctable erosion of the U.S. guarantee, and this when the French withdrawal threatened to contribute to a weakening of NATO by giving other countries a bad example. And there was a related military problem, since a chain reaction leading to a reduction in overall national contributions might lead to the whole apparatus of integrated defense unraveling like a knitted sweater — as well as a strategic problem, since that would only lead to lowering the nuclear threshold in Europe even more.

In the fall of 1966, in an atmosphere of transatlantic crisis related to the offset problem, Washington considered that burden-sharing should be broached as a priority among Americans, Germans, and British. The Johnson administration proposed to the Wilson and Erhard governments opening trilateral conversations on the issue. On October 7, Johnson asked McCloy to make proposals and designated him as representative in the trilateral talks.[94] On April 28, 1967, these resulted in an agreement of wide significance. In the short term, it ended uncertainty over the possible withdrawal of U.S. and British forces from Germany. The three countries agreed on a limited reduction of six thousand men in the BAOR (one brigade) and of thirty-five thousand American troops (one division, which though sent back to the States would remain assigned to the Central European theater and could be quickly sent back).[95]

In the longer term, Washington had at least three reasons to feel satisfied. First, a limited retreat of British and American forces reduced the risk of analogous withdrawals on the part of other allies and appeared prone to reassure Europeans of the survival of the U.S. military presence. Second, the trilateral discussions had increased confidence between Bonn and Washington and laid the bases for better financial cooperation between the two countries (the U.S. military presence in Germany would be offset not only by arms purchases, but also by monetary measures). Finally, Washington had obtained from London and Bonn recognition of the fact that burden-sharing was not only an American preoccupation, but a necessity for the whole Alliance.[96]

McCloy was correct in thinking, once his mission was accomplished in the spring of 1967, that trilateral conversations had allowed "coming a considerable distance from the unpromising situation we faced last autumn."[97] The result indeed diminished the pressure on U.S. engagement in Europe applied by Senator Mansfield's resolution, and it undoubtedly contributed to restoring the confidence of Europeans, shaken by the Gaullist policy, in the commitment of the United States to their security; in this sense, American leadership was strengthened. The 1966 crisis and the trilateral discussions prefigured the 1970s, when burden-sharing would remain the principal preoccupation of the Americans, and American disengagement the prime worry of the Europeans: In this area as in others, Gaullist policy would merely anticipate this situation and fostered an awareness of the problem.

Meanwhile, the United States solved a more technical question linked to the burden-sharing problem: that of force planning, which tried to rationalize the structure of integrated defense (and modify the strategy of the Alliance thanks to a rise in the nuclear threshold) by a better coordination between national programs and NATO force goals, as well as better correspondence between the resources of member-states and their defense efforts.[98] In the wake of the French withdrawal, this double objective, which Paris had obstructed since 1963, was more topical than ever since the United States wanted to demonstrate that NATO integration should and could function without France. In July 1966, the defense ministers of the integrated countries adopted a force plan for 1970, and at the ministerial session of December 1967, the DPC adopted a plan for the years 1968 to 1972. The rupture between France and NATO would have finally made possible the establishment of a process of planning national defense efforts that strengthened the unity and coherence of the integrated military apparatus.[99]

The Loss of French Space

However, the problem remained to be solved of future military relations between France and NATO. The issue of the FFA, already on the right track since the summer, profited from the serious difficulties met in the autumn by the United States, Germany, and Great Britain, who did not want, in addition, to run the risk of the FFA being repatriated. The maintenance of two French divisions in Germany, even nonintegrated, was in effect seen as more preferable than their simple withdrawal, which would be on top of a significant drop in British and American numbers. Moreover, the arrival of the Kiesinger–Brandt government, much more favorable to Franco-German relations, facilitated settling the problem of the status of the FFA, which was eventually settled through a simple exchange of letters between Couve de Murville and Willy Brandt on December 21, 1966.[100] In line with the position adopted by Paris since the spring, French forces were maintained in the FRG outside any constraining redefinition of their mission in relation to NATO. In the difficult climate of the fall of 1966, the FRG and its partners, giving up their initial intransigence, at the end of the day accommodated themselves to a formula that seemed least bad for the Alliance.

In parallel, U.S. forces were departing France on time. The American president insisted that the operation take place on schedule, as he had reiterated during a meeting of the National Security Council in December 1966, so that by the date fixed by de Gaulle of April 1, 1967, the U.S. military presence in France was no more than residual.[101] Moreover, the transplanting of NATO infrastructures and commands, especially SHAPE (transferred to Casteau near Mons and operational by April 1, 1967) and AFCENT (transferred to Brunssum in Holland and operational by June 1) was practically complete. (NATO's Defense College would be moved to Rome in the autumn.)

The possible use of French space by allied forces in case of conflict or crisis, to which the United States attached great importance, was an outstanding issue. It was especially important militarily. At the time when he decided to withdraw, de Gaulle had clearly allowed for the possible availability of French territory and airspace,[102] which was the subject of bilateral discussions in the second half of 1966.[103] But the negotiations between Couve de Murville and Bohlen in Paris went badly. The Americans placed the bar rather high: while taking note of the nonnegotiability of a military presence in peacetime, they wanted to obtain from France the same advantages in times of crisis or war that the United States had enjoyed previously. Paris should guarantee the functioning of the Donges-Metz pipeline in all circumstances and allow the activation of communication networks as well as access to airfields and depots, all on a simple declared alert by SACEUR, without which the Americans let it be known that an agreement could not take place. Faced with these requirements, Paris announced an equally firm position: the United States could not have any depots in France, even under French supervision, or use any base until France had formally declared its involvement in the conflict; similarly, no guarantee could be given in advance about the possible availability of the pipeline and communications installations, which could still be used by the United States in peacetime, but under French control.

Faced with French intransigence, the Americans asked themselves if it was not appropriate to interrupt negotiations over the bases, content to continue to negotiate over the pipeline alone.[104] Couve de Murville's visit to Washington on October 3 advanced things a little. For the U.S. administration, the use of the pipeline in peacetime, even without a guarantee of availability in wartime, was sufficiently worthwhile from a logistical standpoint for an accord to be concluded on this basis (it would be signed on March 24, 1967, and would allow the Donges-Metz pipeline to function for NATO's benefit, with France reserving the right to interrupt it if necessary). For the rest, negotiations made no headway. Paris rejected anything that would lead to maintaining a foreign military presence in France in peacetime and anything that would *de facto* involve automatic French engagement in case of crisis or war. In Washington, the traditional split between the military and the diplomats clearly reappeared. General Lemnitzer and the Pentagon were favorable to a discussion with France on the possibility of the United States using with France's agreement certain bases in time of crisis or war. Such arrangements would at least have the merit of existing, and of keeping up a certain level of dialogue and military cooperation between the two countries. But the State Department stressed a matter of principle that this time would carry the day: "Unless we had an iron-clad guarantee regarding the availability of facilities in an emergency or in the event of hostilities, it would be a waste of our time, effort and money to consider any French proposal"; the French were accused of seeking "an option of neutrality in the event of hostilities in Europe."[105] From this perspective, better to conclude nothing than to sanction such an unacceptable conception of the Alliance.

It was thus for political reasons that the French and Americans would fail to resolve the problem of the availability of French space. In fact, the blame could be shared. On one side, de Gaulle by refusing any prior commitment to reestablish access to French territory and installations in case of conflict, was faithful to his own logic: that of a return to the letter of the Washington Treaty. Was it not the foreign presence in France, even more than the integration of French forces, which since 1958 gave the General the impression of a serious loss of sovereignty (remembering the incident in the summer of 1958)? This partly explains an intransigence that made France vulnerable to the unfair accusation that it was keeping open an option of neutrality in case of Soviet aggression, whereas for de Gaulle it was a matter (the nuance is crucial) of avoiding, as in 1958, being implicated in a non-European conflict for which the United States would have recourse to bases in France. On the other side, while it was true that uncertainty about the availability of installations in France was a serious military disadvantage for the United States, it did not justify (as confirmed by the attitude of Lemnitzer) the refusal to conclude agreements at least stating the terms of their possible reestablishment. It was this mutual intransigence that would result in a logistical rupture between France and NATO that was sharper and more long-lasting than in the operational area. France, whose principal contribution to common defense had been until 1966 the availability to allies of its territory, stopped being NATO's "navel."[106]

The rupture was avoided—albeit barely—over airspace, on which the allies hoped to continue to count, for logistic reasons, in wartime, thanks to a decision to keep the system of annual authorization of overflight. In the spring of 1966, Paris wanted to establish a more constraining system of monthly authorization.

A compromise arose: France would maintain the previous system in exchange for access to information about the air defense alert system (NADGE) that was being set up within NATO. At the beginning of August, the reestablishment of the annual system was announced,[107] which provoked de Gaulle's anger because he had not taken the decision himself.[108] The General could not accept the affair being presented by the press as a "change of attitude, if not policy, which does not correspond to reality."[109] Despite this incident, the annual system, which he recognized as compatible with the "return to sovereignty," would be finally maintained to the satisfaction of the allied military.[110] The episode shows well to what degree the Gaullist motives were of a political nature, often leaving space for compromises.

The Ailleret-Lemnitzer Agreement

The main issue, however, remained to be solved: the future role of French forces in the common defense. A breakdown in this area would be avoided, and this role, as defined by an agreement between France and NATO, was far from expressing a French wish to stand outside the defense of Central Europe. In fact, it left room for a more significant French contribution than in the time of integration.

It would take more than a year to arrive at agreement. Negotiations between Generals Ailleret and Lemnitzer were difficult to start despite the Brussels compromise of June 1966.[111] For Paris, there was no question of the allies posing preconditions. De Gaulle specified that Ailleret and Lemnitzer could not discuss "missions" that French forces might receive from the integrated commands, since this would mean, at least symbolically, reestablishing a form of subordination. The chief of staff of the French army (CEMA) could only discuss with the supreme allied commander Europe (SACEUR) "the organization of liaisons between the two commands in the case that France were at war alongside NATO countries, that is to say, alongside the United States," as well as "certain hypotheses concerning action coordinated between NATO forces and certain French forces," while noting that "France could not make any commitment to action on this subject."[112] For NATO, conversely, the Ailleret-Lemnitzer negotiations should plan a priori a minimum acceptable amount of NATO–France cooperation. In fact, the allies were trying to reduce the impact of the FFA withdrawal from the integrated structure as much as possible. Discussions, which took place between July and October 1966, were thus at an impasse even before having really begun. But at the end of October, the allies realized the risks of failing to achieve something. Brosio played an important role in saving the situation by convincing the Fourteen to accept engaging in negotiations between SACEUR and CEMA without a directive or preordained position.[113]

The first meeting between Ailleret and Lemnitzer took place on November 23. SACEUR approached the exercise pragmatically: for him it was a matter of defining with CEMA which were the French forces that could cooperate operationally with NATO, when, and under what conditions. But negotiations were rocky. By the Council's ministerial meeting in December, nothing had yet been solved.[114] In the spring of 1967, there were still no results. Nevertheless, after agreements concerning NADGE (with which France remained associated) and the pipeline, things seemed more favorable.[115] Finally, on August 22, Ailleret and Lemnitzer arrived at an agreement sanctioned by an exchange of letters approved by the Fourteen.

In line with the position adopted by Paris since the March 1966 decision, the document was presented as simply an agreement of a military nature between CEMA and SACEUR.[116] The Ailleret-Lemnitzer agreement did not have political value from the French standpoint because, for de Gaulle, it was Article 5 of the Washington Treaty and it alone that determined the nature of French engagement in common defense, and there was no question of the Ailleret-Lemnitzer agreement representing more than a practical arrangement aiming to allow this commitment to materialize if necessary. Paris hoped, moreover, to keep the greatest discretion about the Ailleret-Lemnitzer agreement, in order to preserve the image of autonomy acquired by breaking with Atlantic integration. It was thus only by word of mouth that the French authorities would recognize the existence of arrangements for combined operations in Europe; moreover, they put the accent on the bilateral Franco-American aspect of military cooperation (whereas in fact it was Franco–NATO cooperation at issue), to suggest that it placed France on an equal footing with the United States.[117] The United States would respect this discretion, understanding that it was preferable to obtain from France the maximum operational cooperation, even if this meant maintaining the irritating image of its independence, than to risk lessening this cooperation by giving it too much publicity.

Nevertheless, the Ailleret-Lemnitzer agreement was in fact a decisive document.[118] Because it specified the nature of Franco–NATO cooperation that was replacing integration, at least in Central Europe, it had a major political and strategic impact. The Ailleret-Lemnitzer agreement concerned only the French forces in Germany, meaning two divisions of the Second Army Corps, that is, the land units still integrated before 1966. In other words, if France became engaged in case of aggression alongside NATO within the framework of the Ailleret-Lemnitzer agreement, it would do so with the same level of participation as in the time of integration, and in the same zone as before 1966, meaning in CENTAG (the southern half of the FRG). The agreement moreover specified that the limitation of Franco–NATO cooperation to the FFA alone was temporary and that in the future it could be extended to other French units, according to their effective availability.[119] (In 1967, the two divisions of the First Army Corps stationed in the east of France were not yet in a state — due to insufficient equipment and operational capacity — to intervene effectively within the NATO framework.)

The Ailleret-Lemnitzer agreement specified, too, the FFA's role in case of French intervention alongside NATO allies. Although the term "mission" had been proscribed by de Gaulle, it was really this that was at issue. This role fit into the logic that had been in place since the beginning of the 1960s, which tended, well before the 1966 withdrawal, to give France a second-echelon position behind other national forces assigned to the defense of Central Europe. With the Ailleret-Lemnitzer agreement, the FFA explicitly became an operational reserve force whose mission was to accomplish a massive counteroffensive to benefit the integrated forces assigned to the forward line of defense in CENTAG, that is to say, the German and U.S. divisions.[120]

The Ailleret-Lemnitzer agreement also specified the conditions in which the intervention of French forces alongside the allies would take place. First, decision-making autonomy: French forces could only become engaged upon the decision of the French government alone (this was already the case, for France as for other countries, within the framework of integration, but reasserting this principle had a political value); moreover, they could not receive responsibility for a "layer" of the forward defense line, for this would in effect reintroduce a form of automatic engagement, which of course France rejected. In addition, French units would be engaged on a definite mission, at a determined level of strength, and for a determined length of time: France was thus exercising influence over the definition of the mission of French forces, which should remain grouped so as to give the maximum weight to the counteroffensive they effected in order to benefit the integrated forces (and avoid what the French authorities complained of during integration, that once engagement of forces was decided, then SACEUR could use them, even split them up, as he saw fit). The Ailleret-Lemnitzer agreement, accordingly, envisaged the transfer of French forces to the "operational control" (or OPCON, in NATO jargon) of SACEUR and his subordinates (CINCENT, COMCENTAG), while the "operational command" (or OPCOM) would remain national. This meant precisely that if NATO really had French forces under its authority, this authority would be strictly limited to the predetermined mission.

The Ailleret-Lemnitzer agreement ended several months of uncertainty about the role of the FFA and more generally about France's situation in common defense after its withdrawal from the integrated system. In terms of volume, the French military contribution to a possible war in Central Europe would be unchanged and the Ailleret-Lemnitzer agreement even envisaged its buildup (the creation of the First Army in 1969, regrouping the First and Second Army Corps, allowed their extension). In terms of mission, they ratified the evolution since the 1950s and, still more clearly, since the establishment of the forward defense, which tended to give France a reserve role. Moreover, with the Ailleret-Lemnitzer agreement French forces went from a merely defensive role to a counteroffensive role that was certainly more valuable for allied defense.[121] So there was no break in France's participation in the defense of the Alliance.

In addition, the Ailleret-Lemnitzer agreement consecrated a coherent strategic concept, defined by de Gaulle himself, for whom the forces of maneuver, soon to be equipped with tactical nuclear weapons, constituted an essential element of France's general strategy, since they manifested both solidarity with its allies and its determination to rely on nuclear deterrence. This is why de Gaulle thought that the forces of maneuver should operate "grouped, intervening in a concerted action bearing their mark, massively, offensively, with all the land and air support, classic and nuclear, either on our frontiers or further forward."[122] This strategic concept clearly postulated the need to combine French action with that of the allies in Central Europe, a concept that General Emmanuel Hublot put into practice in the winter of 1966–1967, in the form of an exercise at the CHEM, in front of a pleased de Gaulle.[123]

Thus, with the Ailleret-Lemnitzer agreement, which essentially took up this concept, the allies fully recognized the specific strategic role of France in Europe: that of an autonomous nuclear power, placed in the rear of the forward line of defense but which would intervene alongside the allies as the only major available reserve, with all its means, including nuclear, in order to contribute the most to deterrence and to weigh decisively in the unfolding of the conflict. In this sense, the 1966 withdrawal and the substitution of "cooperation" for "integration," far from marking a diminution of France's military and strategic weight in Europe, tended to reconcile its national strategic imperatives with the requirement for a common defense, by combining in one and the same action both intervention in reserve and the "national maneuver of deterrence" theorized by General Poirier at the CPE.

Of course, all this was scarcely evident in 1967. Some in authority understood that France's new situation in relation to NATO was by no means a military rupture, even if they did not acknowledge this publicly. These included some of the allied military chiefs concerned,[124] and especially the most concerned of all, the CINCENT. In fact, General Kielmansegg did not doubt, in taking up his command in July 1966 (hence even before the signing of the Ailleret-Lemnitzer agreement), that France would fight along with the allies in the event of Soviet aggression, in other words, that he would have available for the defense of Central Europe a significant French military contribution.[125] But in circles apart from these informed people, it would take many years to dissipate the impression of a declaratory policy in which both sides had voluntarily amplified the real military significance of the 1966 decision: on the French side to inspire national support for a policy of independent defense; and on the allied side, to stigmatize the "bad pupil" in the Atlantic class.

NOTES

1. Charles de Gaulle, *Discours et Messages (DM)*, vol. 5, "Vers le terme" (janvier 1966–avril 1969), Paris, Plon, 1970.

2. Communiqué à l'issue du Conseil des ministres du 21 juin 1967, au sujet des conflits mondiaux, in Charles de Gaulle, *Lettres, Notes et Carnets (LNC) (juillet 1966–avril 1969)*, Paris, Plon, 1987, pp. 119–20.

3. IFOP poll, May 1967, quoted in Jean Charlot, *Les Français et de Gaulle*, Paris, Plon, 1971, p. 264.

4. NATO Ministerial Meeting, Paris, December 14–16, 1966, Position Paper, "France/NATO: The Constitutional Issue," 3 December 1966; see also "Scope Paper," 7 December 1966, LBJL, NSF, International Meetings and Travels File, box 35.

5. "France/NATO: The Constitutional Issue," p. 2; and LBJL, Administrative Histories, Department of State, vol. 1, ch. 3, "Europe," "French Withdrawal and NATO Countermeasures," p. 8.

6. Hervé Alphand, *L'Etonnement d'être. Journal 1939–1973*, Paris, Fayard, 1977, p. 474; see also "Instruction du 22 février 1966," MAE, Archives diplomatiques, Pactes 1961–1970, box 261.

7. LBJL, Administrative Histories, Department of State, vol. 1, ch. 3, "Europe," "French Withdrawal and NATO Countermeasures"; and *L'Alliance Atlantique. Données et structures,* Brussels, NATO, 1989, p. 71.

8. "Scope Paper," 7 December 1966.

9. "Scope Paper," 7 December 1966, p. 3.

10. Cf. Pierre Maillard, *De Gaulle et l'Allemagne. Le rêve inachevé*, Paris, Plon, 1990, pp. 253–54. See also Renata Fritsch-Bournazel, *L'Union soviétique et les Allemagnes*, Paris, Presses de la F.N.S.P., 1979, p. 131.

11. "Scope Paper," 7 December 1966, p. 2.

12. NATO Ministerial Meeting, Paris, December 14–16, 1966, Position Paper, "Belgian Proposal for Study on Future of NATO," 6 December 1966, LBJL, International Meetings and Travels File, box 35.

13. LBJL, Administrative Histories, Department of State, vol. 1, ch. 3, "Europe," "NATO Political Consultations, The Harmel Exercise," pp. 1–3.

14. "Belgian Proposal for Study on Future of NATO," 6 December 1966, p. 3. On all this, see Frédéric Bozo, "Détente versus Alliance: France, the United States, and the Politics of the Harmel Report (1964–1968)," *Contemporary European History*, 7, no. 3 (1998), pp. 343–60.

15. "Belgian Proposal for Study on Future of NATO."

16. "Belgian Proposal for Study on Future of NATO."

17. "NATO Political Consultations, The Harmel Report," pp. 4–5.

18. EMBTEL, Secto 103, Paris, 16 December 1966, "Personal for President," LBJL, NSF, France, boxes 173–174.

19. EMBTEL, Secto 103, Paris, 16 December 1966.

20. Fritsch-Bournazel, *L'Union soviétique et les Allemagnes*, pp. 134–35.

21. EMBTEL, Paris #9451, 20 December 1966, "Quai View on Kiesinger Declaration and GOF–FRG Relations," LBJL, NSF, France, boxes 173–174.

22. Maillard, *De Gaulle et l'Allemagne*, p. 254.

23. Maurice Couve de Murville, *Une Politique étrangère 1958–1969*, Paris, Plon, 1971, p. 227.

24. "NATO Political Consultations, The Harmel Exercise"; REPAN Telegram #113, 18 March 1967, MAE, Pactes 1961–1970, box 276.

25. NATO Ministerial Meeting, Luxembourg, 13–15 June 1967, Position Paper, "The Study on the Future of the Alliance," 5 June 1967, LBJL, NSF, International Meetings and Travels File, box 35, pp. 2–3.

26. REPAN Telegrams #105, 14 March 1967; #159, 18 April 1967; #178, 8 May 1967; and #208, 24 May 1967, MAE, Pactes 1961–1970, box 276.

27. Position Paper, "The Study on the Future of the Alliance," 5 June 1967.

28. NATO Ministerial Meeting, Luxembourg, 13–15 June 1967, Position Paper, "Issues Paper," 5 June 1967, LBJL, NSF, International Meetings and Travels File, pp. 1–2.

29. NATO Ministerial Meeting, Luxembourg, p. 3.

30. Délégation française au CAN, note, "Plan Harmel," 4 October 1967, MAE, Pactes 1961–1970, box 276.

31. REPAN Telegram #286, 15 September 1967, MAE, Pactes 1961–1970, box 276, and "NATO Political Consultations, The Harmel Exercise."

32. Note, "Rapport Spaak (sous-groupe II du Comité d'études Harmel)," 22 September 1967, MAE, Pactes 1961–1970, box 276; and "NATO Political Consultations, The Harmel Exercise."

33. REPAN Telegrams #296, 26 September 1967 and #305, 6 October 1967, MAE, Pactes 1961–1970, box 276; "NATO Political Consultation, The Harmel Exercise"; and CIA, Directorate of Intelligence, Intelligence Memorandum, "France and the Atlantic Alliance," 6 October 1967, LBJL, NSF, France, boxes 173–174.

34. REPAN Telegram #343–46, 25 October 1967, MAE, Pactes 1961–1970, box 276; and CIA, "France and the Atlantic Alliance."

35. Note en vue du Conseil des ministres, "Conseil Atlantique: Comité spécial sur l'avenir de l'Alliance," 28 November 1967, MAE, Pactes 1961–1970, box 277.

36. REPAN Telegram #294, 25 September 1967, MAE, Pactes 1961–1970, box 259; article by Louis Vallon in *Notre République*, 15 September 1967.

37. CIA, "France and the Atlantic Alliance," 6 October 1967.

38. Note, "Plan Harmel," 14 November 1967, MAE, Pactes 1961–1970, box 277; and also "NATO Political Consultations, The Harmel Exercise," pp. 9–10.

39. "The future tasks of the Alliance," annex to the final communiqué of the ministerial meeting, December 1967.

40. Harlan Cleveland, *NATO: The Transatlantic Bargain*, New York, Harper & Row, 1970, p. 145.

41. Couve de Murville, *Une Politique étrangère*, p. 227.

42. See chapter 5, pp.158-59.

43. See "The Non-Proliferation Treaty," Spurgeon A. Keeny, Jr., 24 December 1968, LBJL, NSF, NSC History, boxes 55–56, pp. 1–3.

44. Position Paper, "Issues Paper," 5 June 1967, pp. 2–3.

45. Paul Buteux, *The Politics of Nuclear Consultation in NATO, 1965–1980*, Cambridge, Cambridge University Press, 1983, pp. 49–50.

46. Position Paper, "Issues Paper," 5 June 1967, p. 4.

47. Note Dictated by the Secretary on the President's Views on Non-Proliferation, as Set Forth at the Recent Camp David Meeting, 3 October 1966, LBJL, NSF, NSC History, boxes 55–56.

48. "The Non-Proliferation Treaty," p. 1.

49. REPAN Telegram #408, 19 October 1966, MAE, Pactes 1961–1970, box 267.

50. Jean Klein, "Vers le traité de non-prolifération," *Politique étrangère*, no. 2, 1968, pp. 225–50.

51. EMBTEL, Paris #9262, Secto #103, 16 December 1966, and EMBTEL, Paris #9216, Rusk to Acting Secretary, LBJL, NSF, France, boxes 173–174.

52. EMBTEL, Paris #9451, 20 December 1966.

53. See chapter 4, p. 120.

54. Daniel Colard and Jean-François Guilhaudis, "L'option nucléaire, le problème des essais et la position de la France sur le désarmement," in *L'Aventure de la bombe. De Gaulle et la dissuasion nucléaire (1958–1969)*, Paris, Plon, 1985.

55. Airgram Paris #A-1335, 22 February 1967, LBJL, NSF, France, boxes 173–174.

56. Airgram Paris #A-1335, 22 February 1967.

57. Colard and Guilhaudis, "L'option nucléaire . . ."

58. See chapter 5, pp. 159–60.

59. Washington Telegram #1037–40, 23 February 1966; Bonn Telegram #1079–82, 25 February 1966, MAE, Pactes 1961–1970, box 267.

60. Fiche d'information, "Problèmes examinés par le Comité spécial ou comité McNamara jusqu'à ce jour," 7 December 1966, MAE, Pactes 1961–1970, box 267.

61. "Scope Paper," 7 December 1966, p. 4.

62. Buteux, *The Politics of Nuclear Consultation in NATO*, pp. 57–60.

63. Press Conference by Robert McNamara, 3 April 1967, quoted in Jane E. Stromseth, *The Origins of Flexible Response: NATO's Debate over Strategy in the 1960s*, London, Macmillan, 1988, p. 184.

64. Stromseth, *Origins of Flexible Response*, p. 175; David N. Schwartz, *NATO's Nuclear Dilemmas*, Washington, Brookings, 1983, pp. 186–87.

65. Communiqué of December 1967, quoted by Stromseth, *Origins of Flexible Response*, p. 175.

66. Communiqué of December 1967.

67. See chapter 5, pp. 151–52.

68. Stromseth, *Origins of Flexible Response*, pp. 176–77.

69. Stromseth, *Origins of Flexible Response*, p. 177.

70. Position Paper, 5 June 1967.

71. Cyrus L. Sulzberger, *An Age of Mediocrity: Memoirs and Diaries, 1963–1972*, New York, Macmillan, 1973, p. 400.

72. See chapter 5, pp. 150–51.

73. Quoted by Jean Lacouture, *De Gaulle*, vol. 2, "The Ruler 1945–1970," trans. Alan Sheridan, New York, Norton, 1992, p. 428.

74. General Charles Ailleret, "Défense 'dirigée' ou défense 'tous azimuts'?" *Revue de Défense Nationale*, December 1967, pp. 1923–32.

75. See Lacouture, *De Gaulle*, p. 429; and Marcel Duval and Yves Le Baut, *L'Arme nucléaire francaise: pourquoi et comment?* Paris, S.P.N./Kronos, 1992, pp. 52–53; see also the comments of General Bourgue and Admiral Sabbagh, in *L'Aventure de la bombe. De Gaulle et la dissuasion nucléaire (1958–1969)*, Paris, Plon, 1985, pp. 201–2.

76. See for example the speech of 3 November 1959 at the École Militaire.

77. Extract from speech given by General de Gaulle on January 27, 1968, to the Centre des Hautes Études Militaires, reprinted in *L'Aventure de la bombe. De Gaulle et la dissuasion nucléaire (1958–1969)*, Paris, Plon, 1985, pp. 210–11, extract in Lacouture, *De Gaulle*, p. 430.

78. See Lacouture, *De Gaulle*, pp. 427–33.

79. See Duval and Le Baut, *L'Arme nucléaire francaise*, p. 53.

80. Ailleret, "Défense 'dirigée' ou défense 'tous azimuts'?"

81. Lacouture, *De Gaulle*, p. 428.

82. Ailleret, "Défense 'dirigée' ou défense 'tous azimuts'?"

83. General François Valentin, "La dissuasion et les armements classiques," in *L'Aventure de la bombe. De Gaulle et la dissuasion nucléaire (1958–1969)*, Institut Charles de Gaulle, Paris, Plon, 1985.

84. See chapter 4, p. 132.

85. Valentin, "La dissuasion et les armements classiques."

86. Personal interview.

87. Valentin, "La dissuasion et les armements classiques."

88. Administrative Histories, State Department, vol. 1, ch. 3, "Europe," The Troop Problem and Burden Sharing," n.d. 1968, LBJL.

89. See chapter 3.

90. See chapter 3.

91. "The Troop Problem and Burden Sharing."

92. See Lawrence S. Kaplan, *NATO and the United States: The Enduring Alliance*, Boston, Twayne, 1988, pp. 127–28.

93. "The Troop Problem and Burden Sharing."

94. "The Troop Problem and Burden Sharing."

95. "The Troop Problem and Burden Sharing"; see also Kaplan, *NATO and the United States*, p. 128; and Stromseth, *Origins of Flexible Response*, p. 179.

96. "The Troop Problem and Burden Sharing"; see also Kaplan, *NATO and the United States*, p. 128; and Stromseth, *Origins of Flexible Response*, p. 179.

97. "The Troop Problem and Burden Sharing"; see also Kaplan, *NATO and the United States*, p. 128; and Stromseth, *Origins of Flexible Response*, p. 179.

98. See chapter 4, pp. 123–25.

99. "The Troop Problem and Burden Sharing."

100. Couve de Murville, *Une Politique étrangère*, p. 85.

101. Airgram Paris #A-1628, 15 April 1967, LBJL, NSF, France, boxes 173–174.

102. See chapter 5, p. 165.

103. Administrative Histories, State Department, vol. 1, ch. 3, Europe, "France."

104. Administrative Histories, State Department; memorandum for the President, Francis M. Bator, "Your Meeting with Ambassador Bohlen," 30 September 1966, LBJL, NSF, France, box 172.

105. Administrative Histories, State Department; memorandum for the President, Francis M. Bator.

106. Details in Frédéric Bozo, *La France et l'OTAN. De la guerre froide au nouvel ordre européen*, Paris, Masson, in series "Travaux et recherches de l'IFRI," 1991, pp. 100–1.

107. See *Revue de Défense Nationale*, May 1967 (p. 909) and July 1967; Michael M. Harrison, *The Reluctant Ally: France and Atlantic Security*, Baltimore, Johns Hopkins University Press, 1981, p. 151.

108. Note au sujet des survols étrangers, 15 September 1967; note au Vice-Amiral Philippon, 20 September 1967, in de Gaulle, *LNC (1966–1969)*, pp. 134, 137.

109. Lettre à Georges Pompidou, 2 October 1967, in de Gaulle, *LNC (1966–1969)*, p. 141.

110. *Revue de Défense Nationale*, February 1968.

111. See chapter 5, p. 174. For all this, see Bozo, "Chronique d'une décision annoncée."

112. Note, 11 October 1966, in de Gaulle, *LNC (1966–1969)*, p. 28.

113. NATO Ministerial Meeting, Paris, December 14–17, 1966, Background Paper, "French Forces in Germany," 6 December 1966, LBJL, NSF, IMTF, box 35.

114. NATO Ministerial Meeting, Paris, December 14–17, 1966.

115. *Revue de Défense Nationale*, May 1967.

116. "French Withdrawal and NATO Countermeasures"; and "De Gaulle's Foreign Policy: 1969 Version," State Department, Director of Intelligence and Research, 20 December 1968, LBJL, NSF, France, boxes 173–174, p. 9.

117. "De Gaulle's Foreign Policy: 1969 Version," pp. 9–10.

118. The agreement has long remained secret. However, for a recent contribution based on newly released archival material, see Bozo, "Chronique d'une décision annoncée." Also see Valentin, *Une Politique de défense pour la France*, Paris, Calmann-Lévy, 1980; Valentin, "La dissuasion et les armements classiques"; and Valentin, "L'arête étroite," *Défense Nationale*, May 1983, pp. 45–56; see also General Lacaze, "La politique militaire," *Défense Nationale*, November 1981, pp. 7–26; and François Maurin, "L'originalité française et le commandement," *Défense Nationale*, July 1988, pp. 45–57. For fuller details, see Bozo, *La France et l'OTAN*, pp. 99 ff., and 109 ff.

119. Valentin, "La dissuasion et les armements classiques."

120. Valentin, "La dissuasion et les armements classiques"; see also Jean-Paul Cointet, François Puaux, and François Valentin, "Les suites de l'action du général de Gaulle en matière de politique de défense depuis 1969," in *De Gaulle en son siècle*, vol. 4, "La sécurité et l'indépendance de la France," Institut Charles de Gaulle, Paris, Plon, 1992.

121. Cointet, Puaux, and Valentin "Les suites de l'action du général de Gaulle . . ."

122. Valentin, *Une politique de défense pour la France*, p. 91.

123. Personal interview; letter from General Emmanuel Hublot to the author, 15 December 1988.

124. Valentin, *Une politique de défense pour la France*, p. 90.

125. Personal interview.

Chapter Seven

Confirmation of the Status Quo (1968–April 1969)

In an East-West context characterized in the first months of 1968 by growing dé-tente between blocs and increased political cohesion of NATO along the lines of the Harmel report, France held to its particular position in the Alliance, even though the climate of relations with the United States began to improve. Never-theless, the May crisis in France and the crushing of the Prague spring in August seemed liable to undermine de Gaulle's foreign policy, especially in its trans-atlantic aspect. But there would be no major upheaval: while seeking to adapt his policy to the new East-West situation, de Gaulle in no way reconsidered its prin-ciples. But he was obliged to acknowledge that France's margin of maneuver was reduced. In fact, to the extent that East-West status quo was now a lasting situa-tion in Europe, the dynamic security policy that de Gaulle had been practicing for years had to give way to a more conservative approach.

During the first months of 1969, time was ripe for a certain normalization, it seemed. With the election of Richard Nixon, relations between France and the United States improved significantly and for quite a while. But although this im-provement dissipated the misunderstandings, it was far from marking the end of transatlantic disagreement. In effect, the United States, while not approving of the French position on the Alliance, now started to understand it; and France, with-out renouncing its vision of this same Alliance, recognized that it was not in a po-sition to impose this vision. The confirmation of the status quo froze France's position in the Atlantic Alliance for many years.

CONTINUITY

The first months of 1968 were marked, on both sides of the Iron Curtain, by progress in the idea of East-West rapprochement. In the wake of the Harmel re-port, France's allies reflected on ways to make détente concrete through arms

control. In this context, de Gaulle's Atlantic policy was characterized by an overall continuity, until the May crisis in France and the crushing of the Prague spring
at the end of August opened a period of turmoil.

From the Harmel Report to the MBFR

At the start of 1968, the situation of relations between France and the Alliance
was clear to de Gaulle. Almost two years after the March 1966 decision, the problem appeared finally solved. Gone was the former—purposeful—uncertainty
about whether France would stay within the Atlantic Pact after 1969: "If I had to
make a decision tonight," he confided, "France would not leave the Alliance." De
Gaulle recalled the phrases of his letter to Johnson in March 1966: only a "substantial" change in the security context could motivate a break with the Alliance
properly speaking. Because such change had not occurred—the East-West opposition and the division of Europe remained—such a break was not on the agenda.
But on the other hand, there was no question of reconsidering France's position
vis-à-vis "NATO" (in the sense meant by de Gaulle); the logic of flexible response, in particular, remained unacceptable.[1]

It is true that the French had hardly any reason to welcome the change in the
strategic context, clearly marked as it was by confirmation of nuclear bipolarity.
Moreover, the now serious prospect of a deployment on both sides of antiballis-
tic missile (ABM) defense systems could only increase French leaders' worry
about the viability of their own deterrence weapons and motivate them to demarcate themselves from the U.S. strategy.[2] As for the integrated military system,
France had finally settled its position on the subject with the Ailleret-Lemnitzer
agreement, which substituted cooperation for integration. De Gaulle thus stuck to
the simple formula of "yes" to the Alliance and "no" to NATO.

At the start of the year, the main parameters of de Gaulle's Western policy thus
seemed unchanging. Franco-German relations, which had improved during 1967
after the arrival of Kiesinger and Brandt, were once more mediocre: What hung
over them was again the issue of the European Economic Community (EEC) and
British application for membership, reopened by Harold Wilson in November
1966, which de Gaulle continued to oppose, while Bonn remained basically set on
it. Brandt, by stating (albeit in private) unflattering opinions of de Gaulle, to whom
he ascribed "the rigid and anti-European ideas of a head of state thirsty for power,"[3]
created an incident that, seen from Paris, ought to have had no repercussions, but
did mean the "honeymoon with the Kiesinger cabinet was spoiled."[4] Although
de Gaulle twice in 1967 gave a blunt refusal to British application—less abrupt
than after Nassau, it is true—the British and those who supported their demand did
not give up. The issue remained more or less open, which did not facilitate relations between Paris and Bonn—nor, of course, between Paris and London.

In this context, the Americans had no illusions about the possibility of a profound change in de Gaulle's policy toward the Alliance. Thus, in early February

1968, Bohlen, ready to leave his post as ambassador to France (he would be replaced by Sargent Shriver, brother-in-law to Kennedy), wrote to Washington that "given the attitude of de Gaulle, there would seem to be very little chance of any real improvement in Franco-American relations . . . even if the war in Vietnam is brought to the negotiating table." He added "I can offer little encouragement to any belief in a change in our relations with France until after the departure of de Gaulle."[5]

This was too pessimistic, or at least too prudent. In the spring of 1968, a slight improvement in relations between the two countries began, thanks to the evolution of the Vietnam conflict. In February 1968, the Tet offensive profoundly upset U.S. strategy and marked a decisive turning point in the Vietnam War. McNamara, who disagreed with the massive bombing of North Vietnam, had left the Pentagon. His successor, Clark Clifford, though a reputed hawk, was of the same opinion. More and more isolated as president and within his own party, in the context of difficult presidential primary elections, Johnson at the end of March made a major military and political choice: he ended the bombing of North Vietnam above the 20th parallel and gave up running for reelection.[6] De Gaulle understood that it was "something serious, a courageous political act by Johnson," a view that he expressed in a short communiqué that provoked an "astounding effect" on the other side of the Atlantic and gave rise to a veritable "wave of gratitude."[7] Nevertheless, de Gaulle was only seeing verified the prediction he had made some years earlier about the evolution of the conflict, which U.S. leaders had hardly wanted to hear at that time. And voilà, now France appeared as a mediator: by common agreement, Paris was chosen by Hanoi and Washington as the site of talks. The first meeting took place on May 13. It was plain that the turn taken by Johnson and the beginning of a peace process were apt to remove an "obstacle that for years had stood in the way of"[8] Franco-American relations and, indirectly at least, hung over France's Atlantic policy.

But the latter's major themes were not questioned. What was at the heart of the disagreement between France and its allies, that is, the logic of blocs, was not questioned, even if it was tempered by a climate of détente that in the spring of 1968 appeared able to last. France was increasingly caught in a dilemma: while wholeheartedly desiring détente, entente, and cooperation, it held itself apart from the policy of "integrated" détente that the allies were pushing. The Fourteen indeed decided in the first months of 1968 to give substance to the Harmel report, which called for "studying disarmament and practical arms control measures, including the possibility of balanced forces reductions." It was a way of satisfying public opinion and the U.S. Congress, ever concerned to lighten the burden of U.S. engagement in Europe (on January 10, 1968, Senator Mansfield had declared the intention of submitting a new resolution along this line to the Senate) and to demonstrate the compatibility between NATO's existence and increasing détente.[9] The allies at the Council level therefore turned to developing a document on mutual and balanced forces reduction (MBFR), which they adopted at the spring ministerial meeting, held in Reykjavik at the end of June 1968.[10]

Yet Paris refused to be associated with "the Reykjavik signal," since the projected MBFR negotiations were in contradiction with the French concept of détente. A bloc-to-bloc approach to disarmament in Europe, it seemed, would indeed consecrate the bipolar logic and strengthen the hold of the two superpowers over the Old Continent as well as their hegemony within their respective alliances. Moreover, France did not accept NATO machinery being used by the Western nations to put MBFR into practice. To participate in the exercise would mean risking giving the impression of a rapprochement with NATO—hence French abstention from a project that, as Paris saw it, had little chance of promoting true disarmament.[11] Of course, the Warsaw Pact would not respond in the coming months to the Reykjavik call and the MBFR negotiations would not begin until 1973. In this affair, however, Paris confirmed its status as a singular member of the Alliance—but at the risk of appearing to reject the progress on détente and disarmament that NATO now made a priority task.

The Impact of May

The May 1968 crisis occurred while de Gaulle's global foreign policy was at its height, even if it no longer won unconditional support from the French people. The stunning "*Québec libre*" and the position he adopted on Middle Eastern affairs after the Six-Day War had appeared both excessive to a public opinion that remained attached to U.S. friendship and largely pro-Israeli (or rather anti-Arab). The charmed relation between de Gaulle's foreign policy and the French people was broken in the last months of 1967. More seriously, people were increasingly skeptical that French policy could be truly independent: 46 percent still thought so at the end of 1965, but only 34 percent in January of 1968.[12] The May crisis is partly explained by foreign policy: ten years after de Gaulle's return to power, the French were no longer disposed to pay the price for such an effort. Asked about what they thought was the most important problem for the country, in August 1967, 22 percent mentioned a foreign issue, in May 1968, 15 percent, and in September 1968, this had fallen to 9 percent, and to 6 percent by June 1969.[13] The French thought they no longer had the means for the great Gaullist policy. More importantly, perhaps, they no longer had the will. The post-May period was thus marked by a shake-up in national priorities and by a shrinking of the country's international margin of maneuver.

This was resented by Georges Pompidou, soon placed—as de Gaulle put it after the latter's resignation as prime minister—"in the Republic's reserve." Pompidou indeed bitterly observed that other nations now gazed "with ironic satisfaction at the image of an unstable and self-destructive country" and were glad that de Gaulle's France was finally "brought down to size": "Good-bye to the war against the dollar. Good-bye to lessons given to the world's great men. Good-bye to our leadership in Western Europe. This [is] the world's reaction."[14] And Hervé Alphand wondered whether, after the legislative elections on June 30, France could preserve the foundation of its independence: free trade and high exports, the deterrent force, and the policy of cooperation in the Third World. "Will there be a new orientation to our diplomacy with regard to the United States, the Atlantic Pact, England and the Common Market, Europe, Germany . . . ?" Faced with these questions, the secretary general of the Quai d'Orsay thought that French diplomacy should first take a pause by holding to "a traditional formula," since it was still too early to measure the lasting impact of the crisis on French international power; but he was convinced that it would be "more difficult for a weakened France than a prosperous and balanced France to be a lone horseman, disdaining opposition and criticism."[15]

For the time being, continuity indeed reigned. The elections of June 23 and 30 sent a large Gaullist majority to the National Assembly. The French chose a return to order. In this context, the surprise replacement of Georges Pompidou by Maurice Couve de Murville as head of the government expressed the General's desire to take over the reins of power. At the Quai d'Orsay the arrival of Michel Debré, the most faithful of the faithful, confirmed de Gaulle's intention to maintain the main lines of his diplomacy. A man of conviction, less given to compromise than his predecessor, Debré promised to defend more inflexibly than ever the principle of national independence; this is why the General had chosen him. "From the beginning you have fought against supranationality," he wrote him. "The supporters of supranationality will try for their revenge after our difficulties. The coming time will be difficult. I need someone unshakable and it's necessary for France. The United States will also want to take advantage of the situation. You will know how to handle their diplomacy."[16] In short, de Gaulle persisted, and as if to better signal this to the world, he ordered the first French thermo-nuclear explosion to be held at the Pacific test site on August 24, 1968. One month after the signing of the nonproliferation treaty, the explosion of the first French H-bomb, like the explosion in Reggane in 1960, had a clear political impact.

The end of the summer of 1968, however, brought a new setback to Gaullist diplomacy. On August 21, Warsaw Pact troops put into practice the principle of proletarian internationalism by quashing the Prague spring. The time was not ripe for Soviet satellite countries to free themselves from its control. After the May crisis, it was a fresh blow to France's international prestige. The English-speaking press "mocked de Gaulle's grand design, now compromised."[17] After the invasion of Czechoslovakia, the General prepared with Couve de Murville and Debré a "very tough" communiqué,[18] stating that the "armed intervention of the Soviet Union in Czechoslovakia showed that the government in Moscow had not renounced the policy of blocs, which had been imposed on Europe by the effect of the Yalta Agreement." As for France, it "deplored the fact that events in Prague, beyond constituting an assault on the rights and destiny of a friendly nation, were likely to hurt European détente, such as she was practicing, and trying to get others to do, and which alone could guarantee peace."[19]

Not only did the incident harm the reactivating of traditional French friendship with the East, but it signaled that any East-West rapprochement in Europe in the future would proceed through consolidation and not through the relaxation of blocs. The first to want to turn the page on the Czech affair were the Americans: Johnson was the first (and not, as has been said, Michel Debré) who saw it, as he declared on September 10, as an "incident" that would have "only temporary consequences."[20] In short, the Czech crisis confirmed de Gaulle's fears about an East-West détente that was managed by the superpowers at the expense of Europeans. Hence the virulence of his denunciation of the "Yalta" order, which in his mind referred much more to the present situation than to the 1945 agreement. This cost him a stinging reply from the diplomat Averell Harriman, then in Paris as head of the U.S. delegation to the Vietnam talks: "There is one thing which General de Gaulle says which is true: that he was not at Yalta; and therefore his impressions have been gained not from a knowledge of what went on, but a lack of knowledge."[21] This was undoubtedly an offensive statement, but it only confirmed the General's analysis that the bad turn taken in East-West relations in Europe resulted from the fact that the French perspective (as was the case at the end of World War II and in the beginning of the Cold War) was not taken into account.

Paradoxically, the Czech crisis appeared to de Gaulle as a confirmation of this perspective. Hence the accentuated criticism of a bipolar East-West rapprochement made to the detriment of the peoples of Europe, and hence, too, the continued French political dissidence in relation to NATO, whose legitimacy and cohesion, in line with the Harmel report, seemed more and more clearly to Paris to be based on the very persistence of the Yalta system, even in the mode of détente between blocs. Nor did the crisis in Czechoslovakia—any more than the May crisis in France—appear liable to modify de Gaulle's Atlantic policy in the near future, since he seemed more convinced than ever that his approach to European security remained the right one.

The Americans, however, peered beneath appearances. At the end of August, some in Washington thought that recent events could well lead the General to begin a policy change within the Western alliance, which might offer "possibilities for accommodation between the United States and France."[22] Their reasoning was simple: in the preceding months, France had suffered reverses and found itself weakened. If de Gaulle decided to modify his policy, the United States could find a way to "accommodate" him by "making a constructive contribution to solving some of the problems France is facing," notably in the economic, financial, scientific, and technical domains. Washington, it was thought, could obtain a softening of Paris's position in the realm of military cooperation, on the issue of the right to overfly French territory, or even on its logistic use by Americans; the latter could also hope that France would prove more favorable to disarmament, and even adhere to the nonproliferation treaty.[23]

Yet the Americans were still wary of hoping for a return to the situation before 1966 with respect to France and NATO. Washington understood that if one wanted to achieve closer Franco-American relations in the months to come, this could only happen on two conditions: first, that neither partner insisted that the other was abandoning its position (e.g., that France was demanding U.S. retreat from Vietnam, or the United States asking for France's return to integration in NATO); and second, that the United States recognized they could not return to a formula of *ex post facto* consultation such as they had practiced, for example, during the Cuban crisis. Such a practice could "only convince France that it is regarded by the United States as a second-class ally."[24]

AN AGONIZING REAPPRAISAL?

However, during the final months of 1968, after the Czech affair, the Americans banked on a French attitude more favorable to the United States and to the Alliance overall. Washington anticipated that from a political standpoint de Gaulle would reequilibrate French diplomacy more on the Anglo-American side. And it was true that in the strategic domain, Paris seemed in the fall of 1968 to revive, for a while and in certain respects, the tripartite ideas of the first years, while, from a military standpoint, cooperation between France and NATO was developing in a satisfactory manner. But the Americans did not fool themselves: the shift in French policy that was perceptible in the autumn of 1968 was by no means de Gaulle's return to the status quo ante, but an adaptation to new circumstances. There would be no "agonizing reappraisal" of French policy with regard to the Alliance.

A New Political Deal

The analysis made in Washington was that the invasion of Czechoslovakia modified the three main parameters of Gaullist policy. The Americans observed first that in the fall of 1968, the Czech affair led to a marked deterioration in relations between France and Germany. De Gaulle indeed did not hesitate, addressing the Americans, to make Bonn partially responsible for the Soviet aggression.[25] For the General, the invasion of Czechoslovakia, even if it was totally unjustifiable, was also a response to "certain imprudence or recent excesses of zeal by the Federal Republic in the direction of Czechoslovakia."[26] He thought that the Germans, in the preceding months by deploying in Eastern Europe very overt activities, especially economic and commercial, had unsettled the Soviet Union, for whom the German danger remained the principal preoccupation. These activities had supplied the pretext for Soviet intervention in Eastern Europe, which for de Gaulle was already blameworthy in itself.[27] And if the latter exaggerated Bonn's responsibility somewhat, it remained true that the problem of the growing autonomy of the FRG in East-West relations was indeed posed, quite apart from the Czech episode, causing an increase in tensions between France and Germany in the fall of 1968. De Gaulle, in effect, could objectively note that the FRG, far from following the example of France in prudently choosing to speak directly with Moscow, had preferred to develop "its relations with the USSR's satellites with the ulterior motive of isolating the GDR and short circuiting the USSR."[28] In addition, during the severe crisis undergone in November by the French currency, weakened by social and economic difficulties, Bonn refused to support the franc.[29] The FRG thus increasingly asserted itself as the real economic power on the Continent. Overall, the fall of 1968 indeed marked a turning point in relations between France and Germany. De Gaulle did not disguise a certain distrust toward the neighbor across the Rhine and the uncontrolled renewal of German power that he was observing.[30]

The second parameter of Gaullist diplomacy, equally modified by the Czech crisis, was the policy toward Eastern Europe. Even though France hoped to preserve the Franco-Soviet entente (everything showed that such was the desire of de Gaulle and his homologues in Moscow), the Americans thought that the invasion of Czechoslovakia sounded the death-knell of the French approach to détente and of the role the General attributed to France in East-West relations, that of spokesperson for Europe and particularly for Bonn.[31] With a Germany possessing an increased margin of maneuver, the conduct of détente could only escape France's control, Washington thought. If the Czech affair had interrupted East-West relations, it was clear that once this "incident" was forgotten, it was the FRG that would play the main role. In sum, as seen from Washington, the unique and dynamic policy of détente practiced by France from 1966 to 1968 was finished.

The third parameter being transformed was the problematic of Franco-American relations. For the Johnson administration, there was no doubt in the fall of 1968 that events would push de Gaulle closer to *les Anglo-Saxons*. Behind the apparent French determination to change nothing in its approach, de Gaulle was undoubtedly "reappraising his policies" toward the West and "looking for new approaches," Washington thought.[32] The Americans thought that there was a serious possibility of improving Franco-American relations. Newspaper articles discussed France's reexamination of its policy on NATO. In this context, Michel Debré went to Washington and met Johnson on October 11. Walt Rostow, who had succeeded Bundy as national security advisor, suggested to the president that he ask the French foreign minister about French views on the state of détente, and whether the French were "willing to work closer in security and other matters with the West."[33]

The weeks that followed confirmed an improvement in the climate. The Americans seized the opportunity of the November monetary crisis to prove their goodwill toward de Gaulle. Unlike Bonn, Washington supported the franc, which after the French "assaults" on the dollar, could only be appreciated in Paris. And a few days after the U.S. presidential elections, Ambassador Shriver suggested to Washington setting up as quickly as possible a meeting between de Gaulle and Nixon "to maintain forward movement in improving the climate of our relations with France" and to explore with de Gaulle "possible areas of cooperation at a time when he may be more flexible because of the way France has fared in 1968."[34] Shriver noted that it would be useful to plan a meeting between Nixon and de Gaulle before the NATO summit in April in Washington, twenty years after the signing of the treaty, a meeting that de Gaulle would probably not attend.[35]

Though they had the impression that after the invasion of Czechoslovakia de Gaulle had doubts about his foreign policy, the Americans wondered to what extent he would really adapt his Atlantic policy. Seen from the State Department, this policy included three paradoxical positions: while continuing to advocate détente as if nothing had happened, de Gaulle took very seriously the rise in East-West tensions, which he thought could lead to a conflict; while continuing to denounce blocs in the East as in the West, various French officials led it be known that Paris would welcome an increase in military cooperation with the United States and Great Britain; finally, while keeping the permanent goal of a closer Franco-German entente, the French had for some months been signaling their distrust of Bonn and doing nothing to reassure the Germans about France's solidarity in case of Soviet aggression. But behind these paradoxes and contradictions, the State Department's analysis of de Gaulle's policy was that, despite the shock of May 1968 and of the Czech invasion, and despite the economic and financial embarrassment of the country, the General was not "likely to abandon the fundamental objectives of his foreign policy." In short, it was concluded, he was merely adapting his tactics and his arguments to the new situation.[36]

A Return to 1958?

This analysis was correct. In the last months of 1968, under pressure from events, de Gaulle adjusted and adapted his approach to European security and to relations with the Alliance, but without changing the basics. This was particularly clear in the nuclear domain, where the General seemed to want to return to the approach of the 1958 memorandum. In early fall, the Americans had the impression that France was perhaps looking for a new formulation for its nuclear doctrine. This was Shriver's hypothesis after his meeting with de Gaulle on September 23. As was his custom, the General explained that "the United States could not be counted on to risk a nuclear war to defend Western Europe."[37] But de Gaulle let it be known that France was itself in a similar situation, meaning that it would not necessarily see an attack against Germany as an attack against France. This remark was unusual, and it gave an indication of the decline in relations between France and Germany after the Czech affair. It also had significance from the Franco-American standpoint. De Gaulle was suggesting to Shriver that if the United States had recourse to nuclear weapons to respond to an attack in Europe, France would do so under the same conditions. To be sure, the General was wary of mentioning the possibility of making firm arrangements about nuclear coordination or cooperation with the United States. But thanks to the comments of certain French officials after this conversation, the Americans interpreted his statements as a signal of a renewed interest in a tripartite cooperation among France, the United States, and Great Britain.[38]

Nothing of this filtered into the public domain, and it remains difficult to have a precise idea of the tenor and bearing of the contacts that seem to have taken place between Paris and Washington—and perhaps London. But it is scarcely surprising that the idea of tripartite cooperation resurfaced in the fall of 1968, even if in the form of discrete trial balloons. Ten years after the memorandum was sent, France's nuclear status had totally changed. From a virtual atomic power, it had become, through its own effort, a confirmed thermonuclear power, thus modifying the problem of nuclear relations with the United States and Great Britain—which Washington was perhaps close to admitting.[39] De Gaulle seemed in any case to think that the next U.S. administration would prove more cooperative with France and might review the nuclear discrimination that Washington had maintained until then between London and Paris, a prospect that was not to be overlooked, due to the financial constraints weighing on the French nuclear effort.[40] Moreover, the political situation in the fall of 1968 was favorable to a return to the tripartite scheme in the strategic realm. After the invasion of Czechoslovakia, de Gaulle wanted to give tangible signs of Western solidarity but without reconsidering integration in NATO. In addition, relations between France and the United States since the spring of 1968 were undergoing improvement and relations with Great Britain appeared to be warming. Finally, relations with the FRG had considerably worsened and de Gaulle was uneasy in the face of renascent German power and, as a consequence, stressed France's status as a nuclear and world power.

All of this could have spurred a return to tripartism. Despite the shake-up of 1968, the international status of France was more solid than in 1958: a full nuclear power, it had better reasons to place itself on an equal footing with *les Anglo-Saxons*; next, France had effectively freed itself from the constraints of integration that hampered its margin of maneuver; and finally, the renewal of the Soviet danger required strong Western solidarity, especially between France and the United States, at a moment when relations between France and Germany were stalled. Such was the late-1968 analysis made in Washington, where it was thought de Gaulle's motivations could be divined: "If something could eventually be worked out [in the nuclear area] with the United States and Great Britain, de Gaulle's prestige and French status as a great power would be much enhanced."[41]

The Americans remained cautious, however. They wondered to what extent de Gaulle really believed that a return to the 1958 formula, even adapted to the new situation, was both practical and desirable. A strategic French/British/U.S. directorate would have serious disadvantages for the United States: first, because such an arrangement would only revive the distrust of the nonnuclear allies (particularly Germany) toward the atomic club, even though the United States had succeeded in reestablishing NATO's nuclear cohesion thanks to the Nuclear Planning Group and the adoption of flexible response; and then because setting up a tripartite strategic directorate would no doubt be seen by the Soviet Union as a hostile act at a time when Washington and Moscow, once the Czech page was turned, wanted to renew dialogue and promote détente, notably at the Soviet-American level. Washington, all things considered, preferred the simple and clear situation created by the French withdrawal and the adoption of flexible response without France. Even if it ratified the strategic partition of the Alliance, this situation at least had the advantage of guaranteeing the nuclear cohesion of the other allies and of ensuring U.S. strategic leadership.

Things remained there, and the idea of a directorate of three Western nuclear powers, once very much in the air, was soon forgotten. In January 1969, de Gaulle returned to a strategic rhetoric more in line with that developed since 1966. Thus, at the Institut des Hautes Études de Défense Nationale (IHEDN) on January 25, he underlined that "it was under the most diverse hypotheses that we should plan and prepare our deterrent action and, if necessary, the use of our forces," unless it was to be admitted "that France no longer is to be counted and has been placed among the accessories of someone else."[42] The General thus appeared to act on the fact that the United States was no more inclined than in 1958 to accept a tripartite formula putting France on a real equal footing with itself.

Military Cooperation

Yet in the fall of 1968 the United States, in the wake of the Czech events that for NATO had been first and foremost a military alert, hoped to make some progress in the military domain. With the maximum discretion in order not to give the USSR any justification for its own policy of aggression, the Fourteen drew lessons from the invasion of Czechoslovakia, as Manlio Brosio suggested at the end of August by proposing that the Defense Planning Committee do an "evaluation of the balance of forces after the Soviet action."[43] These lessons concerned the tactics and logistics used by the Soviets, the defects in an allied alert system that had been caught off-guard by the Warsaw Pact forces, but also NATO force planning in the new context. The allies thought there was no question for the time being of force reductions in the context of negotiations with the Soviet bloc: the Reykjavik proposal made in the spring was frozen. Moreover, the downward tendency of national defense efforts of NATO members appeared halted, at least for a while. Most of the allies let the Americans know, discretely so as not to throw oil on the fire, that they "could do more for NATO if asked to do so."[44]

The Fourteen decided that "even though there is no alternative to the policy of détente," "Western solidarity" should be "tightened" and common defense should be strengthened,[45] not only quantitatively, but qualitatively: what NATO needed in the light of the Soviet demonstration of their capabilities in Czechoslovakia was more flexibility and operational availability to deal with an unforeseen crisis. This was agreed by the defense ministers, meeting in mid-November as the DPC, and they passed an additional budget of more than a billion dollars spread over two or three years. Half of this effort was supplied by West Germany, and only 10 percent by the United States, more and more limited by involvement in Vietnam. In addition, the integrated allies were committed to not withdrawing forces assigned to SACEUR in the foreseeable future.[46]

In this context, how did France behave, having broken with NATO's integrated military system, but also having concluded an agreement on cooperation concerning the defense of Central Europe? The United States hoped that it would prove more inclined to cooperate. Shriver, received by de Gaulle at the end of September, was asked about Washington's views on the Czech affair and seized the ball. Instructed by the State Department, the ambassador stressed that "[the] invasion had created [a] new military situation which in turn required collective action as well as bilateral action by Western European countries to strengthen [the] military deterrent as [the] best antidote to possible Soviet recklessness." And he added that this would require above all "larger conventional forces."[47] Apparently, the General did not react negatively to these statements since, some weeks after this meeting, Shriver observed to Washington that of the many areas for the upcoming discussions between de Gaulle and Nixon, the most important was defense, where "some degree of broadened defense cooperation between France and NATO might be possible." The subject was technical, he said, and if it were taken up at the presidential level, the meetings should be carefully prepared at the bureaucratic level. This said, Shriver insisted the State Department should be "under no illusions of the difficulties" of the exercise. Moreover, de Gaulle was scarcely inclined to inform his entourage about his intentions, and he would want to lay his cards on the table only with the president.[48]

Yet the Czech crisis, occurring almost exactly one year after the conclusion of the Ailleret-Lemnitzer agreement, would not greatly modify military relations between France and NATO, not so much because Paris balked at improving them but because military cooperation in Central Europe was already proceeding along a satisfactory course, even before the events of the summer of 1968. During the year after the signing of the agreement between CEMA and SACEUR, ways of cooperating had been intensively discussed and spelled out by French and allied military authorities. Ailleret-Lemnitzer had been only an agreement in principle, a framework for combined operational planning for possible French involvement. Military efficiency required that practicalities be defined in advance as much as possible: logistics, communications, commands, and of course scenarios and geographic locations of possible French intervention in reserve of the integrated forward line of defense.[49] This planning was undertaken immediately after the signing of the Ailleret-Lemnitzer agreement, on the French side by the chief of staff

(General Ailleret, and then after his accidental death in early 1968, General Michel Fourquet) and his "land" deputy General François Valentin, as well as the commander-in-chief of the FFA, General Jacques Massu. The allied side involved the SACEUR, of course, but also the CINCENT, German general Kielmansegg and the U.S. general commanding the CENTAG zone (southern Germany) where the FFA would operate.

Both sides agreed to envisage France's possible intervention in the form of a counterattack in one of three possible directions in southern Germany, corresponding to the anticipated axes of a Soviet advance: the Nuremberg region, the Ratisbonne region, and, further south, facing Austria in case of a violation of its neutrality by the Warsaw Pact. The elaboration of common plans demonstrated without ambiguity France's desire to be able to play an active role if necessary. De Gaulle himself followed the issue and approved of the plans. And if in early 1968 he issued a directive limiting the Eastern scope of possible French intervention to the latitude of Nuremberg, it was not to let the allies down, but rather to take into account the still-limited operational and logistic capabilities of the FFA.[50]

This planning between France and NATO was well underway when the Czech crisis occurred. In November 1968, de Gaulle received Massu at the Elysée and was informed about the situation of the FFA and relations with the allies. Massu told him that "contacts with the Americans to plan our scenarios are being pursued favorably" and that "relations with the Germans are still excellent, from top to bottom."[51] Moreover, the commander in chief added that after Czechoslovakia, operational planning was more particularly concentrated on the scenario of intervention along the border with Austria, namely the "southeast flank" of the integrated defense. De Gaulle had no comeback on this: it was normal for plans made between France and NATO to take into account the reality of the terrain,[52] and the invasion of Czechoslovakia had changed the balance of forces, at least locally, since Soviet divisions were now stationed there permanently.

Overall, the invasion of Czechoslovakia did not change the principles of military relations between France and NATO. There was nothing surprising in this: de Gaulle, as we have seen, did not conceive of the 1966 withdrawal as leading to distance France from its allies in the face of the Soviet threat. Hence the crisis of August 1968 by no means justified a return to integration, which was not necessary to guarantee France's military solidarity. But it did have the consequence of somewhat changing the declaratory policy. In the fall, French authorities started to mention, more openly but still very vaguely, the existence of close military cooperation with the allies. The accent was placed on the bilateral Franco-American character of this cooperation, as if to put France on an equal footing with the United States. This declaratory change, which did not go unnoticed in Washington, was essentially political.[53] After the Soviet aggression, France wanted to proclaim more clearly its natural solidarity with the other Western nations in case of threat.

This was clearly the main motive of the statements of General Fourquet during a lecture given on March 3, 1969, at IHEDN and later printed in the *Revue de Défense Nationale.*[54] The chief of staff insisted more than ever on the closeness of military cooperation between France and NATO in the defense of Central Europe. For Fourquet, "engaged along the North and East frontiers against an enemy from the East, the battle corps will normally act in tight coordination with our Allies' forces."[55] This presentation, undoubtedly less rigid than Ailleret's a year previously, was widely interpreted in France and by the allies as a shift in French policy toward the Alliance. It seemed the quasi-neutralist "Ailleret doctrine" had been replaced by the "Fourquet doctrine," much more favorable to NATO. After Czechoslovakia, this strategic evolution on France's part seemed to represent a decisive turning point in relations between France and NATO.[56]

It was nothing of the sort. General Fourquet's statements merely reflected the reality of military cooperation put into operation by Ailleret himself back in 1967 and now naturally developing. If there had indeed been a change in strategy, it was not operational, but declaratory: the French authorities were now more careful to stress a military solidarity with the allies that had never been really called into question.[57] Therefore there was no—except at the level of perceptions—real change in the military relations between France and NATO following the Czech crisis.

NORMALIZATION

During the last months of 1968, de Gaulle kept his basic Atlantic policy but tried to adapt it to the new situation in East-West relations and to the new givens of relations among the Western nations. But the political, economic, and social difficulties France was now undergoing limited its strategic room for maneuver. In early 1969, France had no other choice than to accept a form of normalization of its position in the Alliance, favored by the arrival of Richard Nixon in the White House. Without abandoning the very principles of its policy, it basically gave up on imposing them on its Atlantic partners—the Soames affair in February 1969 was the last straw. In other words, while sticking to the 1966 decision, France no longer sought actively to promote its model of transforming the Atlantic alliance.

The Soames Affair

The Soames affair came in the wake of the political shift of the autumn of 1968, which was translated into a certain French desire for rapprochement with *les Anglo-Saxons* and more particularly with Great Britain.[58] Michel Debré, the new foreign minister, played an important role in convincing the General to envisage such a rapprochement, not only because of his personal sympathy toward Great Britain (he approved of its profound distrust of "supranational" mechanisms), but also after an objective analysis of the diplomatic situation in the fall of 1968. The idea of an exclusive Franco-German partnership was becoming distant because of the growing differences of opinion between the two countries; at the same time, it was becoming more and more difficult for France to resist "blackmail over the entry of Great Britain into the Common Market";[59] moreover, Paris was concerned about the growing weight of Germany in Europe. In these conditions, the possibility of a Franco-British rapprochement that might be accompanied by re-examination of the political unity of Western Europe seemed a good option for French diplomacy. It was not incompatible—far from it—with the theme of nuclear tripartism that de Gaulle seemed tempted to revive at the same time. During November 1968 he informed the British ambassador, Christopher Soames, that he wanted to meet him in early 1969.[60]

The meeting took place on February 4, during a lunch at the Elysée, preceded by a long tête-à-tête.[61] De Gaulle explained to the ambassador that he thought closer cooperation between the two countries was possible. The problem of relations between Great Britain and Europe, the main obstacle to this cooperation up until then, could be solved by an arrangement within the EEC. As to the essential issue, the political dimension of European construction, it should be envisaged under the auspices of especially close cooperation between the four principal countries: France, Great Britain, Germany, and Italy. And even though, from such a perspective, NATO (in the Gaullist sense of the term) should subsist for a while, the fact that the Europeans were taking charge of their own security would imply a profound rearrangement of the Alliance.[62]

The perspective thus outlined was neither inconsistent with the current context or in contradiction with de Gaulle's previous policy. The General had always considered that the entry of Great Britain would radically change the EEC, which would then cease being the narrow and constraining organization founded by the Treaty of Rome. On this point, his opinion remained the same. But to the extent that France's European partners' insistence on British membership rendered it inevitable, a mutation in the EEC system toward something closer to a free trade zone appeared to him equally inevitable—but still on the condition that what he considered essential was preserved, that is to say, the prospect of a political and strategic Europe that was autonomous and efficient and based on "realities," that is, in which the most influential nation-states would prevail. Such a construction would result in time in a profound transformation, but not a suppression, of the Alliance, meaning ending Atlantic integration under U.S. command.[63]

Hence de Gaulle did not abandon his long-term objectives. Of course, his statements to Soames appeared to spell an important change—perhaps more imposed than desired—on his part over the issue of British membership in the EEC, but this was secondary to the political dimension of European construction, more of a priority for him than ever. Faced with the probability of British membership in the EEC, de Gaulle tried to separate the economic problematic from the political problematic of European construction. The latter apart (de Gaulle had refused six years earlier to separate the two), the overture to London through the intermediary of Soames really amounted to reformulating the question posed in 1962 to Macmillan: Was Great Britain inclined to work actively for an autonomous Europe? In 1962 London had replied negatively, at least for de Gaulle, but the question remained for him just as decisive. So in his eyes, the February 4 meeting aimed not to make a firm proposal but a preliminary sounding, by submitting to Soames what was certainly only a rough sketch. If London were genuinely interested, then it would be possible to explore this prospect more concretely, at a bilateral level, before widening the discussion.[64]

This exploration however would not take place. London in effect took the "sounding" as a "switch" and the Foreign Office transformed it into a "trap."[65] British concern about what many in London interpreted as a new dilatory maneuver, a desire for "revenge" on France by those responsible in the Foreign Office, and the ambiguity of de Gaulle's language, as usual confusing long-term and more immediate projects, all combined to produce this sorry result, despite the fact that Wilson was at first tempted to accept de Gaulle's proposal. But out of precaution, and to cover himself, he chose, on the advice of his foreign minister, Michael Stewart, to lay it out to Kiesinger on February 11. This produced discontent in Paris, which had insisted on the need for discretion, at least at first, surrounding contacts between the French and British.[66] But worse was to come: the Foreign Office had disseminated to the British ambassadors in EEC capitals both Soames's minutes and the instruction to use them to justify London's position. But some of them went beyond this instruction and presented de Gaulle's proposal as a sort of treachery toward the EEC.[67] From this moment on, things turned venomous and the press in both countries exploited the affair. In an unprecedented move, the British government leaked Soames's notes to certain newspapers, who published them. De Gaulle's statements, ambiguous as they were, were exaggerated: he was said to want to break up both the EEC and NATO, while establishing a "Directorate" of four. This upset the whole of Europe. De Gaulle was furious at the Wilson government, which under pressure from a Foreign Office wanting vengeance for the humiliating veto of 1963, had resorted to an undiplomatic procedure to transform a real overture into a veritable ambush on its initiator.

The episode confirmed that the French margin of maneuver was limited. London's behavior suggested that Great Britain felt sufficiently sure of being able to enter the EEC, soon and in a normal fashion, to reject de Gaulle's proposed approach in an offensive way. The Soames affair would thus put an end to the General's last initiative to make the West's political and strategic organization change. After the East-West status quo, the West-West status quo took root. Now, France's position in the Alliance and relations with NATO no longer had any reason to change dramatically. In Paris as in Washington, the time of normalization had arrived.

De Gaulle and Nixon

The process had been underway for months, aided by the approaching end of Johnson's presidency, which had crystallized (while having begun a real policy change in the spring of 1968, appreciated by de Gaulle) all the main French grievances over the Atlantic system. In early 1969, the tone changed for the better. A Franco-American dialogue that was truly friendly began to be renewed. On January 3, de Gaulle wrote to Johnson that he wished that "the United States and France got together to help in the solution of grave problems that weighed on the world's future."[68] Several weeks later, in his farewell letter to the outgoing U.S. president, the General said he was "convinced that there existed between our two peoples, a deep esteem and friendship that is always manifest in the decisive moments of History."[69] To be sure, de Gaulle even in the worst moments of the Franco-American quarrel had never ceased believing in this esteem and this friendship. Yet with these statements, a page of misunderstandings between France and the United States was finally turned.

The arrival of Nixon in the White House would permit a real normalization. The personal relationship between the two men lent itself to that.[70] De Gaulle had respect for Nixon, whom he had met during Nixon's vice presidency, during his trip to the United States in 1960, and had welcomed him to the Elysée in 1962 and 1967. The General took the new president for a reasonable and well-advised politician and—a real compliment—someone who knew Europe well. He foresaw that this Republican, heir to Eisenhower, would practice U.S. power in a more measured way than Kennedy and Johnson.[71] For his part, Nixon admired de Gaulle, to say the least. First for historical reasons; for Nixon, de Gaulle was quite simply "a genuine hero, one of the towering figures of the twentieth century,"[72] a sentiment shared by his national security advisor, Henry Kissinger. For personal reasons as well: Nixon, a personality tortured in politics as in human relationships, in constant search of recognition, would not forget that de Gaulle had been one of those few who during his own "time in the wilderness" had told him he had confidence in his political future.[73]

Beyond questions of personalities, the new U.S. administration was, as de Gaulle foresaw, much better disposed toward his ideas and his policy than preceding administrations. First, and this was not negligible, the new team in power in Washington understood these ideas and this policy. Kissinger, in his writings on the Alliance, had during the preceding years given proof of a certain comprehension of Gaullist policy, more in any case than the average U.S. expert in Atlantic issues. He saw in de Gaulle "the spokesman of the nation-state and of European autonomy from the United States," a role that could lead him, of course, to be "unnecessarily wounding to Americans," but he did "raise an important theme about the nature of international cooperation." He sympathized, in principle at least (the remainder of his diplomacy would show the effective limits of his tolerance in this area), with the idea that for cooperation between states to be effective, "each ally must—at least theoretically—be able to act autonomously."[74] In a general way, the policy of the Nixon–Kissinger tandem presented itself as springing from a realistic approach to relations among nation-states; therein lay a strong contrast with the more idealistic, even ideological, approach of the preceding Democratic administrations. Especially with regard to Europe and transatlantic relations, the rhetoric of partnership that had irritated de Gaulle for so long now appeared quite removed.

The Nixon administration was looking for a new international policy that in some respects and within certain limits could be compared to Gaullist ideas. Of course, essential things separated France, which de Gaulle had consecrated as a medium power, from the United States, which Nixon had no intention of selling short as a superpower, any more than he could abandon the traditional aims of U.S. policy. But the new president was determined to change "the presentation, the modalities, and the style of American action" and above all to "reconcile the need for active involvement and the desire for some shrinking of burdens" associated with this involvement.[75] After the period of overengagement of the Kennedy and Johnson years, there was indeed an important change (at least virtually) in the conception of U.S. international policy: a stated concern to redefine the relation between ends and means and to find a new balance between them. From the French standpoint, such a reexamination could only appear as positive for Europe and for transatlantic relations, since it would only lead Americans to grasp the extent of the changes on the Old Continent intervening since the post-war period and inspire them to rebalance the Alliance by taking into account the influence and new power of Europeans. At least this was the hope of some people in France on the eve of a new U.S. presidency.

Nixon's visit was thus awaited in Paris with the greatest interest. De Gaulle had written to the newly elected president that "it is with the greatest pleasure and interest" that he would learn of his views on all the issues he thought it opportune to discuss with him.[76] Eisenhower wrote to recommend that he seize the opportunity of Nixon's visit to revive the Franco-American friendship and cooperation so dear to him, and de Gaulle replied, recalling "their old friendship, born in the time of [their] united combat," that he was counting on having "some meaningful conversations."[77] Two weeks before his arrival, Nixon let de Gaulle know that he hoped to establish "frank and sincere" contacts with France; de Gaulle replied by thanking Nixon and telling him that he was in agreement with him.[78]

De Gaulle warmly welcomed Nixon. The General visibly preferred on a personal level dealing with him rather than his predecessor, even though he had the delicacy to confide in Sulzberger that this was "not a question of presidents" and that the improvement in Franco-American relations had begun before President Johnson had left office. It was evidently the political context that mattered most and the General thought it favorable for a Franco-American reconciliation since "the main question," that of NATO, was solved and was no longer even, from his viewpoint, "a subject for discussion." As for Vietnam, on which Nixon and

Kissinger had apparently new and less opposing views to his own, de Gaulle noted the existence of a dialogue that he thought would eventually bring about results.[79]

Nixon's visit to Paris from February 28 to March 2, 1969, the last stop of his first tour of Europe, took place according to the expectations of both parties. From the start, the Americans proved how much their discourse had changed. The first evening, Kissinger officially set the tone for the press: Washington was convinced "that it serves nobody's purpose for the United States and France to have avoidable bad relations." The Europeans, explained the president's special advisor, "do not want to be in the position of having to choose between the United States and France." Therefore, the United States wanted to avoid being "in an organic permanent conflict with France."[80]

The three meetings between de Gaulle and Nixon, of which one took place at Versailles in the Grand Trianon, moved toward normalization and marked a mutual desire to end that "organic permanent conflict" whose principal stake was obviously the Alliance. De Gaulle repeated to Nixon what his predecessors had not understood or wanted to understand, that "France, perhaps paradoxically, rendered the greatest service to the Alliance by being independent." For the rest, he had no objection to other Europeans' accepting the "American protectorate," to which he assimilated integration (a way for the General of putting an end point to the Soames affair that had caused a stir before Nixon's arrival). Moreover, like most of his European counterparts, he considered that détente and disarmament had the "indispensable condition" of strong national defenses.[81] Nixon responded to de Gaulle in pragmatic language: he said that since "there was no way to bridge the theoretical disputes in the Alliance," it was better to "work together on concrete projects of common concern."[82] The General could only approve of statements that broke with the Atlantic rhetoric of the Kennedy and Johnson years, which held that NATO integration was the only possible framework for common action. This was a change, if not in perspective, then at least in discourse, summarized by Kissinger: while rejecting integration of armed forces, de Gaulle approved of the coordination of foreign policies, whereas the United States had until then practiced the reverse, that is to say, military integration without diplomatic coordination; but now Nixon hoped to practice coordination with France "in both fields."[83]

The other subjects discussed by the two presidents raised, if not convergences, at least smaller divergences. The most important point was that Nixon, ending years of U.S. reticence and even hostility to the French nuclear effort, indicated to the General that "he had no objection to possession by France of an independent nuclear force" and that "on the contrary, he thought it useful."[84] On world conflicts, de Gaulle suggested to Nixon ending the Vietnam War by seeking a political solution, including undertaking an immediate military withdrawal. And he recommended avoiding letting China retreat into isolation; Nixon had similar ideas to his on this. As for East-West relations, de Gaulle said

he was favorable to the pursuit of the détente process, which he judged both
necessary and inevitable, but customarily warned the United States against
"Yalta-like arrangements."[85]

On both sides, the Nixon–de Gaulle meetings were considered as positive
overall. On the American side, the good impression made by de Gaulle was manifest. Kissinger, present at one of the meetings, had been able to observe the
breadth of de Gaulle's sense of history, although the former Harvard professor
and specialist in Metternich and Bismarck did not feel he himself made "a lasting impression on the great French leader": when he asked de Gaulle how he
"will keep Germany from dominating the Europe he has just described,"
Kissinger got the single, lofty response: "through war."[86] On the basics, though,
the Nixon team had every reason to feel satisfied with the Parisian stopover. The
dialogue with France was renewed at the highest level: de Gaulle had even accepted the idea of a return visit to the United States, scheduled for 1970. Upon
Nixon's return to Washington, the president was euphoric: de Gaulle was a
"giant" among European leaders. Nixon even appeared converted to the Gaullist
vision of Europe: the world, he said, would be "much more sure . . . if there existed a strong European community that contributed to the balance . . . between
the United States and the USSR."[87] The reality behind the presidential enthusiasm was more modest: the United States could quite simply congratulate itself
that the two countries, while respecting their respective positions, were getting
closer on the principal European and world issues. Kissinger soberly thought that
while the General had not changed his basic principles, he no longer sought so
categorically to impose them.[88]

There was also satisfaction on the French side. For Maurice Couve de Murville,
Nixon's visit, taking place in a "cordial and relaxed" atmosphere, marked a renewal
of dialogue "after years traversed with crises." The main thing was that French positions be "well known and well understood," even if they were not "approved of."
For the rest, Couve de Murville was as usual prudent: the follow-up relations between the two countries would depend, he thought, on the evolution of each. Uncertainty existed about both: France was ready to enter a referendum campaign on
which rested de Gaulle's political future after eleven years in power; and the United
States, while wrestling with them, had not definitely solved the two principal problems that pitted it against France — Vietnam and the dollar. Couve de Murville (who
had, by then, considerable experience in the delicate matter of French–American
relations) concluded that "on each side, as usual, nothing is over yet."[89]

The End

In the spring of 1969, the word "normalization" was best suited to describe the
state of relations between France and the United States within the Alliance. Basically, nothing had changed. The logic of the French position and the U.S. position remained identical. What was new was that communication was reestab-

lished after having been practically nonexistent for years. The French had the impression of finally being understood, if not approved of, whereas the Americans had the sentiment that the French had finally ceased wanting to impose their position, even though they had not renounced it. Everything had changed at the level of form, however, since relations had recovered the kind of proximity and cordiality appropriate for two great allies.

This was the situation as the end of de Gaulle's presidency approached, to be decided in a referendum on April 27 (on the subject of the Senate and regions), a vote on which hinged the General's personal fate. At the end of March, de Gaulle was once again in the United States, attending the funeral of Eisenhower. The death of his companion in arms was obviously emblematic of the close of an era, but also, a herald of the end of the General's political career. Hervé Alphand, who accompanied him on the trip, remarked that he was "the next-to-last of the giants of an era that included Churchill, Roosevelt, Stalin"; of which remained, apart from him, only Mao. De Gaulle had already entered into history and was the "pole of attraction" at the ceremony.[90]

The Nixon administration was appreciative of de Gaulle's gesture in attending "Ike's" funeral. Kissinger admired the courtesy the General demonstrated on this occasion.[91] He was received by Nixon in the Oval Office and they conducted a fresh *tour d'horizon* of the subjects discussed a month earlier. The conversation brought nothing new, but it confirmed in the eyes of the Americans the poor state of Franco-German relations, and, following the Soames affair, of Franco-British relations; by contrast, relations between France and the United States would be better for quite a while.[92]

U.S. officials were undoubtedly aware that this meeting would be the last. For Kissinger, de Gaulle had "a melancholy air of withdrawal, of already being a spectator at his own actions, of speaking in the abstract about a future he knew he would no longer shape."[93] De Gaulle knew the end was coming. It was during the trip to Washington that he confided with detachment to Alphand that he was convinced of losing the referendum on April 27 and that he would be "very happy with this outcome."[94]

This awareness of the approaching end of his mission in a man so imbued with the need to prepare for the long term, well beyond his own actions if not his own existence, and to ensure continuity in a policy he believed was right for the country, illuminates the last great decision taken by de Gaulle concerning the Alliance. He decided on nothing less than tacitly renewing France's membership in the Atlantic Pact, after previously having left a doubt about this. On April 4, 1969, Michel Debré, the foreign minister, represented France in Washington at the twentieth anniversary of the signing of the North Atlantic Treaty. In truth, de Gaulle had given very clear instructions about France's participation in the commemorative ceremonies: "it could not be represented at any military demonstration" by NATO and would not send its defense minister to Washington.[95] But the head of French diplomacy was authorized to declare that the Alliance after twenty years still kept its *"raison d'être"*[96] from the French point of view. The French discretion that surrounded this decision, which was really a surprise to nobody, was the best sign of the normalization of relations between France and the United States and of the appeasement of the great Atlantic quarrel.

On April 27, 1969, a little more than half of the French people said "no" to de Gaulle. At noon on the following day, the General ceased exercising his office.

NOTES

1. Cyrus L. Sulzberger, *An Age of Mediocrity: Memoirs and Diaries, 1963–1972*, New York, Macmillan, 1973, p. 400.

2. The Hague Telegram #346–49, 19 April 1968, MAE, Pactes 1961–1970, box 268.

3. Quoted in Pierre Maillard, *De Gaulle et l'Allemagne. Le rêve inachevé*, Paris, Plon, 1990, p. 230.

4. Hervé Alphand, *L'Etonnement d'être. Journal 1939–1973*, Paris, Fayard, 1977, pp. 499–500.

5. Bohlen to Rusk, 9 February 1968, quoted in Charles E. Bohlen, *Witness to History 1929–1969,* New York, Norton, 1973, p. 520.

6. André Kaspi, *Les Américains,* vol. 2, "Les États-Unis de 1945 à nos jours," Paris, Le Seuil, 1986, p. 531.

7. Alphand, *L'Etonnement d'être*, p. 501.

8. Maurice Couve de Murville, *Une Politique étrangère 1958–1969*, Paris, Plon, 1971, p. 142.

9. LBJL, Administrative Histories, State Department, vol. 1, ch. 3, "Europe," "The Troop Problem and Burden Sharing," n.d. 1968.

10. LBJL, Administrative Histories, State Department, vol. 1, ch. 3, "Europe," "NATO Political Consultations, The Harmel Exercise," n.d., pp. 1–3.

11. Jean Klein, *Sécurité et désarmement en Europe,* Paris, Economica, 1987, pp. 57 ff.

12. Jean Charlot, *Les Français et de Gaulle*, Paris, Plon, 1971, p. 88.

13. Polls cited in Charlot, *Les Français et de Gaulle*, pp. 256–59.

14. Georges Pompidou, *Pour rétablir une vérité,* Paris, Flammarion, 1982, p. 196.

15. Alphand, *L'Etonnement d'être*, p. 510.

16. Letter to Michel Debré, quoted in Bernard Ledwidge, *De Gaulle*, New York, St. Martin's Press, 1982, p. 387.

17. Alphand, *L'Etonnement d'être*, pp. 512–13.

18. Alphand, *L'Etonnement d'être*.

19. Communiqué de la présidence de la République sur l'intervention de l'armée soviétique en Tchécoslovaquie, 21 August 1968, *Politique étrangère de la France,* second semester of 1968, p. 54.

20. Quoted by André Fontaine, *Histoire de la détente 1962–1981,* Paris, Le Seuil, 1982, p. 138.

21. Quoted by John Newhouse, *De Gaulle and the Anglo-Saxons,* New York, Viking, 1970, p. 323.

22. CIA, Memorandum, "Possibilities for Accommodation between the U.S. and France," 28 August 1968, LBJL, NSF, France, boxes 173–174.

23. CIA, Memorandum, "Possibilities for Accommodation between the U.S. and France."

24. CIA, Memorandum, "Possibilities for Accommodation between the U.S. and France."

25. CIA, Directorate of Intelligence, Intelligence Memorandum, "French Foreign Policy in the Wake of the Czechoslovak Crisis," 10 October 1968, LBJL, NSF, France, boxes 173–174.

26. Couve de Murville, *Une Politique étrangère*, p. 282.

27. Cable, Walt Rostow to the President, 23 September 1968, LBJL, NSF, France, boxes 173–174.

28. Maillard, *De Gaulle et l'Allemagne*, p. 254.

29. Maillard, *De Gaulle et l'Allemagne*, p. 262.

30. Sulzberger, *Age of Mediocrity*, p. 505.

31. "De Gaulle's Foreign Policy: 1969 Version," 20 December 1968.

32. "French Foreign Policy in the Wake of the Czechoslovak Crisis," 10 October 1968.

33. Memorandum, Rostow to President, 11 October 1968, LBJL, NSF, France, boxes 173–174.

34. EMBTEL, Paris #24349, for Secretary from Shriver, 23 November, 1968, LBJL, NSF, France, boxes 173–174.

35. Sulzberger, *Age of Mediocrity*, p. 505.

36. Department of State, research memorandum, "De Gaulle's Foreign Policy: 1969 Version," Thomas L. Hughes, 20 December 1968, LBJL, NSF, France, boxes 173–174.

37. "French Foreign Policy in the Wake of the Czechoslovak Crisis," 10 October 1968.

38. "French Foreign Policy in the Wake of the Czechoslovak Crisis"; and "De Gaulle's Foreign Policy: 1969 Version," 20 December 1968.

39. Cf. Henry A. Kissinger, *White House Years,* Boston, Little, Brown, 1979.

40. "De Gaulle's Foreign Policy: 1969 Version," 20 December 1968.

41. "De Gaulle's Foreign Policy: 1969 Version," 20 December 1968.

42. Brouillon de discours prononcé à l'IHEDN, 25 September 1969, in Charles de Gaulle, *Lettres, notes et carnets (LNC) (juillet 1966–avril 1969)*, Paris, Plon, 1987, pp. 283–84.

43. Note du Service des Pactes et du Désarmement, "La crise tchécoslovaque et l'Alliance atlantique," 30 September 1968, MAE, Pactes 1961–1970, box 277.

44. Harlan Cleveland, *NATO: The Transatlantic Bargain,* New York, Harper & Row, 1970, p. 123.

45. "La crise tchécoslovaque et l'Alliance atlantique," 30 September 1968.

46. Cleveland, *NATO: The Transatlantic Bargain*, pp. 124–25; and Lawrence Kaplan, *NATO and the United States: The Enduring Alliance*, Boston, Twayne, 1988, p. 123.

47. Cable, Walt Rostow to the President, 23 September 1968, LBJL, NSF, France, boxes 173–174.

48. EMBTEL, Paris #24349.

49. Interviews; see also Jean-Paul Cointet, François Puaux, and François Valentin, "Les suites de l'action du général de Gaulle en matière de politique de défense depuis 1969," in *De Gaulle en son siècle*, vol. 4, "La sécurité et l'indépendance de la France," Institut Charles de Gaulle, Paris, Plon, 1992.

50. Personal interviews.

51. Jacques Massu, *Baden 68. Souvenirs d'une fidélité gaulliste,* Paris, Plon, 1983, pp. 237–38.

52. Massu, *Baden 68.*

53. "De Gaulle's Foreign Policy: 1969 Version," 20 December 1968, p. 9; *Le Monde,* 31 October 1968.

54. Général M. Fourquet, "Emploi des différents systèmes de forces dans le cadre de la stratégie de dissuasion," *Revue de Défense Nationale,* May 1969, pp. 757–67.

55. Fourquet, "Emploi des différents systèmes . . ."

56. See, for example, Michael M. Harrison, *The Reluctant Ally: France and Atlantic Security,* Baltimore, Johns Hopkins University Press, 1981.

57. Personal interview. See also Jean Lacouture, *De Gaulle,* vol. 2, "The Ruler 1945–1970," trans. Alan Sheridan, New York, Norton, 1992, and Marcel Duval and Yves Le Baut, *L'Arme nucléaire française. Pourquoi et comment?,* Paris, S.P.M./Kronos, 1992.

58. On the Soames affair, see Françoise de La Serre, "De Gaulle et la candidature britannique aux Communautés européennes," in *De Gaulle en son siècle,* vol. 5, "L'Europe," Institut Charles de Gaulle, Paris, Plon, 1992.

59. Maillard, *De Gaulle et l'Allemagne,* p. 262.

60. See the recollections of Ledwidge, *De Gaulle,* p. 389.

61. Since the very tenor of de Gaulle's statements reported by Soames to the Foreign Office is at the origin of the controversy, it is difficult to have a definite idea due to the lack of available archives. It seems, though, that the minutes of the British ambassador reflect in outline the perspective developed by the General. Cf. Ledwidge, *De Gaulle,* p. 396.

62. Ledwidge, *De Gaulle,* p. 392; Maillard, *De Gaulle et l'Allemagne,* p. 260.

63. Maillard, *De Gaulle et l'Allemagne,* pp. 260–61.

64. Maillard, *De Gaulle et l'Allemagne,* p. 260.

65. Maillard, *De Gaulle et l'Allemagne.*

66. Alphand, *L'Etonnement d'être,* pp. 517–18.

67. Ledwidge, *De Gaulle,* p. 395.

68. Letter to Johnson, 3 January 1969, in de Gaulle, *LNC (1966–1969),* pp. 273–74.

69. Letter to Johnson, 29 January 1969, in de Gaulle, *LNC (1966–1969),* p. 287.

70. See Edward A. Kolodziej, "Charles de Gaulle et Richard Nixon. L'exercice du pouvoir et la recherche de la légitimité," in *De Gaulle en son siècle,* vol. 4, "La sécurité et l'indépendance de la France," Institut Charles de Gaulle, Paris, Plon, 1984; and Yves-Henri Nouailhat, "Nixon–de Gaulle: un épisode original des relations franco-américaines," *Revue française d'études américaines,* no. 32, April 1987, pp. 309–18.

71. Lacouture, *De Gaulle,* p. 385.

72. Richard M. Nixon, *Leaders,* New York, Warner, 1982, p. 41.

73. Nixon, *Leaders.*

74. Kissinger, *White House Years,* pp. 104–5.

75. Stanley Hoffmann, *Primacy or World Order: American Foreign Policy since the Cold War,* New York, McGraw Hill, 1978, p. 43.

76. Letter to Richard Nixon, 17 January 1969, in de Gaulle, *LNC (1966–1969),* p. 281.

77. Letter to General Dwight D. Eisenhower, 13 February 1969, in de Gaulle, *LNC (1966–1969),* p. 293.

78. Letter to Richard Nixon, 14 February 1969, in de Gaulle, *LNC (1966–1969),* p. 293.

79. Sulzberger, *Age of Mediocrity,* p. 505.

80. Kissinger, *White House Years,* p. 107.

81. Kissinger, *White House Years,* p. 109.

82. Kissinger, *White House Years.*

83. Kissinger, *White House Years.*

84. Quoted by Nouailhat, "Nixon–de Gaulle."

85. Kissinger, *White House Years*, p. 108

86. Kissinger, *White House Years*, p. 110.

87. Quoted by Frank Costigliola, *France and the United States: The Cold Alliance since World War II,* Boston, Twayne, 1992, p. 164.

88. Kissinger, *White House Years*, p. 88.

89. Couve de Murville, *Une Politique étrangère*, p. 159.

90. Alphand, *L'Etonnement d'être*, p. 520.

91. Kissinger, *White House Years*, p. 384.

92. Kissinger, *White House Years*.

93. Kissinger, *White House Years*.

94. Alphand, *L'Etonnement d'être*, p. 519.

95. Paris Telegram to REPAN, Brussels, 21 January 1969; note de R. de Saint-Légier à M. Haberer, 6 March 1969, MAE, Pactes 1961–1970, box 259.

96. Quoted by Harrison, *Reluctant Ally*, p. 169; see also Michel Debré, *Mémoires, "Gouverner autrement 1962–1970,"* Paris, Albin Michel, 1993, pp. 311 ff.

Conclusion: The Gaullist Legacy

Thirty years after General de Gaulle's departure, his foreign policy, and in particular his Atlantic policy, continue to inform France's international and Western decision making. This statement calls for a series of questions. First, how can we draw up a balance sheet of his actions in this area up to 1969, and how was this balance sheet perceived at that time? Second, in the following years, how did his successors position themselves in relation to the Gaullist legacy, and how did they manage that legacy during the period of status quo between 1969 and 1989? Finally, to what extent did the end of the Cold War affect a policy that from the start was oriented toward an overcoming of blocs, and how has this turn of events governed the adaptation of this policy in the years since 1989?

THE BALANCE SHEET

De Gaulle's policy toward the Atlantic Alliance more than anything else arose from "a certain idea of France." His prime objective, which trumped all others, was in effect to restore the country's independence and sovereignty. By 1969 this national priority had been attained.[1]

This was certainly so from a military standpoint. Until 1958, the autonomy of French defense had been hampered: First, the military, divided between irreconcilable missions (the defense of overseas territory and the defense of Europe) was weak and incoherent. Second, France was marginalized within NATO (in particular in relation to a renascent German military) and its leaders, even before de Gaulle's return to power, were becoming aware that its role in the Alliance did not live up to their ambitions: hence the growing frustration of the waning Fourth Republic with respect to the Atlantic organization. By 1969, French military autonomy had been restored — and moreover, not at the expense of Western security. Far from it. For it was not so much the 1966 decision that led to this outcome, but

245

rather the reverse: after the end of the Algerian conflict, it was by a major restructuring of French defense and by restoring coherence to the French military that the General recovered the country's autonomy, and this recovery, in turn, was inevitably translated into a withdrawal from Atlantic military integration. Meanwhile, the departure of allied installations from French territory put an end to a situation that had represented an impediment—albeit one freely accepted at first—to French sovereignty.

Let us next consider the strategic situation. In 1958, France was merely a virtual atomic power. Within NATO, French feelings of frustration were aggravated by the growing importance to Western defense of a nuclear strategy that increasingly appeared to arise from an American, or Anglo-Saxon, monopoly. Of course, when he came to power, de Gaulle inherited a realization among the Fourth Republic's leaders that only the buildup of its own atomic military power would allow France to claim recognition as having parity status with Great Britain within the Atlantic Alliance. But his ambition went beyond this: there was no question of placing the "*force de frappe*" within NATO constraints, and still less within those of a chimerical multilateral force. Nor could nuclear decisions be shared, due to the fact that the U.S. guarantee was becoming unreliable as a result of the balance of terror. Thus, only a nuclear force that was truly national would fulfill French interests. In this sense, the decisive choice was made by de Gaulle after the Nassau Conference. While by 1969 the French nuclear panoply was still somewhat skimpy (in fact, still limited to an aerial component), its development was well underway, and the advantages of a deterrent independent of the United States were quite evident, especially in contrast with what was seen as a British situation of dependence.

But it was mostly from a political standpoint that de Gaulle had attained his national objectives. In 1958, France appeared to be the sick one of the Alliance. A decade after its creation, the French had the feeling that the Fourth Republic's choice in favor of the Atlantic Alliance had brought them neither an ironclad security, nor the privileged status of a "Big" Western power to which they aspired. Even worse, after the Suez crisis, French leaders considered that their country had been "betrayed" by the United States and let down by NATO. By 1969, a new page had been turned. For de Gaulle, it was a matter of reconciling participation in the Alliance with the imperative of "*grandeur*," and this equation was solved by the 1966 decision. While remaining a full member, France could recover the status of which previous "Atlanticism" had formerly deprived it. And once the Franco-American quarrel had worn down after its 1966–1967 apogee, it was ultimately this new reality of a France that remained a solid ally while being influential beyond the Atlantic horizon that American leaders came to accept, especially after the arrival of Richard Nixon in the White House.

Nevertheless, de Gaulle's Atlantic policy cannot be reduced to a quest for grandeur and the assertion of independence. Rather than a policy of disruption, it was a policy for refounding the Alliance. The national objectives were in fact inseparable from larger Western objectives: to adapt the Alliance's organization to the long-term political and strategic changes that he had been anticipating, and, most of all, to reequilibrate the transatlantic relationship.

Had this second priority been achieved by 1969? The answer here is more ambivalent. In many respects, the 1966 decision can be interpreted as illustrating the limits of the ambition to reorient the Alliance. After the fruitless attempt of the 1958 memorandum (that sought to reorganize the Alliance around a tripartite political and strategic leadership), and after the rejection of the Fouchet Plan (that sought to rebalance it by favoring the emergence of a Western Europe capable of acting in a coherent and autonomous manner in political and strategic realms), and then after the partial failure of the Elysée Treaty (that sought to achieve the same goal by means of a Franco-German entente), France could only acknowledge the impossibility of the Alliance reform that it had constantly called for. Hence, after 1963, there was a policy of obstruction to U.S. projects for consolidating Atlantic integration (among which the multilateral force was the driving force), which would culminate in March 1966 with the withdrawal from military organization.

Nevertheless, even if French policy had failed to effect a transformation of Atlantic bodies in line with the Gaullist vision, the 1966 decision was not without an impact on the Alliance. Even though negative perceptions of the French "withdrawal" were common among the allies, this impact was in fact far from negative: not only was the decision not a rupture, but it permitted a more flexible relation between France and NATO. By preserving for France the possibility of close cooperation, and perhaps of an increased participation in Western defense (this was really the rationale behind the Ailleret-Lemnitzer agreements of 1967), the "withdrawal" in fact moved in the direction of a military strengthening of the Alliance, and would in the long term facilitate its eventual reequilibration. Moreover, the assertion of an autonomous nuclear posture that was independent of both NATO and the United States also implied a strengthening of the Alliance's "global deterrence," which the allies tacitly acknowledged at the Ottawa summit of 1974, and constituted *ipso facto* a kind of Europeanization of this deterrence. Finally, the French decision obliged the allies to ponder the legitimacy of NATO and its political role and led them to search for ways and means for better consultation within the Alliance. In short, far from harming the institution, French policy paradoxically consolidated it, while obliging it to adapt—though in directions remote from what de Gaulle had envisioned.

But the General had by no means renounced this vision or his grand European design. While the 1966 decision, in a way, marked a retreat for Gaullist ambitions, it was a tactical retreat, or at least a strategic one: far from representing an abandonment, the French withdrawal belonged to a forward-looking and dynamic perspective. In fact, the new status of France within the Alliance now constituted a sort of "model" for what in time could be an Alliance that was both Europeanized and freed from bloc politics. He intended this model to gain a following, and even if for the moment he had to reckon with French isolation, it was only in order better to revive a desire to transform the Alliance when the time came—and France's maintained independence within it appeared to be the long-term surety of this desire. From this point of view—to which we will return—the policy thirty years later of his successor Jacques Chirac was by no means a revision of the Gaullist "dogma," but on the contrary marked a return to the active policy of transforming the Atlantic Alliance that had been suspended in 1966.

There remains the third category of Gaullist policy objectives: after national and Western objectives, came East-West ones. The General's grand and long-term ambition was to adapt the Atlantic Alliance to an international system that in his eyes would leave the Cold War behind and even undermine the international status quo by combating the logic of blocs within NATO itself.

Here the assessment may appear the most disappointing. As we have seen, the French withdrawal from the military organization—which occurred a few weeks before de Gaulle's historic trip to the USSR in June 1966—in many respects marked the apogee of the policy of "détente, entente and cooperation" launched in 1963–1964, whose ambition, expressed during the February 1965 press conference—exactly twenty years after the conference of the same name—was to leave "Yalta" behind. Of course, for France this also embodied a national objective, since a loosening of the bipolar system would hasten the country's rise to world status, which presupposed that it free itself from the grip of the Cold War system. But questioning Atlantic integration was also and most especially, for de Gaulle, to contest the bloc system as a whole; could French policy with respect to NATO inspire USSR satellite states that were tempted to take the same steps within the Warsaw Pact? This was a theme the General developed for the benefit of the Eastern countries, notably in Poland in 1967.

Yet events seemed to go against him: the popular democracies were simply not ready, at that time, to take a path forbidden by the USSR, as the Poles did not hesitate to express to de Gaulle during his trip. And the crushing of the Prague spring by the Soviets and their allies in August 1968 would clearly expose the limits to the Gaullist vision: it was a hard blow for a French policy relying on the hypothesis of greater fluidity in East-West relations. Of course, the Czech affair might represent only a brief *"incident de parcours"* on the road to a détente that, far from being undermined, would be asserted in the months and years to come. But while détente was possible, the overcoming of blocs was improbable: the Harmel report adopted by the allies in December 1967—including by the hesitant French—thus found itself validated by the actual evolution of East-West relations. Rather than a Gaullist conception of détente, it was a bloc-to-bloc détente that was taking place, and this implied—at least in the first instance—a consolidation of the same status quo the General had wanted to overthrow.

Nevertheless, the assessment of Gaullist policy in this realm cannot be measured against the standard of the failure of the project to overcome blocs. Indeed, the policy of "détente, entente and cooperation" undertaken after 1963–1964 had a significant effect of entrainment on East-West relations, which were until then still marked by the systematic antagonism of the Cold War, and thus it contributed to the thaw that from now on characterized relations between the blocs on the Old Continent. In addition, Gaullist activism had incontestably led the allies to modify their approach to East-West relations and to integrate the necessity for détente—to the point of making it the "second function" of the Atlantic Alliance, in parallel with its primary mission of defense. Even if the Harmel report was underpinned by a very different conception of East-West relations—bloc to bloc rather than from the Atlantic to the Urals—it can be considered in many respects as a response to the challenge thrown down by the General to the Atlantic and international status quo.

Moreover, the French withdrawal from NATO's integrated military organization was forward looking, like the Western dimension previously discussed. Of course, the 1966 decision somewhat sanctioned the limits of de Gaulle's revisionism: it was because France had not been able to challenge the system of blocs that it unilaterally redefined the modes of belonging to the Alliance; and the events of 1968 merely confirmed the failure of the General's grand East-West design. Nevertheless, in the same way as the 1966 decision constituted in his eyes the pledge of a political and strategic Europe that would take form when circumstances allowed, so the withdrawal from integration prefigured the "post-Yalta" European system that he continually summoned; the new relations between France and the Alliance, in this sense, also constituted a model destined to reign as soon as the Cold War circumstances—which to him were exceptional and transitory—came to an end. In short, the 1966 decision aimed at maintaining a dynamic whose results would sooner or later be felt, which would then confirm the correctness of his thinking.

MANAGING THE LEGACY

When General de Gaulle retired from politics in 1969, the balance sheet of his Atlantic policy could therefore be considered as positive overall, at least from the French standpoint (also no doubt to the allies, but it would take longer for them to recognize it). In any case, it was in the light of such a positive evaluation that his successors would define their own actions in this area; henceforward, if France's foreign and security policy after 1969 was, as a whole, marked by a concern to preserve the legacy, this concern appeared particularly evident in the relations between France and the Alliance, which still constituted the central issue. Between 1969 and 1989—or from the General's departure to the fall of the Berlin Wall—the Gaullist "model," against the background of a durable European status quo, thus remained an incontestable standard of reference for French Atlantic policy. While certain adaptations were made that confirmed the operational flexibility of the model, in no way were its principles questioned. It was truly continuity that reigned.[2]

This continuity was expressed in the constantly asserted desire to maintain "independence." Presidents Georges Pompidou (1969–1974), Valéry Giscard d'Estaing (1974–1981), and François Mitterrand (1981–1995) were all attached, in fact, to preserving a security policy founded on a deterrence and a defense posture that should remain national above all. During these two decades, the French military never stopped being developed, whether in the nuclear area (France possessed as of the first half of the 1970s a strategic "triad" that made it a "minisuperpower") or in the conventional area (its land army and air force were continually reinforced in this period, considerably enlarging its options for intervention in Europe). So while the reality of decision-making autonomy was debatable in 1966, it was not so twenty years later. As a result, France's particular position in the Alliance was never questioned; while remaining a full member of the Alliance properly speaking, it stuck to its posture of military nonintegration and of selective political participation in the organization's other activities. Whether in operational or institutional terms, the situation between France and NATO remained in 1989, in basic outline, what it had been twenty years previously.

Continuity also reigned in the Western dimension, where the model and its capacity to adapt were confirmed. If the buildup of the French military in this period expressed primarily a strengthened capacity for autonomous defense, it also made possible an increased role for France in Western defense arrangements. The paradox is only on the surface: while the "withdrawal" allowed the maintenance and even development of close cooperation between France and NATO, the limits of French military capacity in Central Europe, at the end of the 1960s, in reality made this cooperation very difficult. But twenty years later, this cooperation had reached an unprecedented level, making France a major military partner—and recognized as such—of NATO in the defense of Central Europe. Far from being opposed to each other, the imperative of independence and alliance requirements mutually supported each other, thus proving decisions taken in the 1960s to be correct. For the rest, France's Atlantic policy continued to be determined by the goal of transforming and rebalancing the Western ensemble; the goal of a European strategic entity remained a determining motive in maintaining France's singular position with respect to NATO. Of course, the status quo of bipolar confrontation made such a transformation improbable in the foreseeable future, and France pursued its European strategic goal less actively than in the 1960s. But by the same token, the maintenance of its particular position within the Alliance remained during all these years the surety of the latter's future transformation.

But the French posture within the Alliance also continued, after de Gaulle, to be justified by the wish to overcome the blocs, and his successors continually made the undermining of "Yalta" the main objective of French foreign and security policy. While his departure in 1969 had coincided—in a context of détente, of course, but between blocs—with the confirmation of the East-West status quo he had denounced, successive presidents would keep to this course and continue to make "détente, entente and cooperation" and the organization of a grand Europe "from the Atlantic to the Urals" the focus of their international politics. In the face of a dominant vision of European security organized around the dialogue (or confrontation) between the two alliances, France maintained across two decades the goal of an international order freed from bipolar thinking. Of course, the French policy of getting rid of blocs was principally expressed in institutions or processes devoted to the organization or management of East-West relations; in the 1970s and 1980s, French policy with respect to the Conference on Security and Cooperation in Europe (CSCE) or even France's particular position in disarmament affairs were, accordingly, the most tangible manifestations of the French refusal of "Yalta." But the maintenance of its particular position toward NATO and its refusal of bipolar thinking within the West constituted, in this period and until the fall of the Berlin Wall, France's best argument for its revisionist grand design.

Such continuity in France's Atlantic policy was not a foregone conclusion in the aftermath of de Gaulle's departure. Many domestic and international factors could have led to its revision, thus justifying American hopes during the 1960s that the General's successors would in time reconsider his decisions. If nothing came of this, it was because the effects of the Gaullist legacy were constantly perceived as beneficial, whether nationally or in their Western or East-West dimensions—hence the permanence of a "model" that was never fundamentally called into question during these two decades.

Domestic factors largely account for this outcome: it was primarily because the French people identified with this model that they wanted to preserve it. When the decision was made to withdraw France from Atlantic integration, a national consensus did not yet really exist on this subject. Of course, public opinion had supported the General, and one could speak of true popular consent to this policy as early as 1966. Nevertheless, politicians were still far from unanimous and cleavages between "Atlanticists" and "Gaullists" split the right as well as the left. Quickly, however, a condition *sine qua non* for any pretender to national power was to lay claim to the Gaullist legacy, whether in institutional terms or in the realm or foreign and defense policy. This was evidently the case in 1969 with Georges Pompidou, long the General's prime minister and "dauphin," whose Atlantic policy did not deviate from the line he had laid down. More significantly, the election of Valéry Giscard d'Estaing in 1974 confirmed the rule, since the first non-Gaullist president of the Fifth Republic chose continuity in this area, too. But it was with the election in 1981 of François Mitterrand, the first socialist president and historically an opponent of the General (he had formerly virulently denounced his Atlantic policy) that would consecrate this continuity, since Mitterrand would in turn appropriate the legacy. Meanwhile, the political parties (notably the Communist Party in 1977 and the Socialist Party in 1978) explicitly rallied to it: the consent of the French people ten years after the decision to "quit" NATO had been converted into a veritable "consensus" within the political class, and this consensus powerfully contributed to the continuity of France's Atlantic policy.

International factors also spelled great continuity in the Fifth Republic's Atlantic decision making. If France kept to the posture adopted in 1966, it was also because its leaders consistently saw it as the formula most in line with the defense of their country's interests in the Western ensemble. Not only did France's particular situation regarding NATO allow the *autonomie de décision* reestablished in the 1960s to be preserved, but it was judged by its leaders to have given France considerable influence within the West, compared to what it would have had if it had not broken with "integration." In fact, the allies, and most of all the United States, rapidly came round to recognize not only that France remained a fully fledged ally, but that its solidity as ally was largely due to its particular position. This realization, tacitly admitted by the Americans in the early 1970s and explicitly acknowledged by all the allies in the 1980s, merely strengthened the French in their conviction of the correctness of a policy that gave their country its full weight in the West. The Euromissile crisis at the end of the 1970s and the start of the 1980s startlingly confirmed this: thanks to its independent posture, France remained immune from the pacifist wave that overtook Western Europe and it now appeared as America's most solid ally. Taking a stand unprecedented in the previous twenty years of the NATO debate, François Mitterrand's speech to the Bundestag in January 1983 was undoubtedly the high point of this French independence within the Alliance. Amidst the new Cold War, this stance made a major impact and appeared more than ever to justify the policy pursued by the General's successors.

It is true that the East-West context in this period pushed French leaders to maintain this course. Whether against the background of détente in the 1970s or the new Cold War in the 1980s, the persistence of the bipolar status quo remained the fundamental given of the international system between 1969 and 1989. In these conditions, the French aspiration to a world role continued to rest on denunciation of "Yalta" and on a demand to move beyond blocs. This proclaimed goal conferred on France's international policy a "mission" on a par with this ambition: not only did it structure and give coherence to all actions abroad, but it conferred on its diplomacy—that of a medium power—a more global impact. France could now claim a major role in East-West relations, a role that was particularly expressed by keeping close relations with the USSR (interrupted only during the "detox cure" called for by Mitterrand after his arrival in the Elysée, against the background of the new Cold War). Concomitantly, France could push forward with its role in North-South relations and cultivate a Third World easily seduced by an antibloc discourse that it read as an anti-imperialist policy (despite French efforts in the African "preserve"). For all these reasons, France's particular position within the Atlantic Alliance constituted, for those responsible for its diplomacy, essential political capital that must not be wasted, at least as long as the Cold War persisted.

In many respects, the end of the 1980s coincided with a kind of apogee of a Gaullist "model" characterized by both evident continuity in objectives and real flexibility in application. Of course, the apparent success of the model did not exclude certain questions being posed. Founded on a declaratory policy that since 1966 voluntarily blurred the real importance of military ties between France and its allies in order to stress an "independence" that had always been, even for de Gaulle, relative (for it did not exclude close cooperation with NATO), the "consensus" *ipso facto* suffered from built-in weaknesses. While the *autonomie de décision* remained the asserted priority of French defense, it was becoming difficult to mask evidence of a military rapprochement with NATO—which, however, in no way undermined the correctness of the 1966 decision. So a dilemma arose: either risk jeopardizing the national consensus by admitting the true situation, or risk having to bridle a burgeoning Franco–NATO cooperation that was increasingly appreciated on both sides. Moreover, while France's military and strategic weight in relation to the Alliance had been greatly increased since the start of this period, its real influence *within* the Alliance remained limited. Since 1966 France was no longer represented on the main *nonintegrated* bodies defining NATO policy (except of course for the North Atlantic Council), starting with the Military Committee and the Defense Planning Committee. But what had once been decided for primarily political reasons was less justified twenty years later: Could France continue to improve its participation in common defense without its voice being heard in bodies where decisions were taken that increasingly involved its security? Formulated in a period of rapid change in the international context after the arrival of Mikhail Gorbachev, these questions were not without consequence for relations between France and the Alliance. Yet they bore less on principles than on practice: on the eve of the fall of the Berlin Wall, the 1966 "model" remained therefore an incontestable reference point.

CONTINUING ADAPTATION

The end of the Cold War inevitably had consequences for France's Atlantic policy, which in large part had been justified from the start (and ever since) by an original vision of East-West relations whose aim was the overcoming of blocs. To be sure, the demise of "Yalta," accomplished after the fall of the Berlin Wall, marked the culmination of the Gaullist prophecy; yet it presented a major dilemma: Was the French model of belonging to the Alliance confirmed because this prospect had been realized? Or, on the contrary, was it called into question because the East-West context in which it had been elaborated had become radically outmoded? It is in light of this dilemma that we should analyze the evolution of relations between France and the Alliance in the past decade.[3]

At first, the former kind of thinking prevailed, entailing a renewal of the old Franco-American tensions. For French leaders, the Gaullist vision of European security appeared to be quite validated by the upheavals of 1989 and 1990, which finally made it possible to set up a post–Cold War security order. Hence, the pan-European dimension was privileged and the accent placed on the CSCE (whose summit in Paris in November 1990 consecrated the end of the Cold War), and also on an idea launched by Mitterrand in December 1989 of a "European confederation." In this vision, alliances occupied a secondary place; likely to lose their *raison d'être*, they could only become an ultimate guarantee of security. The disappearance of the Warsaw Pact and then the implosion of the USSR in 1991 merely confirmed this view and cast a spotlight on the different perspectives of France and its allies. Meanwhile, the United States advanced a "new Atlanticism" whose central idea—in line with the Harmel report—was strengthening the role of NATO, thanks to an assertion of "new missions." Paris, on the contrary, was going to try to block this evolution by seeking to limit the Alliance's role to that of an organization for defense in the last resort.

But it was especially in the Western dimension that one witnessed in the immediate post–Cold War period a renewal of transatlantic misunderstandings. While the "new Atlanticism" clearly presupposed maintaining and even reasserting U.S. leadership, the French considered that the fall of the Berlin Wall was opening the way to realizing the European strategic objectives that had been pursued by General de Gaulle. Seen from Paris, the disappearance of the Soviet threat and the probability in time of U.S. disengagement—at least relative—from the Old Continent in effect made likely an emergence of a European entity capable of playing a political and military role on a par with the economic weight of Western Europe. Reviving the ambition of the Fouchet Plan, France envisaged giving the European Union then being born the means to play an autonomous security role by endowing it with a common foreign and security policy (CFSP) and, in the longer term, a common defense policy. This ambition, just as in the 1960s, could not help but lead to a revival of Franco-American antagonism, which would reach a high point with the signing by the Twelve of the Maastricht Treaty in February 1992.

In these circumstances, there could be no question for French leaders of reversing decisions taken in the 1960s. Faced with what they perceived as an American attempt to exceed the traditional missions of the Alliance in order to reinforce U.S. leadership while preserving structures inherited from the Cold War, they felt impelled to maintain France's particular position in NATO. In French eyes, the process of "reforming" the Alliance launched by the allies at the London summit in July 1990 and ratified at the Rome summit in November 1991 seemed to move in exactly the opposite direction to what they wanted: rather than an Atlantic Alliance confined to the role of ultimate guarantor of security and liberated from U.S.–dominated military integration that only the Soviet menace had justified, it was instead a NATO with its scope increased to security at large, whose military was being further integrated and even strengthened, that was emerging on the ruins of Yalta. How, then, could France envisage reassuming a full place within NATO without endorsing a logic of blocs that seemed even more bankrupt than ever and sacrificing the chances of a strategic Europe that still depended on the will of member-states, starting with itself?

This "Gaullo-Mitterrandist" phase, though, would scarcely last beyond the immediate post–Cold War period. Starting in 1992–1993, French leaders sought ways and means to adapt the relation with NATO to a post–Cold War international system that scarcely matched the vision they had had of it after the fall of the Berlin Wall. Far from a pacified Europe managed by collective or cooperative security, the Old Continent saw a revival of the instability formerly contained by bipolar confrontation, of which the collapse of Yugoslavia and the war in Bosnia were the most striking illustrations. In these circumstances, the hypothesis of a diminution of NATO's role found itself contradicted by events: far from the residual defensive role that the French had reserved for it after the 1989 upheavals, the Alliance appeared to be the indispensable instrument of the stabilization of the Old Continent. Even more so: the growing implication of NATO in the management of the crisis in Bosnia confirmed the decisive character of its contribution — to the point, after the dénouement in 1995, of consecrating its preponderance in the architecture of European security.

In the same period, France's strategic ambitions for Europe had to be revised downward. If the Maastricht Treaty somehow marked the realization, thirty years later, of the vision of a political and military Europe that de Gaulle had tried to promote, this diplomatic success was to remain for the time being without a follow-up. As so often in the history of European construction, the swing of the pendulum would interrupt the dynamic of the years 1990–1991 and undermine France's activism on behalf of strategic Europe, against the background of a crisis in political Europe and in an unfavorable economic context. Moreover, the conflict in the Balkans acted both to expose and to catalyze European powerlessness: first, because the breakup of Yugoslavia led to a serious dispute (notably between France and Germany) over recognition of Croatia and Slovenia and demonstrated the limits of political cohesion in Europe; and second, because the military insufficiencies of the Europeans (led by the French and British) were put under a spotlight by the failure of the UN operation in Bosnia. This realization of European failure had its own influence on French politics. Since NATO was increasingly implicated in the crisis, the French were led to rally to the idea that a strategic Europe could not in the future take form unless it worked *with* NATO realities and not *against* them. Hence at the Brussels summit in January 1994 they accepted the perspective of a "European pillar" within the Atlantic Alliance, which they had long rejected in the name of Europe's independence.

As a result, an evolution in relations between France and NATO was necessary — again less in their principles than in their application. From a military viewpoint, the growing involvement of the Alliance in the management of the Bosnian crisis, combined with the major role the French were playing there, entrained the country in a more and more active participation in NATO operations. Without revoking the principle of nonintegration in peacetime, France now accepted the prospect of wholehearted participation in allied operations in times of crisis by means of the Combined Joint Task Forces (CJTF), a project that had been adopted at the Brussels summit. From an institutional point of view, this situation also involved an evolution in relations between France and NATO; now that France was actively participating in military operations of this kind, it could not in effect take the risk of being excluded from political or strategic decisions taken higher up in bodies from which it was absent, notably the Military Committee or meetings of the ministers of defense. Hence, after 1994, there was a policy of selective participation in these nonintegrated bodies in agreement with the allies, evidently favorable to such a rapprochement. Without being undermined, the "model" thus entered a phase of active adaptation in its practical implementation.

With the arrival of President Jacques Chirac in 1995, this adaptation saw a net acceleration. Paradoxically, the first Gaullist president since the death of Pompidou would in effect put into practice a veritable "strategic revolution" that could even seem, initially, of a nature to radically reverse the decisions taken by the General. Almost thirty years to the day after de Gaulle's announcement of France's "withdrawal," Chirac announced in February 1996 that his country was ready to resume its place in the military structures it had quit in 1966. But this offer was obviously subject to one condition: that these structures be thoroughly adjusted to the strategic context of the post–Cold War, and in particular that NATO permit assertion there of a European security and defense identity. Far from unilaterally or unconditionally revising France's particular position within the Alliance, it was a matter of exchanging a "normalization" of relations between France and NATO for an adaptation of the Western alliance, which France had by no means renounced.

If the ways and means of French policy were changing spectacularly, its objectives over these thirty years remained identical. The "new" approach heralded by Chirac indeed aimed first at reasserting a status of great Western power that for thirty years had relied on distancing itself from NATO but that now presupposed, on the contrary, finding a way to influence the Alliance from inside. Moreover, it was a matter of reviving a European strategic dynamic that had too long been blocked by France's partners in the name of the preservation of the Alliance and of the Atlantic status quo, and which now should be promoted by fostering the emergence of European defense in the NATO framework. Finally and most especially, France's initiative—now that it was taking part in the reform process rather than standing apart—consisted of transforming the Atlantic institution from the inside by promoting more flexible military integration and better political control—in short, of finally adapting it to the post–Cold War strategic context. In fact, just as de Gaulle had once taken the decision to "withdraw" France from NATO once he had realized the impossibility of satisfactory reform, so his successor used the prospect of its "return" to obtain such a reform.

Thus behind the appearance of a "strategic revolution" that seemed to upset fundamentals, it was really a continuity in France's Atlantic policy that this episode revealed. For several months, the double perspective of a substantial transformation of NATO and a normalization of French participation seemed close at hand. During the ministerial meeting in Berlin in June 1996, an important advance was made both in the direction of NATO adaptation to its new missions and in its necessary Europeanization. But Berlin in reality marked the apogee of this dynamic. In the autumn of 1996, the limits of NATO adaptation appeared against the background of divergences between the French and Americans over the share of commands of the new integrated military structure. While Paris, which did not contest the maintenance of an American officer in the role of SACEUR, demanded the Europeanization of subordinate commands (CINCENT and especially CINSOUTH), Washington rejected the idea of abandoning the latter to the Europeans. Rapidly becoming public, this conflict between Paris and Washington would lead to an impasse and be translated into the interruption of the rapprochement between France and NATO begun two years earlier. At the Atlantic summit in Madrid in July 1997, the reform of NATO was *de facto* shelved and the enlargement of the Alliance to include Poland, Hungary, and the Czech Republic overtook its adaptation, while France announced that it was suspending, for the moment, the process of returning to the military structure.

Of course, the reasons for this relative failure were to some extent conjunctural. Undertaken in a phase of the strengthening of American leadership and the Atlantic status quo after the crisis in Bosnia and its culmination in 1995, this policy was contracyclical: in such a context, French demands for transforming NATO in the end could merely meet with American indifference, even hostility. If, in 1995–1996, a compromise had seemed possible, it was no doubt due to a certain misunderstanding: the French were overestimating the desire for change among the Americans, who were wrongly interpreting the new approach of the French as a pure and simple return to the Atlantic "fold." So it was not so much a technical obstacle (the devolution of the southern command could have been a matter for compromise) as a fundamentally political dispute that sunk the effort. The principal reasons for the failure were indeed structural. France, despite appearances, was basically still attached to its old goals, while the United States, despite rhetoric favorable to a European security and defense identity within NATO, still considered these goals as incompatible with maintaining the Alliance as it had existed for fifty years—hence, in the final analysis, the stalemate in Chirac's "strategic revolution." Through the enduring Franco-American rivalry, it was still, fundamentally, "two strategies for Europe" that continued to vie with each other.

Thirty years after the General's departure, France continues, therefore, to occupy a unique place within the Alliance, if only because it continues to keep itself formally apart from its "integrated" military structure. Of course, over time, a basic tendency has emerged: the gradual normalization in relations between

France and NATO, particularly pronounced in recent years, which may be explained by a less intransigent conception of "independence." Today, not only does France participate in NATO's nonintegrated activities, but recent policy also shows that the issue of integration is no longer a national "taboo." This tendency is also explained by the declining pertinence of the idea of overcoming blocs: ten years after the end of the Cold War, this goal that long justified France's particular position within the Alliance is itself largely outmoded. Overall, while France remains a "different" ally, the French "difference" had become less systematic than it has been formerly, and the national and international goals that so long motivated it have partly lost their meaning.

However, European goals do remain and they are on the agenda more than ever. If France continues to contest an Atlantic status quo that still causes it to be once again charged (unjustly) with being systematically anti-American, it is because the ambition for a strategic Europe (the most constant theme in French defense and security policy over a half century) has retained its pertinence. After the successful stage of economic and monetary union and the launching of the euro currency, the setting up of a veritable European defense indeed figures in the forefront of Union priorities, and the 1999 crisis in Kosovo merely confirmed its necessity not only for Europe, but for the Alliance, whose reequilibration is more necessary than ever to a better sharing of the transatlantic burden. Were this permanent goal of France's—the constitution of a Europe with a credible defense—finally to be achieved (and several factors seem to favor it, starting with the recent British conversion to European defense, the "normalization" of Germany as a military power, and, for that matter, France's less systematically anti–NATO stance), then the question of relations between France and the Alliance would be obliterated by a much vaster challenge: the definition of a renewed and more balanced strategic partnership between the United States and Europe—for which France has not stopped devoutly wishing.

NOTES

1. For a balance sheet of General de Gaulle's foreign policy, see Maurice Vaïsse, *La Grandeur: Politique étrangère du général de Gaulle (1958–1969)*, Paris, Fayard, 1997.

2. On the influence of Gaullist legacy on French security policy, see Philip H. Gordon, *A Certain Idea of France: French Security Policy and the Gaullist Legacy,* Princeton, Princeton University Press, 1993.

3. On this period, see Frédéric Bozo, "France," in Michael Brenner, ed., *NATO and Collective Security,* London, Macmillan, 1998, pp. 39–80.

Sources and Bibliography

ARCHIVAL SOURCES

France

French Foreign Ministry Archives [MAE], Paris:
–*Série Pactes:*
  1948–1960.
  1961–1970.
–*Série Cabinet du Ministre:*
  Couve de Murville, 1958–1968.
–*Série Amérique:*
  États-Unis, 1952–1963.

United States

Dwight D. Eisenhower Library [DDEL], Abilene, Kansas [on microfiche]:
–*Papers of John Foster Dulles and Christian Herter, 1953–1961*:
  White House Correspondence and Memoranda Series.
  Chronological Correspondence Series, John Foster Dulles and Christian Herter.
  Minutes of Telephone Conversations of John Foster Dulles and Christian Herter.
–*President Dwight D. Eisenhower's Office Files*:
  Part 2: International Series: France.

John F. Kennedy Library [JFKL], Boston, Massachusetts:
–*National Security Files [NSF] 1961–1963*:
  Country File, France.
  Country File, Germany.
  Regional Security File, Europe, MLF, NATO.

Lyndon B. Johnson Library [LBJL], Austin, Texas:
–*National Security Files [NSF] 1963–1969*:
Country File, France.
International Meetings and Travels File.
Memos to the President.
Agency File.
Vice-Presidential Security File.
Committee File.
Files of McGeorge Bundy.
Subject File.
National Security Council History: Trilateral Negotiations and NATO, 1966–1967; Non-Proliferation Treaty.
–*White House Central Files*:
Confidential file.
–*Administrative Histories*:
Department of State, "Europe."

DIPLOMATIC DOCUMENTS

France

Ministère des Affaires étrangères. *Documents diplomatiques français [DDF]*:
———. Vol. 1957. Paris: Imprimerie Nationale, 1990–1991.
———. Vol. 1958. Paris: Imprimerie Nationale, 1992–1993.
———. Vol. 1959. Paris: Imprimerie Nationale, 1994–1995.
———. Vol. 1960. Paris: Imprimerie Nationale, 1995–1996.
———. Vol. 1961. Paris: Imprimerie Nationale, 1997–1998.
———. Vol. 1962. Paris: Imprimerie Nationale, 1998–1999.

United States

Department of State, *Foreign Relations of the United States [FRUS]*:
———. *1955–1957*. Western Europe and Canada. Washington: GPO, 1992.
———. *1958–1960*. Western European Integration and Security; Canada. Washington: GPO, 1993.
———. *1961–1963*. West Europe and Canada. Washington: GPO, 1994.
———. *1964–1969*. Western Europe Region. Washington: GPO, 1995.

OTHER PUBLISHED SOURCES

France

Ministère des Affaires étrangères. *La Politique étrangère de la France. Textes et documents*. Paris: La Documentation française.
de Gaulle, Charles. *Discours et Messages*, vol. 2, "Dans l'attente" (février 1946–avril 1958). Paris: Plon, 1970.

——. *Discours et Messages*, vol. 3, "Avec le renouveau" (mai 1958–juillet 1962). Paris: Plon, 1970.

——. *Discours et Messages*, vol. 4, "Pour l'effort" (août 1962–décembre 1965). Paris: Plon, 1970.

——. *Discours et Messages,* vol. 5, "Vers le terme" (janvier 1966–avril 1969). Paris: Plon, 1970.

United States

Documents on American Foreign Relations.

Public papers of the presidents of the United States:
Dwight D. Eisenhower.
John F. Kennedy.
Lyndon B. Johnson.
Richard M. Nixon.

The Atlantic Alliance. Hearings Before the Subcommittee on National Security and International Operations, Committee on Government Operations, U.S. Senate, 89th Congress, April 1966.

PRESS AND OTHER PERIODICALS

France

Fondation nationale des Sciences politiques. *Dossiers de presse.* Paris: FNSP.
Le Monde.
Revue de défense nationale.
Politique étrangère.
Revue militaire générale.

United States

The New York Times.
Foreign Affairs.

MEMOIRS, DIARIES, AND OTHER

France

Ailleret, Charles. *L'aventure atomique française.* Paris: Grasset, 1968.
Alphand, Hervé. *L'étonnement d'être. Journal 1939–1973.* Paris: Fayard, 1977.
Aron, Raymond. *Mémoires. 50 ans de réflexion politique.* Paris: Julliard, 1983.
de Boissieu, Alain. *Pour servir le Général.* Paris: Plon, 1982.
Burin des Roziers, Etienne. *Retour aux sources. 1962, l'année décisive.* Paris: Plon, 1986.

Chauvel, Jean. *Commentaire*, vol. 3, "De Berne à Paris" (1952–1962). Paris: Fayard, 1973.

Couve de Murville, Maurice. *Une Politique étrangère 1958–1969.* Paris: Plon, 1971.

———. *Le Monde en face.* Paris: Plon, 1989.

Debré, Michel. *Mémoires*, vol. 3, "Gouverner 1958–1962." Paris: Albin Michel, 1988.

———. *Mémoires,* "Gouverner autrement 1962–1970." Paris: Albin Michel, 1993.

de Gaulle, Charles. *Mémoires d'espoir*, "Le Renouveau" (1958–1962). Paris: Plon, 1970.

———. *Mémoires d'espoir*, "L'effort" (1962–). Paris: Plon, 1971.

———. *Lettres, notes et carnets*, juin 1958–décembre 1960. Paris: Plon, 1985.

———. *Lettres, notes et carnets,* janvier 1961–décembre 1963. Paris: Plon, 1986.

———. *Lettres, notes et carnets*, janvier 1964–juin 1966. Paris: Plon, 1987.

———. *Lettres, notes et carnets,* juillet 1966–avril 1969. Paris: Plon, 1987.

Maillard, Pierre. *De Gaulle et l'Allemagne. Le rêve inachevé.* Paris: Plon, 1990.

Malraux, André. *Les chênes qu'on abat.* Paris: Gallimard, 1971.

Massu, Jacques. *Baden 1968. Souvenirs d'une fidélité gaulliste.* Paris: Plon, 1983.

Messmer, Pierre. *Après tant de batailles. Mémoires.* Paris: Albin Michel, 1992.

Monnet, Jean. *Mémoires.* Paris: Fayard, 1976.

Passeron, André. *De Gaulle parle*, tome 1 (1958–1962). Paris: Plon, 1962.

———. *De Gaulle parle,* tome 2 (1962–1966). Paris: Fayard, 1966.

Peyrefitte, Alain. *C'était de Gaulle*, vol. 1, "La France redevient la France." Paris: de Fallois/Fayard, 1994.

———. *C'était de Gaulle*, vol. 2, "La France reprend sa place dans le monde." Paris: de Fallois/Fayard, 1997.

Pompidou, Georges. *Pour rétablir une vérité.* Paris: Flammarion, 1982.

Seydoux, François. *Mémoires d'outre-Rhin.* Paris: Grasset, 1975.

Tournoux, Jean-Raymond. *La Tragédie du Général.* Paris: Plon/Paris-Match, 1967.

———. *Jamais dit.* Paris: Plon, 1971.

United States

Ball, George W. *The Past Has Another Pattern.* New York: Norton, 1982.

Bohlen, Charles E. *Witness to History 1929–1969.* New York: Norton, 1973.

Cleveland, Harlan. *NATO: The Transatlantic Bargain.* New York: Harper & Row, 1970.

Eisenhower, Dwight D. *Waging Peace 1956–1961.* Garden City, NY: Doubleday, 1965.

Johnson, Lyndon B. *The Vantage Point.* New York: Rinehart & Winston, 1971.

Kissinger, Henry A. *White House Years.* Boston: Little, Brown, 1979.

McGhee, George. *At the Creation of a New Germany.* New Haven, CT: Yale University Press, 1989.

McNamara, Robert S. *The Essence of Security.* London: Holder & Stoughton, 1968.

Nitze, Paul H. *From Hiroshima to Glasnost.* New York: Grove Weidenfeld, 1989.

Nixon, Richard M. *Leaders.* New York: Warner, 1982.

———. *Memoirs.* New York: Grosset & Dunlop, 1978.

Sulzberger, Cyrus L. *The Last of the Giants.* New York: Macmillan, 1970.

———. *An Age of Mediocrity: Memoirs and Diaries, 1963–1972.* New York: Macmillan, 1973.

Walters, Vernon A. *Silent Missions.* Garden City, NY: Doubleday, 1978.

Other

Adenauer, Konrad. *Mémoires*, tome 3, 1956–1963. Paris: Hachette, 1963.
Macmillan, Harold. *Riding the Storm 1956–1959*. London: Macmillan, 1971.
——. *Pointing the Way 1959–1961*. London: Macmillan, 1972.
——. *At the End of the Day 1961–1963*. London: Macmillan, 1973.
Spaak, Paul-Henri. *Combats inachevés*. Paris: Fayard, 1969.
Strauss, Franz-Josef. *Mémoires*. Paris: Critérion, 1991.

ORAL HISTORY

Personal interviews

Hervé Alphand (Paris: October 1988.)
Jean-Marc Boegner (Paris: September 1991.)
General Alain de Boissieu (Paris: November 1988.)
Etienne Burin des Roziers (Paris: October 1988.)
Maurice Couve de Murville (Paris: December 1988.)
General Jean Crépin (Paris: December 1988.)
Admiral Marcel Duval (Paris: several interviews.)
General Michel Fourquet (Paris: December 1988.)
Henri Froment-Meurice (Paris: November 1991.)
General Pierre Gallois (Paris: January 1989.)
General Emmanuel Hublot (Paris: December 1988.)
General Kenneth Hunt (Ebenhausen: June 1991.)
General Graf Kielmansegg (Ebenhausen: June 1991.)
Pierre Maillard (Paris: July 1991.)
General François Maurin (Paris: December 1988.)
General Guy Méry (Paris: November 1988.)
Pierre Messmer (Paris: November 1988.)
General Lucien Poirier (Paris: June 1988.)
François de Rose (Paris: November 1988.)
Maurice Schumann (Paris: November 1988.)
General François Valentin (Paris: May 1988, November 1988, June 1989.)
Roger Vaurs (Paris: October 1988.)

Other Unpublished Oral History Sources

GREFHAN. "Le démarrage du nucléaire militaire en France (1952–1956)." Roundtable. Paris: 7 November 1988.
——. "L'évolution du concept français de dissuasion." Roundtable. Paris: 23 January 1989.
——. "Les relations nucléaires franco-germano-italiennes de 1956 à 1958." Roundtable. Paris: 8 December 1989 and 22 June 1990.

———. "Les relations nucléaires occidentales de 1957 à 1972." Roundtable. Paris: 31 May 1991.

——— "Le nucléaire dans les relations internationales." Conference: Troyes, 4 and 5 October 1991.

———. "La crise de Cuba et l'Europe." Conference: Paris, 16 and 17 October 1992.

BOOKS, ARTICLES, AND OTHER SCHOLARLY WORKS

Ambrose, Stephen E. *Eisenhower*. New York: Simon & Schuster, 1983.

———. *Rise to Globalism: American Foreign Policy since 1938*. New York: Penguin, 1985.

Amme, Carl H., Jr. *NATO without France: A Strategic Appraisal*. Stanford, CA: Hoover Institute, 1967.

Aron, Raymond. *Paix et guerre entre les nations*. Paris: Calmann-Lévy, 1962.

———. *Le Grand débat. Initiation à la stratégie atomique*. Paris: Calmann-Lévy, 1963.

———. *République impériale: les États-Unis dans le monde*. Paris: Calmann-Lévy, 1973.

Artaud, Denise. "Le Grand Dessein de J. F. Kennedy: proposition mythique ou occasion manquée?" *Revue d'histoire moderne et contemporaine*, XXIX (April–June 1982): 235–66.

Bahu-Leyser, Danielle. *De Gaulle, les Français et l'Europe*. Paris: Presses Universitaires de France, 1981.

Ball, M. Margaret. *NATO and the European Union Movement*. New York: Praeger, 1959.

Barbier, Colette: "Les négociations franco-germano-italiennes en vue de l'établissement d'une coopération militaire nucléaire au cours des années 1956–1958." *Revue d'histoire diplomatique*, no. 1/2 (1990): 81–113.

———. "La force multilatérale." *Relations internationales*, no. 69 (Spring 1992): 3–18.

Barnavi, Elie, and Saul Friedländer, eds. *La politique étrangère du général de Gaulle*. Paris: Presses Universitaires de France, 1985.

Beaufre, André. *Introduction à la Stratégie*. Paris: Armand Colin, 1963.

———. *Dissuasion et stratégie*. Paris: Colin, 1964.

———. *L'OTAN et l'Europe*. Paris: Calmann-Lévy, 1966.

Beloff, Max. *The United States and the Unity of Europe*. London: Faber & Faber, 1963.

Berstein, Serge. *La France de l'expansion*, vol. 1, "La République gaullienne 1958–1969." Paris: Le Seuil, in the series "Nouvelle histoire de la France contemporaine," no. 17, 1989.

Bloes, Robert. *Le "Plan Fouchet" et le problème de l'Europe politique*. Bruges: Collège d'Europe, 1970.

Bozo, Frédéric. *La France et l'OTAN. De la guerre froide au nouvel ordre européen*. Paris: Masson, in series "Travaux et recherches de l'IFRI," 1991.

———. "De Gaulle, l'Amérique et l'Alliance atlantique: une relecture de la crise de 1966." *Vingtième siècle*, no. 43 (July–September 1994): 55–68.

———. *Deux Stratégies pour l'Europe. De Gaulle, les États-Unis et l'Alliance atlantique (1958–1969)*. Paris: Plon, 1996.

———. "Chronique d'une décision annoncée: le retrait de l'organisation militaire (1965–1967)." In *La France et l'OTAN 1949–1996*, edited by Maurice Vaïsse, Pierre Melandri, and Frédéric Bozo. Brussels: Complexe, 1996.

———. *La Politique étrangère de la France depuis 1945*. Paris: La Découverte, 1997.

———. "France." In *NATO and Collective Security*, edited by Michael Brenner. London: Macmillan, 1998.

———. "Détente versus Alliance: France, the United States and the Politics of the Harmel Report (1964–1868)." *Contemporary European History*, 7, no. 3 (1998): 343–60.

Bozo, Frédéric, and Pierre Melandri. "La France devant l'opinion américaine: le retour de Gaulle (début 1958–printemps 1959)." *Relations internationales*, no. 58 (Summer 1989): 195–215.

Bracken, Paul. *The Command and Control of Nuclear Forces*. New Haven, CT: Yale University Press, 1983.

Buffet, Cyril. "La politique nucléaire de la France et la seconde crise de Berlin (1958–1962)." *Relations internationales*, no. 59 (Autumn 1989): 346–58.

———. "De Gaulle et Berlin. Une certaine idée de l'Allemagne." *Revue d'Allemagne*, XXII, no. 4 (October–December 1990): 525–38.

Bundy, McGeorge. *Danger and Survival: Choices about the Bomb in the First Fifty Years*. New York: Vintage, 1988.

Buteux, Paul. *The Politics of Nuclear Consultation in NATO, 1965–1980*. Cambridge: Cambridge University Press, 1983.

de Carmoy, Guy. *Les Politiques étrangères de la France 1944–1966*. Paris: La Table Ronde, 1967.

Cerny, Philip G. *The Politics of Grandeur: Ideological Aspects of de Gaulle's Foreign Policy*. Cambridge: Cambridge University Press, 1980

Chapsal, Jacques. *La Vie politique sous la Vème République*, tome 1, 1958–1974. Paris: Presses Universitaires de France, 1987.

Charlot, Jean. *Les Français et de Gaulle*. Paris: Plon, 1971.

Clark, Ian. *Nuclear Diplomacy and the Special Relationship: Britain's Deterrent and America 1957–1962*. Oxford: Clarendon, 1994.

Cleveland, Harold Van B. *The Atlantic Idea and Its European Rivals*. New York: McGraw-Hill, 1996.

Cogan, Charles G. *Oldest Allies, Guarded Friends: The United States and France since 1940*. London: Praeger, 1994.

———. *Forced to Choose: France, the Atlantic Alliance and NATO—Then and Now*. Westview, CT: Praeger, 1997.

Cohen, Samy. *La Monarchie nucléaire*. Paris: Fayard, 1986.

———. *La Défaite des généraux*. Paris: Fayard, 1994.

Cohen, Warren I., and Nancy B. Tucker, eds. *Lyndon Johnson Confronts the World: American Foreign Policy 1963–1968*. New York: Cambridge University Press, 1994.

Conze, Eckart. "La coopération franco-germano-italienne dans le domaine nucléaire dans les années 1957–1958." *Revue d'histoire diplomatique,* 104th year, nos. 1 and 2 (1990): 115–32.

Costigliola, Frank. *France and the United States: The Cold Alliance since World War II*. Boston: Twayne, 1992.

Debouzy, Olivier. *The Debate on the American Presence in Europe: A History*. European Strategy Group, 1991.

La Défense: la politique militaire et ses réalisations, Notes et études documentaires no. 3343. Paris: La Documentation française, December 1966.

Delmas, Claude. *L'OTAN*. Paris: Presses Universitaires de France, 1981.

————. *1961–1962, Crise à Cuba*. Brussels: Complexe, 1983.

DePorte, Anton W. *Europe between the Superpowers: The Enduring Balance*. New Haven, CT: Yale University Press, 1979.

Doise, Jean, and Maurice Vaïsse. *Diplomatie et outil militaire 1871–1969*. Paris: Imprimerie Nationale, 1987.

Duroselle, Jean-Baptiste. *La France et les États-Unis des origines à nos jours*. Paris: Le Seuil, 1976.

Duval, Marcel. "Elaboration et développement du concept français de dissuasion." *Relations internationales*, no. 59 (Autumn 1989): 31–383.

Duval, Marcel, and Yves Le Baut. *L'arme Nucléaire française. Pourquoi et comment?* Paris: S.P.M./Kronos, 1992.

Duval, Marcel, and Dominique Mongin. *Histoire des forces nucléaires françaises depuis 1945*. Paris: Presses Universitaires de France, 1993.

Enthoven, Alain C., and K. Wayne Smith. *How Much Is Enough? Shaping the Defense Program, 1961–1969*. New York: Harper & Row, 1971.

Facon, Patrick. "Les bases américaines en France (1945–1958). Entre les nécessités de la sécurité et les impératifs de la souveraineté nationale." *Matériaux*, no. 29 (October–December 1992): 27–36.

Ferro, Maurice. *De Gaulle et l'Amérique, une amitié tumultueuse*. Paris: Plon, 1973.

Flanagan, Stephen J. *NATO's Conventional Defences: Options for the Central Region*. London: Macmillan, 1988.

Fontaine, André. *Histoire de la détente 1962–1981*. Paris: Le Seuil, 1982.

————. *Histoire de la guerre froide*. Paris: Le Seuil, 1983.

Freedman, Lawrence. *The Evolution of Nuclear Strategy*. New York: St. Martin's Press, 1981.

Fritsch-Bournazel, Renata. *L'Union soviétique et les Allemagnes*. Paris: Presses de la F.N.S.P., 1979.

Gaddis, John L. *Strategies of Containment: A Critical Appraisal of Postwar American National Security Policy*. Oxford: Oxford University Press, 1982.

————. *We Now Know: Rethinking Cold War History*. New York: Oxford University Press, 1997.

Gaddis, John Lewis, Philip H. Gordon, and Ernest May, eds. *Cold War Statesmen Confront the Bomb: Nuclear Diplomacy since 1945*. New York: Oxford University Press, 1999.

Gallois, Pierre. *Stratégie de l'âge nucléaire*. Paris: Calmann-Lévy, 1960.

Gerbet, Pierre. *La construction de l'Europe*. Paris: Imprimerie Nationale, 1983.

————. *Le Relèvement 1944–1949*. Paris: Imprimerie Nationale, 1991.

Geyelin, Philip. *Lyndon B. Johnson and the World*. New York: Praeger, 1966.

Giglio, James N. *The Presidency of John F. Kennedy*. Lawrence: University of Kansas Press, 1991.

Goldschmidt, Bertrand. *Le Complexe atomique*. Paris: Fayard, 1980.

Goodman, Elliot R. *The Fate of the Atlantic Community*. New York: Praeger, 1975.

Gordon, Philip H. *A Certain Idea of France: French Security Policy and the Gaullist Legacy*. Princeton: Princeton University Press, 1993.

————. *France, Germany and the Western Alliance*. Boulder, CO: Westview Press, 1995.

————. "Charles de Gaulle and the Nuclear Revolution." In *Cold War Statesmen Confront the Bomb: Nuclear Diplomacy since 1945*, edited by John Lewis Gaddis, Philip H. Gordon, and Ernest May. New York: Oxford University Press, 1999.

Grosser, Alfred. *La Politique étrangère de la Vème République*. Paris: Le Seuil, 1965.

——. *Les Occidentaux: les pays d'Europe et les États-Unis*. Paris: Fayard, 1978.

——. *Affaires extérieures. La Politique de la France 1944–1984*. Paris: Flammarion, 1984.

Haftendorn, Helga. *NATO and the Nuclear Revolution: A Crisis of Credibility 1966–1967*. Oxford: Oxford University Press, 1996.

Harrison, Michael M. *The Reluctant Ally: France and Atlantic Security*. Baltimore: Johns Hopkins University Press, 1981.

Hassner, Pierre. *Change and Security in Europe*. Adelphi Paper no. 45 and 49. London: I.I.S.S., 1968.

Heuser, Beatrice. *NATO, Britain, France and the FRG: Nuclear Strategies and Forces for Europe 1949–2000*. London: Macmillan, 1997.

——. *Nuclear Mentalities? Strategies and Beliefs in Britain, France and the FRG*. London: Macmillan, 1998.

Hill, Roger. *Political Consultation in NATO*. Toronto: Canadian Institute of International Affairs, 1978.

Hitchcock, William I. *France Restored: Cold War Diplomacy and the Quest for Leadership in Europe, 1944–1954*. Chapel Hill: University of North Carolina Press, 1988.

Hoffmann, Stanley. *Gulliver's Troubles or the Setting of American Foreign Policy*. New York: McGraw-Hill, 1968.

——. *Decline or Renewal? France since the 1930's*. New York: Viking, 1974.

——. *Primacy or World Order? American Foreign Policy since the Cold War*. New York: McGraw-Hill, 1978.

Hunt, Kenneth. *NATO without France: The Military Implications*. Adelphi Paper no. 32. London: I.I.S.S., 1966.

Institut Charles de Gaulle. *L'Aventure de la bombe. De Gaulle et la dissuasion nucléaire (1958–1969)*. Paris: Plon, 1985.

——. *De Gaulle en son siècle*, vol. 4, "La sécurité et l'indépendance de la France." Paris: Plon, 1992.

——. *De Gaulle en son siècle*, vol. 5, "L'Europe." Paris: Plon, 1992.

Jouve, Edmond. *Le général de Gaulle et la construction de l'Europe*. Paris: L.G.D.J., 1967.

Kaplan, Lawrence S. *The United States and NATO: The Formative Years*. Lexington: The University Press of Kentucky, 1984.

——. *NATO and the United States: The Enduring Alliance*. Boston: Twayne, 1988.

Karber, Philip A. "In Defense of Forward Defense." *Armed Forces Journal* (May 1984): 28–50.

Kaspi, André. "Unité européenne, *partnership* atlantique." *Relations internationales*, no. 11 (1977): 231–48.

——. *Les Américains*, vol. 2. "Les États-Unis de 1945 à nos jours." Paris: Le Seuil, 1986.

——. *Kennedy. Les 1000 jours d'un Président*. Paris: Armand Colin, 1993.

Kaufmann, William W. *The McNamara Strategy*. New York: Harper & Row, 1964.

Kelleher, Catherine M. *Germany and the Politics of Nuclear Weapons*. New York: Columbia University Press, 1975.

Kissinger, Henry A. *The Troubled Partnership: A Re-Appraisal of the Atlantic Alliance*. New York: McGraw-Hill, 1965.

——. *Diplomacy*. New York: Simon & Schuster, 1994.

Klein, Jean. *Sécurité et désarmement en Europe.* Paris: Economica, 1987.

Kohl, Wilfrid L. *French Nuclear Diplomacy.* Princeton: Princeton University Press, 1971.

Kolodziej, Edward A. *French International Policy under de Gaulle and Pompidou.* Ithaca, NY: Cornell University Press, 1974.

Kraft, Joseph. *The Grand Design: From Common Market to Atlantic Partnership.* New York: Harper, 1962.

Kuisel, Richard. *Seducing the French: The Dilemma of Americanization.* Berkeley, CA: Berkeley University Press, 1993.

Kulski, W. W. *De Gaulle and the World: The Foreign Policy of the Fifth French Republic.* Syracuse, NY: Syracuse University Press, 1966.

Lacouture, Jean. *De Gaulle,* vol. 2, "Le Politique." Paris: Le Seuil, 1985.

———. *De Gaulle,* vol. 3, "Le Souverain." Paris: Le Seuil, 1986.

Lacouture, Jean, and Roland Mehl. *De Gaulle ou l'éternel défi.* Paris: Le Seuil, 1988.

LaFeber, Walter. *America, Russia and the Cold War 1945–1980.* New York: Wiley, 1980.

Le Baut, Yves. "Les Essais nucléaires français de 1966 à 1974." *Relations internationales,* no. 59 (Autumn 1989): 359–70.

Ledwidge, Bernard. *De Gaulle.* New York: St. Martin's Press, 1982.

———. *De Gaulle et les Américains. Conversations avec Dulles, Eisenhower, Kennedy et Rusk.* Paris: Flammarion, 1984.

Legge, J. Michael. *Theater Nuclear Weapons and the NATO Strategy of Flexible Response.* Santa Monica, CA: Rand, 1983.

Le Gloannec, Anne-Marie. *1961: un mur à Berlin.* Brussels: Complexe, 1985.

Leitenberg, M. "Background Information on Tactical Nuclear Weapons." In *Tactical Nuclear Weapons: European Perspectives.* Stockholm: SIPRI, 1978.

Lundestad, Geir. *"Empire" by Integration: The United States and European Integration, 1945–1997.* New York: Oxford University Press, 1998.

Maillard, Pierre. *De Gaulle et l'Allemagne. Le rêve inachevé.* Paris: Plon, 1990.

de Maizière, Ulrich. *Rationalisation du déploiement des forces sur le front central.* Paris: Assemblée de l'U.E.O., 1975.

Martel, André. *Histoire militaire de la France,* vol. 4, "De 1940 à nos jours." Paris: Presses Universitaires de France, 1994.

Melandri, Pierre. *L'Alliance atlantique.* Paris: Gallimard/Julliard, 1979.

———. "France and the Atlantic Alliance: Between Great Power Policy and European Integration." In *Western Security: The Formative Years. European and Atlantic Defence, 1947–1953,* edited by Olav Riste. Oslo: Norwegian University Press, 1985.

———. "Le général de Gaulle, la construction européenne et l'Alliance atlantique." In *La Politique étrangère du général de Gaulle,* edited by Elie Barnavi and Saul Friedländer. Paris: Presses Universitaires de France, 1985.

———. "La France et le 'jeu double' des États-Unis." In *La Guerre d'Algérie et les Français,* edited by Jean-Pierre Rioux. Paris: Fayard, 1990.

———. *La politique étrangère des États-Unis depuis 1945.* Paris: Presses Universitaires de France, 1995.

Mendl, Wolf. *Deterrence and Persuasion: French Nuclear Armament in the Context of National Policy 1945–1969.* New York: Praeger, 1970.

Mongin, Dominique. *La Bombe atomique française 1945–1958.* Brussels: Bruylant, 1997.

Morse, Edward L. *Foreign Policy and Interdependence in Gaullist France.* Princeton: Princeton University Press, 1973.

Mulley, F. W. *The Politics of Western Defence*. London: Thames & Hudson, 1962.

NATO Information Service. *The North Atlantic Treaty Organization: Facts and Figures*. Brussels: NATO, 1989.

Newhouse, John. *Collision in Brussels: The Crisis of 30 June 1965*. New York: Twentieth Century Fund, 1967.

———. *De Gaulle and the Anglo-Saxons*. New York: Viking, 1970.

Nouailhat, Yves-Henri. "Nixon–de Gaulle: un épisode original des relations franco-américaines." *Revue française d'études américaines*, no. 32 (April 1987): 309–18.

Osgood, Robert E. *NATO: The Entangling Alliance*. Chicago: University of Chicago Press, 1962.

Park, William. *Defending the West: A History of NATO*. Brighton, UK: Wheatsheaf Books, 1986.

Paterson, Thomas G., ed. *Kennedy's Quest for Victory: American Foreign Policy 1961–1963*. New York: Oxford University Press, 1989.

Planchais, Jean. *Une Histoire politique de l'Armée*, tome 2, 1940–1967. Paris: Le Seuil, 1967.

Poirier, Lucien. *Des Stratégies nucléaires*. Paris: Hachette, 1977.

———. *Essais de stratégie théorique*. Paris: Fondation pour les études de Défense Nationale, 1982.

Pottier, Olivier. *La Présence militaire américaine en France (1950–1967)*. Reims: Thèse, Université de Reims, 1999.

Reed, John A., Jr. *Germany and NATO*. Washington: National Defense University Press, 1987.

Rey, Marie-Pierre. *La Tentation du rapprochement. France et URSS à l'heure de la détente 1964–1974*. Paris: Publications de la Sorbonne, 1991.

Romer, Jean-Christophe. *Détente et rideau de fer*. Paris: Publications de la Sorbonne, 1984.

de Rose, François. *La France et la défense de l'Europe*. Paris: Le Seuil, 1976.

Rühl, Lothar. *La Politique militaire de la Vème République*. Paris: Presses de la F.N.S.P., 1976.

Ruiz-Palmer, Diego A. "Between the Rhine and the Elbe: France and the Conventional Defense of Central Europe." *Comparative Strategy*, 6, no. 4 (Autumn 1987): 471–512.

———. "France." In *NATO–Warsaw Pact Force Mobilization*, edited by Jeffrey Simmons. Washington: National Defense University Press, 1988

———. "France." In *European Security Policy after the Revolutions of 1989*, edited by Jeffrey Simmons. Washington: National Defense University Press, 1991.

Schake, Kori. *Contingency Planning for the 1961 Berlin Crisis*, N.H.P. Working Paper no. 1, February 1989.

Schlesinger, Arthur M. *A Thousand Days: John F. Kennedy in the White House*. New York: Fawcett Premier, 1965.

Schreiber, Thomas. *Les Relations de la France avec les pays de l'Est (1944–1980)*. Paris: La Documentation française, 1980.

Schwartz, David N. *NATO's Nuclear Dilemmas*. Washington: Brookings, 1983.

Schwartz, Thomas A. "Lyndon Johnson and Europe: Alliance Politics, Political Economy and 'Growing out of the Cold War.'" In *The Foreign Policies of Lyndon Johnson: Beyond Vietnam*, edited by H. W. Brands. College Station: Texas A&M University Press, 1999.

Schwarz, Hans-Peter. "Adenauer et la crise de Cuba." In *L'Europe et la crise de Cuba*, edited by Maurice Vaïsse. Paris: A. Colin, 1993.

——. *Konrad Adenauer: The Statesman 1952–1967*. Providence: Berghahn Books, 1995.

SHAPE. *SHAPE et le commandement allié en Europe. Vingt ans au service de la paix et de la sécurité*. Mons: SHAPE, 1971.

Sherwood, Elizabeth D. *Allies in Crisis: Meeting Global Challenges to Western Security*. New Haven, CT: Yale University Press, 1990.

Sloan, Stanley R. *NATO's Future: Toward a New Transatlantic Bargain*. Washington: National Defense University Press, 1985.

Sorensen, Theodore C. *Kennedy*. New York: Harper & Row, 1965.

Soutou, Georges-Henri. *The French Military Program for Nuclear Energy, 1945–1981*. N.H.P. Occasional Paper no. 3, 1989.

——. "Les Problèmes de sécurité dans les rapports franco-allemands de 1956 à 1963." *Relations internationales*, no. 58 (Summer 1989): 227–51.

——. "Le général de Gaulle, le plan Fouchet et l'Europe." *Commentaire*, 13, no. 52 (Winter 1990–1991): 757–66.

——. "Le général de Gaulle et le plan Fouchet." In *De Gaulle en son siècle*, vol. 5, "L'Europe." Institut Charles de Gaulle. Paris: Plon, 1992.

——. "Les accords de 1957 et 1958: vers une communauté stratégique et nucléaire entre la France, l'Allemagne et l'Italie?" *Matériaux*, no. 31 (April–June 1993): 1–12.

——. *L'Alliance incertaine. Les rapports politico-stratégiques franco-allemands 1954–1996*. Paris: Fayard, 1996.

——. "La France et l'Alliance atlantique de 1949 à 1954." *Cahiers du CEHD*, 3 (1997): 51–74.

Stromseth, Jane E. *The Origins of Flexible Response: NATO's Debate over Strategy in the 1960s*. London: Macmillan, 1988.

Stuart, Douglas, and William Tow. *The Limits of Alliance: NATO out-of-area Problems since 1949*. Baltimore: Johns Hopkins University Press, 1990.

Trachtenberg, Marc. "L'ouverture des archives américaines." In *L'Europe et la crise de Cuba*, edited by Maurice Vaïsse. Paris: A. Colin, 1993.

——. *A Constructed Peace: The Making of the European Settlement 1945–1963*. Princeton: Princeton University Press, 1999.

Vaïsse, Maurice. "Aux origines du mémorandum de septembre 1958." *Relations internationales*, no. 58 (Summer 1989): 253–68.

——. "Une filière sans issue." *Relations internationales*, no. 59 (Autumn 1989): 331–45.

——. "Un dialogue de sourds: les relations nucléaires franco-américaines de 1957 à 1960." *Relations internationales*, no. 68 (Winter 1992): 407–23.

——. "Le choix nucléaire de la France." *Vingtième siècle*, no. 36 (October–December 1992): 20–30.

——. "Le général de Gaulle et la défense de l'Europe, 1947–1958." *Matériaux*, no. 29 (October–December 1992): 5–8.

——, ed. *L'Europe et la crise de Cuba*. Paris: A. Colin, 1993.

——, ed. *La France et l'Atome. Etudes d'histoire nucléaire*. Brussels: Bruylant, 1994.

——, ed. *La France et l'opération de Suez de 1956*. Paris: Addim, 1997.

——. *La Grandeur. Politique étrangère du général de Gaulle 1958–1969*. Paris: Fayard, 1997.

Vaïsse, Maurice, Pierre Melandri, and Frédéric Bozo, eds. *La France et l'OTAN 1949–1996*. Brussels: Complexe, 1996.

Valentin, François. *Une politique de défense pour la France*. Paris: Calmann-Lévy, 1980.

———. "La dissuasion et les armements classiques." In *L'Aventure de la bombe. De Gaulle et la dissuasion nucléaire (1958–1969)*. Institut Charles de Gaulle. Paris: Plon, 1985.

Van Der Beugel, Ernst H. *From Marshall Aid to Atlantic Partnership: European Integration as a Concern of American Foreign Policy*. New York: Elsevier, 1966.

Vandevanter, E., Jr. *Some Fundamentals of NATO Organization*. Santa Monica, CA: Rand, 1963.

———. *Studies on NATO: An Analysis of Integration*. Santa Monica, CA: Rand, 1966.

Viansson-Ponté, Pierre. *Histoire de la République gaullienne*. Paris: Robert Laffont, 1984.

Wall, Irwin M. *The U.S. and the Making of Post War France 1945–1954*. New York: Cambridge University Press, 1991.

Weisenfeld, Ernst. *Quelle Allemagne pour la France?* Paris: A. Colin, 1989.

Williams, Phil. *The Senate and U.S. Troops in Europe*. New York: St. Martin's Press, 1985.

Winand, Pascaline. *Eisenhower, Kennedy and the United States of Europe*. New York: St. Martin's Press, 1993.

Yost, David S. *France and Conventional Defense in Central Europe*. EAI Paper no. 7, 1984.

———. *France's Deterrent Posture and Security in Europe*. Adelphi Paper no. 194–195. London: I.I.S.S., 1985.

Index

About the Author

Frédéric Bozo is professor of contemporary history at the University of Nantes, France, and a senior associate at the French Institute of International Relations (IFRI) in Paris. His focus is on the history and politics of the Atlantic alliance and transatlantic relations, as well as on French foreign and security policy. His recent publications include *La France et l'OTAN 1949–1996* (1996, coedited with Maurice Vaïsse and Pierre Melandri) and *La Politique étrangére de la France depuis 1945* (1997).